SUPPORTING ASIAN CHRISTIANITY'S TRANSITION FROM MISSION TO CHURCH

THE HISTORICAL SERIES OF THE REFORMED CHURCH IN AMERICA
NO. 68

SUPPORTING ASIAN CHRISTIANITY'S TRANSITION FROM MISSION TO CHURCH

A History of the Foundation for Theological Education in South East Asia

Samuel C. Pearson, Editor

WILLIAM B. EERDMANS PUBLISHING COMPANY
Grand Rapids, Michigan / Cambridge, U.K.

Wm. B. Eerdmans Publishing Co.
2140 Oak Industrial Drive S.E., Grand Rapids, Michigan 49503 /
P.O. Box 163, Cambridge CB3 9PU U.K.
www.eerdmans.com

Printed in the United States of America

Library of Congress Cataloging-in-Publication Data

Supporting Asian Christianity's transition from mission to church : a history of the Foundation for Theological Education in South East Asia / Samuel C. Pearson, editor.

p. cm. -- (The historical series of the Reformed Church in America ; no. 68)

Includes bibliographical references and index.

ISBN 978-0-8028-6622-6 (pbk. : alk. paper) 1. Theology--Study and teaching--Asia--History. 2. Theological seminaries--Asia--History. 3. Dong nan Ya shen xue jiao yu ji jin hui--History. 4. Jinling shen xue yuan--History. I. Pearson, Samuel Campbell, 1931-

BV4140.A78S87 2010

230.071'15--dc22

2010025538

The Historical Series of the Reformed Church in America

The series was inaugurated in 1968 by the General Synod of the Reformed Church in America acting through the Commission on History to communicate the church's heritage and collective memory and to reflect on our identity and mission, encouraging historical scholarship which informs both church and academy.

General Editor
Rev. Donald J. Bruggink, Ph.D., D.D.
Western Theological Seminary
Van Raalte Institute, Hope College

Associate Editor
George Brown, Jr., Ph.D.
Western Theological Seminary

Copy Editor
Laurie Baron

Production Editor
Russell L. Gasero

Commission on History
Douglas Carlson, Ph.D., Northwestern College, Orange City, Iowa
Mary L. Kansfield, M.A., East Stroudsburg, Pennsylvania
Hartmut Kramer-Mills, M.Div., Dr.Theol., New Brunswick, New Jersey
Jeffery Tyler, Ph.D., Hope College, Holland, Michigan
Audrey Vermilyea, Bloomington, Minnesota
Lori Witt, Ph.D., Central College, Pella, Iowa

Contents

Abbreviations

AJT	*Asia Journal of Theology*
ASEAN	Association of Southeast Asian Nations
ATESEA	Association for Theological Education in South East Asia
ATSSEA	Association of Theological Schools in South East Asia
B.D.	Bachelor of Divinity
B.Th.	Bachelor of Theology
BTTS	Bible Teachers' Training School
CCC	China Christian Council
CN$	China national currency under Nationalist government
CTE	Commission on Theological Education of China Christian Council
D. Min.	Doctor of Ministry
D.Th.	Doctor of Theology
FTESEA	Foundation for Theological Education in South East Asia
IMC	International Missionary Council
JRPC	Joint Regional Planning Commission
M.R.E.	Master of Religious Education
M.Th.	Master of Theology
NCC	National Christian Council (of China or of Indonesia)
PTE	Programme on Theological Education of the WCC
SEAGST	South East Asia Graduate School of Theology
SEAJT	*South East Asia Journal of Theology*
TEF	Theological Education Fund
UNESCO	United Nations Educational, Scientific, and Cultural Organization
UNRRA	United National Relief and Rehabilitation Administration
WCC	World Council of Churches
WCUTC	West China Union Theological College

Foreword

More than seventy years of history of the Board of Founders of Nanking Theological Seminary and its successor, the Foundation for Theological Education in South East Asia (FTESEA), is succinctly narrated in this monograph, *Supporting Asian Christianity's Transition from Mission to Church: A History of the Foundation for Theological Education in South East Asia,* prepared by Dr. Samuel Pearson. The monograph also includes a chapter on the Association for Theological Education in South East Asia by Dr. Michael Poon. The authors provide a valuable source of information to all those who are interested in theological education in the Protestant churches in China and South East Asia. During the ministry period of the Board of Founders and FTESEA, Asia has gone through radical changes in the political, social, and religious arenas that challenged the organizations continually to examine their operational style and to respond to new forms of relationship with the schools they served.

The growth and vitality of Christianity in the southern hemisphere during the second half of the twentieth century has received much attention from all those who are interested in contemporary Christianity. China and South East Asian countries demonstrate similar vitality. However, the ethos of Christianity that is experienced in Asia has moved beyond the conventional forms of Christian faith that was brought from Europe and North America. The attempts to form united and uniting Protestant churches, along with the quest to indigenize Christianity, have motivated Asian Christians to draw from the local religious and cultural ethos as they practice Christianity and to root their Christian faith in an Asian context. Meanwhile, Asian theologians are also open to new forms of Christianity that are developed and brought from outside the continent.

Furthermore, the presence of a wide variety of Christian communities in a multiethnic and multireligious environment poses challenges for the task of preparing leaders for Christian witness in Asia. FTESEA and its preceding Board of Founders have been constantly attentive to the need for contextual ministerial training and theological reflection. The carefully captured contours of this effort in this monograph will provide a great help to the ongoing engagement of FTESEA in theological education in South East Asia and China.

FTESEA is greatly indebted to Drs. Pearson and Poon for their contributions. Our special thanks are also due to Dr. Charles Forman, Dr. Charles West, Dr. Yeow Choo Lak, and Dr. Wenh-In Ng, who read the manuscript and made valuable suggestions to its authors. The tireless effort of the executive directors, Dr. Marvin Hoff and Dr. H.S. Wilson, in bringing this task into completion is much appreciated.

FTESEA records its thanks to Dr. Donald Bruggink, general editor of the Historical Series of the Reformed Church in America, and his colleagues for their help in publishing and marketing this book.

Benjamin Chan
Chair, FTESEA
May 2010

Preface

The study which follows is based upon minutes of annual meetings of the Board of Founders of Nanking Theological Seminary/ Foundation for Theological Education in South East Asia, papers of individuals who were members of that organization or who participated in its varied activities, earlier histories, and recollections of individuals prominent in the story. For most of the history of the Board of Founders, no one served as archivist and no efforts were made to deposit papers in an archive, a situation remedied in 1999 when the Yale Divinity School agreed to become a repository of the records. Because the Board of Founders received the Swope-Wendel legacy through the United Methodist Church, some papers relevant to the history exist at the church's headquarters in New York and in the Methodist Archives at Drew University in Madison, New Jersey; but these are largely mixed with other church records, and researchers for this history have had only limited access to them.

Chapters concerning Nanking Theological Seminary during World War II and its aftermath were heavily dependent on the papers of Abbe Livingstone Warnshuis, which are located at Union Theological

Seminary in New York. Long a member of the Board of Founders, Warnshuis retained many of its papers, including mimeographed copies of letters from Nanking seminary faculty members in Chengdu and lengthy letters from C. Stanley Smith describing discussions and actions taken at various seminary meetings, which always accompanied the recommendations forwarded to the Board of Founders from the seminary. These documents included extensive discussion of thoughts, plans, and ideas that led to specific actions.

Unfortunately, few records for the period around the time of the Communist victory in the Chinese civil war survive. Therefore, letters written by Western faculty members after they departed China, accounts subsequently published in *Tian Feng*, a journal of the China Christian Council, and later recollections of participants have provided the limited resources for an examination of this period. The library of China's National Christian Council, hidden at the time of the Cultural Revolution, remained intact and is now in the custody of the East China Theological Seminary (Huadong Shen Xueyuan) in Shanghai. This collection has been catalogued but, unfortunately, is not currently open to scholars. It may provide useful information for subsequent studies of Nanking Seminary and its earliest relations with the Board of Founders.

When the Board of Founders extended its work into South East Asia, C. Stanley Smith became its first regional representative. He submitted lengthy written accounts of his trips, and he assessed requests for funding and forwarded them to the Board of Founders in New York. With Sidney Anderson he visited many of the Protestant theological institutions in South East Asia in 1952 and produced the vividly descriptive *Anderson–Smith Report on Theological Education in Southeast Asia*.[1] Documentation for the more recent period is limited. However, after becoming executive director of the FTESEA in 1977, Marvin Hoff made frequent visits to the region and the institutions there that the foundation aided. From 1982, those visits were extended into China. Hoff's extensive reports on these trips to the region were generally appended to the minutes of the annual meetings.[2]

1 Sydney Anderson and C. Stanley Smith, *The Anderson-Smith Report on Theological Education in Southeast Asia, Especially as it Relates to the Training of Chinese for the Ministry* (New York: Board of Founders, NTS, 1952).

2 Additional information regarding Hoff's observations of the Chinese church can be found in Marvin Hoff, ed., *Chinese Theological Education, 1979-2006*, Historical Series of the Reformed Church in America, no. 61 (Grand Rapids: Eerdmans, 2009).

The problem of transliteration of Chinese names into English is complicated by the general use of the Wade–Giles system until the 1950s, when the new government of China introduced the Pinyin system there. All of the older documents used the earlier system, and all of the new ones from China use the new. With regard to place names, I have used the Pinyin spelling wherever possible, indicating the older spelling when the name first appears in the text. All references to Formosa have been changed to Taiwan, the preferred usage today. With respect to personal names, the Romanization is that which appeared in the original text and apparently was the choice of the subject, as few Hanzi (Chinese characters) ever appeared in these materials. Thus Nanjing Seminary personnel with the Chinese name Li appear as president Handel Lee and Dean Li Tien-lu.

South East Asia was still undergoing the process of decolonization when the Board of Founders first began its work there, but in the interest of clarity only current names and spellings of countries and cities are used. The few references to Siam have been changed to Thailand. Generally I have used the name Burma rather than Myanmar except where the context argues for the alternate terminology. Again, South East Asian personal names are reproduced as they appeared in the original documents. Unnecessary titles have been eliminated except where required to establish gender identity.

Finally, the history of this book, like the history of the foundation itself, is a complex one involving the work of many people. In the 1980s, an early effort was made by the executive director and members of the board to document aspects of the foundation's history through a search of files in its office as well as relevant materials in the archives of the General Board of Global Ministries of the United Methodist Church. Subsequently, Charles W. Forman, professor of missions at Yale Divinity School and a long-term member of the FTESEA, who had chaired the board for more than twenty years, undertook the writing of a history. However, Forman found that other commitments made it impossible for him to complete the project, and in 1997 the foundation entered into a contract with a historian who had written previously on related topics for additional research and a written history. That historian engaged in a thorough and careful exploration of sources and produced a lengthy manuscript. However, after six of the foundation's trustees read the manuscript and offered suggestions for revising it, the historian and the foundation found that they could not agree on revisions. The manuscript therefore became the property of the foundation, and the historian asked to remain anonymous. At that point I accepted a contract to complete the manuscript, to consider revisions in light of the readers' comments, and to prepare the book for publication. Some of this text is entirely my work; much of it is the work of others edited and revised in light of my understanding of the story of the foundation. I am profoundly appreciative of that earlier work, as I am of the chapter on the Association for Theological Education in South East Asia that was written by Michael Nai Chiu Poon. All of these people contributed significantly to the successful completion of this project. I appreciate the help received from many librarians and am especially grateful to Martha Smalley and Joan Duffy of the Yale Divinity School Library and to Ruth Tonkiss Cameron and Seth Kasten of Burke Library of Union Theological Seminary in New York for their unfailing assistance to me as I worked through the records of Nanjing Seminary, the Board of Founders, and the Foundation for Theological Education in South East Asia.

For me this project was a very personal one. I am a specialist in the history of Christianity in modern Europe and America, but I have spent eight years teaching in China, including two years at Nanjing Union Theological Seminary. Therefore I know, either personally or by reputation, many of the people whose names appear in these pages. I have also witnessed some of the results of the work of the foundation in contemporary China and in South East Asia. I hope this experience has enabled me to bring greater clarity to the history of the foundation.

Samuel C. Pearson

INTRODUCTION

The history of the Foundation for Theological Education in South East Asia (FTESEA) is a complex tapestry woven from many distinct but closely related threads. The primary thread, of course, is the institutional history of the foundation itself and of its predecessor, the Board of Founders of Nanking Theological Seminary. Yet as the change in name suggests, this story is comprehensible only within the wider framework of the tumultuous historical developments in China and South East Asia[1] during the twentieth century. Thus, the first focus of this work must be on the history of Protestant theological education in China and the emergence of Nanking Theological Seminary as an interdenominational training school for leadership within the Chinese church. Another early focus must be the generous bequest of the Swope-Wendel family of New York for the benefit of Nanjing Theological Seminary.[2] This bequest led to the creation of the Board of

[1] While it is customary in American English to spell *southeast* as a single word, around the world, practices vary. In this volume, for the sake of consistency with the names of the organizations under discussion, the region will be referred to as South East Asia.

[2] Nanjing Theological Seminary had several names during the course of

Founders as an entity to receive and disburse income from the bequest by the denominations participating in the seminary.

Another theme is the development of the relationship between the Board of Founders and Nanjing Seminary. This relationship stretches from the creation of the board through the difficult years of World War II to the creation of the People's Republic of China, reorganization of the seminary as the Nanjing Union Theological Seminary, and a subsequent break in relationship.

Still another is the decision of the Board of Founders, after it became impossible to continue its relationship with Nanjing Seminary, to seek relationships with other theological institutions in South East Asia, a decision that required both court approval and a new name for the foundation. Understanding of this extended work of the foundation in South East Asia requires consideration of the history of the Association of Theological Schools in South East Asia (ATSSEA), later reorganized as the Association for Theological Education in South East Asia (ATESEA). Encouraged and supported by the FTESEA, the ATESEA developed into an institution critical to the development and sustenance of theological education among the Protestant churches of the region. Finally, this volume examines the renewal of relationships with the Chinese church beginning in the early 1980s and FTESEA work with the seminary in Nanjing directly and with the many other Chinese seminaries through the Commission on Theological Education of the China Christian Council.

The city of Nanking (now transliterated as Nanjing) on the lower reaches of the Yangtze River became a focal point for Protestant missions early in the twentieth century. From 1911, steps were taken that led to the merger of Christian Church (Disciples of Christ), Methodist Episcopal Church, and Presbyterian Church (both U.S.A. and U.S.) mission schools into an interdenominational seminary that adopted the name Nanking Theological Seminary in 1917. This cooperative endeavor won widespread support, and the Methodist Episcopal Church, South, and Northern and Southern Baptist churches were soon invited to affiliate. Southern Methodists accepted this invitation quickly and the Northern Baptists a bit later. With the combined resources of several denominations, the seminary quickly became one of the strongest Protestant theological schools in China

its history. Until 1913 it was known as Nanking Bible Training School. From 1913 to 1915 its name was Nanking School of Theology. Thereafter it was known as Nanking Theological Seminary until 1952, when it was reorganized. Since then it has been officially known as Nanjing Union Theological Seminary (Jinling Xiehe Shen Xueyuan).

though it continued, like the others, to struggle with inadequate financial resources. Harry F. Rowe, a Methodist missionary teacher who served for a decade as the seminary's president, solicited funds for the school while in America. Among those whom he visited were Rebecca Swope and Ella Wendel.[3]

While living quite frugally, the Wendel family of New York had accumulated real estate, mostly in Manhattan, for four generations. Consequently, the last surviving members of the family, Rebecca Wendel Swope, who died in 1930, and Ella Wendel, who died the following year, left a fortune for distribution to charities. Among the beneficiaries of their bequest was Nanking Theological Seminary, which was to receive income from a portion of the legacy to be administered by the Board of Foreign Missions of the Methodist Episcopal Church.

China was the largest mission field of American Protestantism by the early twentieth century, but the church in China remained largely a mission church, dependent on the West both for personnel and for funding. This was particularly true with regard to seminary education, which enjoyed little Chinese church support, and Nanking Seminary had developed as a cooperative, interdenominational school in part because the participating denominations lacked the resources adequately to staff a mission seminary of this quality except through the cooperation of several mission boards. Therefore, it was almost incredible to the American and Chinese faculty at Nanking to learn that their seminary would become the beneficiary of a massive bequest from the Swope-Wendel estate to be held in trust for the maintenance of seminary operations.

To meet the terms of the grant, the Board of Founders of Nanking Theological Seminary was established under the laws of the State of New York to receive income from the endowment held by the Board of Foreign Missions of the Methodist Episcopal Church, to guide its spending by and on behalf of Nanking Theological Seminary, and to develop a continuing relationship with the seminary. The board was initially composed of representatives of those denominations participating in the seminary. Generally, board members were individuals who were personally familiar with the seminary's work. Many of them had visited the seminary. Consequently, a very personal

3 Accounts of Rowe's contact with Wendel family members vary; it is likely that he met with the two sisters, but the memorial adopted by the Board of Managers (BM) of Nanking Theological Seminary at the time of his death states only that "he aroused the interest of Mrs. Swope." Minutes, BM, NTS, May 4 and 5, 1948, Abbe Livingstone Warnshuis papers, Burke Library, Union Theological Seminary of New York (hereafter ALW).

relationship developed. Personal relationships between board members and Nanking Theological Seminary became especially significant during the years of World War II when the seminary faculty relocated, some to Shanghai and others to Chengdu. Following the end of the War, the Board of Founders was active in supporting the re-establishment of the seminary in Nanjing. However, the victory of Communist forces in the long Chinese civil war created new challenges both for the seminary and for the board.

With the liberation of Nanjing by Communist forces and the collapse of the Nationalist government, which fled to Taiwan, the seminary was faced with the necessity of defining its position in an officially atheist state. The failure of the United States to recognize the new government of China and the U.S. entry into the Korean police action under United Nations auspices, together with the subsequent sending of Chinese volunteers onto the Korean peninsula, resulted not only in a generation of hostility between China and the United States but also in the effective termination of all contact between the Board of Founders and Nanking Seminary for more than twenty years.

When it became clear that for an indefinite period the Board of Founders would be unable to disburse funds to the Nanking seminary, it explored appropriate alternatives for use of its resources. The board turned its attention not only to Taiwan, which had been considered a part of the China mission scene and whose missionaries had participated in China's National Christian Council, but also to South East Asia and especially to the Chinese Christian communities living there. In an effort to honor the stipulations of the trust under which it operated, the Board of Founders originally offered financial help to South East Asian seminaries specifically to assist their Chinese students. However, when some in Indonesia objected that this policy fostered ill-feelings on the part of other students and appeared inappropriate in the context of Christian ideals, the board reconsidered the situation and turned to the court in New York for a modification of its charter. The court approved the new purpose: "and to receive and disburse funds (1) for any purpose contributing to Christian theological education (a) in China, or (b) in areas of Asia and of the Western Pacific beyond the confines of China, and (2) for educational assistance to Chinese and other Far Eastern students preparing in these or other lands for the ministry or other services in the Christian church when the said corporation shall deem the same advisable because of conditions existing in China."[4] Though

4 Frank T. Cartwright, *A River of Living Water* (Singapore: Board of Founders of Nanking Theological Seminary, 1963), 27.

this expanded purpose suggested the need for a name change for the Board of Founders of Nanking Theological Seminary, it was not until 1963 that the current name, the Foundation for Theological Education in South East Asia (FTESEA), was formally adopted.

During and immediately following World War II, the Board of Founders had stretched the terms of its charter to assist other seminaries in China, especially one in Chengdu that hosted a portion of the Nanking Seminary faculty and students after that city fell to the Japanese. However, with this enlargement of its mission, the number of theological schools that it might appropriately assist increased from one or a few to many. Consequently, the operations of the Board of Founders became more institutionally oriented, and its relationships with recipient institutions and their personnel became less personal than had been the case when it worked almost exclusively with Nanking Seminary. This difference is well reflected in changes in the work of C. Stanley Smith, who represented the Board of Founders in South East Asia in the 1950s. Smith, a Presbyterian missionary, had taught at Nanking and served for a time as the seminary's president. In the earlier years, when he had written the Board of Founders from China, many reading his letters were familiar with the people and the campus about which he wrote. He then became the first regional representative of the Board of Founders in South East Asia. In his new role, Smith corresponded with the board regarding a multitude of theological schools scattered throughout South East Asia. There, responding annually to requests from an ever increasing list of theological institutions, his and the board's participation in theological education was mostly from afar. In South East Asia, too, it became apparent that the Western style of theological education generally involving post-baccalaureate study by residential students was inappropriate to the needs of Asian Christians working in a different culture and facing different political issues. The immediate need in the area was for lower-level institutions, including Bible schools for those with only basic education. The Board of Founders responded to this need, changing its focus from a Western model of ministerial education to a model shaped by and preferred by Asian Christians that appeared better suited to regional needs.

Through its South East Asia office, the Board of Founders assisted in developing a regional sense of Christian community that transcended national boundaries. The mission period had seen the development of both European and American models of Christianity, but the postcolonial period witnessed the emergence of an Asian model of Christianity. The board funded a critical conference on theological education in 1956. Held in Bangkok, Thailand, this was the first conference of its kind in the region and resulted in the formation of the Association of Theological Schools in South East Asia, later reshaped and renamed the Association for Theological Education in South East Asia, the second such international organization in the world. Additionally, resolving the question of graduate level theological education for Asians in Asia, the Board of Founders assisted in creating the South East Asia Graduate School of Theology (SEAGST), which draws on the resources of a variety of regional seminaries and places students from participating countries with the most appropriate faculty mentors within the consortium.

In China, the Nanking Theological Seminary became the site of a reorganized Nanjing Union Theological Seminary (Jinling Xiehe Shen Xueyuan) in 1952, when several additional Protestant seminaries in China merged with the old school, and Bishop K. H. Ting (Ding Guangxun) was appointed president.[5] For more than twenty years there was essentially no contact between the FTESEA and the seminary, but, in the late 1970s, as China began to open to the West and as diplomatic relationships were restored between the United States and China, renewed contact between the two organizations became possible. Since the early 1980s, Nanjing Union Theological Seminary has again been a major beneficiary of FTESEA grants. Other Chinese seminaries have also received special grants on the recommendation of the Commission on Theological Education (CTE) of the China Christian Council (CCC), the official organization of Chinese Protestantism. Thus, while the FTESEA continues its support of theological education throughout Southeast Asia, a major focus of the recent past has been the restoration of relationships with Nanjing Seminary and the Chinese church. Today the foundation works most closely with three partners in South East and East Asia: Nanjing Seminary, the Commission on Theological Education of the China Christian Council, and the Association for Theological Education in South East Asia. As is appropriate for a new relationship with indigenous churches, the FTESEA relies increasingly on the recommendations and oversight of its partners in the region in its work to strengthen theological education.

5 As was the case with NTS, the Chinese name for the seminary uses an older, traditional place name, Jinling. However, in the interest of clarity, the English name is always shown as Nanjing Union Theological Seminary. Clarity, however, produced the unfortunate English acronym NUTS; and I have therefore continued to use NTS for citations that refer to the post-1952 seminary.

CHAPTER 1

Nanking Theological Seminary and its Board of Founders

Nanjing, the name of the city where this narrative appropriately begins, is literally translated as "southern capital." Situated on the southern bank of the Yangtze River, Nanjing lies approximately 160 miles west of Shanghai and is today an urban center and the capital of Jiangsu Province. It is an attractive city with broad avenues and a more-or-less intact city wall. Just to its east lies Purple Mountain, the site of lovely gardens as well as the tombs of Ming Emperor Hong Wu and of Sun Yat-sen, the founder of the Chinese Republic. The city dates at least from the Han dynasty (202 BCE to 23 CE), when it was known as Jinling (formerly transliterated as Ginling). It gained greater political significance as the capital of the Kingdom of Wu in the tenth century. This kingdom, one of several Yangtze states that succeeded the collapse of the Tang dynasty, introduced into Nanjing some of the surviving culture of the Tang. The Wu kingdom was short lived, but the city developed both economically and culturally and in the fourteenth century was chosen by the first Ming emperor as his capital. Though the imperial palace was destroyed and the capital moved to Beijing after the death of Hong Wu, the city continued to enjoy cultural, political, and economic significance from that period to the present.

The city was seized by the British in 1842, and it was there that the Treaty of Nanjing was signed at the end of the first Opium War. This treaty opened four Chinese cities to foreign powers for purposes of trade and residence, and Nanjing itself was added to the list of treaty ports in 1858.[1] However, the Taiping rebels, under the leadership of Hong Xiuquan, made Nanjing their capital from 1853 to 1864; only toward the end of the nineteenth century did Nanjing become important to foreign traders and missionaries.[2]

Nanjing became the capital of the Republic of China in 1928 and, though governmental functions were moved to Chongqing during the Second World War, Nanjing remained the official seat of the Nationalist government until it fled to Taiwan after its mainland defeat by the Communists in 1949. With the creation of the People's Republic of China, the seat of government once more returned to Beijing. Nanjing returned to its present status as capital of one of China's most prosperous provinces.

Protestant missions had commenced in China in 1807 with Robert Morrison's work in Guangzhou (then known in the West as Canton) and among overseas Chinese communities in South East Asia as an agent of the London Missionary Society. Other Protestants followed Morrison into China, and Elijah C. Bridgman, the first American Protestant missionary, sailed for China in 1829. Especially through their efforts to translate the Bible and other Christian literature into Chinese, Morrison and his missionary colleagues laid the foundation for Chinese Protestantism. All such work within the Chinese empire remained illegal, however, and few Chinese were attracted to the new religion.

With the defeat of China in the first Opium War and the subsequent Treaty of Nanjing, mission work within China became legal, and both Protestant and Catholic missionaries began to arrive in significant numbers. This rapid expansion of mission activity in China resulted in part from the favorable terms of the "unequal

1 This treaty was originally known in its English language version as the Treaty of Nanking, and this terminology continues to be used outside China.

2 For an excellent recent biography of Hong, which explores his ideas and the influence of Protestant missions on his thought as well as his military and political actions, see Jonathan D. Spence, *God's Chinese Son: The Taiping Heavenly Kingdom of Hong Xiuquan* (New York: Norton, 1996).

treaties" of Nanjing (1842), Tianjin (1858), and Beijing (1860), which granted missionaries the right to acquire property and work in China and granted them protection of extraterritoriality. It was further encouraged by the almost simultaneous abolition of slavery in the United States and a shift of evangelical Protestant energies from this domestic reform toward foreign missions. Between 1858 and 1861, the number of Protestant missionaries and their wives in China increased from 85 to 618, and by 1898 Protestant missionaries were working in all of the provinces of the empire.[3] In spite of the violent attack on both missionaries and Chinese Christians by the Boxers in 1900, the number of missionaries continued to grow—to 3,445 in 1905 and 5,144 in 1910.[4] The number of Chinese converts also began to grow. While in 1858 there had been less than 500 Chinese converts, that number reached 85,000 by1900.[5]

Significant mission activity in the city of Nanjing commenced later than in most of the treaty ports, delayed by the Taiping rebellion and occupation of the city. Shortly after the defeat of the Taipings, however, Protestants moved into Nanjing, and the city quickly became a center for educational and medical as well as evangelistic mission work. As the number of Chinese communicants increased, it quickly became clear that native leadership for the Chinese church would be a prerequisite for its full development, and that the preparation of this leadership would require educational institutions at every level from primary school through college and seminary.

Among the first Protestants to arrive in Nanjing were representatives of the Methodist Episcopal Church, who established a mission in 1869. By 1888 they had established a college, which bore the name Nanking University. A medical school was added to the university in 1890, and a separate theological seminary was founded a bit later.[6] Missionaries of both the Presbyterian Church in the U.S.A. and the Presbyterian Church in the U.S. were active in the province from about the same time, and the Presbyterian Church in the U.S.A. also established an academy for boys in Nanjing.

3 Kenneth Scott Latourette, *A History of Christian Missions in China* (New York: Russell and Russell, 1967), 405-06, 361.

4 Ibid., 606.

5 Frank Rawlinson, Helen Thoburn, and D. MacGillivray, eds, *The Chinese Church as Revealed in the National Christian Conference* (Shanghai: Oriental Press, 1922), 82.

6 Latourette, *History*, 629; C. Stanley Smith, *The Development of Protestant Theological Education in China in the Light of the History of the Education of the Clergy in Europe and America* (Shanghai: Kelly and Walsh, 1941), 80.

The Christian Church (Disciples of Christ) entered China a bit later and did not commence its work in the city of Nanjing until 1886, when Dr. William Macklin arrived to establish a medical mission. Other Disciples missionaries began arriving in Nanjing the following year. One of them, F. E. Meigs, opened a boarding school for boys that subsequently evolved into Nanking Christian College. Macklin opened a dispensary adjacent to Nanking University and its medical school and near the city's ancient Drum Tower. A hospital building was erected there in 1892.[7] Before the turn of the twentieth century, these several denominational missions, all with interests in medical and educational as well as evangelistic programs, were working in close proximity in the city of Nanjing.

Simultaneously, in both Europe and America the statements of Protestant church leaders began to show an increasing recognition of the waste as well as the theological embarrassment that resulted from rival presentations of the Christian mission. The statements also reflected a consequent growth of interest in cooperative and interdenominational approaches to mission activity. Councils of churches began to appear at local as well as national levels, and the World Missionary Conference held in Edinburgh in 1910 focused on the urgency of cooperation among missionary bodies working in the vicinity of one another.[8] The Edinburgh conference initiated a formal plan for mission coordination. Regional bodies were to be formed both in missionary sending and receiving countries, and all were to be linked in an International Missionary Council. John R. Mott, the charismatic figure behind this conference, was appointed chairman of the Continuation Committee. In this capacity, Mott visited China in 1913. There "with him as presiding officer five regional conferences were held and a national body made up of delegates from these was convened in Shanghai."[9]

Kenneth Scott Latourette reported:

> the findings of the national body included (1) a recognition of the strong plea to the Church presented by the districts in China still unoccupied by Protestant forces, a call for a survey to show the state of the occupation,...a suggested procedure for comity in entering new territory, a note of the need for work

7 Ibid., 81; Edith Eberle, *Macklin of Nanking* (St. Louis: Bethany, 1936), 53 ff.

8 R. Pierce Beaver, *Ecumenical Beginnings in Protestant World Mission: A History of Comity* (New York: Nelson, 1962), 42-80.

9 Latourette, *History*, 669.

> among Moslems, and an expression of the conviction that the missionary body should be heavily reenforced; (2) a statement of the unprecedented openmindedness of the Chinese to the Gospel, a declaration that much of the burden of evangelism could now be assumed by the Chinese churches, and that the work of evangelism should be pushed; (3) an expression of hope that "the Churches...be so developed that the Chinese themselves may recognize them as having become truly native," that "to manifest the unity that already exists among all faithful Christians in China" a common name be adopted, the one preferred being *Chung Hua Chi Tu Chiao Hui,* "the Christian Church in China," and suggested steps toward a larger unity and toward self-support; (4) emphasis upon the training of Chinese leaders; (5) standards for the selection and training of missionaries; (6) a plea for expansion in Christian education, especially in primary, secondary, and theological schools; (7) a statement of the next steps to be taken in Christian literature; (8) plans for more extensive union and cooperation; (9) medical work; (10) women's work; and (11) business efficiency."[10]

Among the specific proposals of this national gathering was a recommendation "that medical, theological, and middle schools and colleges be conducted on union principles...."[11]

This program for greater cooperation in mission was warmly received in China. In fact, to a considerable extent, cooperation in the Middle Kingdom preceded the World Missionary Conference and Mott's subsequent visit. As early as 1807, the China Centenary Conference in Shanghai had advocated similar measures, including the formation of a Christian Federation of China, and the several Protestant missions working in Nanjing moved toward cooperation in their educational work from an early date.

The Christian Church (Disciples) school united with the Presbyterian Academy about 1906 to form the Union Christian College. In 1910 this institution joined with the Methodist Nanking University to become the University of Nanking.[12] Similarly, the Christian Church hospital was working closely with the university's medical school. This is the context of comity and cooperation in which these denominations came to create a union seminary in Nanjing.

10 Ibid., 670.
11 Ibid., 671.
12 Ibid., 80-81.

Though preparation of converts for evangelical and other ministerial work began with the earliest Protestant activity in China, theological seminaries as formal schools for the preparation of clergy were established only from the 1860s. Robert Morrison, China's first Protestant missionary, and his colleague, William Milne, established an Anglo-Chinese College at Malacca, Malaysia, for the purpose of "cultivating the Chinese language and for such other purposes (Literary, Theological, and Philosophical) as are specified...." Yet in his study of early ministerial education in China, Smith observed that the college was not established primarily for the education of a Christian ministry and concluded that "there is no evidence that this first Protestant College ever made any distinctive contribution toward the training of a Chinese ministry."[13]

Thus, in the period prior to the Treaty of Nanjing, preparation of a native clergy was limited to informal in-service preparation in which an individual convert characteristically worked under the instruction and supervision of a missionary. Recruits for such training sometimes came from boys in the mission schools or language teachers engaged by the missionaries or even from converts who had a background in Chinese classical studies. Smith found no evidence of a theological seminary on Chinese soil prior to 1868, when one appeared in the city of Xiamen (Amoy).[14]

With the legal opening of China to missionary activity under the terms of the Treaty of Nanjing and subsequent treaties and the consequent rapid increase in the size and activity of the mission community, the need for Chinese helpers to serve as evangelists, colporteurs, or Bible women also increased rapidly. By 1867 the tradition of informal and in-service training began to give way to formal classes. A Baptist class organized for Bible study in 1867 may have been the first training class, and it evolved into a seminary in 1907. In general, the evolution of formal ministerial instruction was from training class to Bible school and thence to seminary. In general, the Bible schools maintained lower admission standards and a more elementary curriculum that focused on devotional and homiletic study of the Bible.[15]

The development of ministerial training among Presbyterian missions in the lower Yangtze area well illustrates this evolution from individual instruction and Bible classes to Bible schools and, finally, to

[13] Smith, *Development*, 24-26.
[14] Ibid., 29.
[15] Ibid., 39, 40, 49.

seminaries. As early as 1845, a boys' boarding school was established at Ningbo (Ningpo) in Zhejiang Province, a short distance from Nanjing. The founders characterized the enterprise as "our chief hope for raising up a native ministry." A training class for Chinese clergy was formed in 1845, and its first two graduates were ordained in 1864. Early instructors of this class included W. A. P. Martin, who later moved to Beijing, established a Presbyterian mission there, served for a time as president of the Imperial University, and was certainly one of the foremost Americans in China at the time.[16]

As mission work spread, training classes such as the one created in Ningbo were organized in other large mission stations. By 1893 plans were underway for the creation of a theological seminary. However, at the time that proved impossible, and instead a theological class was formed and moved about from station to station in order to enlist the services of a larger number of missionaries. These classes were taught by several missionaries who would become a part of the Nanjing Seminary when it was eventually established. Dr. Joshua C. Garritt and Dr. John W. Davis taught at the Suzhou (Soochow) station between Nanjing and Shanghai, while Dr. J. Leighton Stuart, later president of Yenching University in Beijing and briefly U.S. ambassador to China, and Dr. P. Frank Price taught at the mission station in Hangzhou (Hangchow) in Zhejiang Province to the south of Nanjing.[17]

A second proposal to establish a union theological seminary was made at a general conference of Presbyterian missionaries in Shanghai in 1901, and Nanjing was proposed as a possible site for the school. A provisional committee then presented the proposal to three missions, and two of them approved. A joint committee met in Nanjing January 1, 1904, with representatives from the Presbyterian U.S.A. and the Presbyterian U.S. missions. Dr. John W. Davis of the latter denomination was elected chair, and the group voted to recommend "that the missions concerned unite in the establishment of a Union Theological Seminary under their joint control."[18]

The city of Nanjing was a logical location for this new seminary. Its geographical situation was central to the missions interested in this cooperative venture, and the city was a major treaty port as well as a cultural center. The city was also becoming a center for Protestant

16 Frank Wilson Price, *History of Nanking Theological Seminary, 1911 to 1961* (New York: Board of Founders of Nanking Theological Seminary, 1961), 2.

17 Ibid., 3.

18 Ibid.; Smith, *Development*, 106-07.

mission activities in eastern China. Additionally, large plots of vacant land within the city wall were available as a result of the destruction occasioned by the Taiping Rebellion. A site was chosen near Hanximen, one of the city gates, and each of the cooperating missions was asked for funding for land and buildings.

The new Board of Directors, composed of representatives from each of the cooperating Presbyterian U.S.A. and Presbyterian U.S. missions, met in November 1904 in Nanjing and named the seminary the Presbyterian Union Theological Seminary of Central China. Its doctrinal standards were declared to be "the Word of God as interpreted by the Westminster Confession of Faith, the Catechisms, and other standards as are held in common by both of the Churches controlling the Seminary." Each professor was required to sign a pledge of faithfulness to the Westminster Confession of Faith."[19]

Davis moved from Suzhou to Nanjing in the spring of 1905 to become president of the seminary; and, at its May meeting, the board made plans to construct a main building, a dormitory, and two professors' residences. The seminary opened in October 1906 with ten students in the regular course and twenty-four in a Bible training course. Students came from the adjoining Jiangsu and Zhejiang provinces and from both cooperating denominations. The seminary grew steadily over the next few years with increases in faculty, student enrollment, and facilities. J. Leighton Stuart joined the faculty in early 1909. The first Chinese professor, the Reverend Chen Ching-yung, came to the faculty in 1910 where he joined Davis, Stuart, and J. C. Garritt.[20]

The Christian Church (Disciples of Christ), an American denomination founded in the nineteenth century, initially prepared its American ministers in colleges that combined liberal arts and theological education. In China it initially prepared its native clergy in short Bible training classes for preachers and evangelists that were held after each annual denominational convention. This training was conducted by the Reverend Abram E. Cory, who served a mission station at Lu-chow-fu, but in 1903 he was transferred to Nanjing to develop this Bible study program further. At Nanjing he designed a Bible institute that offered three-week sessions attended by Chinese clergy from various mission stations of this denomination. In 1908 the management of the institute was transferred to a union committee, and the Foreign Christian Missionary Society, the denomination's mission agency, asked Cory to inaugurate a Disciples Bible College and Training

19 Price, *History*, 3-4; Smith, *Development*, 107; Cartwright, *River*, 55.
20 Ibid.

School. This transition reflected the denomination's recognition that Chinese clergy required more extensive education than was available through a short institute course. The Bible college began offering a seminary program in March 1908 in rented quarters with an enrollment of twenty, but it soon moved into mission facilities near the Drum Tower. Its teaching staff consisted of Mr. and Mrs. Cory, Frank Garrett, Charles S. Settlemeyer, and two Chinese teachers. They proposed to provide training to candidates for the ministry who had completed a college course, while a training school associated with the college was designed for students with little or no college training but a fair elementary knowledge of the Bible and Christian doctrine and a desire to become lay evangelists.[21] When the mission received a gift of $6,000 from Myrtle G. Warren for the construction of a building to house the new Bible college, the enthusiasm for union and cooperation was at its peak, and a desire was expressed to join with other denominations in a cooperative venture. Discussions with Presbyterians led to the decision to place the new building on the campus of the Presbyterian Union Theological Seminary.[22]

A third school that would participate in the formation of the seminary was the Fowler School of Theology. That school was established in Nanjing in 1895 by the Methodist Episcopal Church North with a bequest honoring Bishop Charles W. Fowler. Its building was initially on the campus of the Methodist university there and eventually became the administration building of the interdenominational University of Nanking. However, the seminary did not prosper in Nanjing and eventually was moved to Kiukiang where, for two years, it was operated by the Reverend Harry F. Rowe, subsequently president of the Nanjing seminary.[23]

In approving the new Disciples school in Nanjing, the Foreign Christian Missionary Society suggested that it be patterned after the Moody Bible Institute of Chicago and the Bible Teachers' Training School of New York, pioneer ventures in interdenominational cooperation in the preparation of lay evangelists for church service in the United States. Dr. Wilbert W. White, the founder of the Bible Teachers' Training School, traveled to China in 1910 while discussions were underway among the Presbyterian, Disciples, and Methodist missions looking toward a union seminary, and he spoke to a large audience of missionaries in Shanghai. White, whose school was said

21 Smith, *Development*, 81-82.

22 Ibid.; Price, *History*, 2.

23 Price, *History*, 2; Smith, *Development*, 80.

to teach the inductive Bible study method and was described as "interdenominational in character, thorough in intellectual processes, evangelical in doctrine, reverent in spirit, pedagogical in method, and practical in aim," advocated a similar institution for China. A conference at Shanghai shortly afterward, "representing twelve provinces and a large proportion of missionary societies, called for an interdenominational theological school, securely based upon an evangelical foundation, as a conserving and unifying force for the growing Church in China." From this consultation and subsequent meetings emerged a Committee on Bible Training Schools in China, which determined to establish its institution in Nanjing and declared that it would adapt the Bible training school model to conditions in China and provide "all grades of Biblical instruction, in preparation for Christian work, exclusive of denominational teaching," leaving the latter instruction to each cooperating denominational mission.[24]

At a meeting in January 1911, the Presbyterian Seminary Board of Directors voted to lend its buildings to the Bible school. The loan was for an experimental period of thirty months commencing with the autumn term of 1911 and with the expectation that permanent plans would be made during that period. Both the Methodist and Disciple missions agreed to support the Bible school, and it was clear that this interdenominational effort would require a broader doctrinal basis than the Presbyterian school, though the Presbyterian directors were assured that all teachers would "affirm their belief in the inspiration and historicity of the Holy Scriptures and in Jesus Christ, the only begotten Son of God, and His vicarious atonement for the sins of the world." This doctrinal standard would become a source of controversy as the American rift between modernists and fundamentalists was carried to China, where the cooperating missions found they did not understand the standard in the same way. Even this standard failed to satisfy John W. Davis, president of the Presbyterian Seminary. He resigned and was replaced as president by Dr. J. C. Garritt of the Presbyterian, U.S.A. mission.[25]

Thus the newly created Nanking Bible Training School opened September 13, 1911, in the facilities of the Presbyterian Seminary. Its catalogue declared:

24 Price, *History*, 5; Smith, *Development*, 108-09. The Bible Teachers' Training School was established by White in 1900. It was renamed the Biblical Seminary in New York in 1921 and became the New York Theological Seminary in 1966.

25 Price, *History*, 5-6; Cartwright, *River*, 56-57.

> The present affiliation is a measure adopted in hope of attaining the advantages of united effort without delay, while giving the greatest degree of liberty to all cooperating parties. The changing conditions in China, calling for numerous adjustments, and particularly the insistent desire of the Chinese Church at large for unity within its own borders, furnish sufficient justification for this tentative method of cooperation. Those entrusted with the conduct of the institution reverently acknowledge their dependence upon the Divine Spirit who has been leading step by step.[26]

The initial faculty included the following clergy: J. C. Garritt from the Presbyterian U.S.A. mission, P. Frank Price and J. Leighton Stuart from the Presbyterian U.S. mission, Frank Garrett from the Disciples mission, Harry F. Rowe from the Methodist mission, and Chen Ching-yung from the Chinese church. Nonclergy faculty included Chen Li-seng and Li Djao, and Shih Yun-ting and Dsiang Tiao-chin held appointments as tutors.[27] The number of Chinese faculty members offered evidence of the growing maturity of Protestantism in China and an indication of the increasingly significant role that Chinese leaders would assume within the seminary in the following years.

Though the academic year opened with optimism, within weeks the Manchu government was overthrown. When Republican forces moved toward Nanjing, the local imperial military commander resisted the revolutionaries. In the turmoil, the school was forced to close on November 5. However, Nanjing fell to the Republic, and Sun Yat-sen was inaugurated as provisional president in Nanjing on January 1, 1912. Students returned, and the spring term commenced March 5 with an enrollment of sixty-three from six mission groups and six Chinese provinces.[28]

The initial meeting of the Board of Managers for Nanking Bible Training School was held February 8, 1912, after having been scheduled the preceding November but postponed as a result of the siege of the city. Price reported that

> Twelve members, representing the three cooperating denominational families, were present, and four directors-at-large elected the previous summer at Kuling [during a meeting of the

[26] Quoted in Cartwright, *River,* 57.
[27] Ibid.
[28] Price, *History,* 6; Cartwright, *River,* 57.

> Executive Committee of the Committee on Bible Schools], from the China Inland Mission, the Student Volunteer Movement, the Friends' Missions, and the Y.M.C.A.[29]

Officers of the board were selected, including the Reverend C. G. Miller, a Methodist missionary, as chairman and S. K. Tsao of the YMCA as secretary. The initial faculty was approved, and the Reverend Chang Yung-hsun, pastor of St. Luke's Methodist Church in Nanjing, was appointed to the faculty.[30] A budget was adopted, grants (beyond the salaries of their missionary teachers) were requested from participating missions, and additional land purchases were approved. However, the board's primary attention was devoted to clarifying the relationship of its school to the Presbyterian Union Theological Seminary on whose campus the Bible Training School was located. The Presbyterian seminary, which maintained its own board of directors until 1914, was given the authority to appoint its own professors, though these were to be confirmed by the Bible Training School. The Bible school curriculum was also subject to approval by the Presbyterian seminary board. A parallel Women's Bible School was being planned, and it was agreed that, while the women's school would have its own board of directors, "there would be as much mutual consultation and joint action as possible."[31]

During the following year, 1912, the Bible school board and the Presbyterian seminary board entered into discussions looking toward property adjustments and permanent union. The missions of the Methodist Episcopal Church, South, and the Northern and Southern Baptist Conventions were invited "to unite with us in theological instruction, on the same basis of affiliation and cooperation as exists among the present cooperating missions." A new constitution was drafted providing that each participating mission would have two representatives, one Chinese and one Westerner, on the board. Frank Garrett of the Disciples mission was chosen to become acting president when J. C. Garritt went on furlough. The name of the Bible school was also changed to Nanking School of Theology, a title it would use until 1917. The Bible school remained a department of the school of theology. Though the change in nomenclature suggested a broader theological curriculum, and though the new statement of purpose declared that the school would train students for "any form of Christian service,"

29 Price, *History*, 6.
30 Ibid., 6-7.
31 Ibid.

that statement also affirmed that in conducting its instruction, "special prominence shall be given to the study of the Bible."[32]

As the board reached out to additional missions with an invitation to share in the work of the school of theology, the question of its doctrinal position required further clarification. From 1912 forward, the Nanking School of Theology (after 1917 the Nanking Theological Seminary) adopted the following statement:

> The Nanking School of Theology accepts as the basis of its teaching the Word of God, and holds to the fundamental doctrines of our common evangelical faith, which faith has been the strength and heritage of the Christian Church through all its history.
>
> 1. We accept the Scriptures of the Old and New Testament as the inspired Word of God, the supreme rule of faith and practice, and as containing all things necessary to salvation.
>
> 2. We acknowledge the Lord Jesus Christ as the Divine Son of God and His vicarious atonement for the sins of the world.
>
> 3. We accept the divinity and personality of the Holy Spirit and His operation in the work of regeneration and sanctification.
>
> 4. We hold that the Church of the Lord Jesus Christ is a spiritual institution, organized for spiritual ends, depending on spiritual power, and, as a church, has no political authority.[33]

The draft of a new constitution for a union school was sent to the cooperating missions for approval at the May 1913 meeting of the Board of Managers. The constitution was to become effective at the conclusion of the thirty month period of experimental cooperation, i.e., December 31, 1913, contingent on a favorable vote by all missions. The ratification statement submitted to the missions declared "that the Presbyterian Union Theological Seminary, the Nanking Bible College (Disciples), and the Methodist Fowler School of Theology [would] be merged into the Nanking School of Theology."[34]

The change in name from Bible school to school of theology reflected the faculty's interest in strengthening the academic rigor of the institution and seeing it develop as a major training center for Chinese clergy. Additional faculty members were recruited, the study of

[32] Ibid., 7-8; Smith, *Development*, 110.
[33] Price, *History*, 7-8; Cartwright, *River*, 58-59.
[34] Price, *History*, 8-9; Cartwright, *River*, 59.

Hebrew was introduced into the curriculum, and a theological quarterly was launched. However, realization of these academic ambitions would require additional resources. Rowe, by then the vice president of the school, was appointed its special financial agent on his furlough to the United States.[35]

Theological controversies in the United States began to spill over into Nanjing as the North Jiangsu Mission of the Presbyterian Church U.S., one of the two Southern Presbyterian missions supporting the school, complained of liberal theological tendencies. Its representatives failed to attend the meeting of the Board of Managers in 1916 but returned in 1917. Eventually, however, this mission withdrew its support from the Nanjing school.[36]

In spite of this controversy, which continued for more than a decade, Price described the years from 1915 to 1925 as years of "rapid expansion and growing pains." From 1917, new faculty members were required to "submit to the Board of Managers in writing a statement agreeing to teach in harmony with the Constitution, reaffirming his loyalty to the doctrinal standards or declaration of his own Church and declaring his belief in the integrity and historical reliability of the Holy Scriptures."[37]

In 1917 the Board of Managers of the seminary entered into an agreement with the Stewart Evangelistic Fund of California to federate with the fund with respect to its precollegiate Bible Training School. This fund, created by Milton Stewart, represented an effort by Stewart and his brother, Lyman Stewart, to support fundamentalism

35 Price, *History*, 9.

36 Ibid., 10; Kevin Xiyi Yao, *The Fundamentalist Movement among Protestant Missionaries in China, 1920–1937* (New York: Univ. Press of America., 2003), 101-38. J. Leighton Stuart later commented regarding this controversy that "in my whole experience I have never met with *odium theologicum* as implacably virulent and polemical as it was among members of that northern mission. It was strange because as individuals and in personal relationships they were not unlike the rest of us. It may be that the harsh conditions of their life in a poverty-stricken, ill-governed, inaccessible part of the country tended to embitter or at least harden them, for among themselves in matters of internal mission business they showed a somewhat similar spirit. Pearl Buck grew up in that environment and knew little of other missionaries....This largely perhaps explains her reactions to missions." John Leighton Stuart, *Fifty Years in China: The Memoirs of John Leighton Stuart, Missionary and Ambassador* (New York: Random House, 1954), 44-45.

37 Price, *History*, 10.

within American Protestantism.[38] However, this cooperative endeavor was short lived. The Stewart Fund's interest in conservative and precollegiate-level ministerial training ran counter to the seminary's determination to remain open to a variety of theological perspectives, as well as its steady movement toward higher academic standards. A three-year Bachelor of Divinity course for college graduates was introduced in 1918. The Board of Managers ceased admitting new students to the Bible Training School in 1920, extended its undergraduate course from three to four years, and planned a three-year course for junior college graduates.[39] Enrollments grew steadily. In 1919 the faculty reported 146 students from sixteen denominations and eleven provinces and Korea. Four of the students were in the post-graduate program. Three years later the enrollment had reached 168. Though the Methodist Episcopal Church, South, provided an additional dormitory in 1921, facilities remained barely adequate, and the Board of Managers launched a major funding program.[40]

The theological conflict that had erupted in 1916-17 resurfaced in 1922 when Hugh W. White, a member of the Board of Managers representing the North Jiangsu Mission, requested that two books being used in the seminary be withdrawn as textbooks.[41] The North Jiangsu Mission clearly intended to force the seminary to affirm its own fundamentalist doctrinal position, but White found only one supporter among the twenty attending the Board of Managers meeting. Seeking to placate the mission, the board asked Professor C. Stanley Smith to cease using one of the volumes as a textbook, though they added that he might continue to include it along with more conservative titles on his reference list. The board took no action with respect to the second volume, since it was included on the reference list and not required reading for students.[42]

Though the position of the North Jiangsu Mission was not supported by other cooperating missions at Nanking Seminary, it reflected general concerns that had been expressed by the General

[38] Ernest R. Sandeen, *The Roots of Fundamentalism: British and American Millenarianism, 1800–1930* (Grand Rapids: Baker, 1978), 249-50.

[39] Price, *History*, 11.

[40] Ibid., 12, 14.

[41] The two volumes were William Newton Clarke, *An Outline of Christian Theology*, 3d ed. (New York: Scribner's, 1899) and James Hastings, *Dictionary of the Bible* (New York: Scribner's, 1898). Both were widely used in major Protestant seminaries in the U.S. at the time and reflected a liberal view of scripture and inspiration.

[42] Yao, *Fundamentalist Movement*, 111.

Assembly of the Presbyterian Church in the U.S., which had urged the two Presbyterian missions from its denomination to form an investigating committee even while cautioning that "we do not think we ought to take any extreme position in our requirement of concessions from other Missions." The North Jiangsu Mission then pursued its investigation aggressively, found all Presbyterian faculty members "doctrinally sound," but found the views of three others unsatisfactory. A joint meeting of North Jiangsu's investigating committee with that of the Mid-China Mission's committee resulted in submission of recommendations, including closer adherence to the doctrinal standards in the constitution and dismissal of Professor H. C. Ritter, a Methodist and professor of Old Testament.[43]

A meeting of the seminary's Board of Managers with a subcommittee appointed by the two investigating committees was held March 28, 1923. At this critical meeting, according to White of the North Jiangsu Mission, the seminary representatives insisted that

> There is a place here for so-called Progressives and Conservatives.... There is here freedom to search for truth; We want men to be strong, true men, whether they hold to the old or the new views. We are opposed to any form of teaching which tends to undermine the faith of men, whether it comes from the liberal or the over-conservative side.[44]

Clearly the board was unwilling to adopt the strict doctrinal standards of the North Jiangsu Mission, but it was equally unwilling to reject that position out of hand and, instead, sought to accommodate the requests as far as possible. However, it refused to dismiss H. C. Ritter, who was then on furlough in America and eventually decided not to return.[45]

Neither side appeared satisfied by these actions. The North Jiangsu Mission met in August 1923 and resolved to ask the seminary's cooperating missions to accept its interpretation of the constitutional doctrinal basis which reflected the "five points" of fundamentalism.[46]

43 Ibid., 111-14.

44 Hugh W. White, "Nanking Seminary Board of Managers, March 28, 29, 1923, Report to North Kiangsu Mission by Hugh W. White," Hugh W. White Papers, Presbyterian Historical Society, Montreat, N.C., 2-3, cited in Yao, *Fundamentalist Movement,* 115.

45 Ibid., 115-16.

46 I.e., infallibility of Scriptures, deity and virgin birth of Jesus Christ, vicarious atonement of Jesus Christ, bodily resurrection and ascension, and Christ's performance of miracles; ibid, 118-19.

Thus the stage was set for open conflict when the board held a special meeting in November. There the pressures from the North Jiangsu Mission were met with "overwhelming resistance." Yao observed that "the liberal and moderate majority of the board and faculty apparently decided that the requests of the North Jiangsu Mission were too much to take, and they were not willing to accommodate to its conservative agenda anymore." The seminary faculty presented a paper representing its more open position, and Methodist Bishop Lauress J. Birney, a member of the board, appealed for "liberty of teaching in the faculty and liberty of belief on the part of the students," while Edwin Marx of the Disciples of Christ stated that "his church stood for liberty of belief and liberty of teaching on the one foundation of belief in Jesus Christ, and that he felt sure that his church would not stand for any stricter interpretation of the constitution."[47] Subsequently, the North Jiangsu Mission's request was rejected, and the board denied the right of any participating mission to conduct its own investigation of any faculty member.[48]

The North Jiangsu Mission voted to withdraw from participation in Nanking Seminary in January 1924 and so advised its General Assembly through the Executive Committee of Foreign Missions. This mission called upon the Mid-China Mission to leave as well, but Mid-China refused, declaring that "it is our solemn conviction that our testimony as a church and for the whole church in China can best be borne by holding and strengthening a position of large influence and opportunity, rather than by abandonment or isolation." This mission asked the Executive Committee and General Assembly of the Presbyterian Church in the U.S. to allow them to remain in the union, and the latter supported Mid-China's decision. Encouraged by the General Assembly to reconsider its action, the North Jiangsu Mission did postpone its withdrawal, but by 1927 the separation was complete.[49] The withdrawal of the supporting mission with the most conservative doctrinal statement ended this period of turmoil and enabled Nanking Seminary to survive as a union institution offering sufficient doctrinal freedom to serve a broad interdenominational constituency.

As the period of doctrinal turmoil drew to a close, a period of political and military instability followed. When Sun Yat-sen died in 1925, the entire country was faced with warlordism and intensifying rivalry between the Communist and Nationalist wings of the

47 Quoted in ibid., 121.
48 Ibid., 121-22.
49 Ibid., 124-25.

Republican government, as well as antiforeign sentiment aroused and intensified by a fatal attack on protesting students in Shanghai by British-controlled municipal police. Chiang Kai-shek, leader of the Nationalists, seized Shanghai in 1927 and purged Communist leaders in areas under his control. Communist forces from Wuhan responded and entered Nanjing, where foreign missions and other institutions were threatened. Before Chiang's army drove its rivals from the city and established its capital there, missionaries had been threatened, mission property looted, and Dr. John E. Williams, vice president of the University of Nanking, killed.[50] Seminary property was severely damaged during this period, and several missionary professors either fled to Shanghai or took furloughs. The seminary was forced to close for two academic years, reopening in the fall of 1929 in rented quarters with six Western and three Chinese teachers and twenty-six students. This was a dramatic reduction in staff and student body occasioned by this new turmoil. Only gradually did the seminary regain enrollment. Student numbers reached thirty in 1930 and fifty-eight in 1933.[51]

New government regulations at this time forced some changes in the programs offered by the seminary, which was no longer permitted to grant B.A. degrees through other universities and colleges. Yet it was able to strengthen its own diploma course. After 1930 at least half of the members of the Board of Managers were required to be Chinese. In the following year, the seminary chose its first Chinese president, the Reverend Handel Lee, pastor of a Methodist church in Nanjing and an alumnus of the seminary who had studied in the United States.[52] As the seminary began to recover from this period of turmoil and uncertainty, a generous bequest altered its future prospects dramatically.

Professional development officers who are responsible for fund-raising on behalf of universities, cultural institutions, and other charitable institutions speak of "over-the-transom gifts," i.e., significant gifts that appear entirely unexpectedly, frequently when a will is probated. The Foundation for Theological Education in South East Asia and its predecessor, the Board of Founders of Nanking Theological Seminary, owe their existence to one such gift, a legacy established under the terms of the wills of Rebecca Wendel Swope and Ella V. von E. Wendel of New York.

The Reverend Harry F. Rowe, an American Methodist missionary and member of the initial faculty of Nanking Theological Seminary,

50 Price, *History*, 16-17.
51 Ibid., 17-18.
52 Ibid., 19.

became the seminary's president in 1921 after serving for a time as acting president.[53] In that capacity he sought a meeting with some members of the Wendel family of New York, most likely Rebecca Swope and Ella Wendel, in the following year. They gave him $5,000 to help with the construction of a new building. Over the subsequent years, Rowe sent them occasional letters regarding the work of the seminary, but they made no further contributions. Yet, upon the death of the last two surviving members of the family, the seminary became the beneficiary of an enormous legacy from the family estate. The income to be derived from an endowment left to the Board of Foreign Missions of the Methodist Episcopal Church was to be used on behalf of Nanking Theological Seminary. Truly an over-the-transom gift, this legacy was to have an enormous impact on the development of Protestant theological education in Nanjing and South East Asia for many years to come.[54]

The Wendel family was as remarkable as was its legacy to Nanking Theological Seminary. Family members had been accumulating New York real estate, primarily properties in Manhattan, for more than two centuries. They traced their lineage to General David "Fighting Dave" Wendel, who had served in the American Revolution. His son, John D., great-grandfather of the last generation, had begun the family's real estate acquisitions with the purchase of three lots on William Street in Manhattan. His son, John G., had been a business partner of John Jacob Astor in the fur trade. It is said that it was this Wendel who urged Astor repeatedly not to invest in his far-flung fur outposts but rather to concentrate on Manhattan real estate, advice that Astor eventually took. John G. Wendel's dictum was "buy and never sell," a policy carefully followed by other family members.[55]

The final Wendel generation consisted of a brother, John, and six sisters, Josephine J. S., Augusta, Ella V. von E., Georgiana C. R., Mary Eliza Astor, and Rebecca A. D. (Mrs. Luther A. Swope). Though they were not prominent in New York social circles, their reputed wealth brought them to public attention from time to time. Stories concerning them tended to reinforce the perception of family idiosyncrasies. It was reported that the sisters had traveled extensively when young and had mastered several languages, but they and their brother lived in virtual isolation in the family home on Fifth Avenue. The domineering brother, apparently convinced that only fortune seekers would wish

53 Rowe served as acting president from 1918 and as president from 1921 to 1929; Cartwright, *River, 87.*

54 Ibid., 7-8.

55 *New York Times* (hereafter *NYT),* Dec. 6, 1914.

to marry his sisters, forbade them to marry.[56] All their lives the sisters made their own clothes by hand fashioning them in black and in the hoop skirt style popular in their youth, and they wore them until they frayed. Their wardrobes were completed with round straw sailor hats which had been stylish in the 1860s and 1870s.

Of the six sisters, only Rebecca managed to defy her brother on the issue of marriage. Late in life and over the strenuous objections of her brother, she married Luther A. Swope, a professor and a friend of the vicar of Trinity Episcopal Church, which the family attended though they had a variety of Methodist ties. It was said that, following Rebecca's marriage, John discouraged his other sisters from attending church. The only other reported occasion of a sister having defied the brother occurred in 1899 when Georgiana, then thirty-seven years of age, ran away from the family's country home in Irvington-on-the-Hudson and appeared alone at the Park Avenue Hotel. Her brother had her committed to the psychiatric ward at Bellevue Hospital, and she was pronounced insane by a Sheriff's jury. She was released from a sanitarium, however, after the New York Supreme Court declared the commitment unconstitutional. Georgiana then sued her brother for $50,000, but the suit was settled out of court, and she returned to live in the family home with her brother and sisters.[57]

56 As with any reclusive family, there are many conflicting stories in print concerning the Wendels. Most news reports state that neither John nor any of his sisters had children, and certainly at the time of Ella's death in 1931 there were no known direct descendants. However, at the time of John's death in 1914, he was reported to have been at the home of his nephew, H. C. Holwedel, in Los Angeles. Another newspaper account states that Holwedel was the son of the fifth Wendel sister, but as the birth order of the sisters was never reported, it is unclear who was meant. The distribution of the estate following Ella's death suggests that Holwedel was a friend, not a family member. See *NYT*, Dec. 2, 1914.

57 The issue of Georgiana's sanity was extensively covered by the press. At the time she was said to be thirty-seven years old, though press accounts many years later said she was fifty. Her address was given as 19 Harmon Street, White Plains, although other members of the family were reported to live in Irvington. In the midst of the case, a real estate agent, a deputy sheriff, and a lawyer were arrested and arraigned on trespassing and disorderly conduct charges after they visited her home in an effort to secure her signature on a contract to erect a building in Brooklyn. See *NYT*, Jan. 25, 26, 1899; Aug. 24, Sept. 6, 7, 8, 25, 27, Oct. 3, 6, 10, 13, Nov. 3, 9, 1900; Sept. 15, 1901; July 24, 1930; and March 15, 1931. Georgiana's name also appeared in the newspapers when a Turkish man from Tacoma, Washington, tried to enter the Wendel home on Fifth Avenue in 1915 to see her. See *NYT*, July 5, 1915.

Augusta A. S. Wendel died in a sanitarium in Easton, Pennsylvania, January 1, 1912, leaving an estate of $758,677.18.[58] Josephine J. S. Wendel died in June 1914, leaving her estate valued at $3 million to her brother and sisters. To her sister Georgiana, Augusta bequeathed property that had been taken by the Hudson and Manhattan Railroad Company after lengthy litigation. The family apparently never accepted the outcome of that action, for they never claimed the $75,000 granted to them by the court and yearly sought to pay taxes on the property.[59]

John Wendel, the last male member of the family, died in Santa Monica, California, November 30, 1914, shortly after arriving there for a vacation. His obituary appeared on the front page of the *New York Times*, as would those of his two surviving sisters sixteen and seventeen years later. Wendel was termed both "a realty Croesus" and the "recluse of Fifth Avenue" in the headline, and the obituary included stories that would be repeated upon the occasion of the sisters' deaths.[60]

The Wendel home on the northwest corner of Fifth Avenue and Thirty-ninth Street was one of the first houses in that area when it was built in 1830. In 1914 it was valued at only $5,000, but the lot on which it was located was valued at $1,897,000! The windows of the house were never seen open, and the shades were always drawn, giving the appearance that the occupants were away. A large fence enclosed the property, which included "the largest vacant plot on the avenue south of the upper residential section." The *New York Times* reported an unconfirmed story that years earlier John Wendel had received an offer for the property, but that he was weary of repeating that he would never sell any of his property and declared he could not sell because his sister needed a place to walk her dog. As a result, the place had become a favorite of tour guides who liked to point out the "million dollar" yard for a dog.[61]

The Wendel properties included more than 125 Manhattan parcels; the family owned property worth $9 million on Broadway

58 *NYT*, May 14, 1916. Augusta was probably the sister referred to at the time of Georgiana's insanity trial as having had a mental problem from childhood. A trust fund existed for her care, and her death was not mentioned in print until four years after it occurred and then only in connection with a suit filed by the family lawyer asking payment for his services.

59 *NYT*, June 10, 14, 1914; and March 15, 1931. Later, after John's death, there were inaccurate reports that Josephine died intestate.

60 *NYT*, Dec. 1, 1914. Although John's, Rebecca's, and Ella's obituaries were front-page news, John's death was announced at the top of the page, while his sisters' were printed below the fold.

61 When Ella died in 1914, Lord and Taylor sought to purchase the property. See *NYT*, Dec. 1, 1914; and March 16, 1931.

alone. This included an entire block bounded by Broadway and Seventh Avenue, Thirty-eighth and Thirty-ninth Streets; the west side of Broadway between Fiftieth and Fifty-first Streets; and the northeast corner lot at Broadway and Sixty-third Street. The Wendels also owned tenement houses on Grand, Canal, Hester, Division, Spring, Pearl, Essex, Bleeker, Bedford, and Greenwich Streets, and others on West Broadway, Third Avenue, and Avenue D. John rarely improved his properties and seemed indifferent as to whether or not he had tenants. He signed only three-year leases with tenants, and a sign in his office that read "no property for sale."[62]

Though few of his contemporaries were aware of the fact, John Wendel was actually quite well educated. After receiving a degree from Columbia University, he continued his study in Germany and received a Ph.D. degree from Gottingen University. Some of his immigrant tenants, however, were aware that he enjoyed talking with them in their native languages.[63]

The complexity of John Wendel's character and his ambiguous relationship to his community were clearly revealed in an editorial that appeared in the *New York Times* shortly after his death. Declaring that only the accident of birth "had put him in the way to own a considerable part of the surface of the earth in the Borough of Manhattan," the writer described him as lacking in public spirit and disliking progress. Yet it was also acknowledged that he was a man of liberal education who had mastered several languages, traveled widely, and who had refined tastes. While he rarely improved his properties, John was said to be an "easy and generous landlord" who was on record as refusing a $10,000 rent for a building because his tenant who was paying only half that amount was "well established and did not care to move." The editorial writer opined that many would remember him favorably because he refused to allow "glaring electric signs" on the buildings he owned and because he refused to rent to sellers of liquor. In spite of these qualities, the *Times* felt he owned too much of the island for the good of the city and stood in the way of improvement and progress. He was not a "good citizen" and "seemed to feel no real interest in the upbuilding of a great city." Though he was "law-abiding, kindly, [and] temperate," the writer did not believe he was the type to be elevated as a model for the young.[64] A letter to the editor asked what the city would be like if all

62 *NYT*, Dec. 1, 1914.
63 *NYT*, Dec. 2, 1914.
64 Editorial, *NYT*, Dec. 2, 1914.

property owners "bought and never sold and never improved some of the choicest real estate in Manhattan."[65]

Other articles added further insight into the character of John Wendel. One writer had simply walked into his office, gained an interview, and declared that John Wendel was as approachable as "any shoe clerk." Though aware of many stories circulating concerning him—that he refused to rent space for theaters, dance halls, and restaurants, that he was miserly and a misanthrope—Wendel dismissed them as "village gossip." He observed, "If it is true so much the worse for me; if it is untrue the truth will in due time be known. And what difference does it make anyway?"[66]

The *Times* also reported that Wendel liked to collect his rents personally and was willing to allow his properties to remain vacant if he disliked those who wished to rent or their plans for using the property. He reportedly sought a 1 or 1.5 percent return on each of his properties. If taxes increased, he increased the rent, but, if taxes declined, the rent was reduced. The author of this story estimated that he could have doubled or tripled his wealth if he had been more willing to rent on others' terms. Wendel knew all of his tenants and allowed some to remain without payment of rent when their businesses were experiencing hard times, always knowing they would pay him when their circumstances improved. In one case, convinced that a tenant was unable to pay, Wendel allowed him to retain possession of the property for eight years until he was eventually able to resume payment. It was said that tenants never complained of unfairness or of Wendel's breaking a contract. He appeared to treat all, rich and poor alike, in the same manner. When one of his employees robbed him of $80,000 in securities, he refused to prosecute saying he was partly to blame for having put so much trust in the man."[67]

Apparently concerned about children's welfare, Wendel turned one of his properties on West Broadway into a playground for children who lived in the tenements he owned nearby and refused to improve the lot even though it was valued at $81,000. He also contracted with a liveryman near his summer home to transport local children to the beach. He was dissatisfied with the service and refused to renew the contract when it expired, choosing instead to buy horses and buses, build a stable, and hire men to take the children to the beach.[68]

65 *NYT*, Dec. 8, 1914.
66 *NYT*, Dec. 6, 1914.
67 *NYT*, Dec. 6, 1914.
68 *NYT*, Dec. 2, 6, 1914; Feb. 28, 1915.

The *New York Times* reporter who interviewed Wendel found it "an interesting, an amusing, and, in all, baffling experience," and added that Wendel was "a courteous, rather a chipper old gentleman, with a quiet dignity and an intelligent smile. There was nothing about him to indicate cruelty or wistfulness, or intensity or stinginess." The worst he could say was that Wendel was "a bit behind the times." His life seemed to be governed by "nevers." He never dodged his taxes, he never sold property, he never used alcohol or tobacco, he never married, he never had a telephone nor an elevator in his home or office, he never owned an automobile, he had never had his picture taken, he had never made a new friend in the last thirty years of his life, and he never used the front door of his home. Furthermore, Wendel insisted that there was nothing unusual about himself except that he owned a lot of property.[69]

Yet it was unquestionably unusual that a person of such immense wealth should die intestate, but this was apparently the case. When the surviving Wendel sisters realized that their brother had died without a will, Ella and Rebecca, with the consent of their other surviving sisters, Mary and Georgiana, appealed to the Surrogate Court of Westchester County, New York, to be named his heirs. Their request was approved. John's estate was estimated at $50 million at the time of his death, and it was said that he had no debts. At the time of death, he was believed to be the largest individual taxpayer in the City of New York.[70]

While John Wendel had handled all of the family's business affairs prior to his death and was presumed to have held title to all properties in his own name, he had actually transferred title to much of the estate to his sisters over a period of several years. Because this resulted in a diminution of estate taxes, New York sued, and the litigation lasted for years. The sisters were also confronted with a suit by the family lawyer for payment of fees for handling the estates of John and Augusta. This latter dispute led Ella and Rebecca to retain Charles G. Koss of the firm Thompson, Koss, and Warren to represent them.[71]

69 *NYT,* Dec. 2, 6, 1914.

70 The appraisal of the estate was conducted by a prominent Republican politician. One reader complained about the extensive coverage given to Wendel, but the paper responded that Wendel was "most peculiar and therefore highly interesting." *NYT,* Dec. 8, 9, 19, 20, 1914; Jan. 15, 19, 24, 25, Feb. 28, 1915.

71 *NYT,* Jan. 26, 27, 30, 31, Feb. 7, 16, 28, March 13, Sept. 12, Dec. 21, 1915; Feb. 29, March 3, 11, 24, 29, May 3, 5, 6, 14, 20, June 7, Aug. 13, Nov. 12, 19, 1916; March 10, Apr. 22, May 6, 1917; May 30, Sept. 15, 1918; July 24, 1930.

Shortly after the death of their brother, the Wendel sisters were the subject of a page-long story in the *Times* which served to reinforce the general impression of the family as an honorable but curious and rather penurious one. The author wrote of the sisters' life in the mansion on Fifth Avenue. They were said occasionally to entertain members of other old families for tea and to shop at "inexpensive little shops" on Sixth Avenue, paying cash and carrying their purchases home themselves. They had not been seen in church for many years. When they moved to their summer home in Quogue, Long Island, they and their servants walked from their home to the Pennsylvania Station to board the train. In Quogue they used the free community bus that had been purchased by their brother to take local children to the beach.[72]

City real estate developers hoped that John Wendel's death would result in their having greater access to areas of the city, particularly in the Times Square area, where he had resisted development. Yet they feared that the sisters might continue to resist development and grant only short-term leases.[73] However, under the management of Rebecca and perhaps under her husband's influence, the Wendel family real estate practices began gradually to change. In 1917 Rebecca granted a twenty-one-year lease on property to be developed as a theater and office building and began to permit development of estate properties in the Times Square area.[74]

In 1920, the *Times* carried the headline, "Dog's $1,000,000 Lot to Be Improved." The Wendel estate had filed plans to erect a six-story loft and office building on the site of the dog trot. Two days later came a report that another Wendel property on Broadway near Fifteenth Street had been leased for ten years. Four years later the estate leased land on Broadway just south of Times Square to a builder for a twenty-story building, and later in the same year a sixty-three-year lease was granted on eight one- and two-story buildings at Broadway and Thirty-eighth Street. During the same year Luther Swope, Rebecca's husband, died leaving a $90,000 estate, which was added to the Wendel holdings.[75]

Though these reports concerning the Wendel properties appeared from time to time, the Wendel sisters managed to keep their private lives largely out of the public eye. Mary died in 1922, leaving a $5,000 trust to the Methodist church in Irvington, small cash gifts to servants, and

72 *NYT*, Feb. 28, 1915.
73 *NYT*, Jan. 31, 1915.
74 *NYT*, Jan. 10, 11, 28, 1917.
75 *NYT*, July 25, 27, 1920; Jan. 8, Oct. 31, 1924; March 16, 1931.

the remainder of her estate to her three surviving sisters.[76] Georgiana died intestate in 1929 at a sanitarium in Mamaroneck, New York. Notice of her death appeared in the press after her sisters appealed to the Surrogate Court to be named her heirs, and the value of her estate was placed at $2.5 million.[77]

With only two sisters, Rebecca and Ella, surviving, speculation about their wills was rampant. The *Times* again reported the origins of the family fortune as it had at the time of John's death in 1914, when the estate was believed to be worth $60 to $80 million. The sisters, who "dressed in the styles of many years ago," were said to live "frugal and isolated lives," and their sole public appearances were their "annual migration" to and from their country estate at Irvington. That estate was described as "extensive" and surrounded "by a high wall with a massive gate, and...even less known to the public than the town house."[78]

Rebecca lived in a "modern, town house at 249 Central Park West," while Ella continued to occupy the old family residence at 442 Fifth Avenue at the corner of Thirty-ninth Street. Their attorney, Charles G. Koss, said the sisters were "too advanced in years...to live an active modern life." He reported at the time of Georgiana's death that he had been besieged with offers to buy the family home. Although the *Times* reported that these offers ran up to $2 million, Koss insisted that the property was not for sale and that Ella would continue to live there along with the family's long-time servants.[79]

A fascinating account of the private lives of the sisters was given to the press by Isabel Koss, daughter of their attorney, after Ella's death. Miss Koss had met the sisters when she was a child and had known them for more than thirty years. She insisted that they lived full lives, though their father and later their brother had been "very severe in watching out for fortune hunters, and even the girls could never be quite sure that a man was not after their money." Koss reported that they had never expressed regret to her that they had not married. She said that Ella had gone abroad when she was past fifty and that Rebecca had gone around the world when she was sixty-eight.[80]

The Wendel home on Fifth Avenue, where Ella continued to live until her death in 1931, had never been modernized. The home

76 *NYT,* Oct. 20, 1925; March 16, 1931.
77 *NYT*, Feb. 24, 1929.
78 *NYT*, Feb. 20, 24, 1929.
79 *NYT*, Feb. 24, 1929.
80 *NYT*, March 25, 1931.

was a three-story brick with a brownstone front. It was reported that the dining room, parlor, and library remained in the exact condition in which they were left by the builder at his death in 1859. The large backyard was used not only to exercise the dog but also as a place to hang laundry "in defiance of neighbors' protests." Though the home contained gas lights and electricity, it held no radio or phonograph, and a telephone was installed only at the time of Ella's final illness. Isabel Koss related an exchange between her father and Mary Wendel. Considering the value of the property to developers, Koss told Mary that it was costing the family about $1,000 a day to remain in the home. Her response was, "Well, it's home, Mr. Koss, and we don't need the money." When told it was costing her $250 per day in taxes alone, Ella responded that her dog required "a place to run about in." At that time only the Frick and Vanderbilt residences were assessed at higher values.[81] For its part, the *Times* editorialized that the Wendel house was one thing in New York that "money couldn't buy" and that, on the day it was finally demolished, an era would end. A few days later, a letter to the editor commented that the city would have stagnated if everyone refused to modernize but acknowledged that the Wendel house remained as a "quiet but persistent protest against the materialistic fury of our age."[82]

Rebecca died in July 1930. Her will provided for some of the long-term family servants, for her husband's nephew, and for several charities. However, the bulk of her estate, following the death of her sole surviving sister, was to be divided into two hundred parts and distributed among several charities. The *Times* published many of the will's provisions, including the information that "Nankin [sic] Theological Seminary in Nankin, China," was to receive [the income from] thirty-five of the two hundred shares. These shares were given to the Board of Foreign Missions of the Methodist Episcopal Church and were to provide an endowment for the seminary. The will also provided that estate and inheritance taxes would be paid by the estate so that all recipients would receive their legacies free and clear.[83]

After Rebecca's death, Ella left the management of the estate to her lawyers while she remained in the Fifth Avenue home engaged in "household duties." She lived only a few months after her sister's death, and during that time rumors continued to circulate concerning

81 *NYT*, Feb. 20, 24, 1929; March 25, Apr. 12, 1931.

82 *NYT*, July 24, 30, 1930; March 16, 1931.

83 *NYT*, Aug. 2, 1930. Her husband's nephew inherited the property she had received at the time of her husband's death, but the will provided

the eventual disposition of the estate. After Ella's death, the house on Fifth Avenue was assessed at $6,000, while the land was valued at $3,684,000.[84]

Ella Wendel's obituary appeared on the front page of the *Times* on March 15, 1931. The *Times* reported that a small wreath of orchids with a lavender ribbon hung on the door of her home, "a nearer approach to luxury perhaps than Ella Wendel had known in all her seventy-eight years of life."[85]

The *Times* estimated the value of Ella's estate at $100 million in the obituary, and it subsequently published her will. That document contained many identical provisions to those in Rebecca's will. It contained a number of bequests of money and land to family friends, a physician, long-time servants, the nephew of Swope, and, incomprehensibly, established a trust for her sister Georgiana who had preceded her in death. That fund eventually went to the Methodist Episcopal Church in Irvington. The Fifth Avenue home was given to Drew Theological Seminary with the request but not the requirement that the seminary not dispose of it. The remainder of the estate was divided into two hundred equal shares, and thirty-five of these were to go to the Board of Foreign Missions of the Methodist Episcopal Church, the income from which was to be used for the Nankin Theological Seminary in Nankin, China.[86]

The *Times* estimated that those receiving thirty-five shares of the estate would receive about $12.5 million each, though the actual figure proved to be much less, about $2.5 million in the case of NTS.[87]

---

that, should he have no issue, the money should go to Drew Theological Seminary. See also *NYT*, Oct. 31, 1930.

84 *NYT*, March 16, 1931.

85 *NYT*, March 15, 16, 1931.

86 *NYT*, March 24, 1931. The remainder of the two hundred shares were to be distributed as follows: two to the Presbyterian Hospital of New York; five to the American Association for the Prevention of Cruelty to Animals; one to the Massachusetts Society for the Prevention of Cruelty to Animals; two to the Dobbs Ferry (New York) Hospital Association; five to the National Committee for the Prevention of Blindness, Inc.; three to the Northfield Schools in East Northfield, Massachusetts; four to the Methodist Episcopal Church Home in New York City; one to the Methodist Episcopal Church in Irvington; two to the National Kindergarten Association; thirty-five to the Drew Theological Seminary; thirty-five to the New York Homeopathic Medical College and Flower Hospital for the exclusive use of the hospital; thirty-five to the St. Christopher's Home for Children in Dobbs Ferry; and thirty-five to the New York Society for the Relief of Ruptured and Crippled.

87 *NYT*, March 20, 25, 1931. Since most of the estate consisted of real estate,

An organization termed the Protestant Christianization of China provided the comment for the *Times* that the Swope-Wendel bequest was "the largest ever given to a religious institution in the Far East." The money was to be used to "greatly expand the work of training both foreign and Chinese ministers in China." Methodist officials were quoted as saying the money would "be widely distributed to theological seminaries in China and the Nanking Seminary expanded to a scope heretofore undreamed." The school was reported to have forty students and a few old buildings.[88]

Inevitably, because of the size of the Wendel estate and the absence of direct descendants, many people laid claim to the fortune. Koss reported that he had received letters from "every State in the Union" pressing claims. Of the claimants, however, only Rosa Dew Stansbury, whom the lawyers for the estate determined to be a fifth-degree descendant, succeeded in establishing an interest. She had consented to the filing of the will for probate in exchange for $1,000 in cash with the promise of an additional $24,000 if the will were successfully probated. Later she sought to have this consent set aside because she had signed without the advice of counsel. In the course of lengthy litigation, the attorney for Stansbury sought to establish that Ella had been incompetent to make a will because of a "strain of insanity [which] ran through the Wendel family." In addition to a multitude of charges of general incompetence, the attorney alleged that Ella had not gone to church and that no one could recall even a slight interest on her part in church or religious work of any kind. He claimed that she was known to have "professed aversion to all church activities." In reference to the bequest to Nanking Seminary, Stansbury's attorney argued, "The chances are that [Ella Wendel] didn't know where Nanking was or how to spell it." He wrote that in preparing the will Ella was influenced by others, including Koss, and "had about as much to do with it as the man in the moon." Eventually the federal court referred the matter back to the Surrogate Court, refusing to cancel Stansbury's initial agreement to accept $25,000.[89]

---

funds became available over a period of years as property was sold. The figure of $2,531,674.68 was derived by FTESEA executive director Marvin Hoff from minutes of the Board of Founders (hereafter BF). The minutes of the first meeting of the BF on June 5, 1937, indicated that $355,376.14 had been received at that time. Subsequent additional distributions continued through 1955.

88 *NYT*, March 24, 25, 1931. NTS actually had fifty-nine enrolled students at the time.

89 *NYT*, Sept. 27, 28, 29, 30, Oct. 24, 30, Dec. 25, 1931. Distant relatives of the

In the end those named in Ella's will received their legacies. Two centuries of accumulated property passed out of the hands of the family to the great benefit of a group of charities that had somehow come to the attention of Rebecca Wendel Swope and/or Ella Wendel. It is ironic that John, the brother who managed the family estate for many years, left neither a will nor instructions for his sisters on the handling of the family business or the distribution of its assets. Yet the claim of the Stansbury attorney that the terms of Ella's will, which in regard to the distribution of the two hundred shares of the residual estate were the same as those of Rebecca's will, were not those of the last two Wendel sisters appears absurd. These were educated and well-traveled women, and they clearly had a special interest in the Methodist Episcopal Church, two of whose institutions—Drew Seminary and its Board of Foreign Missions on behalf of Nanking Theological Seminary—received in excess of one-third of the estate. Rebecca showed herself a competent business person when she succeeded her brother in managing the properties. Extremely peculiar they may have been, but they seemed to have known what they were doing. When Methodist missionary Harry F. Rowe presented the needs of the Chinese seminary, the Wendel sisters responded generously; and Rowe consequently accomplished far more for the seminary and for Protestant theological education in China and Southeast Asia than he could even have dreamed possible.

While by 1930 Nanking Theological Seminary was gradually recovering from the turmoil and instability of the late 1920s and was enrolling able students from all areas of China, strengthening the curriculum, and gaining and retaining the enthusiastic support of Chinese Christians and the several cooperating missions, the seminary was plagued by a variety of problems over which it had no control. In retrospect it is obvious that the glory days of Protestant missions in China were drawing to a close. Anti-Western and anti-Christian nationalism had emerged with the May Fourth movement of 1919 reflecting Chinese disillusionment with the terms of the Versailles Treaty. Focusing on the inequities of the treaties forced on China by Western powers in the nineteenth century as well as the transfer of German rights in China to Japan after World War I, Chinese nationalism remained a powerful force with which to reckon. If Protestant Christianity were to have a future in China, it would need to become rooted in Chinese soil and independent of Western funding and control. There were probably few who fully understood this issue at the time, but it would continue to drive political forces in China through the years of war and civil struggle that were to follow. The steady increase in appointments of Chinese faculty members to the Nanking Seminary faculty and the selection of a Chinese president in 1931 suggested the seminary's efforts to accommodate the new climate of opinion.[90] Yet the seminary had not escaped the anti-Christian violence that swept Nanjing in 1927. The new republic proved unable to consolidate its power and pacify China, and conflict between warlords as well as occasions of banditry and lawlessness became facts of life in China. If these domestic challenges were not sufficient, signs of waning public support for foreign missions among Americans following the First World War led to the formation of a Laymen's Inquiry of Foreign Missions which, in its final report, *Re-thinking Missions,* may have further undermined such support with its emphasis on the need for Christian cooperation with non-Christian religions and the expression of Christian love less through preaching and personal evangelism than through social services.[91]

Struggling to build a strong union seminary in China under difficult conditions, the faculty of the Nanking Theological Seminary was both pleased and a bit incredulous to discover that the seminary would receive the income from a considerable endowment on the death of Ella Wendel when the terms of Rebecca Wendel Swope's will became public in 1930. The seminary's president, who had asked for and received a $5,000 contribution for a campus building from the Wendel family in 1923, was as surprised as anyone.[92] He had "no advance knowledge that the Seminary had been named as a residuary legatee" of the estate.[93] When the faculty received this news, fifty-nine students were enrolled. The following year, Ella Wendel died and her will confirmed the grant to Nanking Theological Seminary. In anticipation of the receipt of this legacy, the seminary's Board of Managers, composed of representatives of participating missions, renewed efforts to establish a board in New York to protect their interests in the United States. Plans had been initiated for such a board in 1914 to be modeled after the

90 During these years a group of Chinese theologians began to acquire prominence in Chinese Protestant affairs. Among the most significant of these was T. C. Chao (Zhao Zi Chen), 1888-1979, who sought to develop a distinctively Chinese theology. He served as dean of Yanjing (Yenching) University in Beijing from 1928 to 1952 and signed the "Three-Self Manifesto" proclaiming the independence of the Chinese church in 1950.

91 William Ernest Hocking, ed., *Re-thinking Missions, A Layman's Inquiry after One Hundred Years* (New York: Harper & Brothers, 1932). China was one of four countries in which data was collected for preparation of this report.

92 Price, *History*, 19.

93 Frank T. Cartwright to BF, Aug. 22, 1955, ALW.

board for the University of Nanking, which had received a charter from the State of New York to hold property and grant degrees in Nanjing. When New York state authorities refused to grant a separate charter of incorporation for the School of Theology, the University of Nanking's trustees were asked to hold the land, buildings, and equipment of the seminary on behalf of the cooperating missionary societies.[94] However, the interest in a New York board resurfaced at the Board of Managers meeting in 1916, and, in response to circumstances created by the Wendel-Swope bequest, the seminary's Board of Managers voted a constitutional change on June 1, 1932, to provide for a Board of Founders in New York City. The board then referred this proposal to the cooperating missions for their approval.[95]

The first $5,000 of the Wendel-Swope income arrived in Nanjing in 1934, and about that time seminary president Harry F. Rowe prepared a report exploring alternative ways in which Nanking Seminary might use the income from the legacy. His suggestions clearly reflect the seminary faculty's strong ecumenical commitment as well as its desire to create a flagship seminary for Protestant theological education in China.[96]

Since Nanking Theological Seminary was a union institution supported and staffed by five different Protestant denominations, and since it then had enrolled students from twelve denominations, Rowe believed the seminary was in a position to exercise leadership in shaping all Protestant theological education in China. In keeping with this ecumenical vision, he proposed that that the Swope-Wendel funds might be used to:[97]

> 1) Pay all expenses including salaries, maintenance, outgoing, and retirement allowances of all missionaries of the cooperating boards and any subsequently called to such service. Previously the seminary paid only the salaries of Chinese faculty, and dependence on mission board funding for missionary salaries limited the seminary's recruitment of missionary faculty.

94 Price, *History,* 9.

95 Ibid., 9, 20.

96 This report, entitled "Suggestions Towards a Program for the Wise and Useful Expenditure of the Endowment for the NTS at Nanking, China," by Harry F. Rowe was dated May 22, 1934 (hereafter Rowe, "Suggestions"). A copy was located in 1955 and sent to the BF. See Cartwright to BF, August 22, 1955, ALW. Rowe continued in the presidency of the seminary until 1930 when he returned to the U.S. See Minutes, BM, NTS, May 4-5, 1948.

97 Rowe, "Suggestions."

2) Pay all stipends and scholarships for NTS students. He noted that only ten percent of NTS students were self-supporting, though this proportion could be expected to increase with the passage of time or as the churches became able to provide scholarships. He thought that scholarship students at NTS should be recommended by their churches and should spend much of their vacation time in church work, though he added that the faculty should have the final authority regarding acceptance of students by NTS. As an aside, Rowe observed that if the Swope-Wendel funds were used in this manner, church funds currently providing salaries and scholarships would become free for other uses and thus contribute to the entire missionary effort.

3) Strengthen NTS's existing programs. Rowe anticipated that the course for high school graduate would likely "be the most largely attended for some years," but that the course for college graduates would increase in enrollment if the church could "call such men to pastorates and if there is peace in China." He added that the recently introduced religious education project met a real need.

4) Broaden and make effective the new programs designed for rural and urban churches.

5) Strengthen and expand the correspondence course, which had hitherto been limited by a lack of staff and funding. He declared that the program offered a valuable service, that the response from ministers had been good, and that the response would be better if better books were available.

6) Make the seminary's *Theological Quarterly* the outstanding religious journal for all of China. Rowe observed that "it is easy to dream of a journal worthy of China's literary traditions and a true representative of the religious emphasis for which the Christian church stands."[98]

Rowe envisioned Nanking Theological Seminary serving Protestant theological education in China as medical education was served by the Rockefeller Foundation's Union Medical School and Hospital in Beijing. Nanjing was then the capital of the Republic of China as well as the center of Protestant mission activities. The seminary would provide aid to the strongest of the other Bible schools and seminaries in China, and students might be brought there from all

[98] Ibid.

of these schools for a final year of study. He thought that this would free the other institutions to discontinue their final year's study and to concentrate on education for clergy and church workers during their earlier years of study. Such a plan "would bring the men under the influence of [Nanking Seminary's] larger and stronger faculty [and] give them the advantage of a year at the center of the political and social life of the nation, becoming in fact a sort of 'study abroad' opportunity."[99]

While Rowe believed that such a plan might have a "far-reaching influence upon ministerial education in the whole of the Chinese Church," he predicted that it would be resisted and would present "difficulties of the first degree, for denominationalism is strong and local pride is high...." Accordingly, he suggested that "it would be wise to set aside one man who might give a year or two to travel among the seminaries and church groups in an effort to cultivate such relations as would make the plan understood. Results would surely come, though they might come only tardily."[100]

Recognizing the need for Christian literature in the Chinese language, Rowe recommended both translation and writing. He insisted that additional Christian literature was a "strongly felt need in the Chinese church" and that some faculty members should be assigned such work. He thought they might put "the courses they offer into book form" and provide additional volumes for the ministry and for the seminary's correspondence course. Beyond the needs for the ministry, "books for the church membership, books of a religious nature, are almost entirely wanting," Rowe penned. "The difficulty will be tremendous, but difficulties are made to be overcome."[101]

Rowe also urged establishment of a lectureship to facilitate communication between Christians in China and America. He wished that "the American Church [c]ould hear a learned Chinese tell us what China has to offer to the Occident," adding, "exchange professorships are not beyond the range of possibility." He observed that E. Stanley Jones was willing to give part of alternate years to China, "continuing the great work he began in China two years ago." Rowe wrote that "it ought to be possible for some saint from the Church in America to give a half or part of a year to teaching [at Nanking Seminary]....He could teach some classes which are given in English and speak with great effect through an interpreter." Rowe believed that such a person would have great influence in the Chinese church.[102]

99 Ibid.
100 Ibid.
101 Ibid.
102 Ibid.

Rowe believed that the new financial resources provided by the income from the Swope-Wendel fund might enable the seminary to raise its academic standards both for faculty and for students. For those students entering the seminary with only a high school diploma, he wanted to add a year of field work to their program after the second or third year's course of study or, alternatively, a year of preparatory study provided by the faculty before the students began their theological studies. He also wanted Nanking Seminary to have distinguished Chinese scholars on its faculty and thought that they might be sent to America either for a preparatory year of study prior to beginning their instruction or after a few years of service. He also hoped the faculty could be sufficiently large to enable faculty members to spend some time working with the churches, so that they would not become entirely absorbed in theory.[103]

Rowe understood clearly that the magnitude of the legacy might permit Nanking Seminary to become a far greater influence on the Chinese Protestant church than had hitherto been the case. He wrote that "the ideal for such a Seminary as will be built up must be nothing less than a school which can vitally influence the Church which is and is to be in China." Such a seminary must possess both a strong intellectual base and a distinctive quality of life "which is more than any human quality." He declared that "a 'training school' will not suffice. A school which produces prophets of the mysteries and the life of God is demanded."[104] In these suggestions from Rowe, one glimpses his vision for the seminary, a vision that must have inspired the Wendel family when he talked with them more than a decade earlier and one that was apparently shared by his seminary colleagues.

Meanwhile, in New York, staff members of the Board of Foreign Missions of the Methodist Episcopal Church to whom the legacy had been entrusted also began considering ways in which these funds might be used. They learned in 1934 that Luther A. Weigle, dean of the Yale Divinity School, was planning a visit to China at the invitation of the National Committee for Christian Religious Education. Weigle, along with a team of missionaries and Chinese Christian leaders, had been asked to survey the training of ministers and lay people for church work in China. The Board of Foreign Missions asked Weigle to "make a thorough study of [Nanking Theological Seminary] and its possible opportunities in view of the enlarged funds available under the Wendel Bequest." The board also authorized Frank T. Cartwright, its secretary

103 Ibid.
104 Ibid.

for China, Japan, Korea, and South East Asia, to visit his assigned area to study the relationship of Chinese Methodism and the board to the situation at Nanking Seminary. Both Weigle's and Cartwright's reports were presented to the board in 1935.[105]

Cartwright's report included a copy of the seminary's constitution, which contained the provision that a Board of Founders be established in the United States. He explained that the seminary had been under the control of a Board of Managers in Nanking, with the University of Nanking serving as "holding trustees" for the property of the seminary. He noted that, with knowledge of the Swope-Wendel bequest, the Board of Managers had adopted a constitutional change June 1, 1932, to provide for a Board of Founders in New York City.[106] The constitution provided for the Board of Founders to hold in trust buildings, lands, equipment, and all funds for Nanking Theological Seminary. The Board of Founders was further empowered to seek a charter enabling it to confer degrees. However, a New York board had never been formed. Cartwright also reported that during the 1934-35 academic year Nanking Seminary had had four graduate students, thirty seminary students, and seventeen students in the Bible training program.[107]

At the same meeting, Weigle presented his report on theological education in China. China's National Committee for Christian Religious Education had recognized that the Chinese church faced an acute problem in the preparation of students for ministry. Consequently, the national committee had invited Weigle, chair of the executive committee of the Association of Theological Seminaries in the United States and Canada and chair of an interseminary commission for the training of the rural ministry, to lead a study of education for church service in China. Weigle had been in China from February 19 to August 3 and had spent 113 days in conferences and meetings, crisscrossing the country from Hong Kong to Chengdu and from Beijing to Wuhan. Accompanied by T. C. Bau, pastor of the Baptist Church in Hangzhou;

[105] Cartwright, *River*, 8; and *Journal of the 117th Annual Meeting of the Board of Foreign Missions of the Methodist Episcopal Church* (hereafter *Journal*), Newark, New Jersey, November 20-22, 1935, 108-22, MA. Weigle's trip was the subject of an article by Frank W. Price in *Chinese Recorder*, 67 (1937), 153-59; but no mention was made of the Swope-Wendel fund. The periodical of record of the Protestant missions in China, the *Chinese Recorder* was an ecumenical, Protestant periodical published monthly in Shanghai from 1867 to 1941 and circulated to all mission stations in China and to mission boards and church colleges and theological schools in America.

[106] Cartwright, *River*, 9.

[107] *Journal*, 111, 113.

C. Stanley Smith, Presbyterian missionary and teacher at Nanking Theological Seminary; and Chester S. Miao, a Baptist and the executive secretary of the National Committee for Christian Religious Education in China, Weigle surveyed the existing institutions as well as some of the special challenges presented for ministerial education in China. Participants in the study compared their findings with an earlier survey conducted in 1922 and presented the results at an enlarged meeting of the National Committee for Christian Religious Education at Lu Shan (referred to as Kuling by missionaries) from July 18 to 27.[108]

The report submitted by the survey team observed, as had the report of 1922 and the Laymen's Report of 1933, that China lacked a highly educated ministry and that the number of graduate theological schools had actually declined from four to two. Yet with the earlier reports, this report acknowledged that China still had too many ministerial schools working at various academic levels and that further reduction would be appropriate. The report identified thirteen institutions providing academic training above the level of middle school graduation.[109] Many of these, of course, were offering study at a level well below that of a Western seminary. The stronger schools were few in number and clearly identified:

> Yenching School of Religion, Nanking Theological Seminary, and North China Theological Seminary offer the degree of Bachelor of Divinity to qualified college graduates who take three years of graduate work in theology. Shanghai Baptist School of Theology gives the degree Bachelor of Theology (Th.B.) to graduates from senior middle schools who have completed their four year course. Part of this course is taken in the college with which the seminary is affiliated. Nanking Theological Seminary, Canton Union Theological Seminary, and North China Theological Seminary give the degree Tao Hsieh Shih, a purely Chinese degree, but equivalent to the Th.B. degree, to graduates from recognized senior middle schools who have completed a four years' course in theology. St. John's School of Theology and West China University School of Religion give the B.A. degree to students who have taken a combined collegiate and theological course.

108 *Education for Service in the Christian Church in China: The Report of a Survey Commission 1935, with supplementary chapter by* C. *Stanley Smith* (New York: Board of Founders, Nanking Theological Seminary, 1945), 4 (hereafter *Weigle Report).*

109 Ibid., 32, 47.

> Cheeloo School of Theology grants the degree of B.A. in theology to senior middle school graduates who have completed a four years' course in theology.[110]

Following their study, the survey participants concluded that the unique characteristics of the Chinese church argued against defining the task narrowly as one of training clergy. Rather, they suggested defining the task as one of "education for service in the Christian church in China."[111] They found a need for catechist grade lay workers and nonordained, full-time paid evangelists as well as ordained clergy with the equivalent of college and seminary education. Acknowledging the significance of a "thoroughly trained, professional, salaried ministry of the church," they nonetheless recognized that the Chinese church was not yet able to provide adequate maintenance for such clergy. They criticized the theological seminaries in China as too much like those of Britain and America in structure and with curricula that were practically the same. "Has not the time come in China," they queried, "when the Chinese should be free to shake off the limitations of purely traditional forms of organization inherited from the West and to seek from whatever quarter those forms of organization which are best adapted to the needs of an indigenous church?" The result, they opined, would be a curriculum that would be functional, student-centered rather than subject-centered, and directed toward the service that the student would render as a minister of the gospel.[112]

The survey team categorized the Chinese schools as union theological colleges, for which it advocated continuance and development; union theological training schools, for which it advocated a reduction in number; denominational seminaries, which it encouraged to cooperate with the union seminaries; women's seminaries and training schools, which it encouraged toward greater cooperation with men's schools; and graduate schools of theology. These latter included Yenching School of Religion in Beijing and the Graduate School of Nanking Theological Seminary; the team encouraged the further development of both.[113]

Development of adequate libraries was singled out as a primary need of virtually all of the Chinese schools. Only a few of these schools seemed to have adequate libraries with a trained librarian, student

110 Ibid., 46-47.
111 Ibid., 99.
112 Ibid., 38-42; 114-16; 138-39.
113 Ibid.,127-35.

assistants, card catalogues, etc. They reported that "in some cases we found a pitiable situation: a few piles of old books, dust-stained and yellow with age; lack of any proper library space; no catalogue of books; no librarian in charge; books available only at certain short periods of the day and in some cases only on certain days of the week; few if any magazines and periodicals."[114]

The gathering at Lu Shan with representation from all parts of China to which the survey team made its initial report concluded with the organization of the China Association of Theological Seminaries by representatives of the seminaries there represented on July 26, 1935, "to cultivate fellowship, mutual helpfulness and cooperation among all those engaged in preparing an educated ministry for the Christian church in China." In response to the survey team's recommendations and in recognition of the opportunities provided by the Wendel-Swope bequest, this group also recommended that the Nanking Seminary faculty and Board of Managers start a development program with "ample provision for extension and cooperation" with other institutions.[115]

In meetings with faculty members from Nanking Seminary who were attending the conference at Lu Shan, Weigle learned that they supported cooperation with other theological institutions. In a meeting held May 23, two months prior to the Lu Shan meeting, the seminary's Board of Managers had declared that "we acknowledge the responsibility which rests upon the faculty and the Board of Managers of this institution, not only for the adequate development of the institution in Nanking, but also for the undertaking of such service in extension and co-operation with other institutions as may prove advisable and feasible, in the interest of training of leadership for the Christian church throughout China." Representatives at LuShan favored exploring union with Canton Union Theological College and Cheeloo School of Theology as well as the planned West China Union Theological College at Chengdu. They recommended using the common name Nanjing Theological Seminary and operating four centers: Nanjing, Jinan (Tsinan), Guangzhou (Canton), and Chengdu (Chengtu). While they hoped that a single Board of Managers might oversee all, they noted that, because of its remote location, the West China school might require a separate board.[116]

114 Ibid., 121.
115 Ibid.,135; *Journal*, 116.
116 *Weigle Report*, 154; *Journal*, 117.

The seminary's constitutional provision of 1932 for a New York City Board of Founders required the agreement of the mission boards cooperating in the seminary, and attaining this agreement proved to be a lengthy process. Eventually, however, the proposal was approved by the Board of Foreign Missions of the Methodist Episcopal Church, the Board of Foreign Missions of the Presbyterian Church, U.S.A., the Executive Committee for Foreign Missions of the Presbyterian Church in the U.S., the United Christian Missionary Society of the Christian Church (Disciples of Christ), and the Methodist Episcopal Church, South.[117]

Once the several denominational bodies had approved this proposal, the Methodist board, as the recipient of the funds from the Swope-Wendel estate, called a conference of two representatives from each of the five cooperating mission boards in the United States. Appointed to the Board of Founders at the time of its establishment were: Ralph E. Diffendorfer and Herbert Welch from the Methodist Episcopal Church; George T. Scott and its China secretary from the Presbyterian Church in the U.S.A.; C. Darby Fulton and H. Kerr Taylor from the Presbyterian Church in the U.S.; C. M. Yocum and Alexander Paul from the United Christian Missionary Society of the Christian Church (Disciples of Christ); and A. W. Wasson and Sallie Lou MacKinnon from the Methodist Episcopal Church, South. The organizational meeting was held in New York June 5, 1937, and was attended by Diffendorfer, Frank Cartwright as an alternate for Welch, Scott, Courtney H. Fenn as a representative of the Presbyterian Church's China secretary, Fulton, Taylor, and Wasson. Guests at the meeting included Rowe, now retired from Nanking Seminary; P. F. Price, also retired from the Nanking faculty; C. Stanley Smith, then the seminary's vice-president; Louise Rowe; Weigle; and Morris W. Ehnes of the Methodist board. On May 31, 1937, the Swope-Wendel Fund held a principal of $425,376.14.[118]

117 Cartwright, *River*, 9.

118 Minutes, BF, NTS, June 5, 1937, Archives of the Foundation for Theological Education in South East Asia, Yale Divinity School Library, Record Group 180 (hereafter FTEA); Cartwright, *River*, 9, 10, 22. There was some confusion between NTS and the BF with respect to the Swope-Wendel funds, which Diffendorfer and Price sought to alleviate. Diffendorfer wrote, "We have done some unfortunate things in these preliminary days in our relations with [NTS], but with the [BF] now organized we should have no more difficulty. At the same time, we need greatly to overcome the feeling in Nanking, if it still exists, that they have control over the funds." Diffendorfer to Cartwright, Oxford, July 15, retyped July 23, 1937, MA. P.

Diffendorfer was elected chair, Taylor was chosen first vice-chair, Paul second vice-chair, Cartwright secretary, and Scott treasurer. Diffendorfer had extensive prior experience in missions and held the position of executive secretary of the Methodist Board of Foreign Missions. He would serve as chair of the Board of Founders from this first meeting until 1950. Cartwright served as executive secretary until 1961. These two individuals provided a continuity of leadership for the board during the critical years of World War II, the Chinese civil war, and the subsequent refocusing of the work of the board.[119]

Smith presented a report on Nanking Seminary, which was followed by discussion. The board then approved several steps for the development of Nanking Theological Seminary and recommended them to the consideration of the seminary's Board of Managers:

> (1) That the development of a well-educated staff, both Chinese and foreign, is of primary importance. The Chinese members of the staff will have to be secured in China and it would be well to give consecrated and promising teachers opportunities for special training. The Board of Founders will be glad to assist in finding qualified missionary teachers and suggesting their names to the Board of Managers.
>
> (2) That the physical equipment of the Seminary should be developed to meet the needs of the work, with early emphasis on the building of a library and such dormitory facilities as are necessary.
>
> (3) That all building operations should be undertaken in accordance with a plan for the whole development of the Seminary involving both location of buildings and type of architecture, to be worked out in cooperation between the Board of Founders and the Board of Managers.
>
> (4) That insofar as funds allow, and the development of the Seminary warrants, extension work should be carried on outside of Nanking under the direction and supervision of the Nanking Theological Seminary.[120]

F. Price, who attended the founding meeting as a guest, had retired from NTS and was the father of Frank Price, who also served on the faculty of NTS. All subsequent references to Price are to Frank Price unless another person is specified.

119 Diffendorfer's obituary was carried in *NYT*, February 1, 1951.

120 Minutes, BF, NTS, June 5, 1937, FTEA.

The seminary's physical plant was also a matter of major concern at this first meeting of the Board of Founders. Smith's report to the board on behalf of the seminary had addressed building plans, and in response "it was MOVED that we appoint a committee of the three officers, plus Dr. Weigle, to consider these plans and keep in correspondence with the Board of Managers, to the end that the best possible plan may be adopted." The committee was instructed to report at the next annual meeting, and members of the board who were planning to be in China in 1938 were asked to hold a joint meeting with members of the Board of Managers to deal with questions of common interest "including future buildings and general extension of the Seminary's work."[121]

In response to a cablegram from C. H. Plopper, a Disciple missionary and professor at the seminary who wrote on behalf of the Board of Managers, the Board of Founders voted to approve a budget of $30,000 for the 1938-39 academic year and voted, if income exceeded this budget, to begin the creation of a Building and Equipment Fund.[122]

These auspicious initial plans of the Board of Founders for the development of the seminary were to be altered dramatically by the rapid advance of Japanese forces into east central China and a consequent military and political crisis in China. Just a month following the first meeting of that board, the Japanese army commenced open warfare in north China with the Marco Polo Bridge incident of July 7, 1937, on the outskirts of Beijing. This attack drew a Nationalist government response that sent troops north to confront the Japanese. Nonetheless, the Japanese had occupied the city of Beijing by the end of July and immediately began moving into the Shanghai and Yangtze River area. Conflict between Japanese and Chinese forces commenced in Shanghai August 15, and by November the Japanese forces were moving rapidly westward toward Nanjing. The Nationalist government abandoned the capital city on November 20, and it fell to the Japanese on December 12 and 13. The Nanjing Massacre followed.[123]

Nanjing Seminary reopened in the shadow of war September 30, 1937. Few if any people realized the speed with which the Japanese troops would advance up the Yangtze, through Nanjing, and on toward Wuhan. After the fall of Shanghai, however, both the University of

121 Ibid.

122 Ibid.

123 The original English title of Nanking Massacre is still commonly used outside China today.

Nanking and Ginling College chose to move westward to Sichuan Province. The seminary delayed a decision, and no plan had been agreed upon when the seminary suspended classes on November 22 in anticipation of the imminent arrival of Japanese forces. Without a prior agreement regarding relocation and with profoundly differing views as to the challenges likely to be faced in the two proposed locations, some faculty and students migrated westward toward Sichuan along with students and faculty from other Nanjing schools. Others sought haven in the Shanghai international zone. Thus the seminary was divided, and the two campuses survived until the end of the war in 1945 with little contact between them and, following declaration of war between Japan and the United States, with little contact between the Shanghai campus and the Board of Founders in New York.[124]

The Board of Managers met in Shanghai May 26, 1938. President Handel Lee and Dean T. L. Li were among the faculty who had migrated to Shanghai, and the Board of Managers voted to open the seminary in Shanghai in the autumn. Professor Hubert Sone, the only faculty member remaining in Nanjing, was appointed the seminary's representative in Nanjing to protect the interests of the institution and conduct relief work. The fall term commenced in Shanghai with eight returning and twenty-one new students. The Shanghai faculty was assisted by many able Chinese pastors and missionaries resident in that city.

At an Executive Committee meeting of the Board of Founders held March 9, 1938, a decision was reached to proceed, if the entire board concurred, with incorporation in the State of New York. Sympathy, concern, and good wishes were extended to the president, staff members, and students of the seminary facing wartime difficulties.[125] At the annual meeting of the board on June 14, four members of the seminary faculty were present: C. H. Plopper, Frank W. Price, Paul T. H. Chen, and C. Stanley Smith. A verbal report was presented on the "history and activities of the Seminary preceding and following the occupation of Nanking by Japanese troops." Several actions were taken, including commendation of Professor Sone, a grant of funds for replacement of library books lost in the hostilities and for other use in China as well as for scholarships for Chinese faculty members from Nanjing studying in America. Agreement was reached to proceed with incorporation in New York, and the matter of the relocation of the seminary was left to the Board of Managers, which was also encouraged to support the

124 Price, *History*, 27.

125 Minutes, BF, NTS, March 9, 1938, FTEA.

families of Chinese faculty members studying in America. Officers chosen at the inaugural meeting were re-elected, but Morris W. Ehnes of the Methodist Board of Foreign Missions was added to the officiary as assistant treasurer.[126] A month following this meeting, on July 29, 1938, a charter was granted to the Board of Founders by the State of New York enabling the granting of five degrees: Bachelor of Theology, Bachelor of Divinity, Bachelor of Religious Education, Master of Religious Education, and Master of Theology.[127]

Thus within the first few months following the creation of the Board of Founders in New York, the work of Nanking Seminary had been radically disrupted by the extension of the Japanese war in Asia beyond the confines of Manchuria to Beijing and the Yangtze River area. While continuing to seek incorporation and to clarify the scope of its responsibilities under the terms of the Swope-Wendel bequest, the Board of Founders found itself increasingly compelled to respond as best it could to unanticipated developments in China.

[126] Minutes, BF, NTS, June 14, 1938, FTEA.
[127] Price, *History*, 27-26; Minutes, BF, NTS, June 11, 1940, FTEA.

CHAPTER 2

Working amid the Chaos of War

Even as the Board of Founders was being established to disburse funds from the Swope-Wendel bequest, the pleasure and anticipation that news of the bequest had produced in Nanjing was overshadowed by the ominous escalation of Japan's assault on China. Since 1931 the Japanese had occupied the Northeast of China.[1] Just two days after the initial Board of Founders meeting on June 7, 1937, Japan extended hostilities into the heart of China with an attack on Chinese forces at the Luguo (Marco Polo) Bridge near Beijing. Though the armed struggle between China and Japan escalated in the north, Nanking Theological Seminary nonetheless opened for the fall term September 30 and commenced classes October 6. Its vulnerable situation quickly became apparent as the Japanese military proved superior to that of the Chinese. Faculty and student numbers dwindled until there were only eight teachers and twelve students left.

1 The Northeast, or Dongbei in Chinese, is today composed of the three provinces of Heilongjiang, Jilin, and Liaoning. It was long known as Manchuria, and the Japanese established a puppet state termed Manchukuo after seizing the region.

Soon Nanjing, the seat of the Nationalist government, was being bombed. The University of Nanking and Ginling (Jinling) College, a Christian women's college, both mission supported and located near Nanking Seminary, decided to move west to Sichuan Province, where they hoped to be beyond the potential war zone. On November 22 Nanking Seminary suspended classes, but few students remained, and no one had made plans for the relocation of their institution; people simply scattered. Some of the faculty, primarily those in the Rural Church Department, decided to move to Chengdu, Sichuan Province, following the University and Ginling College.[2] From Chengdu they were able to maintain contact with the board throughout the war and were sustained with funding from the Swope-Wendel endowment income. Frank Price, Francis P. Jones, and Tseo Ping-i eventually joined the Chengdu seminary group.[3] Others, including the president, Handel Lee, and the dean, Li Tien-lu,[4] went to Shanghai, which, by action of the Board of Managers, became the seminary's official location. They hoped that Shanghai's International Settlement, governed by Western powers under extraterritorial rights, would afford them protection from the Japanese. Because Shanghai was regarded as the official location of the seminary, those faculty in Chengdu were considered to be Nanking Theological Seminary faculty in Free China on loan to West China Union Theological College (WCUTC).[5]

Hubert L. Sone, the only faculty member to remain in Nanjing, was appointed to protect the seminary's interests. He was soon engulfed by the Japanese attack on the city that commenced December 13, 1937, and the subsequent wild rampage as the Japanese forces were unleashed to rape, murder, pillage, and burn. Sone, like many others,

2 Considerable attention was directed toward the revitalization of rural churches in America and Europe in response to urbanization and rural decline. Such efforts intensified in the 1930s as depression exacerbated problems in rural communities. The Foreign Missions Conference and the U.S. Federal Council of Churches both had offices devoted to rural work. From the outset, the missionary faculty at Nanking Seminary recognized the importance of rural life in China and the need to place emphasis on preparation of clergy to work in rural areas.

3 Tseo had joined the seminary faculty in 1934 as assistant instructor in theology; Price, *History, 24.*

4 Subsequent references to Lee refer to the NTS president unless another person is specified, and references to Li refer to Dean Li unless another is specified. Subsequent references to Jones in this chapter refer to Francis P. Jones unless another person is specified.

5 C. Stanley Smith, NTS Faculty Report, 1945-46, ALW.

was aghast that the soldiers were unrestrained as they sacked the city and decimated its civilian population. "With the coming of the Japanese Soldiers we thought order would soon be restored and peace would come and people would be able to return to their homes and get back to normal life again."[6]

As news of the Japanese advance up the Yangtze reached the city, a group of foreign residents led by John Rabe, a heroic German, organized the International Committee of the Nanking Safety Zone in a desperate attempt to save as many civilians as possible. Rabe was the general manager for Siemens in Nanjing and, ironically, a Nazi. Sone, like other missionaries at Nanking University and the adjacent mission hospital, joined in this valiant struggle against the wanton destruction of the Japanese troops. Sone, who was likely one of the youngest of the foreigners remaining in Nanjing, was made associate food commissioner and was responsible for feeding the twenty-five hundred people, mostly women and children, who were housed at Nanking Seminary. Rabe gathered reports of the army's wanton actions, several of which occurred at the seminary, and forwarded frequent protests to the Japanese embassy.[7] This merciless attack on a defenseless civilian

6 Hubert Sone to Frank W. Price in Shanghai, January 16, 1938, George Fitch Papers, Harvard University.

7 Erwin Wicket, ed., *The Good Man of Nanking: The Diaries of John Rabe*, trans. John E. Woods (New York: Knopf, 1998) is the most horrifying account of the Rape of Nanjing. Rabe made several references to Sone; for example, on February 7, 1938, Sone accompanied Rabe to a field where they found the bodies of nearly 150 people, half of them civilians, who had been machine-gunned, then burned and dumped into ponds (p. 181). Although they make no mention of NTS or Sone, for missionary accounts of the Rape see Martha L. Smalley, ed., *American Missionary Eyewitnesses to the Nanking Massacre, 1937-1938* (New Haven: YDS Library, 1997); and a fuller account in Zhang Kaiyuan, ed., *Eyewitness to Massacre: American Missionaries Bear Witness to Japanese Atrocities in Nanjing* (Armonk, N.Y.: M. E. Sharpe, 2001). See also Timothy Brook, *Documents on the Rape of Nanking* (Ann Arbor: Univ. of Michigan Press, 1999). This book contains Hsu Shuhsi, ed., *Documents of the Nanking Safety Zone* (Chungking: Kelly and Walsh for the Council of International Affairs, 1939) and *The Family Letters of Dr. Robert Wilson*. Numbered documents refer to the Hsu collection. Rabe reported, "Yesterday, in broad daylight, several women at the Seminary were raped right in the middle of a large room filled with men, women and children! We twenty-two Westerners cannot feed 200,000 Chinese civilians and protect them night and day. That is the duty of the Japanese authorities. If you can give them protection, we can help feed them!" (No. 10, Dec. 18, 1937). For Sone's reports see No. 15 on the Dec. 15 rape of thirty women, some by as many as six men, at the University of Nanking; No. 50 on the

population is now known as the Rape of Nanjing, and the Chinese government claims that 300,000 people were victims. It was this service by Professor Sone that was commended by the Board of Founders in 1938.[8]

Following this harrowing experience, Sone returned to the United States in 1940 to pursue graduate study. He later requested an extension of his furlough to complete his doctorate and then went on the list of "Missionaries on Emergency Furlough Temporarily on Other Support," which was a category used by the seminary to protect the faculty rights in all but salary for those separated by the wartime conditions.[9]

The wartime history of Nanking Theological Seminary is actually the history of two campuses isolated from one another by the conditions of conflict. When the seminary's president and dean established a campus in the Shanghai international zone, the Board of Managers met there, and the Board of Founders in New York recognized the Shanghai campus as the legal seminary and the actions taken there as the official actions of the seminary's board. From Shanghai only minimal contact could be maintained with the faculty

---

Dec. 26 attempt to register the refugees and the collection of men who had been soldiers or conscripted laborers in the last year, who having been given assurances they would not be harmed, were taken to the west of the city and used for bayonet practice; Nos. 30, 48, and 56 on rapes at NTS, the Bible Teachers' Training School (BTTS) and private homes; No. 57 on the Japanese order that everyone return home by Feb. 4, and "several hundred women pleading with him [Sone] that they would not have to go home...[saying] they might just as well be killed for staying at the camp as to be raped, robbed or killed at home." They insisted they had survived "half way" but that was useless unless Sone also saved the other half; and the rape with a stick of a sixty-two year old woman who had returned home. No. 21 gives a list of the foreigners who remained in the city. Also see Pei-kai Cheng and Michael Lestz with Jonathan Spence, eds., *The Search for Modern China: A Documentary Collection* (New York: Norton, 1999). One author attributes the first use of the phrase "Rape of Nanking" to George A. Fitch of the Nanjing YMCA in a letter he penned to Price; Masahiro Yamamoto, *Anatomy of an Atrocity* (Westport, Conn.: Praeger, 2000), 177. The activities of the foreigners who remained in Nanjing during this time are featured in the museum at the site of a memorial to the victims of the Rape, which was built in Nanjing in the 1990s.

8 Minutes, BF, NTS, June 14, 1938, FTEA.

9 C. Stanley Smith, "Report of the NTS Between the Sailings of the *Gripsholm*," June 1942-September 1943, in ALW; and a more complete copy in Methodist Archives, Drew University, Madison, N.J. (hereafter MA); and Frank Cartwright to Smith, New York, May 29, 1944, NTS, MA.

and students who resettled in Chengdu. The Board of Founders in New York had much greater access to the latter group, since it remained in Free China throughout the war. The Board of Founders was sensitive to possible problems that might result from this isolation and from its ability to fund the Chengdu operations after funding for the Shanghai operations became impossible.

Wartime communications with the faculty in Shanghai were very difficult. Lee and Li decided on May 26, 1938, that they would resume classes in the fall. They secured the use of three floors of the Christian Literature Society building at 128 Museum Road for classes. Male students were housed on Sichuan Road and the women at the Women's Bible Training School on Lucerne Road. When classes commenced, the seminary had only eight returning students and twenty-one new ones, but another four joined them in the spring of 1939. In addition to teaching, the faculty revived the *Nanking Seminary Review* and also published the *Nanking Seminary News Bulletin* and the *Nanking Seminary Music Series,* which had been the work of Jones. The hustle of Shanghai's business district soon proved to be a distraction, and the seminary moved to a house at 550 Avenue de Roi Albert in the French Concession in October 1939 and remained there until 1946. In the fall of 1939, thirty-two students enrolled, but by 1941 the enrollment had reached fifty-four, thirteen of whom were women. The students represented nine provinces and ten denominations.[10]

Learning that the Board of Founders had been successful in securing an absolute charter from the State of New York Board of Regents, which included authority to grant degrees, the Nanking faculty report of 1939 observed that the charter had been granted because of its "highly trained faculty, adequate endowment, satisfactory curriculum, good record in the past and careful preparation of the materials required by the Board of Regents."[11]

In the summer of 1939, those in Shanghai wanted to purchase a property in the French Concession. However, in sending the request to the Board of Founders, Morris W. Ehnes, who was the assistant treasurer of Nanking Seminary, expressed the view that it was unwise to do so. He also noted that the seminary had $18,383 Mexican and $16,238 U.S. dollars in the bank in Shanghai, adding that he thought it not safe to have so much cash in China, since he feared that the Japanese might seize bank accounts in the concessions. He added that the treasurer had

10 Ibid.

11 Cartwright, *River,* 73.

submitted the budget based on a 3:1 gold ratio but that, as he wrote, the rate was 8:1; therefore they were sure to have additional cash in the future. He thought it was much safer to hold seminary funds in the United States. In New York the Board of Founders agreed not to invest in property in the French Concession at that time.[12]

At its meeting of June 1939, the Board of Founders began to address the new issues created by the war situation in China, the removal of the seminary from Nanjing, and the division of its faculty and student body into two groups. It approved scholarship assistance for teachers on sabbatical leave and for others recommended for study leave as well as for missionary staff members studying during furlough. It considered and approved in principle assistance for members of the staffs of other theological colleges with whom Nanking Seminary was cooperating and for teachers in departments of religion in Chinese universities when recommended by the seminary. However, it also voted to "withhold our approval pending the decision of the lawyer on our ability as a Seminary to make grants to other theological Seminaries for their own purposes unrelated to the Nanking Theological Seminary." The board reelected its officers and approved the budget of $55,174.48, which had been recommended by the Board of Managers contingent on advice of counsel regarding the proposed expenditures for the benefit of other schools in China.[13] Subsequently the Board of Founders received the following opinion from B. A. Matthews, its legal counsel:

> In my opinion, it is perfectly proper for such grants to be made as may in the judgment of the Board of Managers and the Board of Founders operate to carry on the purposes and functions and accomplish the results which Nanking Seminary was established to carry on. Necessarily, the granting of such aid would have to be governed by the sound discretion of those in the field, subject to confirmation by the Board of Founders in America.[14]

Consequently, a special meeting of the Board of Founders was convened December 20, 1939, and the contingent grants of June were confirmed. The board discussed various ways in which Nanking Seminary might strengthen ministerial education in China, especially in cooperation with other institutions. It also considered ways in which

12 M. W. Ehnes to R. E. Diffendorfer and F. T. Cartwright, [Shanghai?], July 12, 1939; and R. E. Diffendorfer to Frank T. Cartwright, [New York], July 14, 1939, both MA.

13 Minutes, BF, NTS, June 13-16, 1939, FTEA.

14 Minutes, BF, NTS, December 20, 1939, FTEA.

it might strengthen that branch of the seminary that had moved west to Chengdu and voted to support studies of conditions and needs both in the West (termed Free China) and in eastern China under Japanese occupation. Professor Henry Pitney Van Dusen of Union Theological Seminary in New York and Dr. A. L. Warnshuis were elected as the first two members at large of the Board of Founders at this meeting. However, lacking a quorum, the board submitted its actions at this meeting to absent members for a mail vote.[15]

Faculty members and students in Shanghai had to face the likelihood that, at some point, the British and French troops in the city would be withdrawn. On a visit to China, Cartwright attended a meeting in Shanghai of the Executive Committee of the Church Committee for China Relief. The committee officially adjourned and then convened informally to hear from Major A. J. Bennett, who was one "of the leading businessmen of Shanghai and chairman of the American Advisory Committee." He reported that, as the European troops were likely to be withdrawn, the Chamber of Commerce and the American Club in Shanghai were asking the U.S. government to station a second regiment of Marines in the city and that they wanted the support of the church groups. Cartwright responded that only the Board of Founders could make such a decision for Nanking Seminary, but he stated that the board was unlikely to change the position it had taken in 1937 that it would not use war or the threat of war to demand protection for its property. In writing to Diffendorfer about the matter, Cartwright stated that he thought a request to increase U.S. troops in Shanghai "would be highly provocative to the extremist element in the Japanese military clique." In this perplexing situation, where any defensive measures taken by the United States would probably lead to greater Japanese control, he reported that he had told Bennett that if it were a matter of policing the settlements, as Bennett insisted, then they should ask the Japanese to strengthen their forces to help in that endeavor.[16]

The troubling uncertainty that underlay these Shanghai deliberations was also reflected in the 1940 annual meeting of the Board of Founders in Swarthmore, Pennsylvania, at which both President Lee and Dean Li were present. The board received reports from them and others recently returned from China. By this time the principal of the Swope-Wendel fund had grown to $1,023,116.23, and the income

15 Ibid.

16 F. T. Cartwright to R. E. Diffendorfer, [Shanghai?], September 11, 1939, MA.

from the fund was exceeding disbursements. The balance that had previously been designated as "reserved for property needs" was now redesignated as "income reserved for future expenditure." Scholarships were approved for Chinese faculty studying in the United States, and the board expressed its willingness to support a literature project if undertaken by the Board of Managers. It also made a grant for the Bible Teachers Training School but declined a request that it support a lectureship at the College of Chinese Studies in Beijing, which the board described as falling outside the scope of its responsibilities. It reelected its officers from the previous year but added the Reverend W. T. Thompson, professor of religious education at Union Theological Seminary in Richmond, as a member at large. The board also asked its secretary, Frank Cartwright, to investigate the possibility of sending theological books to China for the library in Chengdu. While hitherto all missionary teachers at Nanking Seminary had been appointed and paid by denominational boards, the Board of Founders anticipated its own appointment of missionary teachers and agreed that it would pay their salaries directly and that these payments would not appear in the field budget of Nanking Theological Seminary.[17]

The 1941 annual meeting of the Board of Founders returned to New York and was convened by the vice-chairman, H. Kerr Taylor. Professors Plopper and Sone were present as was William R. Leete, who had been appointed to the Nanking Seminary faculty by the Board of Founders on the basis of action taken in 1940 and who was planning to sail for China during the summer. The board formally recognized a temporary branch of the Bachelor of Divinity Department in Chengdu and, in order to strengthen the seminary's work, voted grants for West China Union Theological School, which was hosting the Free China branch of Nanking Seminary; for Cheeloo Theological College and its Rural Church department and library; for the Bible Teachers Training School; for the Committee on Institutes for Religious Workers in Middle Schools in Sichuan; and for the Canton Union Theological School.[18]

Property deeds and receipts from the Chinese government for deeds that had been turned over to government agencies were presented by Professor Plopper and received by the board for safe keeping. The board expressed its pleasure that the Board of Managers in Shanghai had welcomed the Northern (later American) Baptist Convention and

17 Minutes, BF, NTS, June 11, 1940, FTEA.

18 Minutes, BF, NTS, June 10, 1941, FTEA.

Baptist Missionary Society as a cooperating unit, and it authorized its executive committee to expend up to $10,000 in support of a literature program in China.[19]

In 1941 several Chinese members of the Nanking Seminary faculty were in the United States: Chow Ming-I, who had been at Drew Theological Seminary in 1939, had moved to Virginia Polytechnical Institute to pursue an M.A. degree; Lillian Hwang had completed a degree at Westminster Choir School in Princeton, New Jersey, but was having difficulty arranging transportation back to China; and Sone was in graduate study at the University of Chicago Divinity School. Scholarship assistance for these faculty members was approved at the 1941 annual meeting of the Board of Founders.[20]

Following the Japanese attack on Pearl Harbor and U.S. entry into the war, a special meeting of the Board of Founders was convened in Trenton, New Jersey, January 15, 1942. Nanking Seminary professors Sone and Plopper attended, and J. W. Decker was present by invitation, representing the American Baptist Foreign Missionary Society. Recognizing that the state of war between the United States and Japan had made further communication with the Shanghai campus of Nanking Seminary impossible and had also terminated any communication between Shanghai and Chengdu, the board took a number of actions designed as temporary measures until communications could be restored. Francis P. Jones was appointed the board's temporary financial agent in West China and was cabled $25,000 to be expended upon board approval. The board created an Emergency Advisory Committee in Chengdu composed of Nanking faculty members resident there and leaders of the West China Union Theological College host campus. The committee was to counsel with the Board of Founders as the Board of Managers had prior to the war.[21]

At the annual meeting that year, Sone was again present. The Board of Founders received the minutes of the Emergency Advisory Committee (EAC) in West China from Frank Price and confirmed additional members for the committee at that group's request. Mindful of the legal responsibilities of the Board of Managers in Shanghai and reluctant to complicate relationships between the two campuses and faculties, the board declared that the EAC should serve as an informal

19 Ibid.

20 Minutes, Annual Meeting, BM, NTS, April 30 and May 1, 1941, ALW; Minutes, Annual Meeting, BF, NTS, June 10, 1941, FTEA.

21 Minutes, BF, NTS, January 15, 1942, FTEA.

advisory group regarding the seminary's work in Chengdu until such time as the board could formally constitute an advisory committee there.[22] Acknowledging the EAC's request for a return of all Nanking Seminary professors then in the States to China as quickly as possible, the board also observed that wartime conditions created a variety of difficulties impeding such action. The board also discussed issues with respect to the relationship of the group in West China to other institutions there and voted to arrange a conference for discussion of theological education in China to be held in conjunction with the autumn meeting of the Committee on East Asia of the Foreign Missions Conference of North America. The treasurer reported that the income reserve from the Swope-Wendel fund had grown to $272,779.97. In addition to approval of an annual budget, funds were voted for the project to translate Christian literature into Chinese, and officers were reelected.[23] At an emergency meeting in December, a budgetary supplement was approved for the West China campus in response to cables indicating that uncontrolled inflation was compelling reductions in programs.[24]

Once the United States entered World War II and communications between the Board of Founders and the Nanking Seminary in Shanghai virtually ceased, the board received very little information from that campus. One letter was received from a consular official who was a passenger on the first voyage of the *SS Gripsholm* in 1942, which repatriated noncombatants to the United States. Later, C. Stanley Smith prepared a lengthy report on Nanking Seminary in Shanghai in the months between the sailings of the *Gripsholm* in June 1942 and September 1943. According to these reports, the Chinese staff, in addition to Lee and Li, consisted of Peter Ahway Lee; C. H. Wong; Andrew Cheng; Paul T. H. Chen; Shieh Shou-ling; Lillian Hwang (on study leave in the United States); Henry Chou, the associate librarian; and Tsai Ruling, the assistant treasurer. Smith was the only full-time foreign professor teaching in Shanghai at the beginning of 1941, but he was joined later by William R. Leete, a teacher of English. Marguerite Rouse, English secretary to Lee, was the third foreigner on the staff. All three were interned in February 1943.[25]

22 Minutes, BF, NTS, June 10, 1942, FTEA.

23 Ibid.; Ping-I Tseo, "Emergency Advisory Committee, NTS, November 13, 1942, Chengdu"; Frank W. Price, NCC Broadcast, "Theological Education in Free China," Chengdu, July 14, 1942, all ALW.

24 Minutes, BF, NTS, December 16, 1942, FTEA.

25 Smith, "Report of the NTS." Tseo had also been in Shanghai briefly

The Board of Founders learned from Smith's report that the seminary had closed early in the spring of 1941 and that no new students had been admitted for the fall term. Smith reported that he had succeeded in selling drafts on the Board of Founders at exchange rates varying from 15:1 to 25:1 and had received about $16,000. He had deposited the money in twenty different Chinese banks located in Shanghai. He explained, "As it was dangerous to have more than $10,000 in any one account, we spread our accounts out as far as possible." Each professor had been given six months' salary to deposit to a personal account with the understanding that these funds were to be used for personal expenses in case the seminary had to close or as a reserve for the seminary as long as it was able to continue paying the faculty's monthly salaries. The faculty thus had a sense of security for six months, and the seminary was assured of a reserve for as long as it could continue to operate.

When Smith was interned in February 1943, he left enough money to continue paying salaries until October 1943 at the rate then current, but shortly thereafter prices increased dramatically (the cost of a picul of rice, for example, rose from CN $900 to CN $2,000).[26] Therefore, Smith assumed the money had lasted only until graduation in May and that "Lee has probably been financing the school by selling some of the signed drafts on our BF which I left him. (Five drafts for $5,000 each.)"[27]

The fall term enrollment at Shanghai in 1943 was twenty-five, and nine of these students were women. Nanking Seminary tried to avoid Japanese notice, and all foreign members of the Board of Managers resigned in the spring of 1942, but the Japanese knew that the seminary received support from the United States. The house in which the seminary was operating was Chinese owned, but all the

upon his return from the U.S., where he had just received a Ph.D. degree. His family had fled with NTS to Chengdu. Tseo had journeyed there to accompany them back to Shanghai when the U.S. entered the war, making his return to the coast impossible. As a result, he remained in Chengdu teaching in the B.D. course that NTS had established there in cooperation with WCUTC. Price had been in Chengdu since his return to China in 1938, Jones had been in West China since the spring of 1941, and Plopper and Sone had returned to the U.S. on furlough in 1940.

26 The Chinese currency of this period is known in Pinyin as the fabi. It was commonly referred to at the time as the China National dollar (or yuan) or simply as CN$. The inflation of the wartime period continued afterward and contributed to the collapse of the Nationalist government.

27 Smith, "Report of the NTS."

equipment in it was tagged as foreign owned. One Japanese civilian had suggested to Lee that he take down the Board of Founders Charter of Incorporation granted by the Board of Regents of New York in order to avoid problems, and Lee had complied, hiding the charter until it could again be displayed safely.[28]

Beginning in the fall of 1942, increasing restrictions were placed on Americans in Shanghai. Smith wrote that

> [we] had to wear red arm-bands and could not go to theaters or other places of public gathering and it was even inadvisable to go to Chinese churches, although the foreign churches were not interfered with until later. We were free, however, to teach and carry on our work as usual in NTS....Leete and I carried on our teaching work until our internment while...Rouse was in her office almost daily up until about the end of February, 1943.[29]

The seminary completed the fall term at the end of January 1943, and the faculty decided to reopen for the spring term despite the fact that it was extremely difficult to get food for the students. At that time, eight hundred British and American men had already been interned, including Ralph Ward, the former chair of the seminary's Board of Managers. Shortly after classes commenced for the spring term, the seminary received word that Leete was to be interned on February 15. He was sent to the Pudong Civil Assembly Camp for men. Then the Smiths were interned on February 25 at the camp for married couples in the Chapei section of Shanghai. Before leaving for the camp, Smith sent all of his books to the seminary library for safekeeping and removed all of the foreigners' personal belongings from the offices except for Leete's typewriter, which was left for student use. Because of ill health, Rouse was not interned and remained free to come and go until she was repatriated in September 1943. Under the circumstances prevailing in Shanghai, she did not consider it wise to go to the seminary. However, she was in contact with the faculty and attended the Community Church services during those months. Through her, Smith learned that Nanking Seminary finished the spring term with eight graduates and began the fall term September 15. The Chinese faculty remained intact. Li, who had been ill, had returned, and Andrew Cheng was acting dean for the fall term.[30]

28 Ibid.
29 Ibid.
30 Ibid.

Lacking the ability to communicate effectively or regularly with the faculty and Board of Managers in Shanghai, the Board of Founders in New York sought as best it could to provide for their welfare. The income reserve continued to increase, and set-asides were designated specifically to cover expenditures incurred by the Shanghai campus.[31]

Although the president and dean, along with several other faculty members and students, moved to Shanghai when compelled to leave Nanjing, it was with those faculty and staff members who moved to Chengdu in Sichuan Province that the Board of Founders was able to maintain contact throughout the war. Because they were in a part of China that remained under Chinese control, communication was possible throughout the war, and transportation between the United States and this West China campus was sometimes available. Price reported that in Chengdu he was teaching at West China Union Theological College and working with rural churches. He made a journey by bicycle nearly every weekend to "some little country church" and reported that he and his colleagues had started "in cooperation with different church groups several experimental rural parishes...[and] a comprehensive community program." In the summer of 1939, Frank Price traveled back to Nanjing, where he visited his parents, who had returned there from Shanghai. He then went on to Shanghai to meet his wife, Essie, and children, who had been in the States. He reported that his parents were doing relief work day and night among the refugees in Nanjing.[32]

Those who moved west to Chengdu endured considerable hardship in reaching that remote part of China. The Prices' trip westward across China upon their return from furlough in 1939 is an example of travel conditions at the time. It took a month and a day to reach Chengdu from Shanghai. The Prices were the only Americans in a party of twenty, including a two-year-old with whooping cough and an ill seventy-eight-year-old man. Their journey began with a nine-day boat trip from Shanghai to Haiphong, Vietnam (then French Indo-China), from whence they took a three-day train trip to Kunming, Yunnan Province. The train stopped at night, and they had to find their own accommodations and arise before dawn to claim their places on the overcrowded train. They spent a week in Kunming seeking transportation to Chengdu and finally managed to obtain space in an open truck that took them on to their destination. Essie Price observed,

31 Minutes, BF, NTS, March 24, 1944, and June 14, 1944, FTEA.

32 Frank W. Price to Friends, Chengdu, December 2, 1939, Harry Hauser Love Papers, Manuscripts Collections, Kroch Library, Cornell University, Ithaca, N.Y. (hereafter HHL).

"The heavy baggage was piled in the floor of the truck and we sat on that with the smaller pieces at our backs. It seemed a great adventure at first but before the first day was over, that truck was a torture chamber! The sun baked us, the gas fumes choked us, the dust strangled us, and every now and then a cold rain chilled us." She reported that they arrived without serious mishaps, but

> the journey was not without its thrills. The road led us over dozens and dozens of mountain ranges—the highest of which was about 8,000 feet. The curves were so sharp that often the truck ha[d] to back a bit before it could make the turn. At one top we looked back and counted twenty-four road levels. The fact that we saw many wrecked cars at the bottom of deep precipices did not add to our comfort....There were bandits before and behind us but we saw none. We spent our nights in Chinese inns, most of which were clean and more comfortable than the truck!...We did not attempt to carry along any food with us but ate in Chinese restaurants along the way. There was never a dull moment during the trip. It was worth it all to see the gorgeous scenery along the way.[33]

Of the situation in Chengdu, Price wrote to the *Chinese Recorder* in Shanghai in 1940 that the University of Nanking, Ginling College, Cheeloo University, and Central Union Medical College had united with West China Union University, and added:

> in spite of the Japanese invasion, Christianity in West China faces a brighter future than ever before. During the years immediately preceding the war, the Nationalist Government was extending its authority to this area...[and] peace was being reestablished within the province. Opposition to outside influences has practically disappeared; 'down-river' and out-of-province Christians are reenforcing the existing Christian groups, which are awakening to their new responsibilities; and on all sides the Church is discovering new opportunities to preach and to live its message.[34]

The faculty and staff in Chengdu had no legal authority until January 1942, when the Board of Founders, at a special meeting, acknowledged the creation of an Emergency Advisory Committee to handle affairs there.[35]

33 Essie M. Price to Friends, Chengdu, December 2, 1939, HHL.

34 Frank W. Price, "The Church in West China," *Chinese Recorder*, LXXI (1940): 427-35.

35 Minutes, BF, NTS, January 15, 1942, FTEA.

The Board of Founders regularly sent funds to the Emergency Advisory Committee, and in November 1942 it cabled asking if the faculty needed additional support. In reply Price reported that the EAC had already voted to ask for $12,500 to help cover faculty expenses. He also inquired about the return of Miss Kuan Tsui-chen and Andrew T. Roy as well as Hubert Sone and C. H. Plopper, all of whom were in the United States. Price commented on the cooperation of the Nanjing faculty with that of WCUTC: "I believe that the assistance we have given WCUTC these years has been fully justified since they have laid foundations for permanent theological education in the West and have also served as a national theological school during the war years."[36]

Price also reported that the Nanjing faculty then in Chengdu hoped that some of the members of the faculty from Shanghai would come west, noting that while the facilities in Nanjing were occupied, the seminary library was mostly in Shanghai. "We have sent some funds to the Seminary in Shanghai, but are holding the larger amount here pending definite instructions from Shanghai. We surmise that for the present they are drawing on reserves or making loans on security of the [Board of Founder's] grant."[37]

As for the faculty in Chengdu, Price reported that many were kept busy translating Christian works, a project which the Board of Founders was funding. Price quoted from a letter written by Earl Cressy, another American missionary working in Chengdu, praising the seminary's "nation-wide contribution" in support of the program, calling it "a most significant...step in the progress of your Seminary as a national institution, serving the whole Christian constituency throughout China."[38]

Four months later Price again wrote Cartwright concerning faculty for Nanking Seminary. Those in Chengdu wanted the Board of Founders to return Samuel Chu[39] to China that summer. If that were not possible, they recommended that he be given a grant to "travel to rural churches, rural projects and rural training centers" in the United States. Since Newton Chiang[40] was planning to depart for the States,

36 Frank W. Price to Frank T. Cartwright, Chengdu, November 20, 1942, ALW.

37 Ibid.

38 Ibid.; and Smith, "Report of NTS."

39 All subsequent references to Chu are to Samuel Chu unless another person is specified.

40 All subsequent references to Chiang are to Newton Chiang unless another person is specified.

they needed Chu in China to "strengthen our faculty." It was clear that the Chengdu faculty was thinking about post-war reconstruction. If Chu could not then return to China, then the faculty wanted him to visit both government and private rural projects and some good rural training institutes (including Tuskegee) and rural church departments in some American theological schools.[41]

The Emergency Advisory Committee in Chengdu requested $73,741.01 from the Board of Founders in April 1943. Additionally, although it had had no contact with the faculty in Shanghai, the committee asked the board to set aside a minimum of $15,000 in 1942-43 and $20,000 in 1943-44 to cover loans that the Shanghai faculty was assumed to be taking out to cover its emergency needs. The EAC also requested funds for the *Christian Farmer*, which it published.[42]

When transmitting requests to the Board of Founders, Price customarily sent an explanatory letter to Cartwright. With this request he reported that the EAC meeting had lasted for three hours and "the Faculty Executive...spent much time on a study of the budget, endeavoring to maintain our work as well as possible under the severe limitations of abnormal and increasing costs and of restrictions on exchange." He indicated that he was cabling the total amount requested, as he wanted the budget to reach Cartwright in time for the annual meeting of the Board of Founders in June. "When you realize that costs are now seventy times pre-war level and...[we are] including what must be put aside for the institution in Shanghai (to which we have been able to send very little money), we are evidently using up to the limit of our annual endowment income." He asked that the board let him know by cable if it wished to cut expenditures, adding that the EAC had cut rural work and had not asked anything for buildings, although each year since 1939 it had been making building contributions to the West China Union Theological College and Canton Union Theological College (CUTC). "If the exchange rate is lifted from 20:1 to 30:1 or 40:1, our gold budget will be correspondingly lowered, unless the rise of prices is more precipitous than it has been. At present the increase is about eight per cent per month or a doubling of prices each year." Since the Chengdu faculty could not offer its regular program, it was proposing to offer the B.Th. degree to students of WCUTC, CUTC, and Cheeloo School of Theology and hoped the Board of Founders approved this plan.[43]

41 Frank W. Price to Frank T. Cartwright, Chengdu, February 21, 1943, ALW.
42 Minutes, EAC, NTS, Chengdu, April 16, 1943, ALW.
43 Frank W. Price to Frank T. Cartwright, Chengdu, April 17, 1943, ALW.

Price also commented that the faculty was concerned about postwar plans, as was the Council of Higher Education and the National Christian Council executive committee. With regard to faculty matters, Price stated that Cheruthotatil Eapen Abraham, a professor at Serampore College in India, was to visit Chengdu and lecture in the fall. Professor Newton Chiang had obtained a passport and was to fly to the United States from Chongqing. "Christian friends in the government contributed CN $20,000 toward his trip so he could go all the way by air," but Price wanted the board to give Chiang an additional $400, for a total of $1,000." Price on this occasion urged that Samuel Chu remain in the States for the moment.[44]

Francis Jones also wrote to Cartwright from Chengdu about the extreme difficulties he had confronted trying to prepare a budget, saying it was impossible to know what salaries would be needed for the next year. In preparing the budget he had taken the rice and cash bonuses paid to staff in March, multiplied that figure by twelve and added fifty percent to cover the next year. "Elsie Priest thought that might be too conservative an estimate, but we decided to let it go. Miss Priest feels that one can hardly make budgets for six months in advance any more let alone for a year."[45]

The unpredictability of the financial situation was demonstrated the following month when Price reported there was to be a new government subsidy of 50 percent on the exchange of mission funds beginning May 1. This subsidy would have the effect of reducing their request from nearly $74,000 to $54,000, which Price hoped would allow them to draw less than the full income from the Swope-Wendel fund, adding, "I had a long talk with Dr. [H. H.] Kung, [the government finance minister]. He does not feel hopeful about any immediate drop in prices unless there is a sudden victory, radical change in the international situation, greatly increased production and decreased consumption in China, or opening up of foreign trade through Burma road or other routes."[46]

The Board of Founders in its annual meeting approved both the $54,000 budget for the Chengdu campus and a $20,000 reserve for

44 Minutes, EAC, NTS, Chengdu, April 16, 1943; Frank W. Price to Frank T. Cartwright, Chengdu, April 17, 1943, both ALW. In other budgetary matters, the *Christian Farmer* had asked NTS for $10,000 for the second half of 1943 and $2,000 for 1944. The request from the field also included funds for the expenses of students arriving from occupied China who were cut off from church and family support. The total request was $73,741.01.

45 Francis P. Jones to Frank W. Cartwright, Chengdu, April 17, 1943, ALW.

46 Frank W. Price to Frank T. Cartwright, Chengdu, May 7, 1943, ALW.

Shanghai. The Disciples had chosen E. K. Higdon to represent them in place of Alexander Paul, and he was elected a vice-chair. But at this meeting the Disciples sent proxies, including M. Searle Bates of the University of Nanking faculty. Dr. Wu Yi-fang, president of Ginling College, was also present at this meeting.[47] In addition to approving the seminary's budget, the board accepted membership in the Associated Boards of the Christian Colleges in China and again sought to arrange a conference on theological education in China, this time in cooperation with the Associated Boards.[48]

Much of the business of this meeting focused on issues related to the study of Nanking Seminary faculty in America. Philip Cheng had completed his Ph.D. degree at the University of North Carolina. Since he could not then return to China, the Board of Founders granted him assistance for post-doctoral study. Carl S. C. Lee's scholarship for study of psychology at the University of Iowa was extended. Others receiving support from the Board of Founders at this time were N. F. Kwang at San Francisco Theological Seminary and three students at Drew University: David Ling, Katherine Liu, and Samuel Chu.[49]

At this meeting the chair was directed to prepare a list of property lost in China as a result of the war for presentation to the U.S. Department of State. The board also received a report that the principal of the Wendel-Swope fund now totaled $1,068,952.89.[50]

Meanwhile the work of Nanking Theological Seminary continued both in Shanghai and in Chengdu. An undated document, probably from 1943, titled "Christian Theological Education in China," declared that during the 1942-43 academic year fifteen men studied in Shanghai and ten at Chengdu. In 1943-44 the seminary had six men and one woman in its graduate program, which required a baccalaureate degree for admission, and thirty-five men and five women in its "College Grade Schools," which required graduation from senior middle school. Nine men and one woman graduated that year.[51]

47 Dr. Wu, the first Chinese president of Ginling, continued the tradition of executive leadership of this school by women.

48 Minutes, BF, NTS, June 15, 1943, FTEA. The Associated Boards had been established by many of the same individuals and mission boards involved in the BF, and Ralph Diffendorfer, chair of the BF, served for six years as head of the Associated Boards as well.

49 Minutes, Annual Meeting, BF, NTS, June 15, 1943, FTEA.

50 Ibid.; NTS, Swope-Wendel Fund, Comparative Statement of Principal and Income Accounts, May 1 to April 30. On April 30, 1942, the principal account stood at $1,051,367.14, and a year later it was $1,068,952.89.

51 "Christian Theological Education in China," undated [1943?], ALW.

The Chengdu faculty invited T. K. Shen to give a series of lectures, "The Life and Work of the Pastor," which were attended by both pastors and students. In the fall the faculty planned to have Kuo Pen-tao, whom Price described as "an outstanding scholar in this field and an earnest Christian," teach and do research on the history of Chinese religions. In the letter providing this information, Price also observed, "[w]e have had no direct word for some time from the Seminary in Shanghai."[52]

Plans for theological education in China in the post-war years were clearly on the minds of many people in China as the Japanese were forced relentlessly from advance to retreat in the Pacific. Nor was there much awareness in Nationalist strongholds of the Southwest of the growing effectiveness of Communist forces and ideology elsewhere in China and of the challenge this would present both to the Nationalist government and to the Christian presence in China. Francis C. M. Wei, president of Huachung College, wrote Price in mid-1943 asking for a $5,000 grant from Nanking Seminary to commence theological education at his college once the war ended.[53]

On the same subject, Jones informed the Board of Founders that the seminary had funded a conference to consider the entire program of theological education, adding that in Fujian Province there were various small programs run by many churches. He observed that, if Mandarin-speaking students did not participate in these programs, there probably were not enough speakers of the local dialect to sustain a post-graduate program in that important Protestant center in southeast China. However, Carleton Lacy, an American missionary in that area, favored the smaller programs and complained that Nanking Seminary graduates frequently did not return to work with the churches which had sponsored their studies. He cited the "sad experience now with our pastor at Yungan who came back a year and a half ago from Chengdu with his degrees from Nanking University and Nanking Theological Seminary and has twice left his church saying he was [through] and has gone back now only consenting to stay until Conference." Lacy opposed the seminary's plan to set up a theological school in Fujian Province at that time.[54]

In response to rapidly changing circumstances in China, the executive committee of the Board of Founders approved a budget of

52 Frank W. Price to Frank T. Cartwright, Chengdu, May 7, 1943, ALW.
53 Frank W. Price to BF [Chengdu], August 5, 1942, in Frank W. Cartwright to BF, New York, October 8, 1943, ALW.
54 Francis P. Jones, excerpts, August 31, 1943; Carleton Lacy, excerpt, September 3, 1943, both ALW.

$54,000 in July 1943 with the stipulation that, if that amount were insufficient, it would meet again in mid-year to reconsider the situation. The executive committee also cautioned the Emergency Advisory Committee that, although the expenditure had been approved, it should not begin a college level program in theological education in Fujian Province until the war ended and further consultation with the board had taken place. In response to a request and contingent upon the assent of Price and Jones, the board voted $5,000 as an emergency grant to WCUTC to match a similar one from that institution's Board of Governors.[55]

Even while trying to plan for the future, the Emergency Advisory Committee still had to wrestle with the day-to-day challenges of life in wartime Chengdu. In October 1943 the committee voted to ask the Board of Founders for CN$10,000 for repairs, ovens, and equipment for the community kitchen for faculty families of Nanking Theological Seminary and West China Union Theological College. Still concerned with questions about the committee's authority and its relationship to the Board of Managers in Shanghai, the committee agreed to ask the Board of Founders if the EAC needed to appoint or co-opt new members or appoint an emergency Board of Managers to handle Nanking Seminary's affairs. Additionally, it approved a visit of Price to the United States in early 1944 and agreed that Jones would serve as acting chair during Price's absence.[56] It further agreed to fund research on the "Legal Question Affecting Missions and Churches under the New Treaties," a project which was to be directed by R. Y. Lo with the help of Yu Chien-sheng, a student in the seminary's post-graduate course. The EAC also voted, as it had the previous year, to seek the return, as soon as possible, of faculty still in the United States. In another action it invited Sie Ping-teh to join the Literature Department for one year after his graduation from the post-graduate program. The budget was revised and a "quiet financial campaign" was begun among friends of Nanking Theological Seminary in China.[57]

From the south of China, President J. S. Kunkle of Canton Union Theological College in Guangdong Province wrote to Chengdu

[55] Minutes, Executive Committee, BF, NTS, July 12, 1943, FTEA.

[56] The EAC anticipated this would be a brief visit, but Price left in January 1944 and did not return to China until November, when he went to Chongqing to head a liaison group between Chinese and American forces in west China. Price received his mission board's approval for this work, but it deprived the seminary of his services. Price, *History,* 35-36.

[57] Minutes, EAC, NTS, October 4, 1943, ALW.

explaining that conditions had become so acute in his area that he was compelled to ask the EAC to increase its $12,000 grant for scholarships to $28,500 and to increase its $10,000 grant for current work to $75,000. Several months later Kunkle asked for another $2,000 to help with the "extraordinary expenses" that had been incurred in moving the college to Kukong, adding that the school had twenty-eight students, six of whom were university graduates, and some of whom were Mandarin speaking and certainly would have attended Nanking Seminary were it not for the war. He indicated they were practicing economy to the "extent of privation and hardship to loyal students and teachers," and that the situation was complicated not only by the war but also by a famine in that part of the province to which they had moved. He mentioned that they were working in areas not normally theirs; but, as a large proportion of the total Protestant church membership in China was in the south, he thought it might be time for them to expand into an all-China program. He also asked if CUTC could become one of Nanking Seminary's centers after the war.[58] This information was forwarded to the Board of Founders for its consideration.

The financial situation in Chengdu was not much better than that in Guangdong. Tseo wrote the Board of Founders about the poor conditions they were enduring, stating that they were living just above the starvation line. Despite the hardship, the faculty and students were continuing their work. Tseo asked if the Chengdu faculty could establish regular managers to decide their affairs and to give them more authority and a sense of unity.[59]

With inflation in China reducing the value of funds made available there from the Swope-Wendel fund, Price had to write to Nanking Seminary's affiliated institutions just before he left China

58 J. S. Kunkle to EAC, NTS, Kukong, Guangdong, November 10, 1943; J. S. Kunkle to Frank T. Cartwright, Kukong, Guangdong, March 6, 1944, both ALW. The school would later move to Lien Hsien before those in Chengdu lost contact with them, except for one former student who arrived in Chengdu and reported they were spending most of their time on evangelism, Minutes, EAC, NTS, April 2, 1945; Annual Report, NTS, April 2, 1945, both ALW. CUTC was established in 1914, and John S. Kunkle, a Presbyterian missionary, was president from 1917 to 1946. The school was located in Guangzhou until the war. It moved briefly to Yunnan Province but in 1942 returned to Shaoguan (Kukong) where it was associated with Lingnan University. Following the war it returned to Guangzhou but was closed in 1960. See *China News Update* (Presbyterian Church, U.S.A.), April 2005, 1-2.

59 Tseo Ping-I to Frank T. Cartwright, Chengdu, December 4, 1943, ALW.

in January 1944, telling them the Board of Founders had reached the limit of the American funds which could be spent in China. He observed that the board's first obligation was to Nanking Seminary in both Shanghai and Chengdu and to the associated schools. Therefore, he thought they would have to drop all grants "for research projects, literary work and publications, rural extension work, and church workers conferences." He added his personal regret at having to bring this news. Price indicated that Tseo was to be the head of the faculty in his absence and that, in the absence of Jones, F. Olin Stockwell, of the Methodist Mission in Chengdu, would serve as treasurer. He asked for the budget requests for the coming year, indicated he would be present at the Board of Founders meeting, and assured addressees that he would be sympathetic to their needs. He indicated that WCUTC in Chengdu would continue to accept senior middle school graduates for a four-year theological course and that Nanking Seminary would receive college and university graduates for admission to its bachelor of divinity and master of religious education post-graduate courses at Chengdu.[60]

The EAC noted that Nanking Seminary had celebrated its fifth year in west China during the previous November and that it was currently "well overspending" its income as the financial situation deteriorated. The seminary had experienced personnel changes as Francis Jones and his wife returned to the States as a result of Mrs. Jones's illness. Andrew T. Roy was to replace Jones on the Literature Production Program Committee, and they were asking Sverre Holth to join the faculty as a teacher for the 1944-45 academic year.[61]

Despite the hardships being experienced by faculty and students in Chengdu, Abraham, the visiting professor from Serampore who had been there for two months, wrote after his return to India that he was impressed with their work. He had been involved in theological education in India for more than twenty years and said the students at Nanking Theological Seminary compared favorably with those in India. He believed Nanking's graduates were well accepted by the churches he had visited in Free China. He added, "[t]here are many other things about the Seminary which pleased very much indeed, such as the spirit of cooperation and unity that exists between Chinese and foreign members of the faculty, the emphasis on the rural program of

60 Frank W. Price to Friends, [Chengdu], January 4, 1944, ALW.

61 Francis P. Jones, EAC, NTS, January 6, 1944, ALW.

the church and the high place that the study of Chinese language and literature occupies in the curriculum for the B.D. degree.[62]

When Price reviewed the situation in Chengdu for the Board of Founders in early 1944, he noted the financial problems created by a 60 percent rise in the cost of living. In order to cut expenses, Price reported that the board was establishing priorities that eliminated all research projects and subsidies for printing. As Tseo had done earlier, Price again sought advice about the appointment of regular managers, and the Board of Founders discussed this matter but decided not to appoint a formal board for Chengdu. The board decided to continue supporting those in Chengdu within the limits of the annual income from the Swope-Wendel fund but not to use any capital funds. Board members believed that expending funds in Chengdu was somewhat beyond the terms of the Swope and Wendel wills, but they also believed they could justify their action, if it ever became legally necessary to do so, by citing the unusual wartime conditions in China and the existence there of only an EAC, which implied a less permanent body than the appointment of managers would.[63]

By 1944 many of the missionary faculty members from Nanking Seminary were in the United States. Following repatriation, C. Stanley Smith went to New Haven and from there frequently wrote to the Board of Founders offering suggestions and advice. For example, he wrote that Marguerite Rouse and William Leete, who were supported by the board, should be given the $150 outfit allowance which the Presbyterian Church had given to those in their employ who had lost property in China and were repatriated aboard the *Gripsholm.* Smith indicated that, while in New Haven, he had revised all his lectures for a year-long course in his field of historical theology and was eager to return to the Nanjing classroom. "You probably do not realize the kind of insecure feeling one has when all his notes, lectures, and books are gone. You feel almost naked in a cold, cold world," he wrote. He also reported that he was collecting books for the seminary library.[64]

62 C. E. Abraham to BF, Chandernagore, Bengal, no date, ALW.

63 Frank W. Price, Memorandum for NTS, BF, Washington, March 16, 1944, ALW. The capital funds concerned were not the endowment held in trust by the Methodist Board of Foreign Missions but rather funds that had been set aside from unexpended income.

64 Frank T. Cartwright to C. Stanley Smith, New York, May 29, 1944; C. Stanley Smith to Frank T. Cartwright, New Haven, CT, May 22, 1944, both NTS, MA.

Smith also expressed great concern for those seminary personnel in Shanghai whose funds might be nearing total exhaustion:

> Heaven help them when this time comes. We must think of some way to come to their aid. I think that someone from Free China, Chinese, of course, will have to try to get to Shanghai or some other place in occupied China and get some information about our Faculty in Shanghai. I am hoping that [President Handel Lee] is able to borrow on the credit of the Founders but that is dangerous and can not go on too long. Sometimes I wish I were back in [Shanghai], not that I could help them any but I would at least be sharing with them some of the suffering. The thing one misses here at home is the fellowship of those who suffer.[65]

Price reported that those in Chengdu knew nothing about the faculty in Shanghai but continued to seek such information. They requested advice from the Board of Founders on a number of topics. For example, they asked if they should maintain their affiliation with the other theological institutions. The Nationalist government was considering new laws requiring the registration of all religious institutions and organizations, and they wanted to know what name should be used if they were required to register. With respect to the post-war situation, they asked what type of cooperation the Board of Founders envisioned for them with theological schools in India and other Asian countries and how they should restore their program in China.[66]

Responding to rampant inflation and financial crisis in China, the Board of Founders held a special meeting March 24, 1944, and voted an additional $12,000 to cover the deficit at Chengdu as well as a budget of $60,000 for the forthcoming academic year. Concerned about the implications of Chinese inflation for its own budget, the board voted to encourage the seminary to maintain its relationship with other Chinese centers of theological education but without assuming any responsibility for balancing their budgets. At this meeting the Board of Founders, in recognition of the decision of the American Baptist mission in China to cooperate with Nanking Seminary, invited its Foreign Mission Society in the United States to appoint two representatives to serve on the board.[67]

65 C. Stanley Smith to Frank T. Cartwright, New Haven, CT, April 27, 1944, C. Stanley Smith Papers (hereafter SP), MA.

66 Frank W. Price, Memorandum for NTS, BF, Washington, March 16, 1944, ALW.

67 Minutes, BF, NTS, March 24, 1944, FTEA.

Smith raised questions concerning the budget request from Chengdu for the forthcoming year. Chengdu had requested $80,000 for the year, but Smith believed the grant should be limited, as it actually was, to $60,000. He believed that the West China campus needed to cut funding designated for the Literature Production Program, since questions had been raised concerning that funding. The first priority, he insisted, was to maintain the faculty and students. Smith was also concerned about financial planning for the post-war period since he assumed, and C. H. Plopper concurred, that their Nanjing facilities would almost certainly have suffered destruction and that replacement costs would have to be taken from the income fund, not from the principal of the Swope-Wendel fund. He reasonably assumed that post-war prices would be higher than before the war. He wrote that the Board of Founders' decision to keep the faculty intact was a sound one. "The next couple of years at least are going to be chaotic ones in most parts of China and we shall be fortunate if we have anything left of institutions when they are ended. That may sound too pessimistic but the destruction that has already taken place in China will be as nothing to what will happen...[should] the Japanese and American land and air forces really clash in China."[68]

Olin Stockwell wrote from Chengdu in late March that an Emergency Advisory Committee meeting had been held and was described by one person as "the most difficult and discouraging meeting that he had ever attended" in connection with the seminary. While they were meeting, the committee members received a cable from Ralph Diffendorfer giving them another $12,000. Noting that inflation continued to make realistic estimates of expenses impossible, Stockwell indicated that they had huge overhead costs because two of the faculty members and their families were in the United States and another, who had a large family, had several members "down river." This situation necessitated payment of his rice allowance at the local market rate, not in subsidized rice, which was available in Chengdu. Educational costs for the children and the costs of maintaining the cooperative kitchen continued to increase. To stay within the $60,000 allotted by the Board of Founders, the committee dismissed the office coolie and the office secretary (with Essie Price and Stockwell doing that work) and four members of the faculty. One-half of their scholarships had been cut together with all rural and city church extension work,

68 C. Stanley Smith to Frank T. Cartwright, New Haven, CT, April 9, 1944, SP, MA.

all printing subsidies and research projects, and everything else not linked to maintenance of a minimal teaching program. Only four full-time employees remained on the staff: Tseo Ping-I, Yu Moh-ren, Chu Pao-hui, and Hu Ren-an. Kuo Pen-tao continued half time. Stockwell reported that a gift from Chinese sources would make it possible for Kuo to continue some of his work on Chinese religions. "The most important challenge which we are facing today is our preparation for the post-war opportunities in China. To meet these opportunities a trained leadership is absolutely essential. You cannot wait until after the war to begin to train this leadership." Stockwell indicated that the Disciples Church was raising $10,000 to help five students during the next year, since Nanking Seminary did not have a large enough budget to support all of its students. He observed that the seminary had more students in the bachelor of divinity degree program than ever before, and still more were seeking admission.[69]

Stockwell asked the Board of Founders for another $20,000 or for permission to use the gain they received on exchange. He wrote they had had to cut Pan Chun-hsian, Yang Chang-i, and Sie Ping-teh from the faculty, although Pan would continue to study at the seminary and help them part-time if they could give him a scholarship and if the Disciples could provide some of his living expenses. Yang was "one of the most able rural workers," had been Price's right hand man for years, and was "a young man, with a small family, and the possibility of many more years of helpful service." Sie was "well trained, a promising young man in every respect, and if retained...has every promise of growing into leadership and power in our Seminary group." Although they were not contributing to the teaching program, they "are valuable men who ought to be conserved for the Seminary."[70] Jones, who was then in the United States, concurred with Stockwell's observations.[71]

Tseo and Stockwell submitted yet another request to the Board of Founders in May 1944, noting that trying to budget was "like trying to guide a sailing ship through a south China typhoon. No one can tell quite where we are going, what winds of economic disaster will sweep over us in the next few hours, how high the waves of inflation will rise. We can draw up figures, but they do not mean very much." The black market exchange rate had been 150:1, went up to 260:1, then dropped to 180:1; but "there were very few merchants interested in buying checks

69 F. Olin Stockwell to Frank T. Cartwright, Chengdu, March 31, 1944, ALW and MA.

70 Ibid.

71 Francis P. Jones, Comments on March 31, 1944, Stockwell cable, ALW.

for blocked accounts at home." They submitted their budget for 1944-45 at "four times the National Currency figure for the current year."[72]

At their annual meeting June 14, the Board of Founders voted $60,000 for the West China budget and an additional set-aside of $25,000 for Shanghai. It authorized the EAC to ratify temporary appointments of teachers and to consider budgetary needs for the Chengdu campus, and it approved the addition of new members to the EAC. The issue of registration with the government was considered, but no action was taken. As further evidence of the problems created by inflation in China, the Disciples mission board advised the Board of Founders that the Disciples could not send Professor C. H. Plopper back to the field at that time because of the cost of living in West China. The board noted that Plopper was ready to return whenever his board was in a position to send him. Officers were reappointed, and at-large members H. P. Van Dusen and A. L. Warnshuis were asked to serve, along with the board's officers, as the executive committee.[73]

The Chengdu group also forwarded John Kunkle's request for Canton Union Theological College for the 1944-45 year. He asked for CN$140,000 for teachers' salaries, the repair of the mat-sheds in which they were living, travel costs for students in the field, and an "urgently needed building" for the local church. He also asked for CN$60,000 for food for students and observed that the local church scholarships could not support them.[74]

As the fortunes of war steadily shifted in favor of the Allied forces, planning for the future began in earnest. In November 1943 the Board of Founders sponsored a conference in New York on Theological Education in China that was attended by representatives of the Planning Committee of the Associated Boards of the Christian Colleges in China, the Committee on Eastern Asia of the Foreign Missions Conferences, and various theological schools in China, as well as others with an interest in the subject. The project for translation of the Christian classics into Chinese, which Nanking Seminary was helping finance, became one topic of discussion. A decision was reached to continue the work despite wartime limitations. With regard to the work of translation, two primary difficulties were identified: the shortage of qualified translators and long-standing disagreements regarding the

[72] Tseo Ping-I and F. Olin Stockwell to Frank T. Cartwright, Chengdu, May 20, 1944, NTS, MA; Minutes, EAC, NTS, April 2, 1945; Annual Report, NTS, April 2, 1945, both ALW.

[73] Minutes, BF, NTS, June 14, 1944, FTEA.

[74] John S. Kunkle to NTS, Kukong, Guangdong, n.d., MA.

proper terms for accurate expression of theological ideas in the Chinese language.[75]

Presentations at the conference were made by many Nanking Seminary faculty members then in the United States. Newton Chiang spoke on the different needs of urban and rural churches in the area of religious education. Samuel Chu spoke on the church's need for pastors from higher social classes, stressing that money was a source of problems, since the small number of Christians in any community made it difficult for a congregation to support a pastor. He thought the seminary needed specialists in developing self-support among congregations. T. Y. Fong, a layman, insisted that a major weakness of the Chinese church was poor organization. Kuan Tsui-chen's contribution focused on the need for home and children's work. Dr. T. T. Lee stressed the desire in China for greater ecumenicity. Mrs. W. S. New spoke concerning ministry in hospitals. Martin Yang detailed the Chinese church's need for three types of leaders: those who devote all of their time to philosophy and sermons, those who apply religious truths to social problems, and those who carry out the programs of the church. Yang Chang-i expressed his conviction that all of China's religions should be studied in the theological schools. Wu Yi-fang expressed the opinion that all Christian workers, Chinese and missionary, needed a better understanding of Chinese culture.[76]

Luther Weigle directed the conference's attention to his 1935 report, "Education for Service in the Christian Church in China," and observed that his suggestions remained valid and should not be discarded simply because they had not been implemented immediately. Weigle listed as advantages the fact that theological seminaries did not have to register with the government or teach a government-mandated curriculum. He believed China still required three classes of theological education: graduate schools, colleges, and training schools. However, he believed the lower level schools such as the traditional Bible schools should not be training places for clergy but rather for laymen and women and nonordained church workers. He expressed the opinion that Nanking Seminary should be reestablished in Nanjing and should resume its work with regional centers in Guangzhou, west China, and north China.[77]

[75] Minutes, Executive Committee, BF, July 12, 1943; Conference on Theological Education in China, New York, November 10-11, 1943, both ALW.

[76] Conference on Theological Education in China, ALW.

[77] Ibid. Though this description suggests that women were to be excluded from

The Associated Boards for the Christian Colleges in China held its annual meeting in New York in May 1944 with Price as a guest speaker. Price, then in the United States working for the Chinese government, expressed his conviction that those in attendance recognized "China's great contribution to the war" and did not believe the Chinese would "surrender or compromise with the Japanese." He deplored, and expressed the opinion that government educators and friends in government also deplored, "some of the trends toward dictatorial control of universities and university life," but noted that, apart from the "delicate Communist question, many questions are discussed on the college campuses, in the classrooms, and especially in informal gatherings of teachers and students." Price estimated that 20 percent of the leaders in "government, education, business, industry, social work and major fields of effort today in Free China...are either Christians, graduates of Christian schools or men and women who are exceedingly sympathetic to Christianity and we might say Christians at heart." Students from Christian schools were being used as interpreters between Chinese and American forces. He thought it would be a mistake for foreigners or foreign groups to appeal at that time to the government of China for academic and religious freedom. Because such an appeal "would certainly create misunderstanding," he thought they needed to "trust our Chinese colleagues and friends...to make that fight."[78]

Those faculty who were in the United States held a meeting in May 1944. Smith, Plopper, Sone, Price, Leete, and Jones attended, and Dean Weigle attended some of the sessions. Plopper reported that he had given a complete set of photos of deed to the property of Nanking Seminary to the Board of Founder's treasurer, Lloyd S. Ruland, adding that he had a copy and that a third set was presumed to be in Shanghai. All noted that it was impossible to obtain transportation for those who wanted to return to China at that time. Those in attendance recommended that the $2,000 asked for by CUTC be given. On the question of registration with the government, they decided that, if it became a requirement and other similar institutions were registering, then the seminary should do so. They wanted to purchase some

higher levels of theological education and though this was unquestionably the common practice, women would enter NTS in increasing numbers following its return to Nanjing.

78 Frank W. Price, Annual Meeting, Associated Boards for Christian Colleges in China, May 8-9, 1944, MA.

important old Chinese classics such as the Twenty-four Dynastic Histories, which were still available in west China. As they considered post-war plans, they suggested "connections with India, the Philippines, etc." and the possible creation of an All-Asia Theological Association. They hoped to have both a Chinese and a foreign professor in each of the seminary's major departments, and they needed Chinese scholars in Hebrew and Greek since "no really definitive translation of the Bible into Chinese can be attempted" until they had such people.[79]

In late 1944 Price prepared a long memorandum to the Board of Founders addressing many issues and asking several pointed questions: Should the seminary, in spite of financial limitations, continue its organization and program in Free China at all costs until the end of the war? Should it continue both in west China and in Shanghai, or should those in Shanghai be asked to move west? Should the seminary continue to assist WCUTC and CUTC in offering religious programs at the college level? He observed that those in the field needed the counsel of the Board of Founders on what programs to cut, noting that they had already cut the rural extension work. He wanted the board to prioritize the following: post-graduate courses, B.D. and M.R.E. programs, scholarships for students, grants to other theological schools, research in Chinese religions, rural and city church departments, correspondence courses, the rural training center, the Literature Production Program, visiting professors, research projects, the Bible translation project, purchase of library books, and study and writing by members of the staff. Also, as the government was considering a requirement for seminaries to register, he asked the board's recommendation as to whether the seminary should do so and under what name. He reported that Nanking Theological Seminary had many additional questions about the post-war period related to such topics as cooperation with other Asian countries, restoration of theological education in China, restoration of libraries, relations with other movements in China including church union, evangelistic movements, industrialization, and popular education, and ways of dealing with likely economic problems of post-war depression and deflation. The seminary also wanted the board to consider issues of curriculum, types of leadership required, and how the seminary could meet the new needs.[80]

Smith, then in New Haven, wrote to Price about the forthcoming Board of Founders meeting and indicated he had discussed the agenda

79 Francis P. Jones, NTS Furlough Faculty Meeting in New Haven, May 6-7, 1944, MA.

80 Frank W. Price, Memorandum to BF, Washington, March 16, 1944, MA.

with Weigle and that they agreed that the largest post-war question was that of whether the Chinese church and missions would be able to carry on theological education, or whether there would be such destruction that they would simply be compelled to gather up what remained and start to rebuild all phases of Christian work. They needed to know what the various Chinese churches and missions were planning for the training of clergy in the post-war period before they could think much about union institutions. They thought they should turn to lay leaders in Chinese churches, not simply to personnel in the missions or theological schools, to give them a sense of what the churches might need in the post-war period.[81]

Complicating their plans was the fact that Price anticipated having to return to China as one of the ten Chinese-speaking Americans Chiang Kai-shek had asked the United States to provide him. If so, he would not be able to help the seminary. He suggested cabling Stockwell and Tseo asking if they could use some of the missionaries and teachers now evacuated from east and south China, particularly Daniel Nelson who was doing relief work for the Lutherans in Henan Province and whom Price wrote was "one of the best young theological scholars in China."[82] Cartwright replied to Price expressing the Board of Founder's concern over the loss of Price's leadership at the seminary. He wrote that he had read the letter to Diffendorfer but that the board did not know what to advise. He supposed Price had to go to China as the Generalissimo requested, but he did not believe Tseo could replace him at the seminary.[83]

Since the war appeared to be winding down in late 1944, various people were trying to reach decisions regarding return to the seminary. Cartwright was planning a trip to China in early 1945 to represent the Foreign Mission Conference of North America in making plans for post-war work in China.[84] Smith, still in the States, wrote Cartwright asking, in view of the Japanese advance into Guizhou and the threat to southwest China, whether he should search for a job in the United States for the following year. He also asked if Marguerite Rouse were well enough to return to China.[85]

81 C. Stanley Smith to Frank [Price], New Haven, June 1, 1944, MA.

82 Frank W. Price to Frank T. Cartwright, Washington, July 6, 1944, MA. Price confirmed that he would go to China with the group requested by Chiang Kai-shek to help liaison between U.S. forces and the Chinese, Frank W. Price to Ralph Diffendorfer, Washington, July 26, 1944, MA.

83 Frank T. Cartwright to Frank W. Price, New York, July 31, 1944, MA.

84 Frank T. Cartwright to Frank W. Price, [New York], August 29, 1944, MA.

85 C. Stanley Smith to Frank T. Cartwright, Chicago, December 2, 1944, MA.

Leete wanted to return to Chengdu immediately by way of the Holy Land and Cairo so that he could take photographs to make his lectures "more effective." He thought the trip would require two to three months, and he would therefore arrive in Chengdu too late to do any teaching. Cartwright informed him that it was not possible to go to the Holy Land because shipping was unavailable and that the Joint Chiefs of Staff were allowing no one to travel to China. Nonetheless, he hoped that these restrictions would be lifted soon as a result of Chinese victories, and he advised Leete to assure that his passport was valid and that he had a transit visa for India.[86]

Meanwhile Cartwright wrote to those in Chengdu informing them that the Board of Founders was urging Washington to allow Smith to return to China, since Price was then engaged in government work. Leete had taken a United Nations Relief and Rehabilitation Administration (UNRRA) appointment because it was the only way to gain permission to travel to China. He would be available for work at Nanking Seminary sometime in 1946, for he was on a year-by-year contract with UNRRA. The Board of Founders wanted a history of the seminary during the wartime years written while memories were fresh, and it planned to ask President Lee to prepare one as soon as it could contact him. Cartwright noted that, with Price's departure, there was no American on the seminary's faculty and that, as a result, he had requested a military permit for Smith to return to China as soon as possible.[87]

In Chengdu Tseo called a meeting of the Emergency Advisory Committee in January 1945 to discuss the relocation of the seminary in case of national emergency. Price had written that he thought the seminary should continue to work in Free China but thought a remote location like Lanzhou was "probably impracticable." The EAC decided to write the Board of Founders immediately for funds to be used for evacuation if it became necessary and began investigating the possibilities of locating elsewhere. Tseo reported to the Board of Founders that Chiang Kai-shek had called for students to join the army and that one million youths had responded. The Generalissimo also called "all intelligent Christians into active service along the line of

86 William Leete to Frank T. Cartwright, New Haven, Conn., December 5, 1944; Frank T. Cartwright to William Leete, December 12 and 18, 1944, all MA.

87 Frank T. Cartwright to Tseo Ping-I and H. H. Pommerenke, [New York], June 21, 1945; Frank T. Cartwright to whom it may concern, June 19, 1945, both MA.

promoting spiritual life." Tseo added that Professor Ronald Hu (Hu Ren-an) was authorized a leave of absence to become the Protestant chaplain in the new student army. The Board of Founders did not know what to advise with regard to the Generalissimo's call for Christian chaplains for the army and so left the matter to the decision of those in China.[88]

The seminary personnel in Chengdu were concerned about the possible need for evacuation because, as Tseo wrote, "our enemies have taken so many cities and strategic points in China within the last eight months." However, he added that "our primary aim is to keep the integrity of our Seminary in Free China as far as possible in order to carry on our training program for our church leadership wherever [there] is genuine freedom. We esteem freedom far more valuable than security. As soon as our freedom here is threatened we shall move by all means and at all costs." Tseo also quoted from Price's letter advising that they should move to "somewhere in Free China or guerilla territory away from occupied area," adding there were then twenty-two students in the graduate program, though some were enrolled part time.[89]

Andrew Roy also wrote to Cartwright about the Japanese advance and the possible need for those in Chengdu to move again, though he noted that some felt they should not move because of the expense. Yet because Nanking's students were university graduates and came from all over China, they believed they would lose some if they did not move to a Free China area. Roy observed that if they were to remain in occupied territory they might as well go to Shanghai.[90] He declared:

> Years from now the Church will thank God for the wisdom of maintaining this work despite all difficulties. If there were good reasons for having it here in the first place, there are just as good reasons now for insuring that it continues to function in an area where students can reach it, and where it can teach fearlessly and prophetically (in a way which must be extremely difficult at present in a Japanese occupied area).[91]

Upon receiving this correspondence from Tseo and Roy, Cartwright wrote to the Board of Founders, sending copies of its letters and indicating he had contacted the State Department. Officials

88 Ibid., and Minutes, EAC, NTS, Chengdu, January 8, 1945, ALW.
89 Tseo Ping-I to Frank T. Cartwright, Chengdu, January 9, 1945, ALW.
90 Andrew T. Roy to Frank T. Cartwright, Chengdu, January 16, 1945, ALW.
91 Ibid.

there believed the emergency in west China had ended, but Cartwright wanted the board to vote to set aside $20,000 to cover moving expenses if necessary. "In view of the state of mind of the people out there," he wrote, "I think it would be wise for us to express our judgment as to our willingness to pay evacuation expenses. Their cabled request was that we set aside $20,000 for this purpose. I am setting up the vote in that form although I think a flat assurance of our willingness to stand by would give them all the sense of encouragement which they need."[92]

This action was confirmed at a special meeting of the Board of Founders on March 24, 1944. Other more bureaucratic matters also required the attention of the board at that time. For example, the reunion of Methodist churches, two of whom were members of the board, into the United Methodist Church necessitated some changes in the language of board membership, as did the admission of the American Baptist Foreign Mission Society at this special meeting.[93]

The Board of Founders wrote to the various mission boards that supported Nanking Seminary reminding them that the school was operated with the cooperation of several boards and that they should not overlook their commitments to the seminary in budgets for the forthcoming years. They were to supply the salaries of faculty members representing their denominations; and, if they had no faculty, they were expected to make cash contributions. They were also reminded of the need for funds to rehabilitate the seminary facilities after the war.[94]

The Board of Founders observed that three of the students being awarded the bachelor of divinity degree in Chengdu were not college graduates, and it determined to remind the faculty in Chengdu that acceptance of such students into a graduate program was a violation of the charter and that the seminary was prohibited from awarding these degrees.[95]

In other actions the board asked N. F. Kwang, then serving a Chinese church in New Orleans, to return to China to teach Old Testament at Nanking Seminary if he were not needed at CUTC. Scholarships were voted for Tso T. Taan, Newton Chiang, Francis Jones, and Miss Chang Tsai-i. Chang, a graduate in music from Ginling College in Nanjing, was studying sacred music at Union Theological Seminary in New York, and the board observed that "she would fill a need for further workers in a field in which so far very few Chinese

92 Frank T. Cartwright to BF, New York, March 20, 1945, ALW.
93 Ibid.; Minutes, Special Meeting, BF, NTS, March 24, 1944.
94 Frank T. Cartwright to BF, New York, March 20, 1945, ALW.
95 Ibid.

have specialized." The Board of Founders agreed to publish the thesis of Irma Highbaugh, entitled "A Family Centered Program in Rural Reconstruction in West China with Special Emphasis on the Pre-School Child," which was to be sold to individuals and boards working in China. Jones was authorized to purchase books for the libraries of theological seminaries in China.[96]

As the war ended, the faculty in Chengdu drew up an extensive list of questions it wished to discuss with Diffendorfer, chair of the Board of Founders, regarding the seminary's future: What plans and programs were under consideration for Nanking Theological Seminary in terms of buildings, including residences, on the main campus? What could be done to establish a closer relationship with the Board of Founders? Was it possible to reduce the five-year theological course to a four-year intensive one and still award the B.Th. degree granted by the New York Board of Regents? Could the faculty modify the theological curriculum to make it more practical and more Chinese? What was the value of a one-year course for laymen who were unable to enroll in a full theological course? Was it advisable to grant subsidies to graduates who were working as pastors or assistant pastors but could not earn enough to cover living expenses? Considering the changes the war had brought, was the Board of Founders interested in conducting another study like the Weigle study of 1935? What should be the relationship between mission and church with respect to theological education? What advice could the board offer for getting students to Nanking Seminary? Should the Literature Production Program be continued in the immediate future and, if so, to what extent? Was it advisable to have full-time missionary workers in the seminary's Editorial Department?

Additional issues raised included the following: Was it necessary for the Board of Founders to study again its power and duties in relation to the managers in the field in view of the post-war situation? Was it advisable to continue to ask for support from the missions when the seminary had sufficient financial resources? Should Nanking Seminary provide lower level training for preachers, since there was clearly a demand for it? What tasks did the board believe the seminary should undertake in addition to those enumerated in the Weigle report? What work should be given highest priority in the post-war period? What was the board's view regarding new buildings and whether their architectural style should be Western or Chinese? What did the board think about appointing a term-president so that the opportunity to

96 Ibid.

lead the seminary could be given to more faculty members and to prominent Christian leaders? What was the board's opinion regarding rural work? What did the board advise regarding cooperation or coordination or union with other theological seminaries? Could the seminary freely support other theological institutions or Bible schools within the spirit of the Swope-Wendel trust?[97] The extent and complexity of these questions reflected the recognition on the part of the faculty that changed circumstances in China would inevitably demand changes in the work of the seminary and its relationship to the Board of Founders.

Nanking Theological Seminary issued its annual report from Chengdu in the spring of 1945. The seminary reported the largest enrollment since evacuation from Nanjing: seventeen full-time students, six half-time students, and five part-time students, representing ten provinces. Eight came from government colleges, seven from theological seminaries, and thirteen from Christian universities. The largest group, sixteen, were from the Church of Christ in China, but others were Methodists, Anglicans, Baptists, Friends, and Disciples. Only two of the students had mission support, one from the Presbyterians and one from the Disciples. Two hundred fifty-two students from fifteen provinces representing twenty-five denominations were enrolled in correspondence courses. Five students were awarded degrees: two men received the bachelor of theology degree, one the bachelor of divinity degree, and two women, one married and one single, received the degree master of religious education.[98]

To augment the seminary library, the faculty had purchased four Chinese libraries containing a total of twenty-five hundred volumes; one of classical books, one of historical works, one of philosophical works, and one general in nature. One of the libraries had belonged to a well-to-do general who was also a scholar and had purchased old books in Shanghai for more than twenty years. After his death his sons sold the library. For these purchases the Board of Founders granted $1,500, which was exchanged for CN $270,000. However, the books cost CN $450,000; the excess was paid from the contingency fund and the gain on exchange.[99]

The seminary also reported that Tseo was asked to study the difficulties of placing students after graduation and working with

97 "Questions from the faculty of the NTS to be studied and discussed with Cartwright on November 29, 1945," ALW.

98 Minutes, EAC, NTS, April 2, 1945; Annual Report, NTS, April 2, 1945, both ALW.

99 Ibid.

them and the National Christian Council to resolve problems which might arise. Newton Chiang was voted an additional year of study in the United States. Kuo Pen-tao was reported to be working on Chinese religions and, helped by the Reverend and Mrs. H. H. Pommerenke, to have translated some Sui dynasty material into English. They were also working on materials related to the Buddhist doctrine of the golden mean. The National Christian Council (NCC) had paid nothing toward the Literature Production Program in the past year but hoped to contribute $3,500 of the current $7,500 budget.[100]

The faculty continued to share a communal kitchen, and it was reported that a suit of clothing now cost as much as a house did before the war. The Chengdu group had little contact with the seminary in Shanghai and understood that Handel Lee was reluctant to write or to accept letters from them. However, from other sources they had learned that Shanghai had twenty students.[101]

Tseo informed the Board of Founders that Price, who had returned from furlough in the United States but was working for the Chinese government in Chongqing, was being sent to San Francisco by Chiang Kai-shek to assist the Chinese delegation at the United Nations conference. Tseo suggested that Price ask for a one-month leave of absence from his governmental duties to attend the Board of Founders meeting in order to discuss the teaching problems for the forthcoming fall term. Because so many faculty members had left the seminary or had not returned from furlough, Tseo feared the school would be unable to offer instruction in the fall, since only he and one other person were available to teach. Tseo reminded the Board of Founders that he had agreed to be acting chair of the Emergency Advisory Committee only during Price's six-month leave and that consequently his term was over, though he was willing to continue for a time, since they expected Smith to return and take over these responsibilities.[102]

Following the war's end, Cartwright and Smith returned to Chengdu in late 1945 aboard the same plane. Cartwright wrote to Diffendorfer that the EAC was holding its last meeting and that it wanted to be sure that future funds for Nanking Seminary would be sent directly to its account at its bank in Shanghai.[103] Smith reported through Cartwright that he had met with faculty who had been in

100 Ibid.
101 Ibid.
102 Tseo Ping-I to Frank T. Cartwright, [Chengdu?], April 10, 1945, ALW.
103 Frank T. Cartwright to Ralph Diffendorfer, Chengdu, October 22, 1945, MA.

Chengdu and those who had been in Shanghai and "found not the slightest trace of recrimination or suspicion" among them, a situation which, he noted, was not true among other Christian groups.[104]

The annual meeting of the Board of Founders in 1945 was held June 14, following the collapse of Germany and with victory over Japan in sight. Several faculty members were present: Smith, Jones, Chiang, Sone, Plopper, and Leete. The American Baptist Foreign Mission Board had appointed the Reverend E. H. Pruden and Dr. E. A. Fridell as its representatives, and they were welcomed to the board. With the merger of cooperating Methodist denominations and the anticipated merger of cooperating Presbyterian denominations, the board voted to allow uniting boards to be represented "by as many Founders as the sum of the Founders of the Boards which united." The board also memorialized Dr. Joshua C. Garritt, a missionary of the Presbyterian Board of Missions and the first president of Nanking Seminary. It confirmed the EAC's appointment of H. H. Pommerenke as the temporary financial agent until a permanent appointee arrived, voted to take the initiative in collecting books for the theological colleges and seminaries of China, and asked the faculty in China to prepare an account of the significant events in the history of the seminary during the war years.[105]

In order to keep those scholars who had fled to Chengdu fully employed during the war, the seminary had instituted a program to translate the classics of Christianity into Chinese. The program began in 1941, improbably enough, when Jones, driving a truck up the Burma Road to Chongqing en route to Chengdu, met T. H. Sun, one of the secretaries of China's National Christian Council. As they talked, Sun expressed his belief that there was not enough Christian literature available in Chinese and that what did exist was shallow in terms of the philosophical classics of the Confucian, Daoist, and Buddhist traditions. Sun pointed out that the war had freed some of the best translators from their regular work, and he convinced Jones that Nanking Seminary and the NCC should sponsor a translation project employing these people. The project subsequently took shape "in a series of mid-night conversations" involving Sun, W. Y. Chen, and Earl Cressy, all of whom were living in Chongqing in 1941. Sun approached the Roman Catholic bishop, Paul Yu Ping, to ask if his church were interested in participating in the program, since they assumed Catholics would have the same need as Protestants for Christian classics in

104 Frank T. Cartwright, Report to the BF, NTS, Annual Meeting, New York, June 5, 1946, MA.

105 Minutes, BF, NTS, June 12, 1945, FTEA.

Chinese. The bishop was enthusiastic. Pleased with the Protestant-Catholic cooperation, the Emergency Committee in West China of the NCC appointed a Literature Production Committee, chaired by Cressy and Sun. Both Price and Jones supported the program, and the Board of Founders appropriated funds for it in 1941. Suggestions were solicited from persons in the United States as to volumes that should be translated.[106]

By the summer of 1942, fifteen to nineteen people were working in the program. They held what they termed an "ashram" enabling participants to gather away from their regular work for a period of two months, choose materials to be translated, begin the actual translation and editing, and resolve questions of terminology, methodology, etc. P. C. Hsu arrived from Shanghai during the third week to assist in the project. The meeting was held at a secluded Daoist temple forty miles from Chengdu, and those present observed three hours of silence each morning, during which everyone worked on translation. In the afternoons they discussed their work and attempted to resolve difficulties. Collectively, those participating translated a half million words into Chinese.[107]

The Literature Production Program's plan was to translate into Chinese fifty volumes of Christian classics, each containing 200,000 to 250,000 characters, between 1942 and 1951. The works were divided into four groups: (1) pre-Renaissance writings such as Eusebius, Bernard of Clairvaux, Francis of Assisi, the Apocrypha, Augustine, and Thomas Aquinas; (2) Luther, Loyola, Calvin, Bunyan, Fox, Wesley, Kant, and Kierkegaard; (3) Tolstoy, Barth, Schweitzer, and Royce; and (4) general works such as Protestant sermons, church histories, and histories of Christian thought. Several of the Catholic works were being translated by priests of that church.[108]

Those working on the translation project realized that many Chinese did not have an adequate background to recognize the significance of some of the Christian materials that they were translating, but this awareness led to some differences of opinion as to the appropriate resolution of the problem. For example, Bishop Yu Ping

106 Earl Cressy to Ralph Diffendorfer, Chongqing, January 11, 1943, (completed March 3; April 5, second letter), ALW; and Francis Jones, "Beginnings of the Translation Project as reported to the Conference on June 17, 1944," in NTS, MA.

107 Ibid.

108 Earl Cressy to Ralph Diffendorfer, Chongqing, January 11, 1943, and "A Tentative List for Christian Literature Production," both ALW.

wanted books translated that scholars and students could use as source materials; but, as Cressy noted, the NCC and those at the Commercial Press, which was to publish the translations, wanted

> volumes which will give a brilliant outline of the spiritual development of the West, very fully documented, which will appeal to the average educated man, Christian or non-Christian, and not only to research scholars and theological students. One of the outstanding Chinese historians (non-Christian) with whom I discussed this, said that there was a gap in the materials available in Chinese at this point, and that many were feeling the importance of this aspect of the civilization of the West and the need of full treatment of it.[109]

The objective of the Protestants was to make books accessible to average Chinese readers. Cressy continued that the American Dominicans were financing the Aquinas translation, the Quakers the Fox work, and the Methodists Wesley's *Journal*, adding that he wanted to approach other denominations about doing some of the work; for he realized the importance of the introductory material for each volume.[110]

Each evening at the ashram, participants talked about methodology, terms, and the plan of the series. The need for carefully planned introductory material became more evident as the work progressed. For example, "one translator of an apologist stated that many of the arguments used made him laugh and that if the translation was intended as an apologetic for Christianity in the China of today we might as well throw it into the wastepaper basket. However, the discussion brought out the fact that these documents played an important part in convincing the Roman Empire of Christianity [sic]." Cressy added that they hoped to make the books available to a wide range of readers from middle school and university students to pastors and non-Christian scholars.[111]

As Price was about to depart China in January 1944, P. C. Hsu wrote him from Chengdu affirming the wisdom of the seminary in launching the Literature Production Program with Board of Founders

[109] Earl Cressy to Ralph Diffendorfer, Chongqing, April 6, 1943, ALW.

[110] Ibid.

[111] Earl Cressy to Ralph Diffendorfer, Chongqing, January 11, 1943, ALW. At the June 1943 BF meeting, at-large member H. P. Van Dusen and biblical scholar James Moffatt, both from Union Theological Seminary in New York, were invited to work with the LPP, Minutes, BF, NTS, June 15, 1943, FTEA.

support. Enthusiastic about the contribution Christian literature in translation could make to China, he opined that "what the Program is going to mean to the Christian Church in China time alone can tell." He thought friends in America could contribute to the program by making comments and suggestions regarding the tentative list of works to be translated, helping secure books which the program did not have, and providing material for the introductory chapters. Hsu also reported the difficulty the program faced in finding enough people who were well qualified and able to give time to the translation project. The group had translated one million characters during the first year but did not know if it had enough funds to hold another ashram the coming summer. He thought the seminary needed to introduce a Christian literature course in the bachelor of divinity degree program to train translators and writers for the project and indicated that Tseo was doing some work along these lines. Although translators had been paid $25 per thousand characters when the project started and were then receiving $65 per thousand, inflation had increased more rapidly, so that the program's ability to attract translators was declining. Hsu also expressed the belief that cooperation with the Roman Catholics would prove significant though "so far, nothing very definite has been accomplished." He added that he hoped the situation would improve when the bishop returned from the United States.[112]

A list of Chinese and English books published with seminary funds as of January 1944 indicated that they were printing in both Chengdu and Hengyang. The press runs usually produced five hundred or a thousand copies, and the titles ranged from Harry Emerson Fosdick's *The Meaning of Faith* to Kenneth Scott Latourette's *Towards a World Christian Fellowship.*[113]

Two conferences on the Literature Production Program were held in New York in 1944. At the June meeting, those attending agreed that the purpose of the program was to "present the classics as great creative achievements of Christian thought and experience, rather than merely to provide source material for the study of church history." Insofar as possible, translation was to be done from the original language. Conference participants acknowledged there would be problems with the Roman Catholics over "diverging purposes, differing vocabularies, and conflicting points of view" on the writings prior to Luther; but,

112 P. C. Hsu [to Frank Price], Chengdu, January 8, 1944, ALW. Hsu was killed in a truck accident in Chongqing later in January, Frank T. Cartwright to BF, New York, February 11, 1944, ALW.

113 List of Books Reprinted with NTS Funds, January 1, 1944, ALW.

if these could be overcome, it would be a "noteworthy achievement." The series was to include theology, sermons, devotional and mystical literature, and outstanding autobiographies.[114]

The November conference focused primarily on the nature of the works being translated. This conference envisioned readers of the series as including theological students, pastors and other Christian leaders, intelligent Christian laypeople interested in the foundation of their faith, and non-Christians of a scholarly or mystical type.[115] This project, begun in wartime, was to occupy many people over a number of years and continued to receive Board of Founders support after 1949 when the translators moved to Madison, New Jersey, near Drew Theological Seminary.

Clearly there were many questions to be answered in the post-war period, not only those raised by the seminary's faculty but, more significantly, those that would be posed by the renewal of civil war in China. The next few years proved to be busy ones for those associated with Nanking Theological Seminary, and they proved to be a time of many surprises, some pleasant and some unpleasant. But as World War II ended, those associated with the seminary looked to the future with great optimism.

114 Report, Conference on the Translation Project, New York, June 17, 1944, ALW.

115 Roland H. Bainton, Second Conference on Translation of Christian Classics into Chinese, NTS, New York, November 10-12, 1944, ALW.

CHAPTER 3

Postwar Rebuilding in Nanjing

Seminary faculty members in both Shanghai and Chengdu eagerly welcomed the end of World War II in August 1945 and turned their attention to plans for the future of Nanking Theological Seminary. In October C. Stanley Smith, the seminary's vice-president and treasurer, arrived in Chengdu, providing the missionary presence that had been missing since Frank Price commenced work for the Chinese government. After two months of teaching and administrative work in Chengdu, Smith was asked by the president, Handel Lee, to fly to Shanghai in order to assist with arrangements for the return of the faculty members and students there to Nanjing.[1]

As plans materialized for a return to the old campus, Smith and William R. Leete made the trip from Shanghai to Nanjing in January 1946 and reported that Japanese soldiers were evident all along the rail lines doing manual labor or other types of work under the watchful eyes of Chinese soldiers. When they reached the campus in Nanjing, Smith and Leete found that Chinese soldiers were quartered in the chapel and

1 C. Stanley Smith, NTS Faculty Report, 1945-46, ALW.

were sleeping on the students' cots. They also found that the Japanese had built an observation post on the roof of one of the buildings. Smith suggested keeping it as a souvenir, since it provided a good view of the city and of Purple Mountain to the east. Smith also reported that all of the windows in the buildings were broken, though the Japanese had made some improvements. For example, a central heating system had been installed in the main dormitory building, modern toilets and running water had been installed on each floor, and in the basement the Japanese had torn out the old showers and installed toilets. Smith believed they could use this building for a dormitory in the following year, adding that it might also serve as the library, chapel, offices, and classrooms. Most of the seminary's equipment was gone except for one safe and a few stoves. He estimated that it would require $15,000 to repair and restore the campus for use by fifty students. He also observed that the faculty residences were in great need of repair and estimated costs for that work at an additional $10,000. In general, however, Smith reported that the facilities were in much better shape than had been anticipated.[2]

The faculty in Shanghai recommended that it return to Nanjing first and that those in Chengdu finish the term and return to Nanjing with the faculties of the University of Nanking and Ginling College since, if those in the West returned in February as originally planned, there would be no housing available for them.[3] Smith reported to Ralph E. Diffendorfer in March concerning the return of the faculty from Shanghai to Nanjing. On February 20 the group had reserved thirty-two seats on the eight a.m. train between the two cities, but when they arrived at the train station at six a.m., they found that all except six of their places were occupied with no chance of recovery. Those who could find seats or standing room on the eight a.m. train left, and the remainder traveled on the nine a.m. train. Their household belongings were shipped, but few of them arrived without damage. Three pianos and an organ, which could not be crated and so were wrapped in straw, were badly damaged, but Smith thought they could be repaired.[4]

In Nanjing they found that most of the seminary's buildings had been vacated, but "we are still suffering great inconvenience...having a few members of the [Foreign Affairs Bureau] as well as a group of military police living in our library building." Since the military police

2 C. Stanley Smith, "Confidential Report of a Trip to Nanking," January 9, 1946, ALW.

3 Ibid.

4 C. Stanley Smith to Ralph E. Diffendorfer, Nanjing, March 4, 1946, ALW.

were using the school kitchen, the faculty could not prepare meals for the students who had returned with them. As more students were expected that week, the faculty needed to find a way to get the soldiers out of the kitchen. The general in charge of those using the seminary facilities was one for whom Price had worked in his association with the Chinese government; and, with the general's return to the city, the issue was resolved.[5]

Newton Chiang, his family, and a servant returned unexpectedly to Nanjing after a twenty-two-day trip from Chengdu. Housing had not been prepared for their early arrival, and the family was placed in an unfinished house being prepared for another faculty member. Revisiting prewar issues of interest to the seminary and Board of Founders, Smith also reported that he had held discussions on cooperation with the Bible Teachers' Training School in Nanjing, but that there was no foreign representative of that institution then in Nanjing who could discuss the status of their property. Smith added that they were cooperating closely with the University of Nanking, but that this cooperation appeared to be more beneficial to the university than to the seminary. He did not think that they could move the seminary closer to the university, but he did believe they could cooperate by sharing teachers. He asked for the board's advice concerning further cooperation with other theological schools and whether such cooperation as had taken place during the war years could legally continue. He reported that a survey was being conducted to determine the needs of churches in the next decade and expressed the view that one or two good theological schools, centrally located, could provide for the needs of all the churches, adding that before the war there had been twenty-six training schools for Christian workers.[6]

Nanking Theological Seminary resumed classes in Nanjing March 8, 1946, with eleven students, including one senior B. D. student from Chengdu. Smith advised the Board of Founders that the seminary had recovered its houses except for one in which a general was living. The faculty had planned to give CN $50,000 to each family for the purchase of small household items but noted that that amount was no longer sufficient to purchase a single bed! Three additional families had returned from Chengdu, and they were expecting others soon. Smith asked the Board of Founders to make several purchases for them in the United States, including twenty-five rolls of screening for the buildings and three good bicycles with spare tires and parts.

5 Ibid.
6 Ibid.

He believed the bicycles would cost about $50 each in the States but probably four times that amount in China. He added that they needed the bicycles in order to reestablish the rural church experimental station at Shenhuachen.[7]

Smith also attempted to give the Board of Founders an idea of the financial situation. He reported that the Shanghai campus had operated by selling drafts on the Board of Founders. President Lee had managed to obtain CN $3,874,865.09 or $4,300 U.S. that way at an exchange rate averaging 900:1. Smith reported that he was unable to say what expenses those in west China had incurred as he had received no word from Elsie Priest. After Smith's internment in Shanghai in 1943, Lee kept very careful books of expenditures. However, because he became afraid to sell additional drafts on the Board of Founders, which might focus unwanted Japanese attention on the seminary, he had paid the faculty at a reduced rate. Consequently, Smith now asked the Board of Founders to cover these lost wages and added that they would amount to no more than $4,500.[8] In submitting a budget request for the forthcoming academic year of 1946-47, Smith wrote:

> two of the main essentials in making out a budget are an adding machine that is not limited to seven figures and a lively imagination. Our adding machine is so limited in its range that we could not use it on these estimates and you may think when you read the budget that our imagination has been too lively. It is a rather deflating experience to spend one's time with figures that run into the millions and then reduce them to U.S. currency and find that they are only comfortable figures that call for no excitement at all.[9]

Smith thought the budget would be CN $98,345,000, which was only $65,533.33 in U.S. currency at the exchange rate of 1,500: 1. The only unusual expenses were for medical care, which the Board of Founders had not generally paid in the past but which the Chinese faculty so desperately needed that it was asking for a special appropriation. Another special request was for $4,000 for the Literature Production Program. Smith expressed the opinion that, although they had been supporting sister institutions during the war, they should now reduce those contributions.[10]

7 C. Stanley Smith to Ralph E. Diffendorfer, Nanjing, April 3, 1946, ALW.
8 C. Stanley Smith, Treasurer's Report, 1946, ALW.
9 Ibid.
10 Ibid.

Along with Smith's budget, the Board of Managers forwarded to the Board of Founders a report of all the things needed to repair the seminary's physical facilities. The managers needed $25,000 to repair buildings, restore lights and water, and furnish the houses, most of which had only cooking stoves. They noted that they had no bedding when the faculty and students returned from Shanghai and that, for a time, they slept on Japanese tatami on the floor. They reported that the Japanese-installed heating system in the dormitory was in good condition but that they still needed another $31,000 to restore that building.[11]

Smith wrote Cartwright following the meeting of the managers that the faculty members from Chengdu and Shanghai had been together at this meeting for the first time since 1937. He asked the Board of Founders to act quickly on his budget request of $65,000 as well as the request of the managers before the costs of materials increased too much. The managers were quite interested in the research Kuo Pen-tao was doing on Chinese religion in Chengdu, and they wanted to fund his work, but they also wanted Kuo to remain in Chengdu until he could transport his materials by boat to Nanjing. On other personnel matters, they asked that the Presbyterian Board of Missions to support Christopher Tang[12] for another year before they placed him permanently on the seminary's staff and payroll.[13]

Returning with the Chengdu group were two new faculty members: Miss Kuan Tsui-chen who taught in the Department of Religious Education and specialized in work with women and children, and Hu Ren-an, a graduate of Yenching School of Religion, who had served as one of the first Chinese army chaplains. The faculty in Shanghai had been without foreign teachers from February 1943 until late 1945, when Smith came from Chengdu to assist in the move to Nanjing and the Reverend and Mrs. C. H. Plopper returned from the United States.[14]

Smith informed the Board of Founders that between one-third and one-half of the Nanking Seminary students were women. Expressing some concern about the steady increase in the percentage of female students in the seminary, Smith suggested that they might

11 William R. Leete, "Rehabilitation Committee Report to the NTS Managers," Nanjing, May 8, 1946, ALW.

12 All subsequent references to Tang are to Christopher Tang unless another person is specified.

13 C. Stanley Smith to Frank T. Cartwright, Nanjing, May 13, 1946, ALW.

14 Ibid.

need to consider imposing a quota on women students. However, he also thought that the growing number of women was an added reason for uniting the Nanking Seminary and the Bible Teachers' Training School, which was situated very close to the seminary, served a female student body, and whose mission support came in large measure from the same groups that supported the seminary.[15]

When the Board of Founders met in New York June 5, 1946, Newton Chiang and Francis Jones were present from the faculty. Their reports were complemented by Frank Cartwright, who had also recently returned from a six-month tour of China, where he met with faculty members in Chengdu and Shanghai. The Board of Founders considered a request from Lee and Smith that the salaries of Leete and Marguerite Rouse be paid directly to them through the Associated Missions Treasurers in Shanghai and not through the Nanking Seminary treasurer and accounts. The board also observed that it needed to pay for transporting Leete's library from Lushan (Kuling) in Jiangxi Province to Shanghai and to give him the $500 that mission boards were giving for personal losses, though in his case the losses amounted to $825.[16]

The Board of Founders voted funds to cover the drafts issued by the Shanghai campus during the war and for repairing the Nanjing campus. It also appealed to the cooperating denominations to provide additional assistance. It expressed its sympathy for greater cooperation between Nanking Seminary and the women's Bible Teachers' Training School. It responded to a Board of Managers request for special lecturers and considered various prominent leaders for such an assignment. It hoped that Dr. Henry Sloane Coffin of Union Theological Seminary in New York might lecture under the joint auspices of Nanking Seminary, the University of Nanking, and Ginling College. H. P. Van Dusen was planning a trip to China for the Associated Boards for the Christian Colleges in China, and the Board of Founders asked him to visit the seminary. The board also considered inviting Dr. L. N. D. Wells, a prominent Disciples minister in Dallas, to lecture at the seminary.[17]

Meeting in Nanjing April 30 and May 1, 1947, the managers granted president Handel Lee a sabbatical leave; he had worked fourteen years without a vacation and, during the years in Shanghai, under the most trying conditions. Hu was given a scholarship for the

15 Ibid.

16 Frank T. Cartwright to BF, New York, December 1946; Minutes, Annual Meeting, BF, NTS, June 5, 1946, both ALW.

17 Minutes, Annual Meeting, BF, NTS, June 5, 1946, ALW.

1947-48 academic year, provided he could make arrangements to study for an advanced degree in the United States or Canada. Five students received the B.D. degree, four the B.Th. degree, and eight the Tao Hsieh Shih degree.[18] Nanking Seminary continued to seek cooperative arrangements with the Bible Teachers' Training School, suggesting joint registration and joint faculty meetings, a united treasurer's office, a shared library, joint chapel services, a united student organization, a joint committee on curriculum, and joint planning and supervision of field work. Under an agreement between the two institutions, Nanking Seminary's women students were to live and dine at the training school during the following year.[19]

In submitting the treasurer's report, Smith commented that the budget for the previous year had been over CN $324 million but that the thrill of writing such large checks was offset by worries about the rate of exchange and the value of the inflated Chinese dollar. When the fiscal year began in July, the exchange rate was 2,500:1, but by December it was officially 3,350:1, and on the open market it was around 6,000:1. By the middle of February the official rate was the same, but the black market rate had risen to 27,000:1. Smith wrote that "[t]his was followed by the issuance of drastic regulations of penalties attached against all black market transactions....With such fluctuations in exchange, it is little wonder that the life of a treasurer this past year has been one of interest and anxiety."[20]

Smith reported that since the Board of Founders had not approved the request to allow those in China to handle the gain on currency exchange, they were unable to keep pace with steadily rising living costs during the first five months of the year. Many on the faculty were in such straits that they told the administration they would have to resign if something could not be done. Therefore, a committee considered the matter and linked monthly salaries not to the dollar but to the cost of living index issued by the Chinese government with an additional CN $50,000 per month to be given to each family together with an increased rice allowance. This plan was satisfactory for a time, but in October the bonus had to be increased to CN $100,000 per month. When Lloyd S.

18 The Tao Hsieh Shih degree was awarded by NTS with no sanction from the New York State Board of Regents and was discontinued after 1947-48. The Pinyin transliteration is Dao Xue Shi, and it is generally regarded as a professional diploma similar to the Bachelor of Divinity degree but may have represented a less demanding curriculum.

19 Minutes, BM, NTS, April 30-May 1, 1947, ALW.

20 NTS Treasurer's Report, 1946-47, ALW.

Ruland, treasurer of the Board of Founders, visited China in December, he cabled the board asking for approval for those in China to revise the budget monthly based on the exchange rate; prompt permission was granted. By January the bonus was increased to CN $200,000 per month with yet another increase in the rice allowance. On February 18 the government increased the exchange rate from 3,350:1 to 12,000:1, but the black market exchange rate was still double the official rate. When submitting the budget, Smith had eliminated the column that provided figures in Chinese currency, noting that it would have taken up too much space to include the huge amounts! The 1946-47 budget was CN $326,490,452.00 or $45,538.60 U.S.[21]

Smith advised the Board of Founders that the seminary was supporting three projects outside Nanjing: at West China Union Theological College in Chengdu, at Canton Union Theological College in Guangzhou (formerly Canton), and at the North China Rural Service Union. Spending on all three totaled $4,000. Smith added that the seminary was considering decreasing its commitment to these institutions, partly because the decreasing purchasing power occasioned by rapid inflation gave the seminary less surplus than it had previously enjoyed, but also because it believed the other institutions should be encouraged to depend more on their own constituencies.[22]

Commenting more generally upon the situation in Nanjing, Smith wrote:

> the present fiscal year has been one largely of reunion, rehabilitation and readjustment. Our energies have been spent in caring for and teaching the largest student body that we have had since 1927 when our school was broken up by the "Nanking Incident." Limitation of our use of exchange; uncertainty as to the rate of exchange in the face of daily increasing cost of living; and the critical political situation have led to caution in the use of funds for new projects and for needed equipment. In spite of the continuing inflationary trends and the uncertain outcome of the present civil war, there is still a spirit of hope in the air of Nanking this spring and a feeling that we ought to stop marking time and plan to go forward during the coming fiscal year.[23]

Smith enumerated a variety of new as well as continuing programs, including the Literature Production Program, "the

21 Ibid.
22 Ibid.
23 Ibid.

study and use of visual education aids," improvement of the Music Department, and a conference of the four cooperating theological colleges in the forthcoming summer or fall to plan for a larger conference to be held the following summer. The seminary was planning to offer the correspondence course on a reduced scale because of political disturbances that it expected to continue into the next year. The seminary planned to have a circulating library, which had earlier proved effective in Shanghai, and for it the seminary would employ a messenger who would use a bicycle to deliver books to pastors and evangelistic workers throughout Nanjing. The requested grant of $450 would cover the cost of the bicycle, the messenger boy's salary, and some books. Smith reported dropping the short-term Bible course that Nanking Seminary had offered with the Bible Teachers' Training School and granting much smaller stipends to the students on scholarship. The seminary requested $400 to renew the project of librarian Chen Tsing-hsien, a biographical dictionary of outstanding Chinese Christian leaders that he had begun before the war. Kuo had been ill and so had accomplished little work on his research on Chinese religions, and thus the budget request for that project was small. The Literature Production Program had accomplished little because Francis P. Jones,[24] the field director, had only recently returned from the United States.[25] As it appeared that there would be a surplus in the salary category, the Finance Committee recommended that it be used first to pay for the United Nations Relief and Rehabilitation Administration supplies that each Chinese member of the faculty had received and that the remainder be distributed to them to make up for salary deficiencies suffered earlier in the year.[26]

Lee had been on sick leave for three and a half months but was able to return to the seminary July 1 and to be present for the Board of Managers meeting, where he presented the faculty report. The thirty-first commencement was held June 30-July 2, 1946, with Luther Shao, general secretary of the Christian Church (Disciples), preaching the baccalaureate sermon and Y. G. Chen, president of the University of Nanking, giving the commencement address. Four students graduated, of whom two returned to take the fifth-year course for the B.Th. degree, one was "looking after a home," and the other was a teacher of religious education in a girls' middle school.[27]

24 All subsequent references to Jones in this chapter refer to Francis P. Jones unless another person is specified.

25 NTS Treasurer's Report, 1946-47, ALW.

26 Ibid.

27 Handel Lee, Faculty Report, 1946-47, ALW.

By the time classes resumed at in the fall of 1946, the faculty, having been separated for nine years, was reunited. Nanking Theological Seminary then had eighty students enrolled, the largest number since 1927. A few students dropped out during the fall term, but four new ones, pastors of local churches, were added during the spring. The students represented the following denominations: Methodists, twenty-five; Church of Christ in China, twenty-three; Episcopalians, nine; Presbyterians, seven; Disciples, six; two each from the Baptists, English Baptists, and English Methodists; and one each from the China Inland Mission, Congregationalists, London Missionary Society, and the Lutherans. By home provinces, the student representation was: Fujian, seventeen; Jiangsu, sixteen; Guangdong, twelve; Anhui, nine; Zhejiang, six; Hubei, five; Hunan, four; Sichuan, three; two each from Shandong, Shanxi, and Jiangxi; and one each from Hubei and Liaoning. During the fall term, one-third of the enrolled students were women.[28]

Lee observed that Nanking Seminary was emphasizing practical work in all areas. The Young People's Group was headed by Newton Chiang, music by Lillian Hwang, Sunday school by Paul Chen, the evangelistic group by Hu Ren-an, and Bible study by Hubert Sone. All five groups were actively engaged with congregations in the larger local churches, but in some smaller churches only two or three of the groups were at work. In addition to this work at ten local churches, the seminary also maintained a program at a middle school. For students who were only taking the one-year course, Hu had organized a visitation group so that they could observe all aspects of local church work. The seminary also had organized a milk-feeding station with aid from the National Christian Council of China, the UNRRA, the American Advisory Committee, and other organizations. Located at Wesley Church, it fed about five hundred undernourished children under the age of twelve as well as pregnant women. Lee also observed that the seminary was planning a nursery training school, with Kuan Tsui-chen teaching Christian training for children.[29]

The Rural Church Department was conducting research on rural church life and church extension, with students going to the Shenhuachen Rural Training Center either during the summer for several weeks or on weekends. Dr. Lee Ju-lin, a medical doctor associated with the University Hospital Rural Health Department, gave lectures to the students on problems of rural health. Some of the books on rural work that Nanking Seminary had previously published were then scarce, but it had four additional books ready for publication. Three of

28 Ibid.

29 Ibid.

these, *Evangelism in the Rural Church, Principles of Preaching,* and *A Chinese Rural Worker Looks at the Southern States of America,* had been written by Samuel Chu. The fourth, *Mass Education in the Christian Church*, was the work of Yu Moh-ren. The department had also published eight issues of *Rural Church*, a journal begun in Chengdu that it hoped would become a quarterly.[30]

The Shenhuachen Training Center, which had long been used to educate seminary students in rural work, had been the site of warfare for eight years "by the Japanese, the 'puppet soldiers,' and the New Fourth Communist Army." As a result physical destruction had been great, and the people of the area had suffered immeasurably. Lee reported that successive waves of soldiers had occupied the buildings, with the result that some suffered heavy damage and others were destroyed. All the fruit trees had been uprooted, and the only things in good condition were the rice fields and the fish ponds. The health center that had served thousands of people from fifty-two villages had been destroyed, leaving the people badly in need of health care. The Shenhuachen Presbyterian Church, whose pastor was Chu Chi-ih (Samuel Chu), was the center of work there. While it previously had one hundred twelve members, the membership had declined to seventy. Nonetheless, efforts were being made to restore the area. Relief clothing from the Nanjing Christian Relief Committee was distributed to Christians and non-Christians alike. Nanking Seminary wanted to restore the poultry project; all hens had been killed during the war. Though the seminary had received six Guernsey cows from UNRRA, it was keeping these to provide milk for children and sick people in the city.[31]

Lee detailed other aspects of Nanking Seminary's post-war programs. Thirty-nine students, twenty-one men and eighteen women, were enrolled in the short-term course. The correspondence course had resumed with 277 enrolled. Mrs. Sone was giving individual music lessons to thirty-two students, and they were offering courses in music theory and hymnology. The choir was made up of twenty students and was often invited to sing at churches, had been broadcast by the central radio station, had made a recording for broadcast on Christmas day at the request of the Belgian Embassy, had sung Handel's *Messiah* with a city-wide choir, and had sung at an Easter sunrise service together with the choir of the Nanjing Union Church and the American army.[32]

30 Ibid.
31 Ibid. Chu also held an appointment as professor of the rural church in NTS.
32 Ibid.

With respect to seminary publications, Lee reported that the Editorial Department had lost its director, who had returned to his home church. The department had four manuscripts awaiting publication and wanted to translate *Religious Liberty: An Inquiry* by M. Searle Bates into Chinese. Translation of the *Abingdon Commentary* was about 60 percent complete, and the first volume of Old Testament articles was ready for publication. Lee added that the Literature Production Program that had been initiated in Chengdu was to become part of the Editorial Department. During the past year, the seminary library had received 2,395 new books, including about eight hundred in English, and an interlibrary loan system with the University of Nanking and Ginling College was being discussed. Nanking's theology students took a course in library science and met with the librarians monthly to discuss problems.[33]

Regarding the physical plant, Lee advised the Board of Founders that buildings were being renovated; he also indicated that registration with the government was underway. The seminary hoped to obtain real deeds, not simply perpetual leases, to the land under terms of a new treaty between the United States and China. He also reported that, upon return to Nanjing, the seminary found that four pieces of its land had been taken and three built upon; it was now facing difficulties protecting its interest in this property. Increased enrollment had created a serious housing problem, even though the women students were being housed at the Bible Teachers' Training School under a two-year agreement. "Crowded class rooms, make-shift offices, and overflowing dormitories force us again to think of the need for enlarging and changing our plant. New buildings have now become not something just to add to efficiency and appearance, but a positive necessity."[34]

In the accompanying explanatory letter to Cartwright in New York, which was customarily sent with seminary minutes and reports, Smith indicated that Lee was exhausted but had attended some of their meetings. Smith indicated that the primary weakness of the Board of Managers meeting was occasioned by the absence of Chinese representatives of the major denominations participating in Nanking Seminary. For two years neither the Methodists nor the Church of Christ in China had been adequately represented, and that year Z. S. Zia of Moore Memorial Church in Shanghai was the only Chinese person representing the Methodists, while there were no Chinese from the Church of Christ in China. Smith explained that the problem was

33 Ibid.
34 Ibid.

related to the fact that both the Methodists and the Church of Christ in China wanted their representatives selected on a nationwide basis, with the result that some who had been chosen lived too far from Nanjing to attend the meeting. Therefore, it was his opinion that the churches needed to appoint people who lived close to Nanjing with the understanding that they represented the entire country. He added that, for the past two years, the Baptists did not seem to understand that they could send four representatives to the meeting, a misunderstanding Smith attributed to T. C. Bau's absence from China.[35]

Reflecting the hardship conditions in post-war China, Smith wrote that UNRRA food supplies had been given to the faculty and students by the American Advisory Committee the previous fall but that the seminary was required to pay storage and transportation on the goods. The seminary received 1,440 cases of various processed food supplies, soap, and other household goods. Because of spoilage, only about 1,100 cases were actually distributed, about thirty-three cases per person for the twenty-six members of the faculty and staff, including foreign teachers. The seminary charged each person CN $10,000 per case, which was considerably less than the actual cost for storage and transportation. The seminary allowed the faculty to pay for the food over several months, and it had already collected CN $50,000 per person. It proposed to take the remaining balance from those monies due to the Chinese faculty in order to wipe out the debt, but the foreign faculty would still be expected to complete payment for their goods. Smith added that the seminary was using some rehabilitation funds for health needs of the faculty members and their families.[36]

On the subject of publications, Smith noted that a work on Chinese religions had been initiated by Earl Cressy. He had been in west China during the war and there met Kuo Pen-tao, who was living in a Buddhist monastery. Cressy was greatly impressed with Kuo's knowledge of "Chinese ancient lore and saw in him a man suitable to carry out one of his own ambitions, a research project in Chinese religion." Cressy introduced Kuo to the faculty, and Kuo subsequently taught a Chinese philosophy and religion course for the B.D. degree program. For three years he was also engaged in a research program

35 C. Stanley Smith to Frank T. Cartwright, Nanjing, May 5, 1947, ALW. Bau, a pastor of a church in Hangzhou and a leader of Chinese Baptists, had encouraged the Baptist mission to cooperate with NTS and subsequently served on the seminary's Board of Managers. Later he was recommended for the presidency of the seminary but declined that position.

36 Ibid.

studying references to religion in the twenty-four dynastic histories, but ill health forced him to discontinue this work.[37]

Lee had requested a sabbatical leave as a result of the heart attack he suffered in early 1946. He proposed a study of the Chinese church, which would require travel about the country, and Smith noted that the seminary budget provided $1,000 for such travel. The managers wanted Smith, who was vice president, to assume leadership in Lee's absence. Nanking Seminary did not require a Chinese head, it was explained, because it had no connection with the Ministry of Education. Furthermore, the managers had decided not to appoint a Chinese person as temporary president because they believed that, if Lee were unable to resume his duties, the Chinese temporary president would need to be retained in that position to avoid losing face, and the managers' hands would be tied in the selection of a new permanent president. Furthermore, even if Lee were able to resume his post, any Chinese faculty member who served as acting president would expect to be appointed president upon Lee's retirement.[38] This argument proved convincing, and Smith became acting president, a position he continued to hold until he departed for the United States in 1950.[39]

Smith informed the Board of Founders that one-third of Nanking Seminary's students were women. After many years, talks between the seminary and the Bible Teachers' Training School had finally resulted in plans for union, which were being considered by their respective boards.[40]

When the Board of Founders convened for its annual meeting in New York June 4, 1947, the seminary was represented by T. C. Bau, chair of the Board of Managers, and Frank W. Price. T. C. Chao of the School of Religion of Yenching University was also present. The Board of Founders discussed those issues referred to it by the Board of Managers. It voted that when books are closed, any balance remaining should be "given to the Chinese faculty and staff members to make up in part for salary deficits suffered earlier in the fiscal year." It returned to the managers the matter of decreased grants to other theological seminaries in China. According to the Board of Founders' lawyers, they could not fund permanent items in the budgets of those institutions but could fund special projects of the sort carried on at Nanking Seminary. Supportive of the work on Chinese religion that had been

37 Ibid.

38 Ibid.

39 Cartwright, *River,* 81.

40 C. Stanley Smith to Frank T. Cartwright, Nanjing, May 5, 1947, ALW.

undertaken by Kuo in Chengdu, the Board of Founders asked the seminary administrators to look into ways of "setting forward a study of China's religions and religious heritage, making use of this material and of other material which may be now or later available." The board advised the seminary that it would like to help with reconstruction of the library and would consult with librarians to select the best books available. Responding to a suggestion of H. P. Van Dusen, who had recently returned from a trip to China, the Board of Founders also recommended that Luther A. Weigle and Ralph E. Diffendorfer, when they retired from their current work, make a six-month trip to China to assess conditions at Nanking Seminary and its relation to theological education in China.[41]

A special meeting of the executive committee of the managers was called in late October 1947 to consider a variety of pressing issues. Weigle and Diffendorfer, who were then in China, attended this meeting as guests of the Board of Managers. Acting president Smith was instructed to write to the other Chinese theological schools to determine how they were using the funds granted by Nanking Seminary. T. C. Bau and James H. McCallum were asked to study the relationship of the managers and seminary administration with the Board of Founders.[42]

The managers recognized that the Board of Founders had already spent $56,000 rehabilitating seminary buildings and grounds and asked each of the participating missions to make a grant of at least $10,000 to offset some of these costs.[43]

With regard to personnel matters, the managers noted that Price had been assigned to the National Christian Council in China for two years, was working on rural church issues, and therefore had tendered his resignation from the seminary faculty. The managers voted not to accept his resignation, to allow him to continue living in a seminary house, and to ask Mrs. Price to work as a secretary in the administrative office while her husband was not teaching. They hoped he would return to the seminary in the future.[44]

The managers were also negotiating with Ken Yuen-hsieh, dean of students at the University of Shanghai, in the hope that he would accept the position of business manager for the seminary. Dean Li Tien-lu had been appointed as a representative to the General Conference

41 Minutes, Annual Meeting, BF, NTS, June 4, 1947, FTEA.
42 Minutes, Executive Committee, BM, NTS, October 23, 1947, ALW.
43 Ibid.
44 Ibid.

of the Methodist Church scheduled to be held in Boston in May 1948, and he had asked for a four-month leave in order to attend this meeting and to rest from his wartime work. He wished to visit some seminaries in the United States, and the Board of Founders was asked to grant him $600 toward the expenses of such visits. Li was also granted a sabbatical leave for the year 1948-49.[45]

In another action, the managers requested $3,500 to rebuild the seminary's walls, which had been erected inside its property line as a result of a mistake by the city government that had confiscated the land. They also requested $6,500 for work on the chapel and the library, both of which were inadequate for the student body; and they asked for $75,000 from the Board of Founders to build a new women's dormitory. They planned to ask the Bible Teachers' Training School to reconsider its refusal to lease their women's dormitory to Nanking Seminary for another year; but, if that effort failed, they planned to ask the Methodist board if they could use some Methodist mission property for housing. However, if that effort also failed, the managers would have to construct a temporary dormitory building.[46]

With regard to faculty compensation issues, inflation remained a critical and destabilizing problem. The managers explained that current salaries were to be doubled in September and in the next three months increased under the Chinese government's cost of living index. The present salary bonuses were to be discontinued. Rice allowances were still being given based on family size. The salary committee was to review all salaries every three months and make recommendations to the executive committee of the managers.[47]

Smith in his accompanying explanatory letter noted that former president Lee was able to attend part of the meeting of the managers. He reported that Nanking Seminary had twenty-six students in the refresher course, twenty-one in the B.D. course, and fifty-four in the B.Th. course. Of the sixty-two new students, thirty-four were women, and eight of these were enrolled in the refresher course.[48]

With regard to personnel matters, Smith reaffirmed that the seminary did not want Price to resign. The managers hoped Ken would agree to act as business manager until he left for the United States in the following year to study under a scholarship from the Presbyterian

45 Ibid.

46 Ibid.

47 Ibid.

48 C. Stanley Smith to Frank T. Cartwright, Nanjing, October 28, 1947, ALW.

Board of Foreign Missions. Smith supported Li's request for short-term leave. However, Smith had persuaded Li to postpone his sabbatical leave request until 1948-49 because Andrew Cheng also wanted a sabbatical leave if he obtained funding from Union Theological Seminary in New York for the forthcoming year, since he had failed to receive a grant the previous year. The seminary faculty also wanted to consider a policy regarding sabbatical leaves for those who already held advanced degrees from abroad. Smith thought it would be wiser for those faculty members to remain in China and work on a project of concern to the Chinese church rather than go abroad again.[49]

Smith also wrote at length about the kindergarten and feeding station project conducted by Kuan and Leete, both of whom had expertise in this area. The project had been successful, and they wanted to continue it for another year. The project did not depend on the seminary for financial support but was located on seminary property, and students in the Religious Education Department visited the project while enrolled in a course in child welfare.[50]

A week later Smith wrote Cartwright to elaborate upon the issue of the walls and squatters on seminary land. He wrote that the seminary needed to extend the walls because, during the fall, there had been trouble with squatters moving in from the more congested parts of the city and occupying "tempting strips of land outside of our walls" along Hanzhong (formerly Hanchung) Road. In August the police had ordered the people who had erected small shops along a nearby street to move west, and they had moved onto the seminary property. Smith observed:

> One day they came crowding into the land outside our seminary walls with carpenters and building material prepared to put up, not only temporary mat sheds, but more substantial wooden buildings. I warned them that they would not be allowed to do this as seven feet of land on both sides of the road belonged to the Seminary and that they would be building on American Property. They just laughed at me and at the policemen who went around with me later to say the same thing. As the situation was serious we were in danger of having our whole frontage occupied with shops and squatter dwellings, I wrote a letter in English to the mayor telling him of the situation and seeking his help. We also sent a letter in Chinese to the City Council. The result was

49 Ibid.
50 Ibid.

> that the next night the police came and rounded up about thirty squatters and took them to the police station for interrogation. Later they sent a truck with workmen to tear down the buildings if the people did not tear them down themselves. When I came to school the next morning, I found to my delight that all the houses and shacks had been torn down but one. There were some articles in the paper from some of these squatters who claimed to be refugees from Communist territory complaining against their treatment by the police at the instigation of foreigners, but the next day the Public Works Committee answered the protest in a very fair and forthright statement, taking upon themselves the full responsibility for forcing the removal of these buildings since they were violating city ordinances. It was the most successful protest and dealing with the City Government which I have ever had in all my years in China.[51]

In spite of this apparent success, some of the squatters returned, and Smith concluded that the only solution was to move the walls out to the property line. On the other side of Hanzhong Road, squatters had camped outside the wall of Lee's house during the Japanese occupation, and the seminary had sought without success to get them removed. By the time of Smith's letter, they had built second stories on their buildings. Smith hoped for a quick solution because he knew it would be more difficult to move the squatters during the winter.[52]

Regarding other personnel and physical plant problems, Smith asked the Board of Founders to grant Hu, who had a scholarship for study at Union Theological Seminary in New York, $150 for winter clothes, adding that he knew Hu had left China with only summer clothes, no raincoat, and no overcoat, illustrating the desperate need of the faculty for clothing. Smith also reported that they were making changes to the chapel and library, since they recognized that prohibitive costs would make it impossible for them to erect a much needed larger building at that time. Because the Bible Teachers' Training School believed it needed all of its space for its own students, Nanking Seminary had leased a Methodist compound that could

[51] C. Stanley Smith to Frank T. Cartwright, Nanjing, November 5, 1947, ALW. Ironically, this episode, which appeared to Smith to have been resolved satisfactorily in 1947, became an example of American missionary imperialism in the propaganda that followed Liberation. Frank T. Cartwright to BF, October 23, 1951, ALW.

[52] Ibid.

provide housing for twenty to twenty-five women. This space would make unnecessary the $75,000 expenditure for a new building that the managers earlier feared might be required.[53]

A special meeting of the executive committee of the managers was convened in March 1948. Writing to Cartwright about this meeting, James H. McCallum, a Disciples missionary who was then serving as the English secretary for the seminary, commented that the meeting was necessitated because of the issue of salaries, but apparently the arrangement for housing women students had also become critical. The seminary discovered that it was receiving a better exchange on gold than had been the case previously when it worked through the Associated Mission Treasurer and that, as a result, it was paying as well or better than other institutions in Nanjing. Therefore, the managers decided not to increase salaries at that time.[54] The Board of Managers approved the construction of a new women's dormitory, even though it knew the Board of Founders did not favor this action. The lease on the Bible Teachers' Training School would expire in the summer, and the managers were expecting an equal or larger number of women students in the fall. News of this issue was widely known among the churches in China, and as a result, "missions and churches are writing in asking us whether we will be able to receive women students this next school year....Unless we are willing to close down this important department of our work we shall have to have some place to house these students." He observed that the increased exchange rate made it easier to build, so the managers decided to do so despite the unsettled conditions in China, adding there was more building going on in Nanjing at that time than in the whole history of Nanking Seminary. The committee recalled that the seminary "was first built in a time of great political uncertainty and approaching revolution."[55]

McCallum expressed the hope that a recent letter penned by Hubert Sone and the action of the managers would convince the Board of Founders to approve the building. The dormitory capacity was at its limit, and he expected that they would have to take in some of the other theological seminaries that were evacuating north China. Cheeloo University had left its campus that day, but McCallum added that he was uncertain whether the departure involved the entire university or only the medical school. He assumed the university had left because

53 Ibid.

54 James H. McCallum to Frank T. Cartwright, Nanjing, March 16, 1948, ALW.

55 Ibid.

of the Communist victory over the Nationalist forces east of Jinan and the sudden flight of the governor's wife from Shandong. He said the university had only two or three faculty members in theology but added that, if the entire north were evacuated, which would happen if Shenyang (Mukden) fell, Nanking Seminary would have a problem.[56]

McCallum was also concerned about the seminary staff because at that time neither the American Baptists nor the Southern Presbyterians had representatives on the faculty. Furthermore, when C. H. Plopper retired the Disciples mission would be without a representative. While Dean Li had been ill, McCallum reported that he continued to recover and would be in the United States to attend the Methodist General Conference.[57]

McCallum forwarded the Minutes of the Executive Committee of the Managers meeting that had been held March 9, 1948. The seminary had enrolled 102 students for the fall term, including 25 pastors and evangelists, and 99 were enrolled for the spring. One-third of the students were women. A summer conference for the directors of the Forward Movement was being planned in cooperation with the Bible Teachers' Training School. The committee also discussed an audiovisual education program that had been suggested by a delegation on radio-visual education from the Missionary Conference of North America.[58]

Samuel Chu, vice head of the Rural Church Department, reported at this meeting. He advised that it was training students and lay church workers and had held a farmers' institute for forty young farmers. The department had published 1,000 copies of the *Rural Church Quarterly*, but since the journal now had 816 subscribers, the department planned to publish 1,200 copies of future issues. Yu Mo-ren had made trips to Wuxi (Wusih), Suzhou (Soochow), and Shanghai to study rural work, and Chu had surveyed thirty rural churches. The department was planning visits to Taiwan and other places known for effective rural work. In addition to engaging in agricultural extension, research, and social work, it was promoting cooperatives, health programs, and measures for prevention of animal disease, and was developing a cannery project.[59]

Smith prepared the 1948 faculty report. He noted that U.S. ambassador and former Nanking Seminary faculty member J. Leighton

56 Ibid.

57 Ibid.

58 Minutes, Executive Committee, BM, NTS, March 9, 1948, ALW.

59 Report, NTS, Rural Church Department, 1947-48; C. Stanley Smith, NTS Faculty Report, 1947-48, both ALW.

Stuart had given the commencement address in Chinese. Regarding personnel matters, he reported that Price had declined the offer to take a leave of absence while working for the National Christian Council and to live on the campus, so that his wife could provide administrative help to the seminary. Therefore, Price's resignation had been accepted. Smith added that the Rural Church Department had suffered since Price's departure. He also commented that, in spite of the unrest in China, they had experienced no interruptions in school work and had ended the year on schedule. He reported an increase in chapel attendance and, while observing that the students in the refresher course were older, sometimes much older, than the other students, he affirmed that there had been great communication among all the students.[60]

On what had clearly been a controversial matter, Smith revealed in this report that he believed coeducation in theological education was valuable. He observed that for many years Nanking Seminary had been open to women students on the same basis as men:

> We have had plenty of opportunity to observe the results of their freedom of relations between men and women students. There have been a few criticizable [sic] incidents but very few, and the normal wholesome relationship in classroom, library, worship, and recreation has been beneficial to the whole life of the institution. This mutual contact in the life of the school will make for better cooperation when these men and women go out into the life of the Church. We are glad that it is going to be possible for us to build a new dormitory for our increasingly large number of women students who now make up practically one-third of our student body. Whether it will be wise to increase this proportion or not is worthy of consideration but there does not seem to be any good argument for its decrease. With our student body now filling all our available dormitory space we shall have the opportunity of selecting from future applicants those who are better prepared and who give more promise of effective work after their graduation.[61]

This subject had produced considerable discussion, and some wanted to limit the number of women in the various programs. Others wanted to reduce the enrollment in the refresher course, which accepted some students without senior middle school education who could not meet

[60] C. Stanley Smith, NTS Faculty Report, 1947-48, ALW.
[61] Ibid.

the standards for the regular programs. Regarding these issues, Smith explained why a decision had been reached not to impose arbitrary limits on these programs:

> while the difficulties and dangers attendant on the unlimited admission of women students, and the Refresher Course students were recognized,...it was felt that the large number of young women students coming to us for their training for service in the churches should not be discouraged, provided they fulfilled the entrance requirements of the Seminary; and that the recognized service which the Seminary was rendering through its Refresher Course to pastors and both men and women evangelists who had seen active service in the church for several years, especially during the war period, should not be curtailed....The problem of women students was not only one as to the wisdom of accepting a larger proportion than one-third of our total student body, but was also tied up with our relationship with the BTTS.[62]

Smith added that it appeared that plans for greater cooperation with the Bible Teachers' Training School appeared to lack support at the women's school and that this factor led to the decision to build the new dormitory. He also observed that the large number of students in the refresher course reduced the dormitory living space for men preparing for the ministry in the regular programs.[63]

Smith reported that the audiovisual department planned to produce records, filmstrips, and broadcast materials. The library had recovered 2,000 books that the Japanese had moved to Wuhu during the war, and therefore the seminary holdings stood at 15,724 volumes, 7,704 in Chinese and 8,020 in English. It received 160 magazines, 140 of them in Chinese, published by various church bodies throughout China. In October it had resumed the circulating library using a bicycle messenger; and, in seven months, nearly one hundred people had borrowed more than five hundred books through the service. The Literature Production Program had been reorganized, with all work being done by Nanking Seminary, since the National Christian Council had withdrawn its support. The faculty who were working in the project had held consultations with Roman Catholic scholars and had agreed to push for completion of five volumes: *The Apostolic Fathers*, Augustine's *Confessions* and *City of God* (the latter in two volumes), and Eusebius's

62 Ibid.
63 Ibid.

Ecclesiastical History. Most of the translation work was complete, but additional editing was required.[64]

The seminary's Editorial Department had published Hsieh Shou-ling's translation of Williston Walker's *The History of the Christian Church*, though Smith added that Hsieh had been recalled to the Lutheran seminary where he had taught before the war. Other works published included Harry Emerson Fosdick's *A Guide to the Understanding of the Bible*, translated by Tang Chung-moh; Walter Rauschenbusch's *Christianity and the Social Crisis*, translated by Yeh Chih-fang; M. Searle Bates's *Religious Liberty*; the first volume of the *Abingdon Commentary*; and Paul Chen's *Church Library and Control*. The seminary had also reprinted a number of other works. It had resumed publishing the *Nanking Seminary Review* with Christmas and Easter issues. The periodical was begun in February 1914 but had been suspended for five years during the war. One thousand copies of each issue were being printed, but Smith noted that subscriptions barely covered the cost of postage.[65]

Smith advised the Board of Founders regarding the physical plant that extensive repair work on pipes was required after the winter's freezing weather. All the teachers' residences had been screened, and furniture had been purchased to accommodate the increase in student numbers. The library and chapel were being enlarged. The new women's dormitory would provide housing for eighty-eight students and apartments for three women teachers. The architects of the Presbyterian and Methodist churches were assisting the seminary in planning for the future development of the campus. Mrs. Lee, Mrs. Sone, and Mrs. Plopper had been serving as a special committee to improve the appearance of the grounds and had arranged for the planting of shrubs, trees, and plants, and the erection of a small pavilion.[66]

On the crucial matter of the deeds to the Nanjing property, Smith reported that early in 1937 they had made photostatic copies of their deeds and taken them to the land office for registration. When Nanjing was captured by the Japanese, the deeds were still in the land office, but photostatic copies of the deeds and the receipts given for them at the land office had been taken to the United States and given to the treasurer of the Board of Founders. In 1946 these documents were returned to China, and the process of re-registration begun in order to replace the "perpetual leases" that had constituted their right of ownership. Smith wrote:

64 Ibid.
65 Ibid.
66 Ibid.

> The matter of registration of deeds is still underway, and our deeds are still in the land office. We are expecting to receive new deeds for all our property in place of the perpetual leases and other papers we have had heretofore. This is in accordance with the treaty between China and the United States....We have at last come to the place where the Land Office agrees to give us such deeds, in case we can show proof that the State of New York, under which the Seminary legally holds land, allows Chinese nationals to hold land. (This is a treaty stipulation)."[67]

Smith reported that city work was centered at Wesley Church under the direction of Hu Ren-an, who had joined the staff six years earlier and was currently a student at Union Theological Seminary in New York. The Child Welfare Station at the Wesley Church was operated jointly by Nanking Theological Seminary and the Wesley Church Committee, and Hubert Sone was chair of the program. This was the only child welfare station in the city, and so it had attracted the attention of the American Advisory Committee, which gave it liberal support. It had also received a grant from the Nanking International Women's Club for special projects.[68]

All of the Nanking Seminary students were working with local Christians in the areas of Sunday schools, women's and social services, youth work, evangelism, music, and rural church work. A special observation group composed of students from the pastors' refresher course tried to maintain contact with every church in Nanjing, and the students had been working with eleven churches and two Christian institutions. Five students had completed internships during the previous summer as required by the B.Th. program.[69]

Smith wrote that though they were working in many different areas,

> looking over China, and indeed the world, today it is evident that the greatest need is for Christian leadership; not only for devoted and practically minded pastors and evangelists, both men and women, but for those who, through study, hard thinking, and meditation under the guidance of the Spirit upon the deeper meanings of the Christian faith and their application to the life

67 Ibid. The U.S. and China revised their treaties eliminating the extraterritoriality provisions in 1943, thereby making it necessary for all foreign missions in China to adjust the legal provisions of their property holdings.

68 Ibid.

69 Ibid.

> of today, may go forth to lead the earnest and often bewildered members of the Christian churches to a deeper knowledge of, and devotion to, the will of God as revealed by Jesus Christ.[70]

Smith warned that "the growing industrial life of the nation brings with it the menace of a non-Christian industrialism and the growth of slums and the exploitation of women and children for profit. The city churches must face these conditions." He believed they needed reinforcement in order to meet this challenge.[71]

When the managers gathered for their annual meeting in May 1948, representatives were present from the Methodists, Northern and Southern Presbyterians, the China Baptist Council, the Disciples Church, the East China Synod of the CCC, and the Alumni Association. With President Lee on leave and Smith serving as acting president of the seminary, Smith chaired the meeting.[72]

The managers recommended reinstatement of a pension plan that had been instituted in 1939, and they offered suggestions for handling the contributions for the wartime and immediate postwar years. They also urged that, for the duration of the current inflationary period, faculty contributions should be converted into U.S. dollars.[73]

In other personnel action, the managers granted Chen Tsing-hsien, the librarian, a sabbatical leave for 1948-49. Sie Ping-teh was sent to the Yale School of Graduate Studies for advanced study in the history of Christian thought to better prepare him to work with the Literature Production Program upon his return. The Board of Founders was asked to provide scholarship and travel funds for both. Approval of a furlough was granted for William Leete. The managers approved Mrs. Andrew Cheng's accompanying her husband to the United States in 1948-49 and payment of his prewar basic salary in U.S. currency while he and his wife were there, but they noted that this arrangement would apply only to faculty members whose spouses were with them on sabbatical leave in the United States. However, the managers also voted that those on seminary scholarships in the States should receive 60 percent of their salaries in China, not 40 percent as previously.[74]

The managers asked for a Board of Founders grant of $800 to assist the China Sunday School Union in restoring the lithographic plates

70 Ibid.
71 Ibid.
72 Minutes, Annual Meeting, BM, NTS, May 4-5, 1948, ALW.
73 Ibid.
74 Ibid.

of religious pictures for which they had received a grant in 1943. The experimental nursery school and kindergarten was discussed by Kuan, and the managers approved a recommendation from the Governing Faculty that this project be continued on its present experimental basis for another year and that $700 be placed in the 1948-49 budget for its operation. The managers acknowledged that the number of female students at Nanking Seminary continued to increase but voted to table a recommendation of the administrative-finance committee that the number of women students be limited to no more than one-third of the total enrollment.[75] The managers also recommended the granting of degrees and diplomas at the spring 1948 commencement: four M.R.E. degrees (one to a woman); three M.R.E. diplomas; two B.D. degrees; two B.Th. degrees (both to women); four Tao Hsieh Shih degrees (one to a woman); and one Tao Hsieh Shih diploma. Additionally, twenty-one Pastor's Refresher Course certificates were recommended (five to women).[76]

Z. T. Kaung was appointed representative of the managers to the Board of Directors of the North China Rural Service Union. In the area of curriculum and long-term personnel planning, the managers approved the Governing Faculty's recommendations that the immediate faculty needs were for a missionary in the field of church history, either a Chinese or a missionary to teach Old Testament, a missionary to teach religious education, a missionary or Chinese in audiovisual education, a Chinese or a missionary in homiletics and voice culture, a missionary in rural church, a Chinese for the correspondence department, a Chinese to serve as the editorial committee secretary, a Chinese to serve as business manager and dean of women, and a missionary as the English secretary. Within the next five years, they anticipated needing a missionary in systematic theology (whom they assumed would be Samuel H. Moffett, then engaged in language study in Beijing), a Chinese in pastoral theology, a Chinese or a missionary in Christian ethics, a Chinese or a missionary in philosophy of religion, a Chinese in psychology of religion (whom they assumed would be Chen Tse-ming), and a missionary for the Music Department. Within ten years they anticipated needing faculty in Old and New Testament and English language. The Presbyterian China Council had recommended "cooperation and perhaps organic union of NTS with BTTS" [Bible Teachers' Training School], and the Board of Managers declared that

75 Ibid.
76 Ibid.

this recommendation "represents the conviction of the majority of the cooperating bodies in the BM of the NTS."[77]

The managers reported to the Board of Founders that they had authorized building a wall around part of the seminary property and a two-story house at Shenhuachen to be used as a rural training center and replacing two one-story houses that were destroyed during the war. They indicated that they were trying to buy a water shop and its property adjoining their land and that, if that were not possible, then to trade some of their land for it.[78]

In his covering letter accompanying the report of the managers, Smith stated that because of the large number of missionaries present and because they came from so many different dialect areas, the meeting was conducted in English with interpreters. The issue of sabbatical leaves had again been raised for discussion. Some of the managers believed that those faculty members holding advanced degrees from the United States should spend their leaves in China learning more about the Chinese church. Lee had proposed such a plan for himself, and it was very favorably received by the managers, but Lee was prevented from carrying out the travel requisite for his project by virtue of ill health. Others who had been through the war years in China felt the need for a complete change of place and opposed entire exclusion of overseas leaves for such people.[79]

Among financial issues, salaries continued to be a problem because of exchange rates, though recently the rates had been quite favorable and had covered the increase in cost of living. The managers had agreed to continue the nursery school project for another year, since it was helpful to the women students of the seminary and had made a good impression on the faculty and visiting Americans, even though some questioned whether it should be operated by the seminary.[80]

Budgetary matters remained critical and were aggravated, of course, by uncertainties created by hyperinflation as the Nationalist government gradually collapsed. Therefore, a week after forwarding the annual report of the managers, Smith wrote the Board of Founders again, this time specifically about the fiscal situation. During the previous year, the managers had allowed for inflation in their budget, but now the Chinese government was allowing them to exchange money under the special arrangements extended to the American

77 Ibid.
78 Ibid.
79 C. Stanley Smith to Frank T. Cartwright, Nanjing, May 8, 1948, ALW.
80 Ibid.

army, American Embassy, and the United Nations. This meant that the seminary would receive 80 percent of the black market rate on drafts against the Board of Founders' New York treasurer. As a result, the managers had some surplus in the budget. There would be increases in expenditures for insurance, which they once again were paying on seminary property, and for taxes which the Chinese government demanded and which, through the intercession of the American Embassy, Nanking Seminary had not yet paid on the grounds that it was a school. However, Smith believed it inevitable that they would soon be required to pay the disputed taxes. They had also budgeted $200 for prizes for students, which Smith justified with the observation that similar awards were commonly made by U.S. seminaries.[81]

Just prior to the annual meeting of the Board of Founders in New York in June 1948, the seminary learned that two houses in the block where it owned three other houses were on the market. They were Western-style houses, and the owner, who lived in Shanghai, wanted to sell them to the seminary. It in turn sought permission from the Board of Founders to purchase them for not more than $35,000, since they were needed as housing for members of the Chinese faculty. Smith wrote that if the board was concerned about purchasing property in Nanjing at that moment, it should know that most mission organizations were purchasing property there and that more building was going on than in anyone's memory.

When the Board of Founders met in New York on June 9, Dean Li Tien-lu and Professor Hu Ren-an of the faculty were present. Li gave an informal presentation, and the principal of the Swope-Wendel Fund was reported to have risen to $2,333,909.39. A budget of $66,613 for the forthcoming year at the seminary was approved, with $59,064 to come from the Board of Founders. Approval for the property purchase was also granted, and a month later Sone reported that they needed a letter from the Board of Founders to meet new legal requirements and hasten the process of buying the houses, which they had agreed to purchase for about one-third less than the $35,000 that had originally been asked. The board also learned with regret of the retirement of Professor Plopper and recorded "their sense of obligation to Dr. Plopper for his long, faithful service as a member of the faculty and as Treasurer of the Seminary."[82]

81 C. Stanley Smith to Frank W. Cartwright, Nanjing, May 14, 1948, ALW.

82 C. Stanley Smith to Frank T. Cartwright, Nanjing, June 6, 1948; Hubert Sone to Frank T. Cartwright, Nanjing, July 4, 1948, both ALW; Minutes, Annual Meeting, BF, NTS, June 9, 1948, FTEA.

Sone also reported to the Board of Founders in July 1948 that many faculty members were traveling to conferences, but that he had not left Nanjing because he was involved in two relief projects, one constructing 250 houses for fire victims whose homes were destroyed in the early spring and another feeding destitute people. He wrote that at one location they had been feeding fifteen thousand refugees from famine, flood, and war, and at another they fed thirty thousand of Nanjing's destitute people. He added that the financial situation was most confused. A U.S. dollar was officially worth CN $480,000, but sellers could usually get at least CN $2,000,000. The American army and consulates received the black market rate, which had also been approved for the seminary. At that time the official quote for one ounce of gold was CN $18,960,000, but the black market rate was about CN $210,000,000 per ounce. Soft, very poor coal cost CN $3,000,000 for one hundred pounds, and charcoal was sold at CN $8,000,000 per one hundred pounds.[83]

China's political situation was changing rapidly in late 1948, and the increasing success of Communist forces against the Nationalists posed new challenges for the seminary. Smith wrote the Board of Founders in early December that he had been in Shanghai for a meeting of the National Christian Council when Shenyang and Changchun fell "and the Nationalist cause seemed to be pretty well defeated in Manchuria."[84] When he returned to Nanjing, Smith learned that the seminary students from South China, from Fujian Province to Hainan Island of Guangdong Province, wanted to return home. Then some left for Fuzhou, the capital of Fujian Province, asking permission to enroll in the seminary there. By December 1, fifty-five students had left Nanjing, and the seventy-five who remained asked for early examinations so that they could leave before the Communist forces occupied the city. The faculty held a meeting to discuss the situation. Some thought they should end the term and move immediately, but others believed that a precipitous move would be too expensive and that they should remain in Nanjing. They decided to hold examinations December 12 and to close the school on the fifteenth. Later the closure was moved up to

83 Hubert Sone to Frank T. Cartwright, Nanjing, July 4, 1948, ALW.

84 The term Manchuria, applied to the three northeastern provinces of China, was commonly used until mid-twentieth century and is still commonly used in the West. However, the Chinese prefer the term Northeast (Dongbei in pinyin) and consistently use it in contemporary references to the provinces of Heilongjiang, Jilin, and Liaoning. In 1948, Guangdong Province included Hainan Island; today Hainan is a separate province.

December 11, but with hope that the seminary would be able to reopen in the spring.[85]

Smith wrote that "from all indications...nothing but a miracle can stop the Communists from occupying Nanking in a very short time." A friend at the American Embassy had told him it would probably not happen before the end of the year, but Smith thought that the occupation would occur earlier. He did not know what would happen, since there was no precedent, but he gathered that there were no theological seminaries operating in Communist areas and "most people think that we will be among the first of the Christian schools to be closed down." He wrote that his wife was in Shanghai but that he thought he would not flee, as he would likely be caught before he could get away. He did not fear personal mistreatment by the Communists, but he feared there would be looting between the time the Nationalists withdrew and the Communists arrived. Smith thought that the Christian churches should take a stand against communism, but he was unclear as to how this could be done. Pondering the situation, he thought it might be time for a reevaluation and reorientation of the mission movement in China, because the church had become the church of the upper classes. He noted that schools had developed that way because they were required to be self-supporting and that second-and third-generation Christians tended to forget the class their grandparents came from. He added that the situation was chaotic as there was practically no government in place to enforce laws and regulations. He had been unable to get money and therefore had sold some drafts on the Board of Founders in New York. The streets were no longer lighted at night, and they had no electricity half the time. Yet he noted that the city seemed generally under control. There had been some rioting at rice shops recently, but it had been contained.[86]

When the executive committee of the Board of Managers met on December 6, it decided to carry on in Nanjing for as long as possible. If it seemed unwise to reopen in the spring, then a small committee of the managers would meet with the faculty and decide what to do. Smith reported that the Associated Mission Treasurers were considering establishing a branch in Hong Kong. Lee, who had verbally resigned the presidency earlier, was asked to put his resignation into writing.

[85] Letter fragment, C. Stanley Smith to Frank T. Cartwright [Nanjing], December 3, 1948, ALW.

[86] Ibid. For an excellent account of the Communist movement into Nanjing see Knight Biggerstaff, *Nanking Letters, 1949* (Ithaca: China-Japan Program, Cornell Univ., 2001).

Only about twenty students remained in Nanjing, and they planned to stay during the turnover. Ginling College and the University of Nanking would attempt to continue their operations. Smith had asked the Friends' Service Union to take over part of the seminary plant for medical relief and social services. He wrote, "There has been much in the last couple of weeks to lead us to believe that the Communists have greatly altered their attitude towards religious work and activities. Such optimism may be unwarranted and we may find the situation much more serious than we now anticipate, once the city falls, but we are more hopeful than we were a month ago." Yet he also reported that a split was developing between those on the seminary faculty who wanted to flee and those who did not. Those who had been in Chengdu during the Japanese occupation were the ones who wanted to flee, while those who had remained in Shanghai under the Japanese occupation were more confident that they could work under Communist rule.[87]

The Communist armies did not appear in Nanjing until April 23, 1949. Nanking Theological Seminary was able to reopen in the spring, and the executive committee of the Board of Managers met in late February 1949. The committee reported that fifty-three students had been enrolled during the fall term and that they had followed a modified curriculum. All members of the faculty had been present for the beginning of the new term except Tseo Ping-I, who had become president of West China Union Theological College; Christopher Tang, who was in Hunan; and Newton Chiang, who was in Hangzhou (Hangchow) pending a decision on a leave of absence he had requested so that he could work with the National Christian Council. Both Chiang and Tang were being urged to return to Nanjing because of the shortage of faculty.[88]

T. C. Bau reported for a search committee that the committee had begun seeking nominations for a president to replace Lee. In spite of the difficult and uncertain circumstances in Nanjing and all of China at the time, the committee had established the highest possible qualifications for applicants including theological training, ordination, and pastoral experience, Chinese nationality, administrative experience and ability, good health, acquaintance with Chinese culture, a cooperative spirit, spiritual depth and evangelistic zeal, known widely in China and abroad, preferably between forty and fifty years of age, and preferably from one

87 C. Stanley Smith to Frank T. Cartwright, Nanjing, December 11, 1948, ALW.

88 Minutes, Executive Committee, BM, NTS, February 25, 1949, ALW.

of the denominations cooperating in the operation of the seminary.[89] In the United States, Cartwright responded with a letter to the Board of Founders and to faculty members in the States in which he observed that this list of qualifications was the source of "a little amusement." However, he assumed that people would understand that "the seminary [is] looking for the best possible man, and while we realize he cannot embody all of these qualifications we would like to have him embody as many as is humanly possible." He added that a letter in English and Chinese giving the qualifications and asking for nominations had been sent to 150 people.[90]

Cartwright circulated to Board of Founders members a letter in which Smith detailed some of the ways in which Nanking Seminary was anticipating the directives of the new Communist government even before Nanjing's conquest. He reported that the Rural Church Department had given each worker and each student a plot of land at the seminary to be farmed under the supervision of Li Chen-kang, director of the Rural Church program. Li was also thinking of offering a course on beekeeping, while Samuel Chu was offering a course on poultry raising. Students were also studying first aid and elementary medical health in anticipation that they might earn their living in part with this knowledge, if they were assigned to rural areas where there were no medical facilities. The superintendent of the government hospital, himself a Christian, was assisting with this endeavor and had offered to teach the course. Smith wrote:

> You will see from the above that [the seminary] is trying to move with the times and to anticipate the times. Gardens, chicken pens, bee hives, and medical clinics, may look a little strange on the campus of a theological seminary but they are part of our program to enable us not only to meet the challenge of Communism, but to perform some services to underprivileged members of society which should be a part of our Christian work.[91]

Smith also commented on some "rather confidential" reports from T. C. Chao in Beijing regarding the Communists, which he thought were helpful "with the exception of a too uncritical acceptance of the new Regime. I doubt whether Chao has a very realistic understanding

89 Ibid.

90 Frank T. Cartwright to BF and NTS Faculty in U.S., New York, April 20, 1949, ALW.

91 Ibid.

of what is involved in Russian Communism." Others who were "living at present behind the 'bamboo curtain'" had also written positive reports. He continued:

> Personally, I feel that while there has been a tactical change in some of the methods used that it is too early as yet to say whether there has been any fundamental change or not in the attitude towards the Christian religion and Christian work. I think we have reason to be more hopeful than we were last fall but we do not want to let our hopes carry us further than the realities of the situation will allow.[92]

Despite the impending political change and its potential implications for religion in general and Christianity and Nanking Seminary in particular, the faculty had decided to continue its program and therefore was compelled to continue dealing with ordinary administrative problems. Three days prior to the arrival of Communist forces in Nanjing, Smith, who had been serving as treasurer for about a year, submitted a treasurer's report to the Board of Founders. He addressed difficulties that arose as a result of the physical separation of the board in New York from the seminary that it was funding in China. He observed that there was an item in the budget for English books that had customarily been purchased in the United States, but no one in China knew how much was expended or what books were purchased. Smith knew that the seminary had paid for five hundred copies of Price's *The Rural Church in China*, which were to be distributed free in Nanjing, but he did not know whether they had been charged to the English books account. He explained that the seminary received invoices along with books but never knew exactly what had been ordered or whether it had received everything ordered. Furthermore, book purchases were not a separate line in the budget. Therefore Smith suggested that the book purchases be handled as a direct budget transfer in New York. The seminary had also requested that $1,000 per annum be placed into a pension fund, but he did not know whether this had been done in 1947-48. He estimated the budget for the 1949-50 year at $65,020 but indicated that the new People's Banknotes had not been issued nor an exchange rate established.[93]

In his new position as president of West China Union Theological College in Chengdu (WCUTC), Tseo Ping-I wrote to Cartwright asking

92 Ibid.

93 C. Stanley Smith, Treasurer's Report, April 20, 1949, ALW.

for funds to support two projects for students so that they might respond to the Communists who "strongly urge[d] that the educated men with others should be making some practical contribution to the livelihood of the members of the community in which they work. We feel that this will help our graduates to associate more closely with the membership of their churches and to feel that with them they live a common life." Apparently failing to appreciate the implications of the Communist revolution for women's work, the students were teaching agriculture and carpentry to the men and sewing and weaving to the women. Tseo requested $1,000 gold from seminary funds and committed WCUTC to contribute an additional $1,500 gold. He also informed the Board of Founders that the seminary managers had been scheduled to meet in Nanjing on April 27. However, since the Communists gained control of the city April 23, that had proven impossible. Price was in Shanghai, and Bau was in Hangzhou, and they were unable to gather a quorum in Nanjing.[94]

The Board of Founders held its annual meeting in New York June 2, 1949. Dr. Andrew Cheng and his wife, together with Professors Sie Ping-teh and Hu Ren-an of the seminary faculty, were then in the United States and attended this meeting. The Board of Founders acknowledged that communications with the seminary in Nanjing had broken down and that they had received no letters or cables from Nanjing since the Communist takeover and did not know if the meeting of the managers had taken place. Apparently some individual members of the board had received messages giving them some idea of the situation in Nanjing, but details were not included in the minutes of the meeting. Despite the uncertainty, the board voted $15,000 for apartments and a residence, $3,000 for WCUTC to fulfill obligations which had been assumed during the war, and a scholarship for Andrew C. Y. Cheng. It also approved a $66,000 budget for the forthcoming academic year, granted $14,000 for scholarships, and $13,000 for pensions. Tseo's request for funds for WCUTC was referred to the executive committee, which was given the power to act on it. Diffendorfer was re-elected chair of the board, and Dr. E. A. Fridell and E. K. Higdon were named vice-chairs. Dr. J. W. Decker was named a member at large and Professor R. Pierce Beaver an alternate for the members at large.[95]

Meanwhile, with conditions in Nanjing uncertain, the managers held their annual meeting in Shanghai, July 13-15, 1949. They accepted

[94] Tseo Ping-I to Frank T. Cartwright, Chengdu, May 16, 1949, ALW.
[95] Minutes, Annual Meeting, BF, NTS, June 2, 1949, ALW.

the resignation of Lee, who had been president since 1931. He was to receive his salary and a house off campus until he was sixty-five and then receive a pension. The managers asked the mission boards of those denominations supporting Nanking Seminary to send their chosen faculty personnel to China immediately. They urged that, if such persons could not reach Nanjing, they be directed to study Chinese language and the Chinese church elsewhere in the country. The American Baptists and the Disciples were asked to nominate professors from their denominations who might be elected to the Board of Managers. The managers reported that, at the end of the spring term, they had awarded one B.D. degree, two B.Th. degrees, one Tao Hsieh Shih diploma, and seven refresher course certificates. After much discussion, T. C. Bau was elected the new president of Nanking Seminary.[96]

Writing to Cartwright concerning the meeting and Bau's election, Smith pointed out that Bau had been chair of China's National Christian Council and chair of the Board of Managers for three years. Smith commented that the Chinese thought it was more important to have a good administrator as head of Nanking Seminary, whereas the Westerners wanted an academic. However, given the present critical situation, Smith believed that the Chinese were probably right. One of the major issues discussed at the managers' meeting had been Lee's stated desire to continue teaching at the seminary. Smith did not think this would be a problem with Bau as president, though it might have been if one of Lee's students had been elected president. Though not included in the minutes of the meeting, it had been agreed that the new president could call upon President Emeritus Lee to "give such special lectures or addresses to the students as seemed wise." It remained unclear what Lee's relationship to Nanking Seminary and the church in Nanjing would be, but Smith thought that should be determined by the Methodist mission and Lee's own physical ability. Significantly, Smith also reported that Bau was very reluctant to accept the presidency and had said that, if he were chosen, he would not accept. Smith believed the Chinese managers had put great pressure on Bau to reverse his position, but Smith remained uncertain as to whether Bau would accept. Smith noted that requests for $3,000 for vocational training materials and $2,000 for rural service unions, items requested by Price, had been approved without any real faculty discussion, a practice that Smith believed was unwise. Smith said that the additional funds could

96 Minutes, Annual Meeting, BM, NTS, Shanghai, July 13-15, 1949, ALW.

be effectively used because of the terrible rise in the cost of living that they were then experiencing. However, he believed that the funding of the rural service unions might create difficulties since, during the war, the unions had engaged in rural activities on too wide a scale and had been criticized for it. More urgently, Smith observed, there was a problem of salaries occasioned by the continuing rise in the cost of living.[97]

A week later Smith wrote that Bau might not accept the presidency. If he did not, his strongest rival, Zia, pastor of the Moore Memorial Church in Shanghai, likely would be elected. Smith wanted the new president chosen and in place before the fall term to obviate problems created by having a foreigner in the job:

> The position of an American in any institution today and even in Church work is becoming increasingly difficult. The... propaganda that is being uniformly carried on by press, radio, and propagandists at every street corner against American imperialism and capitalism, coupled with the serious economic situation for which Americans are more or less blamed, is beginning to affect the people. It would not take much to incite them to violence against foreigners, especially Americans. So far I think the position of the American business man is particularly difficult but if the agitation against Americans continues it will be hard to discriminate between business men and missionaries.[98]

The strain imposed by the unresolved political situation was clearly apparent in the seminary as it was throughout Chinese society. It affected individuals in many ways and seemed to open doors for endless mischief. Smith reported, as an example of difficulties created or aggravated by changes taking place in China at the time, that he had experienced severe problems with a student from Manchuria. The student had arrived with a letter from the president of the Mukden Theological Seminary and during the first year had created no conflict. Then, during the summer, he commenced excessive smoking in the dormitory and "drinking to the extent of becoming intoxicated." Smith, as acting president, had discussed these matters with the student, who promised to reform; but he did not, and "it was evident that he had a nervous strain or a serious emotional derangement, if not a mental one." Before the city was liberated by Communist forces, the

[97] C. Stanley Smith to Frank T. Cartwright, Nanjing, July 21, 1949, ALW.
[98] C. Stanley Smith to Frank T. Cartwright, Nanjing, July 29, 1949, ALW.

student associated with the Nationalist soldiers. Yet after liberation he "openly boasted that he was a Communist but we did not believe him. He began to quarrel with the students to the extent of slapping them in the face and to grow increasingly antagonistic against some of the foreign teachers." Smith and a Chinese colleague had tried to talk with him, and Smith reported "it was the most painful experience I have ever gone through and I have a new idea of what demonic possession is." That conference produced no results. When the Presbyterians refused to provide support for the student, Smith asked the Methodists, who also refused. Lee and the Chinese business manager tried to convince the man to return to his wife and children in Manchuria, but he refused unless they would give him several times the cost of his ticket. Smith continued that

> the latest word is that he has refused under any conditions to leave, that he is going to stay in the Seminary and make trouble. He has no means of support but he will try to terrorize the students or the Faculty to give him his living expenses. He has been trying to stir up trouble amongst the servants and claims he will be an informer against both student body and Faculty to the Communists. I am afraid when the word gets out that he is going to stay that some of our students will refuse to return. I have gone into detail in this case just to give you one concrete situation. Many other institutions are facing not only one man but whole groups who are trying to terrorize and blackmail the institution. The University Hospital is also having serious trouble. Under these conditions it is imperative that we get a strong Chinese President as soon as possible. There is no telling when conditions may become so serious that we may all be compelled to leave—if we can. In many respects things are going along very auspiciously for Church and Mission work, and they may continue to do so, but always hanging over our heads is the menace of serious trouble resulting from the extremely hostile propaganda which is being spread broadcast.[99]

By August Bau had finally and definitively declined the presidency of Nanking Theological Seminary. A committee on the election of the president was appointed and recommended that Li Tien-lu be invited to become president and Andrew C. Y. Cheng become dean. The committee clarified Lee's position by deciding he could live in

99 Ibid.

any seminary residence except the president's house, could hold no administrative duties, and, although he was not a member of the Governing Faculty, could be invited to teach any course. With these issues apparently resolved, Smith resigned as vice president of Nanking Seminary.[100]

Yet the issue of presidential leadership remained unresolved. Li was unable to accept the presidency because of his own ill health, even though he expressed the hope that he might be able to serve at a later time. Consequently, Smith was asked to continue serving as acting president until someone else could be found. The managers decided that, once Cheng returned from the United States, a committee composed of Cheng, Li, and Samuel Chu would assume administrative responsibility for the seminary with Smith serving as treasurer and an ex-officio member of the committee.[101]

Smith clarified for Cartwright and the Board of Founders in New York the political considerations that underlay the selection of Li as president by the managers. Personally, Smith thought Zia, who had been Bau's rival in the earlier discussions, would have been a good choice, but his name had not even been suggested this time. Li had had several heart attacks during the previous year, the most recent only ten days before the meeting at which the Chinese members of the managers insisted upon electing him president. Smith believed the vote may have been designed to honor him for his long years of service to the seminary or else to install a caretaker president for a year while they searched for a long-term appointee. Smith also indicated that the alumni may have wanted either an alumnus or a long-time faculty member such as Li chosen for the position. Once Li was elected, he was notified by telegram and immediately declined, but the reply was not received until after the meeting had adjourned. Smith also reported that Cheng had not yet arrived in Nanjing and that therefore, although Smith had resigned as vice president, he was still acting president and teaching a full load of classes.[102]

Smith advised the Board of Founders that President Emeritus and Mrs. Lee had moved to a house in the nearby Methodist compound. The house had been vacant, but the mission wanted to retain it rather than having it taken over by the seminary. Smith believed that the resolution of the issue of Lee's teaching was a good one. He concluded his letter with the observation that there were only fifty-four students then

100 Minutes, BM, NTS, August 25-26, 1949, ALW.

101 Minutes, Executive Committee, BM, NTS, September 15, 1949, ALW.

102 C. Stanley Smith to Frank T. Cartwright, Nanjing, October 4, 1949, ALW.

enrolled, eight or nine in the pastors' refresher course, and only three holding college degrees and enrolled in the B.D. degree program.[103]

Cheng finally reached Nanjing from the United States by way of Hong Kong about November 1, and Smith reported to Cartwright that although Cheng did not want to head the administrative committee, he was persuaded to do so. Whatever Cheng's decision, Smith realized the urgency of removing foreign missionaries from administrative posts and wrote that, had Cheng refused the leadership of the administrative committee, Smith would have asked his doctor to declare that he was no longer able to continue as acting president while teaching full time.[104]

Regarding the seminary property, Smith commented that the president's house on campus was still empty and that government officials had been out measuring all the property. The seminary was expecting a huge tax bill. He wrote that there had been little or no interference in its work and that a greater number of younger people were then enrolled in seminary classes in preparation for careers in the church. While very few were college graduates, many had completed middle school. Since there were fewer opportunities for Christians to hold teaching jobs or official posts, Christian youth were looking to the church for careers. Low salaries were no longer a deterrent, since everyone was being paid at the subsistence level. Smith reported that anti-American propaganda was having its impact and worried that, if the United States delayed recognition of the new government for long, Americans in China would suffer. Few letters, magazines, or books had arrived from the United States, but they did have the radio. Smith advised that "there will be quite an exodus of missionaries from several denominations next summer if transportation is available."[105]

Cartwright also received a letter from Cheng reporting on his return to Nanjing and sent excerpts to members of the Board of Founders in February. Arriving in Hong Kong, the Cheng family waited twelve days for third-class deck passage to Tianjin (Tientsin) and then had a rough and stormy trip northward. In Tianjin they had to wait another ten days for transportation to Nanjing. Even as he wrote, Cheng said that four of the sewing machines he was bringing to Nanking Seminary were still in Tianjin. He added that the faculty was giving a series of lectures on the topic of Christianity and Communism

[103] Ibid.

[104] C. Stanley Smith to Frank T. Cartwright, Nanjing, December 1, 1949, ALW.

[105] Ibid.

in order to "acquaint our students with the policy and constitution of the New Regime."[106]

Smith wrote Cartwright from Nanjing in early March that the seminary had closed for winter break January 30 and reopened February 24. A few students had finished their course, but thirteen new ones had arrived, and sixty-four students were then on campus. The Methodists continued to send their pastors for refresher courses, which helped sustain the enrollment. Smith advised that a Chinese person should take over as treasurer and that all accounts should be kept in Chinese. If the Board of Founders wished for a missionary to remain in the treasurer's office, that person should have the position of financial agent of the Board of Founders, a position Jones had held in Chengdu during the war. Smith observed that the Chinese appeared to want a foreigner to continue as treasurer and added that other institutions were facing similar problems. The Nanjing Methodist Conference had just appointed its first Chinese treasurer, as had the Church of Christ in China Presbytery in Nanjing. If Smith could find a Chinese person to take over this work for the seminary, Rouse would prepare a monthly abstract in English for the Board of Founders. He also advised that, if the board wanted a financial agent in Nanjing, there were only three possibilities since Smith was leaving for furlough: Leete, who was really too old; Sone, who was chair of the property committee and teaching full time; and Jones, who would probably have to assume the task.[107]

Smith also described for the board details of the breakdown of civil society in Nanjing. He sent a full account of a robbery of Miss Rouse, Nanking Seminary's English secretary, who lived in the seminary compound. She had been awakened one night at about 10:30 by a man sitting on her bed with his fingers around her throat; and, for the next seven to eight hours, nine men held her captive with her hands tied behind her back and a sweater over her face for most of the time. She was threatened with knives and an axe and was ordered to reveal the location of gold bars that the intruders believed were hidden. About daybreak her captors apparently decided she had no gold bars and left taking all of her possessions except her nightclothes. Smith reflected on the fact that, wishing to remain in Nanjing until summer, Rouse had passed up an opportunity to leave on the *SS General Gordon*. He concluded, "Things are outwardly very quiet but there come periods of strain from time to time which make one realize that the situation may

106 Frank T. Cartwright to BF, New York, February 17, 1950, ALW.

107 C. Stanley Smith to Frank T. Cartwright, Nanjing, March 6, 1950, ALW.

change very suddenly....Quite a number of our Nanking community are leaving including the entire American Consular staff."[108]

A report of the property committee filed with other materials from 1950 revealed further evidence of lawlessness in Nanjing. The seminary had been renovating one of its buildings for use by staff and was installing two modern bathrooms when "eight or ten men scaled the wall at night, intimidated the caretaker and his wife and stripped all of the equipment from both bathrooms except the two tubs. The same thing also happened to one of the bathrooms at the West Hanzhong Road residences. These, of course, had to be replaced."[109]

For the administrative committee, Cheng reported to Cartwright that Jones was to be treasurer for the managers for the coming year. Smith would return to the United States on furlough. Both Hu and Sie had been asked to return to the seminary, but they would need permits from the government for permission to land in China. Mrs. Hu had applied for a permit for her husband, but Cheng indicated that the people in Nanjing did not know whether Sie wanted to apply. Reflecting the impact of deteriorating relations with the United States and the difficulties of international travel, Cheng added, "The Board of Managers are not very enthusiastic about sending people to America for training or for sabbatical leave at the present time."[110]

Cheng also forwarded the minutes of the annual meeting of the managers that had just concluded to Cartwright. Therein were laid out the policy and program for Nanking Seminary: "In order to understand the fundamental purpose of the Seminary, we wish to call attention to the statement of purpose as revised by the Annual Meeting of the Board of Managers in 1935."[111] Reflecting the immediate situation, the minutes continued:

> The administrative and business affairs of the Seminary, with the exception of policy and finance, which are related to and under the control of, the Board of Managers, must be carried out in accordance with the following principles: (1) The administration must be in the hands of Chinese leaders. (2) The principle of

108 Ibid.

109 Report of the Property Committee, NTS, n.d. [1950?], ALW.

110 Andrew C. Y. Cheng to Frank T. Cartwright, Nanjing, May 12, 1950, ALW.

111 The 1935 statement of purpose is reproduced in Cartwright, *River*, 68-69. It represented the NTS commitment to administer the Swope-Wendel bequest wisely in the development of leadership for the Protestant church in China.

democracy must be followed, that is, things should be decided by mutual consultation."[112]

Other actions taken at this meeting included the stipulation that costs of extension work could not exceed 10 percent of the total budget each year. With regard to the curriculum, the Board of Managers voted that "all courses offered at the Seminary, except those which are regularly required by an advanced school of theology, should be adjusted to meet the needs of (1) the Chinese Church (2) the new situation in China (3) Church supported students and their financial conditions." The managers also voted that "because of the changing situation, the Seminary should re-examine and discuss the teaching methods employed in different courses in order that they may be adapted to the real conditions."[113]

The managers wanted "the relation of the...Managers to the [Board of Founders]...more clearly understood. We, therefore, ask...Smith, while in America, to take up on behalf of the...Managers the problems involved so as to clarify and strengthen the relationship between the two Boards." The managers also declared that "the Seminary funds... [should] not be used for missionary teachers." Regulations concerning sabbatical leaves for advanced study needed revision "in accordance with present needs and conditions."[114]

The managers discussed the issue of administrative leadership and agreed that a single president was preferable to a committee and so elected Cheng to a three-year term as president. In other business, they voted $1,500 for WCUTC for the 1950-51 year and a scholarship of $300 for Smith to attend Princeton University and Theological Seminary during his 1950-51 furlough.[115]

The managers declared that they would not support other theological institutions on a regular basis but would consider requests for special, nonrecurring grants. They reported that one person received the M.R.E. degree, three (all women) received the B.Th. degree, and five received pastors' refresher course certificates.[116]

The treasurer's report for the year was very brief. Lin Tsun-yuan, who had taught bookkeeping at the Yi Wen Business College operated by the Presbyterian mission in Chefoo, Shandong Province, had recently

[112] Minutes, Annual Meeting, BM, NTS, May 5-6, 1950, ALW.
[113] Ibid.
[114] Ibid.
[115] Ibid.
[116] Ibid.

joined the seminary staff and submitted this report, though later treasurer's reports would be submitted by Jones. The report indicated that Nanking Seminary was returning $3,000 that had been allocated for new faculty, since it could locate none.[117]

Cheng also forwarded a faculty report, which listed seventy students from eight denominations and thirteen provinces. Ninety-seven people from thirteen provinces, eighty-six of them men and eleven women, were taking the correspondence course, which was based on required and optional readings as well as reference materials. More than eighty books appeared on the course syllabus, including some of the "latest study group series on the New Democracy, Dialectic Materialism, Marx and Lenin, Mao Tse-tung, etc." The seminary was still operating the experimental nursery school, and the report indicated that most of those enrolled were children of Christians.[118] Evidence of the sensitivity of the students and faculty to the new political situation is clearly revealed in this comment:

> Another new feature of this last year was the formation of small study groups by both students and Chinese members of the faculty. Six small groups were divided in the Spring Term and the purpose of such groups is to acquaint ourselves with the program and policy of the New Regime, to learn the principles of the New Democracy and to keep in touch with the general trends of thinking in the nation as a whole. These study groups were initiated entirely by the students themselves and the Chinese Faculty appointed....Hsieh Ching-sheng to make out plans with them. While these study groups were intended for Chinese nationals, foreign members of the Faculty are also welcome to join any group if they wish to. The value of such groups, so far as experience shows, is not only to promote interest in the new learning but also to deepen the spiritual fellowship between students and faculty members by weekly contacts in an informal way.[119]

With limited current information available on conditions in Nanjing and with great uncertainty as to the immediate future of the seminary, the Board of Founders held its annual meeting June 9, 1950, voted to authorize remittance of $60,460 to the field for the

117 Treasurer's Report, NTS, 1949-50, ALW.
118 Faculty Report, NTS, 1949-50, ALW.
119 Ibid.

forthcoming academic year, and recognized with pleasure the selection of Andrew Cheng as seminary president.[120]

Smith, who left Nanjing for the States July 3, 1950, prepared a lengthy report to the Board of Founders summarizing experiences at Nanking Seminary from the fall of 1948 until his departure. With regard to some of the matters in the 1949-50 faculty report, Smith wrote that the Chinese faculty and students had voluntarily organized the classes and study groups to consider Marxism, the "New Democracy," and the new constitution after its adoption by the People's government in Beijing. The servants and foreign faculty had been invited to attend, but Smith added that the foreigners did not attend because of their belief that "Chinese colleagues would feel freer without [our] presence." Smith did attend one study group and reported that it was a "free-for-all discussion period on certain issues that had arisen in the student groups. It was a lively meeting with plenty of give and take between students and teachers."[121]

Smith also believed that the ascendancy of communism in China with the challenge it posed to Christianity had led to a new level of seriousness among the students:

> This new interest in Christian theology in China is one of the most interesting and perhaps paradoxical things that has arisen out of the Communist occupation. I think I can say without exaggeration that I have never in all my thirty-two years of teaching theology in China, enjoyed teaching as I have this past year and a half since we have been "liberated." In many ways China today is a theologian's paradise! Unfortunately, however, the paradise, so far as missionary teachers are concerned may soon be barred with a flaming sword![122]

Smith observed that the Communists were instructing everyone at required meetings what it meant to be a Communist and that learning was often a matter of life and death even for the family, since one could lose a job if the tests were failed. He believed this situation had led Christians to want to understand more fully what they believed in order that they could defend their faith, even to their children. Seminary students, when meeting with students from government schools, were asked such questions as, "'Was man developed from monkeys?' 'Can the ideal social kingdom be established on earth by a

120 Minutes, Annual Meeting, BF, NTS, June 9, 1950, FTEA.
121 C. Stanley Smith to BF, New York, October 30, 1950, ALW.
122 Ibid.

process of dialectical materialism?' 'Did Labor create the world?' 'Has the individual no intrinsic value and no hope of immortality?'" Smith declared that these questions had led the Christian students to demand answers from their professors and had created a new interest in subjects which previously may have been less important to the students. He concluded that the students were beginning to understand that Christian action was rooted in Christian theology:

> Too long has the Chinese student, like the American student, tended to think that practice arose out of itself and could stand by itself. Communism is teaching him differently and he has to heed their teaching if he is to exist as a Christian. He must not only outlive the Communist in social action but he must out think him as well. Hence the new interest in Theology in Communist controlled China.[123]

Regarding the relationship of the seminary to the new government and its materialistic ideology, Smith reported that there had been some looting in the city but that it did not affect the seminary and that their worst fears had not been realized when he left on July 3. However, from more recent reports, he gathered that "these days of almost complete freedom from government inspection and interference are coming to an end. There have been some requests from the authorities for reports on our work and program." Smith revealed the depth of the ideological struggle for Chinese Christians when he noted that some were happy with the noninterference while other students and faculty felt that "we were being isolated and cut off from a great movement in Chinese history—something which, if we did not feel that we could wholeheartedly join, we should at least try to understand and cooperate with in its more constructive aspects and which we should try to influence along Christian lines as much as possible." Smith observed that there were daily marches of young people in the city from which the seminary students and the churches were largely isolated. On the one hand, the Christians could not agree with the antireligious aspects of the Communist program, but, on the other hand, many of the more thoughtful Christians believed that the new government was far wider than ideological communism and contained many positive attributes which Christians, as citizens of China, should endorse and support. The internal struggle was over how this might be done with integrity.[124]

123 Ibid.
124 Ibid.

Smith also reported an increase in Nanking Seminary's enrollment. The Synod of Guangdong had sent six pastors and women evangelists to the one-year refresher course, and the Methodists were increasing the number of their students in this program as well. The number of students in the regular course for ministerial preparation was also rising. Total enrollment had doubled with fifty new students. The number of women students had increased from nineteen to twenty-eight. Smith observed that the seminary still needed a new dormitory for women, but he granted that "it has not seemed wise to build it under present conditions."[125]

Smith wrote that the transition from Nationalist to Communist government in Nanjing had occurred "almost uneventfully as the city, deserted by its would-be defenders, waited to welcome its new masters. The strain of the new situation was unending. No foreigner should have been in the position of head of a Chinese school under these circumstances." Smith, of course, had been acting president at that time, and he added the sad news that he experienced a heart attack and was bedridden for two months following the spring graduation.[126]

Reviewing for the Board of Founders the process of presidential selection, Smith reported that Cheng had been reluctant to accept the presidency under the existing political situation but that faculty, students, and friends insisted that he do so. He was assured of a strong supporting administrative committee. Cheng's selection was complicated by virtue of the fact that he had never been ordained, and his installation as president was therefore delayed until his ordination by the Church of Christ in China Presbytery of Nanjing in the summer.[127]

When the Board of Founders convened a special meeting in New York October 30, 1950, in addition to this lengthy appraisal from Smith, they also had correspondence from Jones and Cheng in Nanjing. Jones advised them that a new salary schedule had been adopted based on the cost of rice, oil, fuel, and cloth with the result that salaries had actually been reduced by about one-third, a fact made more palatable by virtue of the fact that prices had also dropped. However, he expected that they would need to revise salaries upward soon. He informed the board of the very good news that over one hundred students were then enrolled, about half of them new students. Methodists had sent students from

125 Ibid.
126 Ibid.
127 Ibid.

nearly every conference in China, and 150 people had attended a week-long young people's conference on the campus.[128]

With this information in hand, the Board of Founders authorized new faculty positions, and it also agreed that pensions would be paid to long-time employees. The Literature Production Program was reviewed, and the board urged that outstanding manuscripts be collected and that Jones speed up the publication schedule. Ralph E. Diffendorfer, J. W. Decker, and R. Pierce Beaver were instructed to assess the entire issue of the translation and literature project and to report to the board. The executive committee was instructed to meet as necessary to study the changes that would be needed at Nanking Seminary to meet the current conditions there.[129]

The Board of Founders itself experienced some membership changes at this meeting. The Presbyterian Church in the U.S.A. had elected Dr. Henry Pitney Van Dusen, previously a member at large, to represent the denomination on the board. The United Christian Missionary Society (Disciples) had chosen Dr. Virgil Sly for board membership. Dr. Lloyd S. Ruland became the new chair, with E. K. Higdon and Dr. Eugene L. Smith as vice-chairs. Ralph E. Diffendorfer, a charter member of the board who had previously served as chair but who had rotated off the board, was elected to serve as a member at large, filling the place previously occupied by Van Dusen.[130]

In his lengthy report prepared for this October meeting, Smith presented a variety of concerns that arose from the change in government and the new ideological situation in China. He recognized that the seminary's constitution was now out of date and indicated that the seminary managers, meeting August 30-31, 1950, had appointed a committee to suggest revisions. It was clear, for example, that foreign missionaries should be taken off the various seminary boards. Smith was personally concerned about the potential lowering of academic standards in response to pressure to shorten courses, to offer more short-term programs, and to lower entrance requirements. His personal opinion was that in response to well-reasoned Communist publications, Nanking Seminary needed longer and better courses to teach all aspects of Christianity. There was a critical need for teachers in the theological fields as many of the older ones were reaching retirement age, and

128 Francis P. Jones to Frank T. Cartwright, Nanjing, September 15, 1950; Andrew C. Y. Cheng to Frank T. Cartwright, Nanjing, July 28, 1950, both ALW.

129 Minutes, Meeting, BF, NTS, October 30, 1950, ALW.

130 Ibid.

missionaries would almost certainly leave. Smith estimated that there were only three or four men in China "adequately trained to teach theology," and all of them already held vitally important positions, two as heads of theological schools. He realized that recruiting teachers from other institutions would only weaken the programs from which they were taken. Smith noted that there was interest in abolishing denominations in China and uniting the Protestant church. He believed that the Christians should do this themselves before they had it forced upon them. If this unification occurred, Smith believed there would be only one or two theological schools in the country, and he asked the board to consider what it would do if asked to fund another seminary in addition to Nanking. Smith also realized that it might soon be impossible to use the Swope-Wendel legacy in China. He wrote that their bank drafts had so far been welcomed, but

> we have also been informed that strong pressure is being exerted in high places to compel the Chinese church and all its institutions to become self-supporting as a condition of survival....Some would have this done at once...others would allow a reasonable amount of time for financial adjustments to be made. The goal of self-support, however, seems to have been set. Any immediate demand for self-support would seriously threaten to wipe out most of the existing theological schools, especially those of the larger denominations which are over 90 percent subsidized from abroad. Under a demand for self-support the NTS would be in serious danger of extinction in China.[131]

Smith raised the possibility of establishing or reorganizing Nanking Theological Seminary in Hong Kong as the Lutheran Church had done in the case of its theological seminary in Hubei. Graduates from the Hong Kong-based Lutheran program were finding their way back into China, and Smith believed graduates of other schools might also do so. He believed that the publication program could not be continued in the People's Republic, but he thought it might be carried out in Hong Kong under the direct auspices of the Board of Founders, rather than under the seminary directly.[132]

Smith advised the board that there were three significant problems requiring immediate attention: the pension plan had to be revised, since it was based on a currency that no longer existed; the publication

[131] C. Stanley Smith to BF, New York, October 30, 1950, ALW.
[132] Ibid.

program needed to be continued, since some manuscripts had not yet been completed; and the Board of Founders should assist the Nanking Seminary by locating Chinese scholars outside the country who would be willing to return to the seminary and assist personnel there.[133]

Sone had remained in Nanjing, and he wrote to Cartwright in March 1951 describing the adjustment to the three-self principles of self-control, self-support, and self-propagation. He reported that he was no longer teaching or attending committee meetings and that the seminary's constitution was being revised to eliminate all references to the Board of Founders. He wrote that Nanking Theological Seminary could expect no support from local churches for two or three years because they were also undergoing three-self programs. Sone wrote the Board of Founders that the curriculum then included a great deal of agricultural work and that the campus had been altered accordingly.[134]

Sone also commented on the sensitive issue of property ownership with which the seminary had struggled under the Nationalist government and which apparently had not been resolved satisfactorily. In any event it became an issue once more with the establishment of the People's Republic. In January 1951 Cheng had sent a cable to the Board of Founders in New York requesting that Nanking Seminary's property be transferred to those in Nanjing. Under the circumstances and without U.S. diplomatic recognition of the Chinese government, such action from the board seemed impossible. In response, a cable was sent declaring, "Seminary Founders favor transfer property but legally impossible present conditions. Founders recognize seminary directors in China for possession and use property.[135] Sone wrote that "the cabled statement regarding the transfer of the property to [NTS] seems to be adequate" as all property was being registered.[136]

In a mood of uncertainty, the executive committee of the Board of Founders met March 19, 1951, to consider future activity. Leete had cabled that he was in Bangkok and had advanced the seminary $500 of his own money before leaving Nanjing. The committee voted to reimburse him. It appeared obvious that the Board of Founders could no longer assist the seminary directly, so the committee commenced to identify and explore the various challenges the board faced. Three committees were created. A Translation and Literature Production Committee was to be chaired by Henry P. Van Dusen. A Committee on

133 Ibid.
134 Hubert Sone to Frank T. Cartwright, Nanjing, March 7, 1951, ALW.
135 Minutes, Special Meeting, BF, New York, April 11, 1951, ALW.
136 Hubert Sone to Frank T. Cartwright, Nanjing, March 1951, ALW.

Legal Aspects, composed of Ruland, E. A. Fridell, and the legal counsels of the Presbyterian and Methodist boards, was instructed to explore the bequest and charter in order to ascertain how the Swope-Wendel legacy could legally be used. A Committee on Location, chaired by Cartwright and including Smith and Decker, was asked to explore locations outside China where the objectives of the Board of Founders might be realized. The executive committee also voted to call a special meeting of the entire board "to consider the future of the Seminary during whatever period it is impossible to use Seminary funds in China."[137]

Smith prepared another lengthy report for this meeting of the executive committee of the board. He indicated that he had discussed the seminary's situation with Weigle and that they thought plans should be made on the assumption that the present situation in China would not continue indefinitely and that the board would be able to resume funding the seminary at some point in the future. However, they recognized that there was no way to know how long the present situation would prevail and cautioned that, even if the Communists left, the old ways of conducting mission activities would have to be altered significantly:

> Just how these changes will affect an institution like [NTS] which is dependent on income from abroad we cannot foresee. However, the Chinese are a very reasonable people and once the present period...has passed, it may be that, since this income is from an endowment with no political strings attached, there would be no objections to its use in China even under a Communist regime.[138]

Smith believed that the Board of Founders needed to steer a cautious pathway mindful of its mission, of legal constraints imposed by the terms of the Swope-Wendel bequest, and of the situation in China and sensibilities of the faculty still in China. He declared that the board should establish

> some policy by which the BF can carry on some aspects of [its] program during this period of isolation. We shall have to keep in mind the limitations which the legal aspects of our legacy will impose and also the very delicate question as to what the attitude

[137] Minutes, Executive Committee, BF, NTS, March 19, 1951, ALW.

[138] C. Stanley Smith, "The Program of the NTS with Relation to Work Outside China," March 19, 1951, ALW.

> of those now in Nanking, both members of our faculty and of the Managers, will be toward our carrying out any Seminary work outside of Nanjing and especially outside of China.[139]

Smith recalled the problems that arose during World War II, when the board supported the group of faculty in Chengdu while its contact with the official seminary was terminated by the Japanese occupation of East China. The subsequent return of both the Shanghai and the Chengdu contingents to Nanjing, while cause for celebration, entailed significant adjustments. "Although the healing of this division was greater than we had hardly dared to hope for, we cannot overlook the fact that there was a division and that there are some of its results still evident among the faculty...to this day." Nonetheless, Smith thought the board should carry on its work outside of China and, since it would be impossible to get permission from those in Nanjing, he thought the decision was up to the board. A recent arrival in the United States from Nanjing had reported that Nanking Seminary was to be "nationalized," and he thought that meant teaching would be required to "adhere strictly to the Communist, or at least New Democracy, line." Even if the school were not nationalized and subsidized, he thought it would have to close down or carry on "a very precarious existence in cooperation with other theological schools in like condition. I would look for the amalgamation of all the larger schools into one or two seminaries that might be supported on a low economic level by the united churches of China and which might be staffed in most departments from the staffs of all the present schools." In either case the relationship with the Board of Founders would cease to exist.[140]

To the board Smith posed the question: "What is the duty and opportunity of the BF in trying to carry on at least part of the teaching program outside of China for as long as is necessary?" He thought it would be possible to find students, not necessarily all Chinese but a majority Chinese, for such a program. He also thought it would not be necessary for them all to return to China to take up ministry, for some could work among the extensive overseas Chinese communities in South East Asia. He noted that several Nanking Seminary graduates had served overseas Chinese churches and that students from Korea and Taiwan had attended Nanking Seminary in the past. The previous year it would have been possible for Chinese students to travel to Hong Kong and study there with professors unable to return to China and

139 Ibid.
140 Ibid.

then, upon completion of their studies, to return home. However, the U.S. entrance into the Korean War had precipitated more restrictive travel policies in China. Therefore study in Hong Kong was no longer an obvious option.

> Some might still be smuggled out of China but their reentrance would be very difficult and dangerous now from all reports. Such students, however, could go to overseas churches where they are badly needed. Some might be willing to take the risks involved to return to China as missionaries to Communist China even as foreigners did to imperialist China in years past.[141]

Considering these factors, Smith reasoned that the board might recruit from "among overseas Chinese Christians and from Chinese students now in America who may not wish to return to China under present conditions or who might be willing to go to churches in southeast Asia until conditions changed in China." He believed that the closer an academic program was to China the better it would be at facilitating re-entry. He thought some of the returned missionary faculty might be willing to teach in such a school but did not think it wise to have too many of them. Chinese theological students in the United States and mature Chinese Christians studying abroad could be recruited as teachers, and native teachers could be recruited if the emphasis were to be placed on work among overseas Chinese. While there had been earlier consideration of assisting members of the faculty who might want to leave China, the "unexpectedly favorable conditions" under which Nanking Seminary continued to operate led to putting such plans aside.[142]

Smith wrote that Hong Kong or Manila might be an appropriate site for the location of an institution supported by the Board of Founders. He had visited the Lutheran Theological Seminary in Hong Kong, where two former Nanking Seminary faculty members were teaching, and believed that this location had advantages. "Certainly if we decided to attempt to organize a school [in Hong Kong] we would not want to put much capital investment in it nor do I think it would be necessary," he wrote. Manila would be another attractive possibility. There they could work with one of the existing union seminaries, and there was a fairly large Chinese population there. Yet Smith acknowledged that there were ethnic frictions between Filipinos

141 Ibid.
142 Ibid.

and Chinese. Another possible location might be Singapore, which he reported that some favored since it had a theological seminary and some of the Methodists there had studied at Nanking Seminary.[143]

Continuation of the translation and publication program had been endorsed at the last board meeting, and Smith recommended that Jones be asked to continue with this project on a full-time basis, together with a group of Chinese assistants. However, it appeared certain that the project would extend far beyond Jones's date of retirement, and Smith considered a variety of options for locating the program. Hong Kong was attractive because assistants would be available and publication costs would be low. Singapore, Manila, and Hawaii were alternative options. William P. Fenn was in Singapore to study education issues for the British government, and Smith had asked him to look at the theological seminary there. Smith expected his report in a few weeks. He also indicated that there was a possibility of establishing a board-supported educational program in Honolulu. He assumed that anti-Chinese sentiment would be less of a problem there than elsewhere in the United States if conflict between the U.S. and China intensified. Smith believed that the likely enrollment in any Board of Founders' theological education program outside China would be small and that such a program should be linked to the Literature Production Program.[144]

Smith argued for expansion of the Literature Production Program. He had seen the impact of the Communists' literature program and how ill-prepared the Christians had been to respond in this ideological struggle. He also recommended that the program be expanded to provide literature for "other countries of the Orient not yet under the control of the Communists before it is too late." He recommended that all theological students read the Communist literature, wherein "every effort is made to bring these usually highly esoteric subjects within the understanding of the common man." He explained that in China there was a fairly adequate literature concerned with

> exegetical studies of the Bible, devotion, worship and piety in its individual aspects. We are lacking in a literature that gives to students and to the public generally an intelligent view of life as a whole, such as the Communists aim to give them and especially making clear the relation between Christian beliefs and the problems of society. It is my conviction that [the Board

143 Ibid.
144 Ibid.

> of Founders] could find no more profitable use of some of the income of the Wendel legacy at this time than by taking the initiative in an attempt to provide a more adequate literature with which to combat Communism in China and other parts of the Orient.[145]

Such books could be written by young men in theological schools with the help of some who had recently lived in China so that "their writings might be oriented toward the students and intelligentsia of China rather than toward American readers." These books could then be translated into Chinese. He reiterated that it would be impossible under present conditions to consult the people in Nanjing, and that the Board of Founders must make the necessary decisions on its own.[146]

Jones, who had been in charge of the Literature Production Program in China, developed a plan for continuing the work in the United States and submitted it to the Board of Founders in April 1951. He observed that the translation of the Christian classics into Chinese had been the subject of three conferences in New York between 1944 and 1946, that many in China were working on the project, but that by 1951 only one volume was ready for publication. Five additional works were near completion, another eight were partially done, but on at least six others no work had commenced. Nanking Seminary had terminated its work on the Literature Production Program because of lack of funds, and some who had worked on the project earlier could no longer be contacted. Sie was in Hartford, Connecticut, where he had been preparing for two and a half years to work on this project. Tang was expected to come from Nanjing within the following year to participate in the project. Jones recommended that the board continue the program as one aspect of its work in Nanjing, but he also observed that, if the Christians in China were isolated for ten or twenty years, there would be fewer and fewer people competent to undertake this project. There were currently Chinese people who could not or would not return to the People's Republic who were capable of doing the translation, and undertaking the project in the United States would have the advantage of immediate access to many volumes that were out of print and unavailable to translators in China. However, there were offsetting disadvantages: the costs would double in the States, and it seemed unlikely that such translated books would be permitted entry into China, though they certainly could be circulated among overseas

145 Ibid.

146 Ibid.

Chinese. Jones noted the program did not translate "journalistic literature," which would become outdated. As to the Christian classics, he observed that the commonly used English translations were often quite old, and he reasoned that even if the Chinese translations could not be sent to China for years, they would remain valuable whenever sent.[147]

In response to a query from Abbe Livingstone Warnshuis, a member of the Board of Founders, concerning legal restrictions on the use of the Swope-Wendel fund, Cartwright advised that the wills of Ella Wendel and of Rebecca Swope contained identical provisions, namely, "And the remaining Thirty-five equal shares or parts thereof to the Board of Foreign Missions of the Methodist Episcopal Church incorporated under the Laws of the State of New York, the income of which is to be used for the maintenance of the Nankin [sic] Theological Seminary at Nankin, China."[148] This provision, coupled with the isolation of China and the seminary from the West, was the source of the many difficulties the Board of Founders faced as it searched for an appropriate mission after it could no longer support the seminary in Nanjing.

In April, Cartwright shared with the Board of Founders information received from Sone in a confidential letter. Sone and his wife had reached Hong Kong, and they reported that the situation for Christian religious leaders in China had become more difficult. Widespread xenophobia appeared to be directed at Christians, and communication between Nanking Seminary and the Board of Founders had to be terminated in the best interest of the personnel in Nanjing.[149]

Following a mail vote that gave unanimous approval for granting $1,000 to the Christian Literature Society to speed production and circulation of Bates's *Religious Liberty*, a special meeting of the Board of Founders was convened May 7, 1951. Samuel Moffett gave a verbal report on conditions at Nanking Seminary when he left Nanjing in January 1951, and Sone's letter was read to the entire board. Then Kenneth Murray and Howard Vail, attorneys for the Methodist and Presbyterian churches respectively, introduced the following statement:

> There is a history of extension of the work of NTS in the past. The question as to whether the wording of the bequest in the Wendel

[147] Francis P. Jones, "Proposal for Translation Center for NTS in the U.S.," April 1951, ALW.

[148] Frank T. Cartwright to Abbe Livingstone Warnshuis, New York, April 11, 1951, ALW.

[149] Frank T. Cartwright to BF, New York, April 18, 1951, ALW.

and Swope Wills created a legal trust was referred to outside counsel in 1934 at which time an opinion was given to the effect that the bequest did not create a legal trust and that in view of the fact that it was an absolute gift to the Board of Foreign Missions for one of its corporate purposes, the Board could feel that it had a considerable say in whatever plans were made for the Seminary or its activities. In the light of this opinion, extension work was carried on outside Nanking and this was especially true during the Japanese War. There did not seem to be any definite restriction to the Nanking area, although, it is true that during the Japanese War the Seminary remained within the borders of China.

The question is now raised as to whether it would constitute a violation of the terms of the bequest to carry on the work of the Seminary at some place outside the borders of China. It is our opinion that a temporary relocation of the work outside the borders of China can be justified under the circumstances. We feel that the phrase "at Nanking" in the two Wills is deemed to be more specifically a description of the location of the institution, and was not intended as a limitation to a geographical area, and would fully justify a complete immigration to some place like Bangkok, Manila, or Singapore. It could further be justified as an emergency measure in view of the fact that Chinese students cannot leave or reenter Nanking since it is under Communist control.

While on the one hand there might be some risk of straining our authority, it seems that the risk of criticism would be greater by holding the funds inactive, possibly for a considerable period of time.

We feel that a strong case could be made to justify the extension of the work at one of the locations mentioned above, principally to carry on the vital work of translation, to train Christian ministers to minister to Chinese in free areas throughout Southeast Asia, and to maintain, in so far as possible, the continuity of student relationships and of faculty.[150]

The committee on translation recommended that the board establish a center for five years or longer to work on the completion of translations of a series of Christian classics into Chinese with a view to their publication. The committee also urged "a publication program

[150] Minutes, Special Meeting, BF, NTS, May 7, 1951, ALW.

of substantial contemporary works with relevance to the problems confronting Chinese Christians inside and outside of China." The committee realized that the budget would depend on the scope of work to be done but set a maximum figure of $25,000 per year for such a project. The committee suggested that Chinese scholars in Europe with command of German and other languages useful in such a program should be involved.[151]

The committee on location recommended that "for the immediate foreseeable future" the board cooperate with projects in existing institutions rather than seek to establish a new institution. The committee also recommended approaches along those lines to Union Theological Seminary, Manila; Trinity College, Singapore; Higher Theological School, Jakarta; McGilvary Theological Seminary, Chiang Mai, Thailand; and Insein Theological Seminary, Burma. It recommended that each of these institutions be informed that

> we want no worthy Chinese turned away for lack of funds. This would imply the setting up of a scholarship fund by the [BF]....We invite proposals from these institutions for limited projects which promise benefits to Chinese and to other nationals in preparation for work in the ecumenical church...[such as] libraries, rural experimentation, visiting professors from other Asiatic lands, especially available and qualified Chinese.[152]

By "limited projects" the committee meant year-to-year projects to last no longer than three years and projects requiring small amounts of funding in several places in preference to a few large projects. The committee also suggested that one or more qualified representatives of the board visit Burma, Indonesia, Japan, Malaysia, the Philippines, and Thailand for a thorough study of their theological institutions. Having made a decision to work with existing institutions at least for the present, the Board of Founders expanded the committee on location, which would pursue these new relationships, and $25,000 was voted for its work. In an effort to keep Nanking Seminary's missionary faculty from dispersing during this period of uncertainty, the board asked the various mission boards not to appoint those missionaries elsewhere without consultation, since the board maintained the hope "of resuming a service in Nanking at some time in the not distant future." The fiscal year was to end at the end of the month, and the budget for

151 Ibid.
152 Ibid.

the seminary from the Swope-Wendel fund had been $76,807.37, of which $55,150.01 had been sent by draft to China.[153]

Significant personnel changes on the board occurred at this meeting. R. E. Diffendorfer, a founding member of the board, and Dr. Albert E. Beebe, the assistant treasurer, had recently died and were memorialized. Professor Clarence T. Craig was elected to replace Diffendorfer.[154]

In October 1951, Cartwright received and circulated to the Board of Founders some articles that had appeared in *Tian Feng*, the official magazine of the Protestant Church in China, in which the work of Protestant missionaries, missionary teachers, and the Board of Founders in support of Nanking Theological Seminary was criticized as constituting acts of American imperialism.[155] It was clearly apparent that further contact with seminary personnel in Nanjing was unwise and that the Board of Founders and Nanking Seminary were not going to be able to escape the propaganda war that intensified along with the growing military conflict between China and the United States in Korea.

One of the Americans denounced in China at this time was Frank W. Price, who had worked for the Nationalist government in China and had represented that government at the San Francisco peace conference. His denunciation was understandable but somewhat ironic, since Price had written to U.S. Secretary of State Dean Acheson on November 29, 1949, urging that the United States immediately extend diplomatic relations to the Communist government.[156] Price and his wife were detained in China but never arrested nor imprisoned. They were permitted to leave in September 1952. Price, who never returned to China, was elected moderator of the Presbyterian Church in the U.S. in 1953 and later that year translated into English and published a Chinese hymn penned by Ernest Y. L. Yang entitled, "Fount of Love."[157]

While the members of the Board of Founders were left to contemplate the changes that had occurred in China and this latest

153 Ibid.

154 Ibid.

155 Frank T. Cartwright to BF, New York, October 23, 1951, ALW.

156 "The Moderator: Biographical," *Presbyterian Outlook*, 135 (June 15, 1953): 1; and Frank W. Price to Dean Acheson, November 29, 1949, Price Family Papers, George C. Marshall Foundation, Lexington, Vir. (hereafter PP).

157 Price to Friends on Our Mailing List, Richmond, Vir., December 10, 1952, Frank Price Papers, Davidson College Archives, Davidson, N.C.; "The 1953 General Assembly," *Christian Observer*, 141 (June 24, 1953), 2; and "Fount of Love," *Presbyterian Survey*, 43 (July 1953), 33.

outbreak of antiforeign sentiment that seemed to have alienated them from Nanking Seminary and from Chinese friends they had long known and loved, many of whom had suffered with them during World War II, they also were compelled to decide what they should do with the proceeds of the Swope-Wendel fund. They felt it would be irresponsible simply to hold the money and wait; it needed to be spent in furtherance of the intentions of the bequest. Although many Chinese missions from the mainland reestablished themselves on Taiwan under the Nationalist government, the Board of Founders, probably influenced by Smith, continued to hope for an early renewal of relations with Nanking Seminary and, meanwhile, chose to turn its attention toward the Chinese diaspora, particularly that in South East Asia. The decision brought impressive results that none could have imagined as 1951 drew to a close.

CHAPTER 4

Expanding Programs into South East Asia

The critical decision reached by the Board of Founders at its special meeting of May 7, 1951, to seek cooperation with existing institutions in South East Asia serving Chinese students compelled exploration of how this decision might best be implemented. Over the next year, a plan was developed by the board to send C. Stanley Smith and Sidney B. Anderson on a visit to various institutions in Burma, Thailand, Singapore, Indonesia, and the Philippines. Proposed to board members by the executive committee and confirmed by mail vote, the study began early in 1952.[1]

Smith journeyed to South East Asia by way of Britain and India so that he could familiarize Christian groups in those places with the purpose of his trip. In February 1953 Smith wrote Frank Cartwright from Singapore reporting some of his preliminary observations about the schools he had seen. Later that year a complete report was made to the Board of Founders and subsequently published as the *Anderson-Smith Report on Theological Education in Southeast Asia.*[2]

1 Minutes, Special Meeting, BF, NTS, May 7, 1952, FTEA.

2 C. Stanley Smith to Frank T. Cartwright, February 8, 1952, ALW; C. Stanley

In England Smith conferred with the secretaries of several mission boards to acquaint them with the purpose of his trip and to solicit information regarding their interests in theological education in South East Asia. The London Missionary Society expressed special interest in Singapore's Trinity College, where one of its former missionaries was stationed, but expressed regret that it was unable to provide financial support for the college at that time because of a lack of funds.[3]

In India, Smith surveyed a theological textbook series of forty to fifty volumes then being edited by Marcus Ward for the National Christian Council of India. He also visited the Christian Institute for the Study of Religion and Society at the United Theological College in Bangalore, where the primary emphasis was on the study of communism and other political ideologies in India. He was then joined by Anderson, and the two of them visited the Theological Faculty of Serampore College, where the principal, Cheruthotatil Eapen Abraham, had been an exchange professor at Nanking Theological Seminary in Chengdu in 1944. Their report noted that the senate of the Serampore College set the standards for and granted all theological degrees in India. They believed that the same arrangement might be made for South East Asia. Smith and Anderson believed that unless Chinese students attended Serampore College the Board of Founders could not extend grants to it; nonetheless, Smith observed that, since the college had contributed

---

Smith, "A Report on Theological Education in Southeast Asia, Especially as it is Related to the Training of Ministers and Church Workers for the Ecumenical Church in that Area, Made to the BF of the NTS" [1952], 39 pp. At the September 12, 1952, meeting of the BF, Smith reported that publication could not be accomplished for $800, for Charles Scribners Sons wanted $1,920 for 1,000 copies. That amount was then voted; see Minutes, BF, NTS, September 12, 1952, ALW. A typescript of the report is among the Warnshuis Papers at UTS in New York. The published version is [Sidney R. Anderson and C. Stanley Smith], *The Anderson-Smith Report on Theological Education in Southeast Asia Especially as it Relates to the Training of Chinese for the Christian Ministry: The Report of a Survey Commission, 1951-52* (New York: Board of Founders of Nanking Theological Seminary, 1952). References here are to the published version. Henry P. Van Dusen published a review of the report in which he stated Anderson and Smith had correctly identified the problem of three levels of theological schools; i.e., theological colleges requiring an undergraduate degree for admission, theological schools which admitted middle school graduates, and Bible schools for the training of nonordained Christian workers. See H. P. Van Dusen, "Theological Education in Asia," *International Review of Missions,* XLII (1953), 332-34.

3 Anderson and Smith, *Report,* 1.

to Abraham's services in Chengdu, a small grant to assist them in preserving their early records would be appropriate.[4]

While surveying theological education in the region, Anderson and Smith also inquired into the presence of ethnically Chinese people in all the countries of South East Asia as well as the influence in the area of Buddhism and Islam, which they termed "other strong religions." They reported that in every area they visited they found a problem of "foot-loose, free-lance Chinese evangelists" whose influence had been "pernicious." Only in Indonesia where the Dutch had placed a high priority on theological education was there an ability to withstand the work of these evangelists. Many of the evangelists, they reported, were not connected with any church and were not ordained. They placed great emphasis on Pentecostal and millennial expressions of Christianity; and, with large contributions from wealthier Chinese churches, they had established schools in Hong Kong to propagate their ideas. Smith noted that, in the Philippines particularly, these independent Chinese churches were isolated from the indigenous churches and were being further isolated by independent evangelists. He expressed his conviction that all these countries needed "Biblically-grounded, theologically-trained, ecumenically-minded leadership—a leadership with a genuine evangelical passion to guide the churches to keep Christians from being led astray by every 'wind of doctrine' that comes their way." He also noted that among the Presbyterian and Reformed churches there was a "rather strong tendency toward a somewhat extreme form of Congregationalism."[5]

Anderson and Smith became convinced that the real need of Chinese Christians in South East Asia was for a better-educated ministry and that the critical problem was how to train such a ministry, particularly since each country had its own unique needs. For example, they noted that Burma had perhaps 300,000 Chinese, of whom 30,000 were in the city of Rangoon. The Methodist church in that city had 616 Chinese members and 980 others, mostly from the Karen ethnic group. The Insein Theological College relied mostly on part-time teachers because the student body was so small. There were so many different ethnic groups in Burma that Smith and Anderson thought any minister who expected to work there needed an education that would include exposure to a variety of regional ethnicities. The theological college at

4 Ibid., 4-5. Serampore, about sixteen miles upriver from Calcutta, was the site at which pioneer Protestant missionary William Carey had established a mission and college.

5 Ibid., 10-11.

Insein would welcome a Chinese teacher, and Smith believed David Yu might be an appropriate candidate if he would agree to go there. Yet Smith also reported that it seemed likely that the country would eventually fall under Communist rule.[6]

Smith and Anderson reported that the situation for theological education for Chinese in Thailand was "the most unsatisfactory of all the countries we visited." Thailand had perhaps three million Chinese, of whom about a thousand were Christians. They were organized into twelve churches, three of them in Bangkok. This thriving Christian community did not need money, but it did need Chinese-speaking clergy. Local social conditions worked against producing a Chinese-speaking clergy there, since most Chinese families preferred to educate their sons in Chinese-language elementary schools, with the result that they could not compete effectively with Thais for places in secondary schools where the language of instruction was Thai. Without secondary school education, it was impossible for Chinese students to attend McGilvary Theological Seminary in Chiang Mai. Some of the Thai Christians seemed unaware of this problem, and the Thai director of the Bangkok Christian College, a middle school, told Smith he would reserve three places at his school for Chinese boys who wanted to study for the ministry, though Smith was unable to say whether that was being done. Smith added that Prince Royal Academy, a Christian middle school in Chiang Mai, might also be able to help, but its language of instruction was also Thai. As a result of this language problem, Smith wrote, many Chinese Christians there sent their sons to a lower-level Bible college in Bangkok, which taught them middle school subjects in Chinese. This was contrary to government policy, however, and the practice was attacked by the government shortly after his visit.[7]

Smith proposed a variety of possibilities for responding to the educational needs of Chinese Christians in Thailand. He thought it might be best to send prospective ministers for Chinese churches in Thailand to Singapore for high school education instead of trying to establish a school for them in Thailand. But this plan would be complicated, since the students would be required to return home once a year to maintain valid residency. Smith suggested that perhaps mature Christian men could be given a year's course and trained as pastors for these churches. He added that McGilvary Theological Seminary had

6 Ibid., 12-15; C. Stanley Smith to Frank T. Cartwright, Singapore, February 8, 1952, ALW.

7 Anderson and Smith, *Report*, 15-20.

only two full-time faculty members, a foreign teacher who headed the school and one Thai professor. All other faculty members worked part time. Smith recommended that the Board of Founders hire a Chinese professor for them and provide scholarships for Chinese students, provided this could be accomplished without violating Thai law. He added that Rajah Manikam, a distinguished Indian theologian and East Asian secretary of the World Council of Churches and the International Missionary Council, had said that, while the Christian church in South East Asia was generally weakest in Thailand, the Chinese churches there were the strongest.[8]

Smith and Anderson visited Singapore but no other places in Malaya. They noted that the majority of Singapore's population, about 80 percent, was Chinese. The Chinese born in Singapore tended to speak Mandarin, but many preferred their dialects, and church services were commonly conducted in dialects. Trinity College's courses were taught in English, but there was demand for a Chinese course that they had opened in 1951 with the assistance of Frank Balchin from the London Missionary Society and John Lu from the English Presbyterian mission. Lu had received education at Princeton Seminary, and Frank was formerly a missionary in China. Most of Trinity's students were part time and were teaching in Christian or government schools to finance their studies. Smith judged that most of these students wanted teaching careers, not careers in the church, but he thought there would be more applicants committed to church work if adequate scholarships were available to cover expenses. If scholarships were inadequate to cover full expenses, Smith argued that students should be given four years to complete the course rather than the three then permitted.

Smith painted a rather sad picture of academic standards at Trinity. Most of the students devoted only fifteen to seventeen hours a week to their studies, and one person close to the college told Smith the classes were "so elementary that it took no effort to get through [them]." Few students were enrolled in theology courses. Additionally, since most of the faculty was part-time, there was little contact between faculty and students. Nor was the school yet ecumenical. Smith described it as "thoroughly Methodist." Only two students came from other denominational backgrounds. Smith believed that other denominations needed to participate in the program. In spite of all of these problems, Smith and Anderson recommended that the Board of Founders provide substantial aid to Singapore's Trinity College, though

8 Ibid., 16-17.

not to the exclusion of assisting other institutions. The leaders of Trinity College looked favorably on establishing a relationship with the Board of Founders, and Smith favored the board entering into a three-year agreement with Trinity to strengthen it, improve its physical plant, assign Nanking Seminary missionary faculty to teach there, and join in the work of its Board of Governors. He hoped that the theological course it then offered could be extended for an additional year or two, that it could offer the B.Th. and perhaps even the B.D. degree, and that eventually Trinity might become a center for theological education in South East Asia. In Singapore Smith met with C. S. Leung, a leader in the Chinese Christian community, who also urged that the Board of Founders distribute its resources among the countries that most needed aid rather than investing all resources in a single program. Smith agreed with this judgment.[9]

Anderson and Smith also visited Indonesia, which, Smith observed, was an area difficult for Americans to understand because there had been "so little [American] mission work carried on there." He reported that they were welcomed warmly by Indonesians, Chinese, and the Dutch. Most of the Chinese they met were from the Xiamen area of Fujian Province and spoke the Hokkien dialect. A Council of Chinese Churches there participated in the National Christian Council of Indonesia. Smith preached at the Ketapung Chinese Church, probably the largest in Jakarta, which had been established by American Methodists. Pouw Le-gan, a seventh-generation Chinese in Indonesia and a Methodist, interpreted into Indonesian. The congregation of about one thousand "understood English and some [Mandarin] Chinese but apparently they all understood Indonesian." The following week he preached at a church of four to five hundred in Bandung where Pouw's father was pastor, and again his sermon was translated into Indonesian. Smith wrote that 60 percent of the Chinese in Indonesia were born there, but in the churches of recent immigrants they needed dialect-speaking clergy, a situation that he anticipated would probably influence theological education there for fifteen to twenty years.[10]

The position of the Chinese in Indonesia was complicated by political factors. In 1910 a Dutch law made those born in Indonesia Dutch subjects but not Dutch citizens. At the time of Smith's visit, the government was requiring Chinese to register at their consulates

9 Ibid., 20-30; C. Stanley Smith to Frank T. Cartwright, Hong Kong, March 10, 1952 ALW.

10 Anderson and Smith, *Report,* 31-32.

or automatically become citizens of Indonesia. Many recent Chinese immigrants hesitated to register because, they believed, the Communist government had "extorted large sums from overseas Chinese." Smith reported additionally that there were secondary schools for Chinese, but many had recently had their textbooks seized by the government because of content sympathetic to communism. He added that Communist literature was sold openly in Chinese bookstores and that Communist Chinese newspapers circulated in Indonesia as they did in all the other countries which had recognized the People's Republic of China.[11]

Smith advised that if missionaries planned to work in Indonesia, they "should make it one of their main concerns to avoid increasing tensions or fomenting new ones. Tensions do exist and will undoubtedly continue to exist for a generation at least." He noted there were about three million Christians in Indonesia's population of seventy million. Two and a half million of these were Protestants. The Christians were located primarily in two areas: the Minahasa region in the northern Celebes, where the population was 90 percent Christian, and the Batak region of northern Sumatra, which was 50 percent Christian. Only 1 percent of the population of Java was Christian.[12]

Though there were fewer American missions there than elsewhere in South East Asia, American Methodists had been engaged in mission work in Indonesia since the early 1900s. The Christian and Missionary Alliance had been in Borneo for several decades, and the Salvation Army had been in north central Celebes for several years.

Protestant churches in Indonesia were of two kinds: ecumenical and sectarian. The ecumenical groups federated with the National Christian Council of Indonesia. Sectarian groups distanced themselves from the council. Among the latter group, many had been established recently by American missions. For example, the Southern Baptist Convention recently had obtained permission from the Ministry of Religion to commence work in Java. Some thirty autonomous groups federated with the Indonesian National Council. These included the Batak Church, 600,000 members; the Protestant Church of Minahasa, 360,000 members; the Protestant Church of Timor, 280,000 members; the Malaku Church of Amboina, 200,000 members; the Nias Church on an island off the west coast of northern Sumatra, 175,000 members; the Sangi-Talaud Church on the islands in the northeast corner of

[11] Ibid., 35.
[12] Ibid., 38-39.

the archipelago, 100,000 members; and the Irian (West New Guinea) Church, 100,000 members. The smaller groups numbered from 1,726 to 80,000 members; and four Chinese groups together numbered 14,000 members.[13]

The Dutch colonial government controlled mission work strictly, and overlapping efforts were not permitted. At the time of the Anderson and Smith visit, the Ministry of Religion, in cooperation with the National Christian Council, determined the area in which each mission was permitted to work. Smith reported that the ministry had wanted the council to approve the proposal of the Southern Baptist Church, but it had been reluctant to do so because the Southern Baptist Church was not an ecumenically minded church, and the council preferred approving the United Church of Indonesia, which was affiliated with the World Council of Churches. Also, the National Council did not wish to see the colonial pattern of ministry control of mission activity continued. The Southern Baptist Church finally received its permission, but William Decker, secretary of the International Missionary Council (IMC), had written a letter to the Ministry of Religion stating that the National Christian Council did not endorse the work of the Southern Baptist Church. Consequently, there were hard feelings on both sides. Smith was uncertain as to whether Southern Baptist mission activity would be restricted to a specific area.[14]

Smith reported that the National Christian Council of Indonesia was a council of churches, not a council of all Christian institutions. Members were appointed by church judicatories, and there were members neither from missions nor from groups like YMCA, YWCA, or Bible or literature societies. The council had no relations with mission boards; rather the judicatories of individual churches worked with mission boards and made their own decisions as to whether they would accept mission funds and personnel and how those resources would be used.[15]

Since the council had no coordinating functions, Smith wrote that mission groups wishing to work in Indonesia would have to make contact directly with individual churches. While this was an impediment, Smith discouraged mission efforts to strengthen the National Council since he believed that such efforts should come from the "grass-roots."[16]

13 Ibid., 39-40.
14 Ibid., 41-42.
15 Ibid., 42.
16 Ibid., 44.

With regard to the Chinese churches in Java, Smith reported that they were

> vigorous, growing, prosperous bodies living a full life of worship, activity, and service....Pouw gives credit for "the present vigour and growth" of the Chinese- and Indonesian-speaking churches in large measure to the ministry of itinerant evangelists from China, evangelists like John Sung, Leland Wang, Dzao Sze-kwang, etc. It is very interesting, and worthy of further study, that these foot-loose evangelists from China who, in other parts of Southeast Asia, have been such divisive influences as to have done in many cases apparently, more harm to the Chinese churches than good, have yet in Indonesia apparently been such constructive forces.[17]

Smith attributed the positive influence of the itinerants here as opposed to their more controversial influence elsewhere to unique cultural characteristics. He specified:

> the better integration of the Chinese churches into the general Christian life of the nation; 2) the sound, Biblically-grounded, theologically-inspired religious education which the Dutch and other European missionaries have given to the churches under their care; 3) the equally sound, Biblically-grounded and theologically-inspired education which the Dutch controlled and generally staffed theological seminaries have given to the ministers of Chinese as well as Indonesian churches.[18]

Theological education in Indonesia was conducted in Bible schools, usually based on primary school preparation; medium theological schools, requiring lower secondary school graduation; and higher theological schools, requiring graduation from secondary school for entrance. However, Smith reported the absence there of a seminary fully comparable to Nanking Theological Seminary or the seminaries in India, which granted the B.D. degree. In fact, he wrote, the only such school in South East Asia was in Manila.[19]

However, Smith regarded the Higher Theological College in Jakarta as offering the best theological program in Indonesia and one very nearly comparable to that of Nanking Seminary and the stronger Indian seminaries. "It may in reality be nearly equal to the B.D. degree

17 Ibid., 46.
18 Ibid.
19 Ibid., 46-47.

grade," he wrote. A two-year preparatory course was required for admission to the regular theological course because of the "general lowering in the standards of the secondary school education." He added that the two-year course was "largely devoted to linguistic and Biblical studies, the regular course of the school required three years in residence; to this is added a year of supervised field work, half of which has to be done in a local church." Considering all aspects of this program including the preparatory studies, Smith believed that the program at Higher Theological College ranked with Nanking's B.Th. degree, which required five years' study beyond the middle school.[20]

Smith expressed concern that there was only one Indonesian professor at Higher Theological College in Jakarta; all others were Dutch or other Europeans, and instruction was in Dutch "though German and Indonesian may also be used." A single course in English was offered, and instruction in Dutch was becoming an increasing problem. Students no longer wished to study Dutch, and one Chinese leader claimed that in another year the students would not know enough Dutch to handle the courses at Higher Theological College. Additionally, the seminary was totally financed by a Dutch endowment and controlled by the Dutch. The churches were welcome to contribute funds and board members to the school, but only one church was then doing so. Smith thought some Indonesian church leaders would have liked to have had control of the school under the Indonesian churches through the National Council but "fear[ed] lest the lower educational background of many of the Indonesian pastors who would probably serve on a church-elected governing Board might seriously lower the educational standards of the school." Even more sensitive was the fact that the Indonesian churches could not finance the school, which then had an annual budget of about $2,500, and hesitated to ask the Dutch for the endowment. Smith believed the larger problem was that of language. Professors taught in Dutch, with which many students were unfamiliar. Some of the professors could lecture in English, but it seemed unlikely that many students would have adequate English language skills for study in the near future. While the professors might learn Indonesian, Smith thought that would not be easy. Therefore, Smith worried that "the standard of theological education at HTC seems to be in serious danger of being lowered considerably."[21]

Regarding the problem of theological literature, Smith noted a serious lack of such materials in either the Indonesian or Chinese

[20] Ibid., 47.
[21] Ibid., 47-48.

language. The head of the Christian Literature Society of Indonesia had shown him some fine Dutch books but said few had been translated. Positively, there appeared to be no serious theological conflict between the Dutch Reformed Church and the more conservative Christian Reformed Church, both of which were conducting mission programs in Indonesia. The Christian Reformed Church controlled the seminary. Smith thought that a grant of $1,200 would assist it in translating some valuable works into Indonesian or Chinese, adding that he had been told that "there had been a promise of a contribution from America to the [Christian Literature Society] but that none had been received."[22]

Rajah Manikam had told Smith that the medium level theological schools or, in some cases, the Bible schools were most important for the Indonesian churches. He recommended assistance for the theological school at Jogjakarta, but only if it united with a nearby school at Malang. Later Smith and Anderson discovered there was little likelihood of such a union. However, after visiting the school at Jogjakarta "at the earnest request of the school authorities," Anderson and Smith recommended grants to it. They were convinced that this school would probably be more effective in training Chinese for the ministry of Chinese churches than would the Higher Theological College in Jakarta. They noted that classroom instruction at Jogjakarta was conducted mostly in Indonesian and thereby avoided the language problem that plagued the Jakarta institution.[23]

Smith recognized that language constituted a major problem for the Chinese churches throughout South East Asia. In Indonesia the language of instruction in most theological schools was Dutch, while in the Philippines, Singapore, and Thailand it was English. Trinity College in Singapore had a Chinese Department, and the seminary at Chiang Mai had begun a Thai language course. While young Chinese were increasingly learning the language of the country in which they lived, parents still wanted the young to study Chinese in anticipation of a return to the homeland. As a result, Chinese were reluctant to master additional languages. In Indonesia, Smith doubted that the Chinese would learn Dutch or English, so it would be difficult for them to matriculate in a theological school that did not offer instruction either in Chinese or Indonesian. Smith and Anderson believed that theological schools that enrolled Chinese students should have at least one Chinese-speaking missionary or Chinese person on the faculty to assist Chinese students in resolving their language difficulties.[24]

22 Ibid., 48-49.
23 Ibid., 49.
24 Ibid., 49-50.

The report discussed the development of a new theological school at Makassar in southwestern Celebes, which was then operating in makeshift quarters in Timor. Various mission boards had promised $100,000 for the school, and thirteen churches were cooperating in it. Once the school moved to Makassar, the Dyak Bible School in Borneo expected to unite with it. The Makassar School offered a medium level theological curriculum requiring higher middle school completion for admission and offering a four-year course in theology. Since it required the entrants to take a one-year preparatory course focusing on linguistic and introductory Bible study, the curriculum could be considered a five-year one. In the fall of 1951 it enrolled seventy-four students, mostly married men but a few women as well. The school hoped to admit twenty-five new students each year, and admission required recommendation by a church. The school had five full-time missionary teachers, four part-time ones, one full-time Indonesian teacher, and two part-time ones. The head was Dutch, but he was eager for an Indonesian to lead the school and also wanted an American missionary to supervise field work. There had been some question as to the appropriateness of the site chosen for the new school, but the governor, a Muslim, wanted it built there.[25]

Anderson and Smith reported that there was great interest in theological education in Indonesia. The first finding reported from a theological conference held in Bandung in January 1952 was that "churches must give their full attention to theological education." Indonesians attending the conference wanted theological schools founded by the churches and answerable to them, and they wanted assurance that certificates awarded to students reflected real learning. They also wanted to establish a way by which students of "outstanding academic ability" who finished a middle school could be prepared for study in a theological college.

> Here the conference was trying to meet the vexed problem that confronts all theological schools: how to deal with the student who has not had an adequate pre-theological education on which to erect his theological structure and tries to overcome this difficulty by seeking degree after degree from theological schools where he generally studies more and more of the same subjects with little broadening of the basis on which he began to build.[26]

25 Ibid., 50-51.

26 Ibid., 52. In the unpublished version of this report, Smith noted, "I write this after having just talked with a theological teacher-student from one

The manuscript version of the *Anderson-Smith Report* to the Board of Founders concluded with comments on government accreditation and the production of theological literature. It also proposed a conference on theological education in South East Asia and suggested that such a meeting be held in Singapore or Bangkok under the auspices of the International Missionary Council, the World Council of Churches, and the Committee for the Production of Literature for Overseas Chinese. Anderson and Smith asked the board to provide $3,000 for the travel expenses of those who attended.[27]

As theological educators in South East Asia learned of the interest of the Board of Founders, they sought support. Theodore Runyan, for example, who had recently taken a faculty position at Trinity College in Singapore, pointed out that there were fifty thousand Protestant Christians on the Malaysian Peninsula of whom forty thousand were Chinese. Most of the clergy had been trained outside the country, several of them at Nanking Theological Seminary, but they were no longer able to meet the needs of the rapidly growing church. Furthermore, most of the clergy had received only a superficial education. Runyan added that Trinity College had been established to remedy the situation but that the three churches supporting it were unable to provide adequately for its needs. The most pressing needs at the college were for housing, staff, and scholarship aid. The school had three buildings: a men's hostel; a women's hostel which also contained the library, chapel, refectory, and classrooms; and a third building then under renovation at the cost of $13,000 with a loan from the Methodist church. It would contain the Chinese Department, staff, library, and classrooms. Runyon explained that the school needed additional funds to cover its debt but felt that it had been essential to proceed with renovation, since the school could not function without a Chinese Department, which required the additional space.[28]

Runyan also advised the Board of Founders that the twenty-one courses then being offered were being taught by eighteen different people

---

of the younger churches who has already attended five theological schools of varied levels in three different countries and who is now seeking aid to enable him to try another seminary before he returns to his position in a theological college that is crying for his assistance to meet the teaching load. He is, of course, pursuing the *ignis fatuus* of an advanced theological degree. It will be interesting to see whether the theological school of Indonesia will be able to work out any new solution to this vexatious problem," Smith, "A Report on Theological Education," 38.

27 Smith, "A Report on Theological Education," 39.

28 Theodore Runyan to BF, Singapore [n.d., 1951-52?], ALW.

and that they were relying heavily on "local ministers, missionaries, and school masters to come in and teach a course each on a voluntary non-remunerative basis." The three full-time teachers were all Methodists: the principal, who taught church history and homiletics, administered the school, and had other administrative duties assigned by the church; a woman missionary, who taught two courses in religious education, was dean of women, librarian, and matron of the women's hostel; and Andrew K. T. Chen, who taught advanced Chinese and the history of Israel in the Chinese course, supervised the men's hostel, and received $75 per month from the college. Runyan added that the London Missionary Society had promised to send a full-time person at mid-year.[29]

Runyan observed that neither Chinese nor Indian families thought it necessary to support children in study for the ministry and generally preferred to see their daughters married well and their sons engaged in profit-making work. Therefore, theological students generally received no support from home. Churches could offer little scholarship assistance after meeting their own operational expenses. Consequently, students were required to support themselves, and most did so by full- or part-time jobs as school teachers. He recognized that this was primarily a problem of the church but did not believe that a solution could be found at that time. Trinity was compelled to turn away some students because there was no financial aid for them. He noted the existence of a strong system of church-operated, grant-in-aid schools in Malaya offering Christian education but explained that they too were in need of qualified teachers. Runyan concluded that he hoped that Trinity would become known as the Chinese vernacular college of the region and asked if it might affiliate with the Board of Founders for three years to inaugurate its programs.[30]

After the conclusion of the Anderson-Smith study, Smith met with the Board of Founders at a special meeting May 7, 1952, to summarize the study's findings and recommendations. The board had written to various schools in South East Asia prior to the Anderson and Smith trip in order to explain the purpose of their visit. When their travel had to be postponed for several months, the board, in a move that would foreshadow its relationship with these institutions in the years to come, decided to send some of them small grants as an indication of its sincerity. Smith reported that this gesture had been very wise and "was especially appreciated in Jakarta where there had been a number

[29] Ibid.
[30] Ibid.

of surveys carried out by visitors from American Mission Boards, some promises made and little realization of the promises." When he and Anderson had met with the Board of Curators of the Higher Theological College in Jakarta, its chair had introduced them by saying, "It is a pleasure to introduce representatives of an organization that acts before it speaks." Smith believed that these grants had prepared the way for them and "was part of the reason we were so warmly welcomed wherever we went."[31]

Smith informed the board that the native churches primarily served animistic peoples like the Karen of Burma and the Minahasas and Bataks of Indonesia, while the Chinese churches were generally vigorous and needed little assistance except in the area of education. Especially in Thailand, there was need for secondary education for the Chinese youth who were interested in ministry. The churches would welcome missionaries with experience in China who spoke Mandarin or one of the dialects of southeast China that were common there. Smith's report included a census of population and church membership in South East Asia:[32]

Country	**Tot. Pop.**	**Protestant**	**% Prot.**	**Chin Pop**	**Chin Prot**	**% C Prot**
Burma	17 m.	312,500	1.91	300,000	800	.27
Thailand	25 m.	15,000	.06	3 m.	1,000	.033
Malaya	6 m.	50,000	.83	3 m.	40,000	1.35
Indonesia	80 m.	2.5 m.	3.1	2 m.	16,000	.8
Philippines	20 m.	400,000	2	200,000	8,000	5.8
Total	**148 m.**	**3.2775 m.**	**2.2**	**8.5 m.**	**65,800**	**.77**

Smith believed that even though the percentage of Chinese who were Protestant was less than the Protestant percentage of the overall population, the Chinese community would be especially open to Christian evangelism. "The very forces of nationalism, fear, and prejudices that are tending to separate the Chinese from the native populations are making the Chinese in their insecurity, anxiety, and isolation open to the friendly approach of Christian missionaries,

31 C. Stanley Smith, "Summaries and Recommendations from the Report of the Study of Theological Education in Southeast Asia" [1952], 1, ALW; Minutes, Special Meeting, BF, NTS, May 7, 1952, FTEA.

32 Ibid.

especially if they can speak even a little Chinese, and of Chinese pastors," he wrote, adding that the number of Chinese-speaking missionaries and Chinese clergy in all of the countries was "pitiably small."[33]

Smith suggested that the Board of Founders could assist the Chinese Christian communities in South East Asia in solving their leadership problem. He appeared to see board work in this area as a logical extension of its work with Nanking Theological Seminary. In the past, he observed, the Chinese churches of the region had sometimes found pastors from Nanking Seminary. More generally, they had previously given little thought to pastoral preparation, since they could rely upon China-educated leadership. With a new situation in China, they were discovering how difficult their leadership problem had become, particularly in Thailand where the language barrier made it all but impossible for Chinese to obtain a high school education, a precondition for study at McGilvary Seminary in Chiang Mai, the only theological school available to them within the country. Elsewhere, in Indonesia, Burma, the Philippines, and Singapore, language was also a problem for Chinese students who often did not have adequate English or, in the case of Indonesia, Dutch language fluency for the theological course. Trinity's Chinese Department in Singapore would certainly help address the problem there. Another concern was that the theological schools in South East Asia did not have alumni among the local Chinese pastors, and a gulf of misunderstanding often existed between churches and schools.

> This gulf of misunderstanding and distrust was sometimes created and more often widened by the carping criticism of the institutions by the free-lance evangelists coming from China or Hong Kong. All too often also the sources of trouble were the pastors invited from China who had graduated from Bible Schools or Fundamentalist theological schools of lower grade which stressed particular modes of baptism as essential to salvation or emphasized literalistic, Pentecostal, or millennial interpretations of Scripture. In all fairness, it should also be said that sometimes the theological schools were partly to blame for this distrust.[34]

[33] Ibid., 3. Smith noted in the report itself that "perhaps the most outstanding characteristic of the five countries included in our Study was the increasing jealousy, resentment and suspicion of the Chinese on the part of the nationals in these nations," Anderson and Smith, *Report*, 84.

[34] Smith, "Summaries and Recommendations," 4.

In every country except Indonesia, they had found among the churches this type of distrust of the theological schools "established and controlled by the more ecumenically-minded Missions and Churches." In the Philippines, the Chinese churches were fundamentalist and were unwilling to send their students to the "liberal" theological schools. They seemed to want a separate Chinese faculty of their own choosing at the seminaries, as well as separate facilities. Smith hoped that the migration to the Philippines of some of the Reformed Church in America missionaries from the Xiamen area in China would resolve this problem, for these missionaries were conservative but not fundamentalist and strongly supported church union. Realistically, however, Smith did not expect rapid change.[35]

In Thailand where the only available seminary was McGilvary Seminary, a Presbyterian school in Chiang Mai, this problem of distrust was acute. Smith reported

> distrust of the very "sound" Presbyterian Theological Seminary at [Chiang Mai] on the part of many in the Chinese churches... [which] had been aroused by the bitter theological controversy which has existed...within the Presbyterian Mission...and ha[d] been heightened by the attitude of certain Chinese pastors and Bible School teachers from China.[36]

In Singapore, Smith found that those of Presbyterian background were distrustful of Trinity College. In Indonesia, while such distrust was minimal, language was a primary barrier to Chinese participation in the theological schools. In the entire region except for Indonesia, very few Chinese had ever graduated from a theological school. In Indonesia, the Jogjakarta seminary had been founded in 1934 and, of its sixty-two graduates, twenty-five were Chinese. These graduates served Indonesian-speaking Chinese churches. Currently, only at Trinity College was there a significant Chinese enrollment, and most of the Trinity students probably would not become clergy.[37]

Smith reported that Chinese preparing for church careers in South East Asia frequently enrolled in the Bible schools of the region. For example, in the Philippines many Chinese were enrolled in the Bible schools around Manila, which were generally operated by the less ecumenically minded churches though, Smith observed, some

35 Ibid.

36 Ibid.

37 bid., 4-5.

ecumenical churches were considering creating such schools "in self-defense." These Bible schools were generally "either independent, though often receiving financial aid from churches abroad or [had been] established by Pentecostal and Millennial sects, the China Inland Mission, Oriental Missionary Society, Christian and Missionary Alliance, or...the Seventh Day Adventists." Smith added that such schools were increasing in number and that there were many new ones in Taiwan. He saw them as a challenge to the survival of ecumenically minded Protestantism among Chinese Christians. "These ex-China sects are not sparing either funds or personnel in their efforts to capture the overseas Chinese in Southeast Asia and they have a fair chance of success. If they do it will be a serious blow for the ecumenical movement."[38]

Yet the Bible colleges were not all cut from the same cloth. Smith observed that some of them were doing a good job. The Chinese Bible School at Bandung offered an evening program in theology taught by Dutch teachers for men and women working during the day that "would have done credit to a good theological seminary." In Singapore, the China Inland Mission was planning a school that Chao Tsz-kuan, "one of the most outstanding of the Chinese evangelists," hoped to lead. Smith wrote that he "has ambitions for making it into a theological seminary." In Bangkok, the Chinese Bible School accepted students with only six years of primary education, that which the government allowed to be offered in the Chinese language. In the Philippines, they found six Bible schools in the Manila area, one of which had been founded by American veterans who were members of the Pentecostal Baptist Church in America. The school appeared vital. It had a radio station, and its student body included five or six Chinese. Unfortunately, it refused to cooperate with any nonfundamentalist churches. While Smith and Anderson found several Chinese students in this school, there was only one in the Union Theological Seminary at Manila, the strongest theological school in the Philippines. In summation, Smith reported that the situation was "not a very encouraging one in some ways so far as theological education for overseas Chinese is concerned" and that the situation would prove "very challenging." He wondered if the Chinese could find ways to make use of the existing schools and if these schools could find ways to offer courses in a vernacular that Chinese students could handle."[39]

38 Ibid., 5.
39 Ibid.

Smith believed that the Board of Founders could best assist in addressing the leadership problems of Chinese churches in South East Asia by offering scholarships for theological students and, in Thailand, by offering scholarships at the secondary school level to prepare students for theological study. He hoped the board would encourage the Baptists to strengthen the school at Insein, Burma, and the Presbyterians to do the same at the McGilvary Seminary in Chiang Mai, Thailand. Even though neither school had Chinese students at that time, they were willing to accept them, and Smith urged the Board of Founders to give both schools grants for the current year, since both had theological education programs consistent with the board's policy. Smith was encouraged by the fact that these two schools were willing to make adjustments to train Chinese, and in any event both were located in countries with significant Protestant leadership needs. However, he thought that after the 1952-53 year, further grants should depend on their attracting Chinese students.[40]

The immediate issue before the Board of Founders, according to Smith, was whether the financial resources of the board and the missionary faculty from Nanking Seminary should be used to underwrite establishment of a theological school in Asia offering the B.D. degree to Chinese who wished to prepare for ministry or for teaching in theological schools. He believed that an early return to Nanjing was quite unlikely and that there was no question as to the need for well-educated Chinese theological teachers to work in the existing seminaries. If the Board of Founders established a school, Smith believed the board should support the former Nanking Seminary missionary faculty or ask the participating mission boards that had previously supported them to continue doing so in order to keep the faculty together. Such a school should not be limited to Chinese students, but their needs should have highest priority.

Of the existing schools in South East Asia only two, Union Theological Seminary in Manila and the Higher Theological College in Jakarta, taught at a level approaching that of Nanking Seminary and the best Indian seminaries. Union Seminary awarded the B.D. degree on the authority of its own Board of Trustees but was so lacking in faculty that B.D. students shared classes with B.Th. students, who had only high school educations prior to matriculation. As to the possibility of strengthening instruction for Chinese, the Philippine government refused to allow any Chinese into the country, even if requested by the

40 Ibid., 9-10.

churches. The Higher Theological College maintained a high standard of education, but its use of Dutch as the language of instruction made it inaccessible for Chinese students. If the college were to teach in English, some college-educated Chinese students could attend, but if it offered instruction in Indonesian, few Chinese could enroll. Smith believed that the seminaries in Thailand and Burma were not sufficiently advanced to be considered for major Board of Founders support. He believed that Trinity College in Singapore might be a likely candidate for Board of Founders support, but it would require a great deal of funding, and the British societies might not welcome such assistance from America. The Lutheran Seminary in Hong Kong did not wish to cooperate with an ecumenical and interdenominational institution. It would welcome some non-Lutheran students and faculty but would insist upon Lutheran church control of the school.[41]

Reflecting on the situation he and Anderson had found in each of the countries they visited, Smith thought the Board of Founders might wisely continue to make small yearly grants to the schools throughout the area and attempt to integrate former Nanking Seminary missionary personnel into the faculties of regional schools as they were needed to fill vacancies, replace faculty members on leave of absence, etc. In order accomplish these goals, Smith thought the board should consider establishing an office in the region to "promote and coordinate" information from this region and consider ways to help the Chinese Christian community. He believed it would be helpful for a board representative to continue making short visits to South East Asia from time to time. A South East Asian office could also promote the production and distribution of theological literature in the area and act as a clearing house for requests from the region's theological seminaries.[42] Such an office could also support planning for the proposed South East Asian Conference on Theological Education, which had been endorsed by the Conference on Theological Education that met in Bandung, Indonesia, in January 1952 and by the faculty of Manila's Union Theological Seminary.[43]

41 Ibid., 6-7. Smith added that he had earlier raised the possibility of Honolulu, but no one on the board appeared interested in that site.

42 Smith, "Summaries and Recommendations," 9-10. The latter suggestion had also come from a conference on theological education in South and South East Asia that had been held at Stony Point, N.Y., in November 1951.

43 Ibid.

Smith advised that, should the Board of Founders proceed to establish an office in South East Asia, it should consider factors such as the ease and cost of travel about the region, the areas with the greatest need for teaching or counseling assistance, the availability and cost of housing, the need for assistance in promoting better integration of the Chinese community into the ecumenical church, the centrality of local theological schools in relation to the strategy for theological education in the region, and the best locality for the use of the language of the director, either Mandarin or a Chinese dialect. Considering all these criteria and all possible locations, Smith concluded that the choice was between Singapore and Manila with Singapore "somewhat more favorable."[44]

Smith also identified the four people he viewed as potential directors to staff such an office. They were Francis Jones, then directing the Literature Production Program; Herbert L. Sone, engaged in graduate study at the University of Chicago; Samuel H. Moffett, who had been working for the Presbyterians in Korea; and himself. He was awaiting assignment from either the Presbyterians or the Board of Founders. Smith added that Sone was eager to return to Asia for theological teaching and preferred Singapore.[45]

Following Smith's presentation, the Board of Founders took steps toward granting support to many of the institutions visited by Anderson and Smith. The preamble to each proposed grant declared that it was being "made pursuant to the Board of Founders' policy of fostering theological leadership for Chinese churches and upon recommendation of the Committee on Extension." The board also voted to continue the Literature Production Program by establishing a translation center at Drew University, to appoint a special committee "to consider the advisability of establishing a separate institution for higher theological education outside the mainland of China," to authorize the appointment of a representative of the board for South East Asia, and to commence negotiations with mission boards regarding the appointment of the four NTS missionary faculty now in the United States to the work of NTS, perhaps in separate center or centers."[46]

At this same meeting, Lloyd S. Ruland resigned from the board and was replaced by Dr. J. LeRoy Dodds. To replace Ruland as chair, Dr. H. P. Van Dusen was elected. The board also voted to invite the

44 Ibid.
45 Ibid.
46 Minutes, Special Meeting, BF, NTS, May 7, 1952, FTEA.

Reformed Church in America to cooperate with the board and to inform the Canadian Presbyterian Church of the board's interest in Taiwan and to express hope for that denomination's continued cooperation. Finally, the board went on record supporting the proposal for a conference on theological education in South and South East Asia to be scheduled for 1953.

At the annual meeting of the Board of Founders on May 26, 1952, the first grants were awarded to theological seminaries in South East Asia based on the recommendations of Smith and Anderson. The grants, all of which were under $5,000, were mostly for libraries, scholarships, and Chinese faculty salaries and were made to the Baptist English Divinity School, Insein, Burma; McGilvary Theological Seminary, Chiang Mai, Thailand; Higher Theological College, Jakarta, and Jogjakarta Theological School, Indonesia; Union Theological Seminary, Manila, and College of Theology, Silliman University, Dumaguete, Philippines; Lutheran Theological Seminary, Hong Kong; Theological College, Taipei, and Tainan Theological College, Tainan, Taiwan; and Trinity College, Singapore. Trinity College also received $25,000 for a building, and Serampore Theological College in India was granted $500 for the protection and translation of early Indian mission documents.[47]

Other awards went to Liang The-hui, a faculty member of Tainan Theological College in Taiwan and a Nanking Seminary graduate, for study at McCormick Theological Seminary in Chicago, for a series of theological textbooks under production in India, and to the Christian Literature Society of Indonesia for translation of Dutch theological literature into Chinese and Indonesian.[48]

The *Anderson-Smith Report* had posed a number of perplexing questions that were considered at the meeting, including: "May we give scholarships to non-Chinese students? How should grants for translation projects be handled? Should they aid the Bible School in Bangkok?" These were discussed, along with the more general questions of support for Bible schools and theological schools that were operating at the undergraduate or even the precollegiate level but that the *Anderson-Smith Report* indicated were providing greatly needed education for Christians in South East Asia. The Board of Founders also received a report from Francis Jones regarding the Literature

47 Minutes, Annual Meeting, BF, NTS, May 26, 1952, ALW. Grants were awarded based on the "Recommendations to the BF for grants to Theological Seminaries and other projects in South and Southeast Asia, Arising Out of a Study of Education in these areas by Dr. S. R. Anderson and Dr. C. Stanley Smith, December 1951-April 1952."

48 Ibid.

Production Program. The program had finished translating nine works, had another nine partially complete, and had twenty-one people working on other books.[49]

The Board of Founder's committee on extension recommended the initiation of a legal study of its situation in light of current conditions in China. The committee recommended establishing a separate institution outside China and appointing a director of extension to deal with the institutions in South East Asia. It recommended that the four Nanking Seminary missionary faculty members then in the United States, Jones, Moffett, Smith, and Sone, be sent to other theological seminaries or assigned to translation work. It also decided to circulate the *Anderson-Smith Report*.[50]

Comments were received from various Board of Founders members and former missionaries once the report was circulated. H. A. Poppen, a former Reformed Church in America missionary who had worked in Taiwan, thought Smith was in Indonesia too short a time to understand all of the problems there and that he had met only those who would cooperate with the Board of Founders. Poppen thought Union Theological Seminary in Manila "should be further explored with a view to fuller cooperation" but concluded that "Trinity College in Singapore presents a very interesting opportunity and [is] the best bet of them all." Poppen also thought that the emphasis on support of Bible schools might be good, as "I do not think the Chinese are too interested in the theology end of the whole problem." As Chinese were finding restrictions on movement from place to place, he thought that "it would be logical to develop in more than one area."[51]

Abbe Livingstone Warnshius, a member of the Board of Founders, suggested that a Chinese instructor should be placed at Insein in Burma and that there should be a "somewhat greater emphasis on the idea of integrating these Chinese churches and Chinese people in the life of the country, instead of developing a sect or a colony. Has not our American church life and service been weakened by the perpetuation of language-churches?" With regard to British missions' support of Trinity College, he wrote, "I know the British boards are financially straightened," but he added that both the London Missionary Society and the English Presbyterians had evacuated their China missions. He recommended that Smith return to London "to try to work out a real

49 Minutes, Annual Meeting, BF, and Francis P. Jones, "Report of the Translation Project," May 26, 1952, FTEA.

50 Minutes, Annual Meeting, BF, NTS, May 26, 1952, ALW.

51 H. A. Poppen to A. L. Warnshuis, Kalamazoo, Mich., June 17, 1952, ALW.

united support for the college in Singapore. It is just too easy for them to think that Nanking has lots of money, and so they need not worry. Too easy money may be their ruin."[52]

By late summer in 1952, the Board of Founders was beginning to take action in response to the changed conditions in China and suggestions in the *Anderson-Smith Report*. Van Dusen visited seminaries in South East Asia and reported at an executive committee meeting June 23, 1952. At that gathering the committee voted to begin providing support for three of the missionaries in the United States, Francis P. Jones, C. Stanley Smith, and Hubert L. Sone. The committee also invited Smith to become the Board of Founders representative in South East Asia beginning July 1. The committee recorded that "the Special Committee considering the advisability of establishing a separate institution expressed the judgment that the time is not ripe for deciding this question...."[53]

At a special meeting on September 12, the board adopted a motion to extend its work to "any purpose contributing to Christian theological education in China, or in... Asia and...the western Pacific..., and for educational assistance to Chinese and other Far Eastern students preparing in these and other lands for the ministry or other services in the Christian Church...because of conditions existing in China." The board authorized its officers to petition the Regents of the State of New York for an amendment to its charter and submitted the legal forms that its legal representative, Harold Harper of Harper and Matthews, thought necessary. This amendment to the charter was granted on November 21, 1952, adding the following statement of purpose:

> and to receive and disburse funds: (1) for any purpose contributing to Christian theological education (a) in China, or (b) in areas of Asia and of the Western Pacific beyond the confines of China, and (2) for educational assistance to Chinese and other Far Eastern students preparing in these or other lands for the ministry or other services in the Christian church when the said corporation shall deem the same advisable because of conditions existing in China.[54]

Seeking further clarification of the founders' legal situation, an approach was made through the Division of Foreign Missions of the

52 A. L. Warnshuis, "Some notes on...Smith's report," July 7, 1952, ALW.
53 Minutes, Executive Committee, BF, NTS, June 23, 1952, FTEA.
54 Minutes, BF, NTS, September 12, 1952, and May 25, 1953, FTEA.

Board of Missions of the Methodist Church to the Surragote's Court of the County of New York. That body on March 16, 1953, issued identical decrees regarding the bequests of Rebecca A. D. Wendel Swope and Ella V. VonEchtzel Wendel directing that the monies bequeathed "for maintenance of the Nankin Theological Seminary at Nankin, China" should be paid to Nanking Theological Seminary, a New York educational corporation.[55]

At the meeting initiating these legal actions, the Board of Founders also noted that Smith would go to Bangkok, working half time for the board and half time for his denomination.[56] Promptly after Smith's arrival in Bangkok, he was urged to accept the presidency of Trinity College. Its board of governors asked him to assume the post as of January 1, 1953, for a three-year term while the governors searched for someone to assume the post permanently. They also asked for Board of Founders assistance in locating a permanent president.[57] Smith agreed to accept the appointment but could not do so immediately; therefore, for the interim, Sone served as acting president of Trinity College.[58]

Upon arrival in Bangkok, Smith began to function as the South East Asia representative of the Board of Founders. In one of his first letters to the board, Smith expressed surprise that churches in Taiwan expressed interest in locating a seminary there, since little interest had been expressed the previous year. He believed that, since there were already two theological schools on the island, there would be little justification for the Board of Founders to support a third, particularly as he did not believe that churches in Taiwan were any better prepared financially to support a minister with a B.D. degree than had been the churches in mainland China.[59]

Smith forwarded a request to the Board of Founders for $1,000 for support of a pastors' conference in Indonesia and expressed the opinion that the grant should be made only if Chinese pastors were included in the meeting. He expressed concern that, if all legal restrictions on the Board of Founder's use of funds were removed, it would receive constant requests such as this one. In the same letter Smith reported that he had gone to Indonesia and again visited the

55 Frank T. Cartwright to BF, New York, August 11, 1952; and Minutes, BF, NTS, September 12, 1952, both ALW.; Minutes, BF, NTS, May 25, 1953.

56 Minutes, BF, NTS, September 12, 1952.

57 Robin Woods to Frank T. Cartwright, Singapore, October 4, 1952, ALW.

58 "President's Report," *Sophia: The Magazine of Trinity College Singapore,* 1 (1953), 3.

59 Smith to Frank [Cartwright], Bangkok, January 7, 1953, ALW.

Bible school in Jogjakarta. He believed it was "of a much higher grade than the average school of this type would be in China" and found five Chinese students enrolled. He found the general view of church leaders in Jakarta to be that the church in central Java was conservative but not fundamentalist and that it was liberal in its acceptance of biblical criticism. The impression Smith gained was that it was "scholarly, conservative, [and] orthodox in the best meaning of that word." Both the Chinese and the Indonesian churches in the area were growing and were integrated into community life.[60]

Upon his return from Indonesia, Smith visited Singapore and met with Sone and Runyan about the presidency of Trinity College. Smith agreed to accept the position but insisted on the condition that he could retain his position with the Board of Founders. He also reported to the board following this meeting that Trinity had increased its full-time faculty and, as a result, had been able to enrich its curriculum. The renovation of the old building had been completed, and it now housed residences as well as classrooms and social rooms for the Chinese Department. Smith reported an improved relationship between the college and the Chinese churches with Presbyterian connections. Smith remained concerned about reliance entirely on the Methodist board for funding, about the school's entrance requirements, and about the inadequate scholarships that compelled students to be employed while studying. Yet he thought these problems would be resolved in time.[61]

Meanwhile, in the People's Republic of China, Nanking Theological Seminary had been reorganized as Nanjing Union Theological Seminary in 1952. Upon Smith's departure, Andrew C. Y. Cheng, newly returned from graduate study at Hartford Seminary, reluctantly accepted the presidency, a post he held until reorganization. In the immediate aftermath of the Communist victory in 1949 and governmental reorganization, a struggle ensued among factions of the Protestant community as to how the church should relate to missions and to the government. With the entry of the United States into the Korean War and the subsequent expulsion of missionaries from China, those who advocated greater autonomy for the Chinese church prevailed. The Chinese Protestant church committed itself to the "Three-Self Principles" of self-support, self-administration, and self-propagation. Independent Chinese Protestant churches had long existed, and therefore a model already was available for the reorganization of church life apart from the Western missions.

60 Ibid.
61 Ibid.

However, there were no seminaries or Bible schools in China that had been self-supporting or had the resources to become self-supporting either in terms of faculty or of fiscal resources. Thus, an immediate and critical question arose as to how the Chinese Protestant church would educate its leadership. Nanjing Union Theological Seminary, having enjoyed the support of several major mission boards as well as the Swope-Wendel fund, was clearly the strongest Protestant seminary in China and had finally consummated the long negotiated merger with the Bible Teachers' Training School (BTTS), a women's Bible school located on a campus adjacent to the seminary and previously supported by some of the same mission boards. A reforming committee of the church in late 1951 completed the merger and consolidated the two schools on the BTTS campus, relinquishing the seminary's campus and residential properties to the government.[62]

Y. T. Wu, then president of the China Christian Council and chair of the Three-Self Patriotic Movement, convened a meeting in Shanghai in 1952 to address this critical issue of leadership education in the church. There it was agreed that twelve schools, thirteen if one considers Nanking Seminary and BTTS as separate institutions, would be merged in Nanjing under the name Nanjing Union Theological Seminary. Anglican Bishop K. H. Ting, who had recently returned to China from study and work in North America and Europe, was named principal of the united seminary. The schools that merged into the reorganized Nanjing Union Seminary constituted a remarkable array of denominational and theological traditions, including liberal and conservative Presbyterians, Southern Baptists, Anglicans, and others. It opened in the late fall of 1952 with two vice presidents, Andrew Cheng, the former president of Nanking Seminary and a theological liberal, and Ting Yu-chang, formerly at North China Theological Seminary and a theological conservative, and with parallel curricula under a policy which the principal termed one of "mutual respect."[63]

62 Interview of Professor Chen Zemin of NTS by Samuel C. Pearson, Nanjing, July 1, 2005. Chen had been educated at the Shanghai campus of NTS during the years 1941-44 and served as a hospital chaplain after his graduation. He returned to the seminary in 1950 to teach history of Christian thought. Though retired from administrative duties, Chen continues to teach and advise students at NTS.

63 Ibid.; Frank W. Price to Frank T. Cartwright, Richmond, Vir., January 24, 1953, ALW. The Chinese name for the reorganized seminary is Jinling Xiehe Shen Xueyuan, Jinling being a traditional name for the city of Nanjing. The Pinyin form of Ting's name is Ding Guangxun, but prior to the introduction of the Pinyin system, he was widely known in the West

Dr. Frank Price made a report to the Board of Founders' meeting of May 25, 1953, based upon information he had received from President Ting.[64] However, little detailed information on the reorganized seminary was available to the board at this time, and the board continued to focus its attention elsewhere in South East Asia where Smith, as its regional representative, continued to provide the board with information and requests for assistance.

Smith strongly urged that any scholarships granted by the Board of Founders in South East Asia should be given to or through specific schools, which would then be responsible for the students. He had received several requests from the Higher Theological College in Jakarta, and one concerned scholarships for non-Chinese students. When he and Anderson had been asked about this the previous year during their visit to Indonesia, they had responded that, for legal reasons, the Board of Founders could make grants only to Chinese students. This year in Jogjakarta, D. C. Mulder, a Dutch missionary teacher at the seminary there, again asked if some scholarship funds could not be used for non-Chinese students. Mulder

> thought that too rigid restriction to Chinese might create bad feeling and undo much of the good we were trying to do. Trusting that the court might liberalize our use of the income a bit, I told Dr. Mulder that he might use one scholarship for non-Chinese. After I told him this I wondered whether I had done right in making this concession so kept quiet when they raised the same question again in Jakarta. I think that their feeling that it is a mistake to make a too rigid application of the scholarships to Chinese is a sound one. It makes for jealousy and bad feeling against the Chinese. If we can legally moderate this regulation a bit, I think it will be wise to do so. I would still keep the large majority of scholarships for Chinese to carry out the intention of the donor but I would not make them exclusively so.[65]

Smith reported to Cartwright that the Board of Founders scholarships given to students studying for the ministry at Higher Theological College in Jakarta had resulted in a significant increase in the enrollment of Chinese there. However, as a result of this increase,

as K. H. Ting and continues to use that form in relations with Christians outside China.

64 Minutes, Annual Meeting, BF, NTS, May 25, 1953, FTEA.

65 C. Stanley Smith to Frank T. Cartwright, Bangkok, February 25, 1953, ALW.

the school no longer had adequate housing facilities and had asked for a grant of $10,000, half the cost of building a new dormitory. Smith inquired as to whether it would be possible to make a grant for the building and, if it were, recommended a grant of $7,000 or $8,000. If the board could not assist with construction costs, he would not grant the additional six scholarships, since the school would have no housing for the students.[66]

Once the legal uncertainties related to the use of the Swope-Wendel funds outside of China were resolved, the Board of Founders began to formulate a new policy for itself. At the annual meeting of May 25, 1953, C. Stanley Smith submitted his report as field representative, and Dr. E. L. Smith, a member of the board, presented a draft proposal which, after further study, was adopted at the following annual meeting.[67]

This policy document stated, "It shall be and is the policy of the Board of Founders of Nanking Theological Seminary, in accordance with its amended charter, to use the funds at its disposal in places of major need or strategic importance for the strengthening of Christian theological education in Asia, recognizing however special responsibility for eastern and southeastern Asia." The board would give attention to the needs of Chinese communities and Chinese students. It would continue support for the translation project. It would provide grants for theological students to pursue advanced study outside their homelands, with preference going to those from union schools but, under special circumstances, to those from denominationally sponsored schools. The board would balance its grants among translation, scholarships, and operating and capital expenses.[68]

Smith's report covered his first six months in Bangkok. Though he was supposed to divide his time equally between the work of the Board of Founders and that of the Presbyterian Church, Smith wrote that he actually spent 80 to 90 percent of his time on Presbyterian Church work. Yet much that he had learned would prove valuable in his work as regional representative of the Board of Founders. He had learned some Thai language, and this had broken down some barriers between himself and Thai Christians that arose out of existing tensions

66 Ibid.

67 Minutes, Annual Meeting, BF, NTS, May 25, 1953, FTEA.

68 Minutes, Annual Meeting, BF, NTS, May 25, 1953, FTEA; Proposed Text of Policy for the BF of NTS, Draft of November 3, 1953, ALW; the policy statement was adopted at the Annual Meeting, BF, NTS, May 27, 1954, 1954, FTEA.

between Chinese and Thai communities. The Thais knew he had lived in China and was in Bangkok to study the problems of the Chinese there.[69]

In Thailand Smith discovered that there were leadership problems not only in the Chinese church but in the Thai church as well. He wrote that Thai Christians would make few converts from Buddhism until they had a better trained leadership. Many of the smaller and more sectarian Christian groups that had been active in China were then in Thailand, and they emphasized evangelization rather than institutional work. Smith thought that "it will be interesting to see whether this direct approach to Buddhism on its lower levels will be any more effective than the institutionalized approach of the Presbyterian mission. Personally," Smith continued, "I think it will fail largely because of lack of educated leadership which can approach Buddhism on its higher levels."[70]

Smith's observations regarding the problems of developing an educated Chinese clergy reinforced concerns already expressed in the *Anderson-Smith Report*. Among the Chinese, there was a problem of lack of secondary education. Only Bangkok Bible Center admitted students with no more than a primary education. The Christian high schools were making available more places for Chinese students, but the number of Chinese students who possessed the Thai language skill required to attend was quite small. There were only thirty-three Chinese students at the Bangkok Christian College, a high school. Yet without a secondary school certificate, no one could hope to attend McGilvary Theological Seminary in Chiang Mai. Smith doubted if many of the students at the Bangkok Christian College would actually be able to meet admission requirements at the seminary.[71]

The Thai church appeared to face a major problem in convincing young men to enter the ministry. McGilvary Seminary had graduated only five students from the four-year course in the previous year. The grants from the Board of Founders for a Chinese teacher and Chinese students there had not been used because such people simply could not be found. Smith thought that further Board of Founders grants should be for audiovisual equipment and a refresher course for pastors. He also recommended that a missionary or a national, preferably a national, be trained in comparative religion so that the approach to Theravada Buddhism might be made by someone knowledgeable concerning that

69 C. Stanley Smith, "Report of the Field Representative in Southeast Asia to the BF of NTS," Bangkok, 1953, ALW.

70 Ibid.

71 Ibid.

tradition. He added that he thought Singapore was the place where the education of Chinese clergy was most likely to take place.[72]

During the first six months in Bangkok, Smith had received reports from various institutions in the region, many of which he had visited. Fairly typical was a report from C. H. Hwang, principal, and Boris Anderson, vice principal of the Tainan Theological College in Taiwan, which was a seminary of the Presbyterian Church of Taiwan.[73] They reported eighty-three regular students, five full-time, and seven part-time faculty members in theology as well as two full-time faculty members in religious education. Tainan Theological College had used its Board of Founders grants to renovate the library, which had a collection of two thousand volumes, and to remodel an old hospital compound into a men's dormitory, dining hall, and music room. The scholarship grant was used to give forty-eight students five dollars each month for food. A refresher course for pastors, which had proved quite popular, was offered with board funds. Tainan Theological College reported that it trained pastors for the southern synod of the Presbyterian Church of Taiwan and for work among aboriginal tribes. It was responsible for supplying 142 churches, but 22 were then lacking pastors. Each year the synod added six or seven new congregations through its program of evangelization. Most of the college's students needed financial aid. Few were from wealthy families, and "a fair proportion are sons of ministers," but the school claimed to have turned away no student for financial reasons. Since 1948 it had required graduation from senior middle school as a prerequisite for admission, and in that year it had extended its course from four to five years. It had begun a Religious Education Department, which admitted eight women for a two-year course in kindergarten teaching, since "many of the city churches run week-day kindergartens, and are badly in need of trained staff." Tainan college asked the Board of Founders for a grant to enable it to give each graduate a library of twelve books including commentaries, a Bible dictionary, and a concordance as a nucleus for a personal library. It also requested books for the Taiwanese staff. The *Anderson-Smith Report* had commented on the weakness of the staff, and the college hoped to remedy that situation by sending two or three of its faculty abroad for advanced graduate education.[74]

[72] Ibid.

[73] Hwang was also known as Ng Chiong Hui and as Shoki Coe, an Anglicized version of his Japanese name. Most sources refer to him as Hwang, and that is the form used in this text except in quoted material.

[74] C. H. Hwang and Boris Anderson, Report on TTC, Taiwan, April, 1953, ALW.

In submitting his recommendations for funding for the forthcoming year, Smith mentioned the difficulties of mail service in the region and the fact that some requests never arrived and had to be resubmitted. At the time of writing, he had still received no response from the school in Jogjakarta but asked that its $2,100 grant be renewed, for he had visited the school in December and observed that it was doing good work with both Indonesians and Chinese. Smith indicated he would hold the grant until he received a report on the expenditure of the previous year's grant.[75]

Smith also suggested that the Board of Founders consider grants to denominational schools under some circumstances. He pointed out that there were two types of such schools. Some, like the Baptist Divinity School at Insein, Burma, and the two Presbyterian theological colleges in Taiwan, prepared clergy primarily for their own churches. However, there were other denominational and interdenominational schools which, while mission controlled and supported, trained ministers for national churches that were union churches. Schools in this category included the Higher Theological College in Jakarta, the Theological School in Jogjakarta, and the McGilvary Theological Seminary in Chiang Mai, which was the theological school of the Church of Christ in Thailand, though it received most of its support from the Presbyterian Church.[76]

In South East Asia, Smith noted there were really only two union institutions—Union Theological Seminary in Manila and Trinity College in Singapore—and he thought there should be no question about continuing to aid them. In Indonesia and Taiwan where Chinese students were enrolled in theological schools, he felt the Board of Founders should continue to offer assistance even if the schools were operated under the auspices of a single denomination. However, Smith had reservations about indefinite support for the schools in Burma and Thailand, since they were denominational schools and "seem to be unable to attract Chinese students or secure a Chinese member for their faculties." Smith did not advocate immediate termination of aid for these schools but rather making reduced grants for 1953-54 and advising them that in the future the Board of Founders could not support schools in which no Chinese were enrolled. With respect to the Thailand situation, the American Baptists and Disciples of Christ cooperated with the Presbyterians in the Church of Christ in

75 C. Stanley Smith, "NTS Requests for Grants 1953-54," Received May 13, 1953, ALW.

76 Ibid.

Thailand, but only the Presbyterians funded the theological school. He thought the Board of Founders should encourage all cooperating denominations both to assist in supporting the seminary and to make a more substantial effort to recruit Chinese students as a condition of receiving board funding in the future, even though he recognized that the recruitment problem was complicated by the fact that few Chinese students possessed proper educational credentials for admission.[77]

Smith's specific recommendations for 1953-54 funding from the Board of Founders included a grant to the Baptist Divinity School, Insein, Burma, for Chinese and English library books, audiovisual equipment, a lay leadership course, and a refresher course for pastors. Chen Hsu-yong, who was the pastor of Rangoon's Chinese Methodist Church and husband of the headmistress of the Methodist Chinese High School, where he also taught, was recommended for $250 to complete the final year of his theological education. He held a B.A. in education from Peking University and had completed two and a half years of study at the Shanghai Bible Seminary before he fled the Communists. He had been recommended by the East Asian secretary of the WCC, and Anderson and Smith had met him during their earlier visit to the region.[78]

Smith recommended that McGilvary Theological Seminary in Chiang Mai, Thailand, receive a grant for the library, audiovisual equipment, a refresher course, and scholarships for Chinese students. Smith recommended that the previous salary grant for a Chinese professor be canceled, with the understanding that the Board of Founders would entertain a special request for such funding if the seminary could locate a Chinese faculty member. Higher Theological College in Jakarta, Indonesia, was recommended for scholarships for Chinese and non-Chinese students and for half the cost of a new dormitory needed because of the increase in the number of Chinese students. Smith noted that the seminary had not requested funds for the salary of its Chinese faculty member, Pouw Le-gan. He recommended that the board set aside $1,500 for this item but not publish the grant until he could learn more about the situation. He justified the request for non-Chinese scholarships with the observation that

> the question of granting scholarships for non-Chinese has been frequently raised in Indonesia and elsewhere. There is fear lest the grant of a scholarship exclusively to Chinese may

77 Ibid.
78 Ibid.

> cause jealousy and bad feeling against them on the part of the other nationals. I think there is some justification for this fear, especially in Indonesia, but it would also be true in Thailand and the Philippines. I would recommend, therefore, that in making grants for scholarships this year in Indonesia, we include a few for non-Chinese.[79]

For the Theological School at Jogjakarta, Indonesia, Smith recommended a grant for a Chinese professor to teach Chinese history and culture, for library books, and for scholarships for Chinese and non-Chinese students. For the Presbyterian Theological College in Taipei, Taiwan, a grant was recommended for books and scholarships. Tainan Theological College in Taiwan was recommended for funds for library, for "as many [scholarships] as possible," for a refresher course, for scholarships for faculty study in the United States, for book grants for teachers and graduating students, and for buildings. Smith wrote that this school had seventy students and an income of $8,776 composed of $2,300 from the Board of Founders, $4,600 from local churches, and $1,876 from England, adding that "this is the most remarkable showing of local support for theological education that I know of on any Mission Field." Smith added that, except for its failure to be a union institution, this school came closest to being the kind for which the Board of Founders' legacy had been intended. Smith also recommended a grant of $800 for the Lutheran Theological Seminary in Hong Kong.[80]

The College of Theology at Silliman University in Dumaguete, Philippines, was recommended for a grant for library and scholarships for Chinese students, but only if it had used the previous year's grant. Union Theological Seminary in Manila, the other Philippine school, was recommended for a grant to cover the salary of a Chinese professor, for Chinese student scholarships, for a refresher course, and for scholarships for agricultural work. However, some of these grants were renewals of unspent grants committed the previous year.[81]

Trinity College in Singapore was recommended for significant grants. It had received $25,000 for construction of a building, and Smith wrote that he believed Sone had sent a report on that project to the Board of Founders, but he had not received a copy and therefore could not comment. Sone's request for the forthcoming year was for

79 Ibid.
80 Ibid.
81 Ibid.

scholarships, the library, and the salaries of two Chinese professors. Sone indicated that Trinity needed scholarship funds for the full year, since the overseas students from Borneo, Sumatra, India, and Hong Kong could not gain summer employment and could not afford to return to their homes during the summer break. Trinity had only one full-time Chinese professor, and Sone believed it would need more if it was to attract Chinese students. That year Trinity had enrolled twenty-eight students, nine in the Chinese program and nineteen in the English.[82]

Sone forwarded the minutes of a meeting of Trinity's Board of Governors to the Board of Founders, and those minutes revealed that Trinity had closed the Music Department because it had only one student, but Mrs. Sone was teaching piano to nineteen students so that they would be able to play simple hymns for religious services. The minutes also indicated that the college was strengthening its entrance requirements. Students were required to have graduated from a senior middle school or to present a Cambridge certificate for admission to the three-year course leading to the Licentiate of Theology. Students lacking these requirements could take the course, but they would not receive the degree. The board had decided to reject students without the necessary qualifications as well as those who wanted to enroll part-time, live in their hostels, and teach or study at other schools, since these students overtaxed the facilities and "often create other problems for the College." There were then five full-time faculty members, four missionaries and one Chinese, and nine part-time volunteers, four Westerners and five Chinese. Fifteen students came from the Methodist church, seven from the Presbyterian, seven from the Missouri Synod Lutheran, five from Anglican churches, and one from a Baptist church.[83]

The importance of the issue of libraries for South East Asian theological seminaries was underscored in early 1954 when Cartwright returned from a visit to South East Asia, reported to a special meeting of the board, and then drafted a longer report to all Board of Founders members. After a visit to Silliman University in 1953, H. P. Van Dusen had suggested that the Board of Founders might assist the theological schools in the region by sending a professional theological librarian to consult and offer a workshop. Smith was asked for his views but did

82 Ibid.; Hubert L. Sone to Frank T. Cartwright, Singapore, April 16, 1953, ALW.

83 Minutes, Board of Governors of Trinity College, Singapore, March 6, 1953, ALW.

not have a strong recommendation. He believed the library at Union Theological Seminary in Manila was in very good shape and that the Higher Theological College library in Jakarta was catalogued, though he added, "I doubt very much whether [the cataloguing system] follows anything that would be intelligent to an American-trained librarian." The library at Trinity College in Singapore had been catalogued, but the general library service there was not good because the library did not have dedicated space but was in a hallway through which students had to pass going to meals and classes, no one was in charge, and anyone taking or returning a book simply recorded it in a notebook. The library at McGilvary Seminary in Chiang Mai was in a separate room, but Smith did not know if it would welcome someone coming there to work on it. The Baptist Divinity School in Insein, Burma, which had been rehabilitated with a Board of Founders grant, had a cataloguing system, but Smith did not have specific information regarding it. He thought the theological seminary at Silliman University and Trinity College could profit from a librarian's visit and that others might welcome such a visit.[84]

Smith moved from Bangkok to Singapore in December 1953 to assume the presidency of Trinity College. From Singapore he reported in April 1954 that he had met in Bangalore with Rajah Manikam and Marcus Ward, who suggested holding a conference on Asian theological education. They were considering a small conference in Singapore at the end of the year. Participation was to be limited to those who were actually engaged in theological education in the region.[85]

Smith also forwarded requests from various theological institutions for Board of Founders' support. Most wanted renewed funding for projects the board had supported the previous year. However, Union Theological Seminary in Manila was asking for salary for a qualified Chinese professor, a proposal which Smith endorsed, though he noted the school had only two Chinese students. With regard to the Tainan Theological College request, Smith wrote that he thought C. H. Hwang, the principal, believed in "ask and thou shalt receive" but added that Hwang generally asked for appropriate things and made better use of Board of Founders grants than some of the other institutions. Smith therefore recommended that Tainan Theological College be given $10,000 to help defray its building costs.

84 Minutes, Special Meeting, BF, NTS, January 8, 1954, FTEA; Frank T. Cartwright to BF, New York, February 19, 1954, ALW.

85 C. Stanley Smith to Frank T. Cartwright, Singapore, April 5, 1954, ALW.

He also suggested that the board should not continue granting the school $200 for books for its graduates unless other schools were advised that they, too, could request such grants.[86]

Smith had visited the theological school in Jogjakarta again on a recent trip to Indonesia and expressed some ambivalence in his report to the Board of Founders. On the one hand, the school had lower academic standards than the board would like, but on the other, Smith reported that he found good cooperation between the Chinese and non-Chinese there. The school did not yet have a full-time Chinese teacher, but it had secured a part-time one who taught Chinese history and culture. The school offered a five-year course beyond junior middle school and had a good relationship with the local church. Ten Chinese students were then enrolled, and Smith believed that, since the number of Chinese students there was growing, the Board of Founders was wise in continuing its policy of aiding Chinese students with scholarships.[87]

Smith praised the policy of the Presbyterian Theological College in Taipei, which gave scholarships only to students in actual need and required that they do satisfactory academic work and a certain amount of manual labor for the college while receiving aid. He hoped he would be able to implement such a policy at Trinity College asking, for instance, that scholarship students assist in the library.[88]

Though Smith was then in Singapore, his annual report to the Board of Founders in May 1954 reviewed the year he had spent in Bangkok working half time for the board and half time for his church. He had visited Taiwan, Singapore, Sri Lanka, India, and Burma during the year. He had also drafted a constitution for the Board of Directors of McGilvary Theological Seminary in Chiang Mai, though the principal of that school had been on furlough for the year and Smith had not been able to discuss the draft with him. Smith observed that the seminary lacked adequate facilities and well-qualified candidates for the ministry and reflected "the general weakness in leadership and number of Christians in the whole church in Thailand." There seemed little chance for a more ecumenical approach, since the Presbyterian mission had been in Thailand for nearly a century and was well-established while "the Church of Christ in Thailand is too weak to run a good Seminary alone." He noted some progress in providing opportunities for Chinese to attend secondary school in Thailand, but these efforts had not yet produced any candidates for the ministry, a

86 C. Stanley Smith to Frank T. Cartwright, Singapore, April 29, 1954, ALW.
87 Ibid.
88 Ibid.

situation Smith described as "extremely frustrating." He did report positively on his contacts with Theravada Buddhist leaders and his participation in a YMCA consultation on Buddhism in Kandy, Sri Lanka, in November 1953.[89]

Smith expressed his pleasure at having returned to academic work, as it gave him a better perspective on what the schools needed, adding that such perspective "makes a great difference in one's judgments or criticisms." He added that he would probably appraise Trinity College "somewhat differently after seeing it from the inside for four months, though on the whole our judgments in 1952 were very sound. The problems, if anything, on closer experience with them, seem more acute."[90]

Smith observed that his work at Trinity College was his first in a union enterprise that was "international as well as inter-denominational and which is an attempt to work in unity by those with an Anglican background and those with a free church tradition." Most of the property of Trinity College belonged to the Women's Board of the Methodist Church in the United States, and, since it was extremely difficult to incorporate in Singapore, Smith doubted that Trinity College could do so. Without being incorporated, the college could not own property or hold investment accounts, and this became a problem when the college received grants from the Board of Founders for capital improvements. However, he thought such grants could be given to the Methodists and an agreement reached with them, since Sone was the secretary of the Methodist property committee and made the final decision on such questions. If such an arrangement were reached, Smith recommended a $40,000 grant to Trinity College for capital use.[91]

Smith commented in his report on the difficulties of movement about the region. He had been able to fly from Singapore to Jakarta and Jogjakarta for less than $100, but it was difficult for a resident alien to enter and leave Singapore, as he had to report his movements to the government. However, he had obtained a year's permit to return to Singapore. He also commented on the red tape involved in gaining a tourist visa to Indonesia. As a result of friendship with an official in charge of such visas, Smith had been able to receive one in only two days instead of the normal six weeks to two months and at the nominal cost of $15 Straits. The Indonesians were skeptical regarding the likelihood of a missionary spending much in their country, but Smith did support

89 NTS, Report of Field Representative in Southeast Asia, May 5, 1954, Singapore, ALW.

90 Ibid.

91 Ibid.

their economy by "replenishing some Jogja and Bali works of art that I had purchased on my first visit and had given away to relatives and friends as Christmas presents."[92]

In Jakarta, Smith had met with various missionaries as well as the secretary of the National Christian Council of Indonesia, Wilhelm Johanis Rumambi, concerning the proposed conference on theological education. He discovered significant differences in vocabulary among those with different church backgrounds, and he thought they needed a conference to clarify the vocabulary they were using. He found the churches in Indonesia were proud of their relations with the WCC and the IMC and wanted any conference to have the approval of these world bodies. Smith wrote that he understood this concern but also thought they could convene a conference on local and regional issues without having to wait for the WCC and the IMC to approve procedures and protocol. He pointed out that he and Manikam had proposed a conference on theological education, not on the ecumenical church, and he suggested that the issue might better be discussed with the faculty of the Higher Theological College. This suggestion was accepted, and Smith paid the expenses for the principal of the Jogjakarta school to attend this meeting. He was the only person at the meeting from outside Jakarta and gave the meeting a wider scope. At the meeting, two young European missionaries, Muller Kruger and Christoph Barth, were present; and Smith judged that they were more sensitive to the issues in Indonesia than were some of the older Dutch missionaries. Plans were underway for a Christian university, and the Higher Theological College would probably merge with it if arrangements could be made to assure the seminary some independence in managing its own affairs.[93]

At the Jogjakarta school, Smith found that relations between the Chinese and Indonesians were "excellent." He had taken pictures of the student body, the faculty, and the Chinese and Indonesian recipients of Board of Founders scholarships. He had also visited Hindu temples and a mosque in the area and taken photographs that he hoped to use in a slide presentation on theological education in South East Asia. Smith reported that Jogjakarta "is the center of a region where the conversions [to Christianity] from Islam are probably the highest of any place in the world. I was told that they average around five hundred a year." He also noted a very high interest in the forthcoming theological education conference among the people he met in Jogjakarta.[94]

92 Ibid.

93 Ibid. Kruger was German, and Barth was Swiss and the son of Karl Barth.

94 Ibid.

After studying the situation of theological education in the region, Smith recommended that the Board of Founders not establish and operate its own theological school in South East Asia but rather concentrate on assisting four existing schools with capital and annual operating grants. The four Smith singled out were Tainan Theological College in Taiwan, which Smith believed should be urged to become a union college and whose principal was sympathetic to such a move; Union Theological Seminary in Manila; Trinity College in Singapore; and Higher Theological College in Jakarta. Smith recommended continuing to make smaller grants to other schools as long as they used them wisely.[95]

For the four high-priority schools, Smith recommended that the Board of Founders strengthen the faculties by giving two- or three-year grants for salary assistance for new hires and scholarships for current faculty members to encourage study abroad to advance their special fields of work. He also recommended the "assignment and support of missionary teachers upon invitation of the school authorities if such support cannot be secured from mission boards" and scholarships for prospective teachers to study abroad after two or three years in assistant positions at the schools. Scholarship grants should be based on need, good character, and scholarship, with recipients required to give some service to the school each week. Library grants should be designed to provide technical training for librarians as well as library equipment. From the Board of Founders' reserve fund, i.e., income from previous years that had not been spent when received, Smith recommended that up to $200,000 be used for capital grants to the four schools. Smith hoped that another $100,000 could be used for grants on a nonrecurring basis, special grants for library reference books, audiovisual equipment, increasing the staff by assuring salaries for a period of years, literary production by supporting temporary assignment of a teacher to produce literature, and advanced study for current staff members. Smith acknowledged that his recommendations would benefit others than the Chinese, but he thought the objectives fell within the expanded purpose of the Swope-Wendel grant.[96]

The Board of Founders considered Smith's report and recommendations at its annual meeting in May 1954. In addition to adopting the new policy proposed a year earlier "to use the funds at

95 C. Stanley Smith, "Future Program of the BF," Singapore, May 5, 1954, ALW. "It is not an accident that some outstanding schools in ATESEA today were the four prophetically singled out by Stanley Smith some fifty years ago...." Yeo Choo Lak to Samuel C. Pearson, Hawaii, April 15, 2008.

96 Ibid.

its disposal in places of major need or strategic importance for the strengthening of Christian theological education in Asia, recognizing however special responsibility for eastern and southeastern Asia," the board considered Smith's recommendation regarding selection of a few schools for special aid. The board was unable to reach agreement on this matter and voted to "continue to consider whether long range policy should be to aid many schools and students or to develop one or more theological college(s) of university grade.[97]

Francis Jones also reported at this meeting on the progress of the Literature Production Program. Participants in the program had been trying to standardize Christian terminology in Chinese. Hunt's *Theory and Practice of Communism* had been translated and sent to John R. Fleming, general secretary of the Malayan Christian Council, for publication in Singapore. Translations of the first Calvin volume and the volume by Archbishop William Temple had been sent to Hong Kong, where nine hundred paper and one hundred cloth-bound copies were being printed for $1,000. The budget for the program was $30,500, including $10,000 for salaries.[98]

Smith's Field Representative's Report, which was read at the meeting, indicated he had expended $3,710 for operation of the Board of Founders' office exclusive of his salary. Mrs. Smith was doing the housekeeping because they had been unable to keep a servant as a result of inadequate quarters. He wrote the board that he had found his servant "actually burning incense in front of her room in an effort to appease or drive out the evil spirits which had invaded her room and were making her life so unhappy." He explained that the evil spirits were "chiefly a leaky roof, a concrete floor through which the water seeped in the heavier rains and bad odors from a toilet nearby. We have had these matters taken care of we hope and are now trying to find another servant who is either a Christian or is willing to brave the haunted condition of the quarters."[99]

The South East Asian conference proposed by Smith and others proved to be even more controversial than he had expected after his trip to Indonesia. He wanted to hold a small, regional conference to discuss issues of particular interest to people involved in theological education. However, a great deal of opposition was expressed as news of the plans spread. Much of the opposition centered on whether it was appropriate for the Board of Founders' representative to convene such a meeting or

97 Minutes, Annual Meeting, BF, NTS, May 27, 1954, FTEA.
98 Ibid.
99 Ibid.

whether it should be held under the auspices of the IMC or the WCC. Many also believed that it should involve representatives of all of the churches concerned, rather than just those involved in theological education. As a result, the conference was never held.[100]

After the failure of Smith's initial effort to sponsor a conference on theological education in Asia, the Board of Founders convened a meeting in Williams Bay, Wisconsin, April 9 and 10, 1954, to discuss the general question of theological education in South East Asia as well as the possibility of holding a conference there. The meeting was scheduled to coincide with the Evanston, Illinois, assembly of the World Council of Churches in order to reduce travel costs and assure maximum participation of people involved in this work. Invitations were extended widely to those involved in Protestant theological education in South and South East Asia, and participants came from Taiwan, Indonesia, India, the Philippines, Thailand, Hong King, and Singapore. Raymond Maxwell represented the World Council of Churches and Charles Ranson the International Missionary Council. C. Stanley Smith participated as the Board of Founders' field representative, and eight members of the board participated.[101]

Rajah Manikam presented an introductory statement in which he acknowledged that other aspects of Christian education might be taken over by governments but asserted that theological education could not be. He also observed that government assistance was available for other types of education but not for theological education, while the latter was very expensive since there was a low student-faculty ratio at seminaries. Except in India, Japan, and the Philippines, there was no standardization of theological education, a situation which "makes for much initiative and individuality, but little coordination or unity." Manikam continued that in South East Asia there were four models of theological education: British, Continental, American, and local adaptations. There were also different types of schools. Generally, the theological schools accepted students after middle or high school and provided four to six years of education. Theological colleges accepted students after four years of liberal arts study and granted a B.D. degree, but only the Philippines and Japan had this system. The region also had independent Bible schools, unrelated to any church, which were generally operated by fundamentalists.[102]

[100] C. Stanley Smith, "Report of Field Representative: The Conference on Theological Education," [1954], ALW.
[101] Consultation Regarding Theological Education in Southeast Asia, Williams Bay, Wis., August 9-10, 1954, 1, ALW; Cartwright, *River,* 26.
[102] Ibid., 1-2.

H. P. Van Dusen summarized the deliberations of the Board of Founders, saying that the board could support many institutions, a few, or even one. He indicated that the board was leaning toward support for a single school. Charles Ranson and Manikam supported the plan, but, according to C. H. Hwang, principal of Tainan Theological College, who wrote about the conference years later, "it was an exciting idea which fascinated everyone, but no one apart from the 'big three' regarded it as a realistic possibility."[103] Hwang indicated that the Asians at Williams Bay favored the position taken by Smith that "the three options need not be put as three clear-cut and separate possibilities." Hwang and others believed that concentrating on one school was not practicable in South East Asia with its diverse countries and cultures; there were a few leading schools in the area which could be strengthened by extra financial help; and, while some schools were not strong, they should not be ignored when they were fulfilling strategic needs in their countries.[104]

Hwang remembered that Van Dusen spoke to him at dinner the evening Hwang had spoken in favor of the board supporting many schools in South East Asia, "half-joking and half-seriously,...'you lost yourself half a million dollars by what you said this morning. But go ahead with your application for capital grants now, for [Tainan Theological College] is definitely regarded as one of the three or four leading theological schools in Southeast Asia.'" Hwang mused that, at least, Van Dusen was not "displeased" with him.[105]

The conference provided additional evidence of the great need for ministers in South East Asia. In Thailand, it was reported there were only thirty-five ordained ministers, none of them college graduates, for seventy-five thousand Protestant Christians. India had only three thousand ordained clergy, one for every seven churches. Among all Asian countries, only Japan had a sufficient supply of clergy. Related to this problem was the fact that there were insufficient theological colleges in the region. Only one institution in Indonesia and one in Taiwan could be considered to be operating at the higher level, and there were none at this level in Malaya or Burma. Perhaps, some suggested, the academic

103 Hwang indicated that this idea resurfaced at the Bangkok Conference in 1956 where it was dubbed "Charles Ranson's Grand Idea—a Higher Theological Faculty in Asia" and then again at the Asian Institute of Theology and Culture in Kyoto in 1987.

104 Shoki Coe [Hwang], *Recollections and Reflections,* 2d ed. (Taiwan: Taiwan Church News, 1993), 218-19.

105 Ibid., 219.

demands should be adjusted in terms of the actual situation. Manikam asked if they should not recognize that middle school graduation with four to five years additional study was an appropriate goal for the present time.[106]

Smith presented an overview of theological education in the entire region. In Taiwan, the Theological College in Taipei offered a five-year course beyond middle school, had a current enrollment of forty-five students, and had forty-five full- or part-time faculty with several educated in Japan. James Dickson was the principal, and the college also operated a Bible school. Tainan Theological College, under the leadership of C. H. Hwang, offered a five-year course for middle school graduates and was more closely related to churches in the area than any other school in the region. Many of the faculty members had been educated at Westminster College in England, and Smith believed this school had "great possibilities."

Smith mentioned two schools in Hong Kong. The Lutheran Theological Seminary had moved to Hong Kong from Sheko, China. It offered a thorough course with a largely European or American faculty and had produced a considerable amount of Christian literature in Chinese. The Southern Baptist Theological Seminary offered the Th.B. and B.D. degrees, had a large enrollment, and a good faculty. He did not have information on the admission and graduation requirements for their degrees.[107]

In the Philippines, the Union Theological Seminary in Manila was patterned on American institutions, and Benjamin Guansing was president. The Theological College of Silliman University offered courses primarily for high school graduates but enrolled some college graduates. James McKinley was president. The Baptist Theological College and St. Andrew's Episcopal Seminary were mentioned, but little detail was provided.

McGilvary Theological Seminary in Chiang Mai was the one Protestant seminary in Thailand. Smith reported that it had many long-range problems, including student recruitment, placement, and finance. In Malaya, Trinity College was a union of Anglican, English Presbyterian, and American Methodist missions. It had grown from one and a half part-time teachers to five Western and one Asian teacher over a span of five years and required high school graduation for admission. To the west of Thailand in Burma, Smith reported that

106 Consultation Regarding Theological Education, 2.
107 Ibid.

the Baptist Theological School in Insein was moving toward becoming a union school and had added Anglicans and Methodists to its board of directors. At the time it enrolled fifty students, and Smith remarked that "it is important in an area where there is a great resurgence of Buddhism." Higher Theological College in Jakarta offered a six-year course beyond middle school. Other schools were at Makassar and Malang in southeast Java, an area "surrounded by Moslems;...[in which was found] the largest group of converts from Islam, 40,000." Though Smith had visited the theological school at Jogjakarta, he did not mention it in this report.[108]

As the conference participants discussed the vastly differing approaches to theological education taken in various countries of the region, the depth of the problems became evident. In Indonesia, students specialized immediately after high school, so there was a need for a lengthy, six-year program. Hwang explained that the 130 students at Tainan Theological College were required to master Mandarin, Taiwanese, Greek, Hebrew, and English; again a lengthy course seemed required. He added, "the major need is for evangelists, not theologians; the latter can go abroad to learn the traditions and heritage."[109]

Keith Bridston of the WCC observed, "There is a need for greater interchange between the theological schools within Asia. The traditional lines of communication leave total ignorance of one's neighbors." He also opined that "theological education is too much formed by Western traditions, and this perhaps is one of the reasons effective evangelists for the local churches are not produced."[110]

Van Dusen suggested that if pretheological students attended state universities after high school, the theological program might be shortened to three years. However, the students would not necessarily receive adequate preparation for theological school and might be under heavy non-Christian influence while at the university. If, alternatively, they enrolled directly in theological schools after high school, they could take some arts courses along with languages and theology. Yet, he also declared, "Unless a man has been to arts college, he is likely to get second rate arts work, and if he enters theological school directly out of middle school, he has never rubbed up against the university mind and the secular mind, so how can he speak to educated men?"[111]

[108] Ibid., 3-4.
[109] Ibid., 4.
[110] Ibid.
[111] Ibid., 4-5.

Bishop Enrique Sobrepena of the Philippines said, "The problem of meeting the urgent need for pastors and the problem of having pastors prepared for other types of groups [led] him to favor two types of theological training: one, a two-year liberal arts program, followed by theological work leading to a Th.B., and a four-year liberal arts program, followed by work leading to a B.D."[112]

Smith addressed issues related to the integration of Chinese Christians into the work of the church in South East Asia. In Indonesia and Thailand they were becoming more integrated, but in the Philippines "we find one of the most difficult places; the separateness of the Chinese has its effect on theological education. Most of the Chinese are 'self-made' and do not feel that an educated Christian ministry is worth paying for. In Malaya and Indonesia there is also a tendency to divide the Chinese from the national churches." He continued that the Board of Founders had helped some schools in the past two years, and there had been a slight increase in the number of Chinese in theological institutions; from two to eight or nine in Jakarta and from none to five at Insein.[113]

Smith presented an analysis of the challenges of theological education in the region based upon his observations. The first of these was difficulty in communication; i.e., the enormous variety of languages used in the area. Smith said that "probably no [other] area has such a communication problem." A second challenge was the preparation of students; i.e., the educational systems of the various countries did not prepare students for theological education. How, for example, can theological students study church history without some knowledge of European history? Either additional training must be provided or standards must be lowered. He favored a two-year junior college program followed by three years of theological education. He did not agree with earlier comments to the effect that liberal arts courses offered at theological schools necessarily were of lower quality. Still another issue was adequate staff. Smith said it was almost impossible to find qualified Asian teachers, since so few had appropriate educational backgrounds. If they could be found, provision of adequate compensation would be a challenge. Missionaries were supported by home boards and taught without the need for local salaries, but if Asian faculty were recruited, means had to be found for paying them. He observed, "In the west, we don't realize the demands we put on these schools; all of ours are

112 Ibid., 5.
113 Ibid.

endowed. Theological education is the field in which mission help will be needed longest." Standardization of curricula was another area of potential difficulty. "There is the problem of diversities; one must begin at the bottom, integrating the schools in any one given country, then branching out into regional areas, learning of each other's problems." The Bible schools constituted still another problem. They had lower academic standards, and Smith observed that the churches had lost control of them in most countries including Malaya, Philippines, and Taiwan, though he found "some control of them" in Indonesia. "Most of the countries want, and feel [the] importance of Bible Schools," he noted, adding that some groups [supporting Bible schools] were cooperative but that other groups were not.[114]

The issue of the Board of Founders focusing its aid on Chinese people was discussed at length. I. P. Simandjuntak from Indonesia stated that the board's emphasis on aiding Chinese constituted a problem and insisted that "quality, not race should count." Van Dusen pointed out that there were similar problems regarding other European and American scholarships that were handled through the WCC and allocated to seminaries through the national councils. However, Manikam stated that the Board of Founders needed to face this question, noting that

> if the BF were helping Chinese in Nanking, there would be no objection; but now, since that was closed, [should] it just barge in on the whole area saying our primary responsibility is for Chinese? Suppose Indians did the same? At a time when we want to pull together, this creates a picture we don't want to see, and it did not take into account the history of theological education in Asia.[115]

Manikam continued that even in Indonesia integration was not as effective as it was thought to be and that there were Bible schools there that the Board of Founders did not help. He also noted that in Thailand there were separate Bible schools for Chinese and Thais. He thought the entire question of which schools the Board of Founders assisted needed to be reconsidered in consultation with the national Christian councils and suggested that the board's South East Asia representative needed an advisory council. Van Dusen responded that "the [Board of Founders] finds itself with an inner tension, not between members of

114 Ibid, 6.
115 Ibid.

the [board], but between a concern for all these larger issues, *and* for the Christian Church in China and Chinese Christians."[116]

Conference participants then discussed the possibility of convening a conference in South East Asia, who should attend such a meeting, and from what geographical areas. Cartwright recommended that a large proportion of the representatives be from church bodies in the ecumenical movement, since the seminaries were an arm of the church. He thought the conference could accommodate up to 120 people and still accomplish its work and that at least half and preferably more of the participants should be Asian. As to location, Taiwan was first favored until it was explained that the Indonesian delegates would be unable to secure visas. At that point, either Bangkok or Singapore was recommended. An agenda was discussed, it was proposed to convene the conference in February 1956, and it was agreed that the conference would be sponsored by the IMC-WCC through their East Asia Secretariat and by the Board of Founders.[117]

Regarding other issues, Smith asked whether the Board of Founders should strengthen any one of the regional schools to offer a post-graduate curriculum. Hwang argued against this, since students wishing advanced study could receive it in Japan or Western countries. He also pointed out that only the church considered South East Asia to be a single area and that the international situation was such that any central school "would not be available to all" who lived in the region. Smith replied with the suggestion that advanced education could be offered in the form of two-month summer programs bringing together top leaders from Europe, the United States, and South East Asia. He thought the Board of Founders should fund such a program for five years to determine its value. Bishop Ralph A. Ward of Hong Kong was enthusiastic about this proposal, terming it the best idea suggested in the two days of the meeting. Van Dusen reiterated that the first priority of the Board of Founders was to strengthen existing schools but agreed that it would be easy to secure Western scholars to participate in a short course such as Smith had suggested.[118]

Smith commented that he had initially been unsympathetic to the Bible schools but had come to recognize that they fulfilled a need. Sobrepena said that need should be thought of in terms of quality, not quantity. Hwang reported that sixteen Bible schools had

[116] Ibid., 6-7.
[117] Ibid., 7-8.
[118] Ibid., 9-10.

been established in Taiwan over the previous five years and that they currently enrolled more than five hundred students. Previously he had also opposed Bible schools, but he had come to realize that they played a valuable role in evangelism. For example, they served a critical role in the Presbyterian Church of Taiwan, which was attempting to double its membership over the next ten years even though it already had thirty vacant pulpits. Therefore, for the foreseeable future, the church would depend on many part-time pastors who would not have full seminary education. He also observed that most of the seminaries had begun as Bible schools.[119]

The Williams Bay Conference was meant to be deliberative, and no effort was made to secure resolutions or findings. However, Board of Founders members at the conference decided to hold a special meeting of the board. Though a quorum was not present, they discussed a number of issues and asked J. W. Decker, an at-large board member present at this meeting, to circulate proposals to the entire membership for a mail vote. They asked that the board pay for the conference and for a later one to be held in Evanston. They also supported a request for a grant of $40,000 to purchase a house for the Literature Production Program in Madison, New Jersey, and for grants of $4,000 for a translation project in India and $1,000 to underwrite a refresher course in Indonesia.[120]

The Board of Founders received a request from Burma for clarification of the board's policy with respect to granting scholarships to married couples. Reflecting its growing awareness of the enormous diversity of circumstances throughout the region, the board returned the matter with the observation that a decision should be made at the discretion of the school concerned. Since Taiwan was the only place in which the Board of Founders was engaged where there was no overall agency through which the board could work, those present at this meeting expressed their desire that any board members attending the forthcoming conference on theological education in February 1956 should spend some time in Taiwan looking into the situation there.[121]

Smith reported that in Singapore all the churches continued to express interest in participating in the program of Trinity College. The Anglicans had recently erected a hostel for their students. The Methodists provided 67 percent of the students and covered 25

119 Ibid., 11.

120 Minutes, Special Meeting, BF, NTS, August 10, 1954, Williams Bay, Wis., ALW.

121 Ibid.

percent of the costs; Anglicans, 17 percent of the students and 13 percent of costs; Presbyterians, 14 percent of each; and the Board of Founders covered the remaining 21 percent of the college's costs. All those attending this meeting agreed that the school needed to move to quarters closer to the university.[122]

Smith reported that Union Theological Seminary in Manila hoped to move to a new campus and had approached him regarding possible funding. The board agreed to invite the seminary's Board of Governors to present its plan. A special committee was also appointed to consider conducting a two-month summer regional institute for up to fifty participants each summer.[123]

South East Asia was beginning to hold greater interest for Americans, and the Board of Founders found no difficulty in convincing American theologians to visit the region. For example, E. G. Homrighausen, chair of the Department of Christian Education at Princeton Theological Seminary, planned to visit the region, spending two weeks in Taiwan, six in Indonesia, one in Singapore, and shorter visits in Bangkok and India. When Smith learned of his plans, he asked the Board of Founders to provide some travel funds, but he also cautioned that he thought there should be more careful planning for such trips of theologians to South East Asia in the future.[124]

Paul H. Vieth, professor of Christian nurture in the Yale Divinity School, whom Smith had hoped would undertake the trip that Homrighausen made, had accepted a Fulbright grant to Japan but still was able to make a two-week trip to Taiwan and another two-week trip to Manila on behalf of the Board of Founders. In Taiwan, Vieth visited Tainan Theological College and a coeducational Christian high school. At Taichung he met Donald MacInnis, a former student of his, who showed him the campus for the new Tunghai University. He reported that many of the 2.5 million mainlanders who had moved to Taiwan with the Nationalists following the Communist victory in China's civil war had brought their churches with them, and that the missions had followed. Yet the Nationalist government took a very restrictive attitude toward Christianity. No religious activity was permitted in the military, Bible classes and chapel services were prohibited even in Christian schools, and one principal of a Christian high school had

122 Ibid.

123 Ibid.

124 Nelson Chappel to Frank T. Cartwright, n.p., October 5, 1954, and Excerpt, C. Stanley Smith to [Frank T. Cartwright], n.p., November 2, 1954, both ALW.

been told to remove a cross from the school's gate. Canadian and English Presbyterian missions had partnerships with the Presbyterian Church of Taiwan and supported its efforts toward self-direction and self-support, but other denominational missions were luring away ministers with promises of better salaries and funds for church building. The Chinese Sunday School Union was selling materials from one of the most conservative publishers in the United States. There was little leadership in Christian education on the island, and the emphasis appeared focused entirely on evangelism, not on balanced church programs and education for children and young people.[125]

Both of Taiwan's theological colleges, that in Taipei and that in Tainan, emphasized traditional academic subjects but placed little emphasis on practical training for the ministry. Both accepted students directly from secondary schools. The Tainan school had a five-year course and Taipei a six-year one, but neither offered significant liberal arts courses except in language, and neither granted a college degree. The government allowed them to operate as religious schools but did not grant them the status of colleges. Since their curricula offered so little in the liberal arts, it was difficult for their graduates to meet admission requirements of American theological seminaries. Those graduates who did go to the United States usually attended extremely conservative Bible seminaries and returned to "make a conservative church still more conservative."[126]

Vieth reported that a disproportionate amount of class time was given to Bible study; in Taipei thirty-two semester hours in New Testament alone were required for graduation. Vieth contrasted this requirement with Yale's four-hour requirement. While acknowledging the value of knowledge of the Bible, he objected that in Taiwan the excessive Bible study came at the expense of "liberal arts and the more practical training for ministry such as work in Christian ethics, social ethics, Christian education, counseling, etc." He believed that students graduating from these schools were poorly trained for pastoral ministry. He also noted the problem of duplication in instruction occasioned by dependence on ministers who came to campus for an hour or two per week for part-time instruction. Yet budgetary constraints compelled dependence on such instruction. In Taipei there were only two full-time faculty members among the twenty-six on the staff. Fifteen were missionaries who taught a course or two, and the remainder consisted

125 Paul H. Vieth, Report on a Visit to [Taiwan], November 28-December 8, 1954, ALW.

126 Ibid.

of local pastors. Of the Taiwanese faculty members, seven had been educated at seminaries in Japan and two at schools in the United States. Vieth also noted that these seminaries catered primarily to the Taiwanese. However, the Southern Baptists had opened a seminary exclusively for mainlanders.[127]

Vieth summarized the problems of theological education in Taiwan as including preparation for a time when church leaders would need to include both Taiwanese and mainlanders, preparation for addressing issues related to "liberation" of the mainland if that should occur, and preparation of a better prepared faculty. He suggested to the Board of Founders that the theological institutions should merge with Tunghai University or, at the very least, cooperate more closely with one another in offering their curricula. He indicated that he had not mentioned these recommendations to anyone in Taiwan.[128]

The Board of Founders received reports regarding other regional theological institutions in which it had an interest in late 1954. Smith wrote that Union Theological Seminary in Manila wanted to purchase land outside the city for a campus, though some questioned the wisdom of the plan. Smith recommended that the school follow the example of Nanjing Seminary: retain the seminary in the city but establish a rural station on the outskirts, where all students could receive some instruction in rural church issues and those specializing in the rural church could spend a more extended period in study. Union seminary had requested that the Board of Founders grant $150,000 for the move and said it intended to use its current property for church offices rather than sell it. Smith opposed such a grant but suggested a Board of Founders grant of $50,000 for land and some buildings for a rural center.[129]

Regarding theological education in Indonesia, Smith reported that the reorganization of Higher Theological College in Jakarta was complete. The number of professors had been increased from four to seven. One visitor had written that, at the opening ceremonies

[127] Ibid.

[128] Ibid.

[129] C. Stanley Smith to [Frank T. Cartwright], October 5, 1954; Excerpt, Winburn Thomas, [Jakarta], October 26, 1954, both ALW. Less than a year later, Benjamin Guansing wrote to Cartwright that the price of land they wanted to buy had doubled and that they were therefore requesting $150,000 for the purchase, adding that the cooperating churches were to supply some of the money. They planned to keep the other land as an endowment for the seminary, see Benjamin Guansing to Frank T. Cartwright, Manila, September 12, 1955, ALW.

September 27, "the professors in their Dutch gowns looked like a Rembrandt painting." The seminary had the right to grant degrees and might one day affiliate with the new Christian university which was then being planned.[130]

As plans progressed for a South East Asia conference on theological education, which had been discussed earlier at Williams Bay and strongly supported by Asians at that gathering, the Board of Founders suggested that it be held in February 1956 in Chiang Mai, Thailand, and that it be sponsored jointly by the IMC, the WCC, and the Board of Founders. The board wanted invitations sent broadly to people associated with regional theological institutions, churches that were members of the WCC, the national councils of churches, and the missions working in the area. It also anticipated special consultants from South East Asia and abroad and representatives of sponsoring organizations. The board suggested that each theological school send an administrative officer, a faculty member, and a member of its governing board, and that each country's national council of churches send a representative. As a cost control measure, the board expressed the hope that, wherever possible, the national council representative would also be a governing board member. The Board of Founders planned to send each participant a list of topics to be discussed and suggested that prepared papers should be distributed prior to the meeting so that study groups in each country could consider them in preparation for the conference. The board also suggested that, by late 1955, groups in each country hold small preliminary conferences followed by a national conference to discuss the issues that would form the agenda for the regional conference. Suggested topics were pretheological preparation, recruitment and maintenance of students, instruction and curriculum, textbooks and administration, faculty, departmentalization and libraries, standardization, objectives in theological education, and postgraduate theological education in South East Asia or abroad.[131]

Smith reported to Cartwright in December 1954 on a meeting he had attended in Manila in which the proposed conference was

130 Ibid.

131 Rajah Manikam and C. Stanley Smith to Secretaries of the NCCs and Councils of Churches and Principals of Theological Institutions in Southeast Asia, Reyapuram, Madras, India, December 1, 1954. See also Rajah Manikam to Colleagues, Circular Letter #5, Southeast Asian Theological Education Conference, Madras, December 17, 1954. Confirmation that the IMC would help sponsor the conference can be found in William Decker to Frank T. Cartwright, February 14, 1955, all ALW.

considered by representatives of many denominations. Smith observed that the Anglicans had a large theological seminary in the suburbs of Manila and educated clergy both for their own churches and for the Aglipayan Church, which had split from Rome and was described by Smith as "catholic, but not Roman."[132] Other representatives at the Manila conference were from the Southern Baptist Church's Far Eastern Bible Institute and Seminary, which conducted radio broadcasts from Manila and conducted a school for Chinese which had begun as a Bible school.[133] Of the Southern Baptists in the Philippines, Smith wrote:

> They are an extremely conservative group, if not indeed a fundamentalist group, and have had very little relation with the other denominations in the Philippines. There was great pleasure, therefore, in seeing them entering into this Conference on Theological Education. It is extremely interesting that there seems to be more ecumenicity in Theological Education in the Far East than in any other form of Christian work. This is the more amazing because one would naturally suppose that Theological education would be one of the tenacious strongholds of denominationalism.[134]

Those attending the Manila conference discussed ideas that had been developed at the Indonesia and Wisconsin conferences and added further issues to be discussed at the regional meeting in February 1956.[135]

Regarding the location for proposed two-month summer institutes, Smith advised the Board of Founders that Trinity College was not a suitable location because of inadequate facilities and reminded the board that Trinity had requested an additional $10,000 for construction of a larger building. Smith had written the heads of the theological schools in South East Asia to ask if they could host a summer institute in 1955, but he was reasonably sure there were only two possible places for such a meeting, Singapore and Bangkok. Singapore had a favorable climate, and, despite its poor facilities, Trinity College was on vacation from mid-June until the end of September. In

132 The Aglipayan Church or Philippine Independent Church had severed ties with Rome. Its clergy were ordained by the Anglican Church from 1948, and it joined the Old Catholic Union of Utrecht in 1965.

133 C. Stanley Smith to Frank T. Cartwright, [Singapore], December 30, 1954, ALW.

134 Ibid.

135 Ibid.

Bangkok, which lacked a suitable school site, the Church of Christ in Thailand maintained a church center. If the institute were to be held in Bangkok, Smith recommended that it be held in December and January because of the weather. The Philippines would be very hot from March to May, when schools there were closed for long vacations, and it would be difficult for other South East Asians to secure visas because of Philippine governmental restrictions. Commenting on Indonesia, Smith noted that it was expensive to reach and that it might be difficult to find an appropriate time. However, he thought that, because of the importance of the church and theological education there, an institute should be held in Indonesia at a future time.[136]

Smith forwarded a request from Higher Theological College in Jakarta for $1,000 to help support the first nationwide conference on religious education. Smith anticipated some ambivalence regarding this request on the part of the Board of Founders. He reminded the board that it had previously supported the travel expenses of E. G. Homrighausen of Princeton Theological Seminary to South East Asia, and that he had spent most of his time in Indonesia. Smith thought that the churches should support their own evangelical work, but he also noted that the conference would be helpful to the theological schools in Indonesia and that the board had supported a conference on religious education two years earlier following his and Van Dusen's visit to the area. Therefore, Smith recommended that the Board of Founders grant the $1,000, adding that, except for Taiwan and Manila, there were no other places in the region that were prepared to carry on such an extensive program in religious education as Indonesia.[137]

Smith was especially supportive of the idea of the Board of Founders supporting study institutes for teachers and theological colleges because he believed "the BF should use its funds largely for the purpose for which they were given, namely the training of Christian ministers and theological education related to this training." He believed there had been a "tendency to broaden the basis of financial support," but he thought the board should again narrow the range of projects it supported, even though Manikam and "possibly some of the NCCs in the Far East" would like to see the funds used for general church projects. If the institutes were designed for theological seminary faculty, Smith thought they should be scheduled for six to eight weeks. If designed for pastors and church workers, he recommended that they

136 Ibid.

137 C. Stanley Smith to BF, [Singapore], January 27, 1955, ALW.

last not more than six weeks. He thought that such institutes should be sponsored directly by the Board of Founders:

> I think this is reasonable, as the Institute is looked upon as part of the [BF]'s program for theological education, but again I am inclined to think that it will arouse a bit of opposition in some quarters. The whole relationship of an organization like the [BF] to the [WCC], and the [IMC] and to the East Asia Secretary of these organizations, is very much to the fore out here at present. It is part of the whole situation which has political as well as ecclesiastical aspects.[138]

Smith explained that the national councils of churches were very sensitive and did not like "anything initiated from abroad, about which they have not been first consulted." He had seen this demonstrated recently when the Malayan Christian Council complained of not being consulted about the study institute. Smith responded that the institute had not yet been decided upon and no site for it had been set. Therefore, he thought that consultation was premature. However, the council insisted that anything related to South East Asia was of concern to them.[139]

The Board of Founders voted to sponsor the first of the summer study institutes at a special meeting in January 1955. It established the probable site as Singapore, and funding was appropriated. The board was troubled by the sluggish development of plans for the 1956 regional conference and expressed the hope that a central theme could be decided upon and that clearer priorities could be established for discussion of items on the preliminary agenda in the hope that the conference might reach "creative conclusions." Dr. Paul E. Johnson became a Methodist representative to the Board of Founders at this meeting, replacing the recently deceased Clarence Craig.[140]

When Smith wrote the various regional theological schools in early 1955 asking for their requests for the following year, he explained that the Board of Founders was reconsidering its policies with respect to the region. Instead of supporting many schools with small grants, a policy followed since 1952, it might support a single school as it had in Nanjing. Alternatively, it might support several higher level schools

138 C. Stanley Smith to Frank T. Cartwright, Singapore, February 19, 1955, ALW.

139 Ibid.

140 Special Meeting, BF, NTS, January 21, 1955, ALW.

in order to enable them to hire Asian faculty and improve facilities. He cautioned the principals that the board might cut aid to some institutions in order to concentrate on others. Other possibilities included extension of the service area to include India, Japan, and Korea or to focus on support of theological education through conferences and study institutes. Smith also advised that the Board of Founders might seek to adhere more closely to the original idea of the donor and use its funds only where there was a large Christian or non-Christian Chinese population. Because of these possible changes, Smith asked each institution for a statement as to how it had used past grants, how enrollments had grown, the number of Chinese and non-Chinese students enrolled, buildings and equipment purchased, etc. He also asked that the proposed study groups preparatory to the 1956 conference send him reports of their discussions and of their preferences for topics to be discussed at that conference. He added that he had small grants available to support these meetings. Smith also advised that he was circulating copies of the *Anderson-Smith Report* in preparation for the conference.[141]

Smith visited Hong Kong in 1955, both to recruit students for Trinity College and other South East Asian theological schools and also to survey the state of theological education there. He reported that conditions were much calmer in Hong Kong than a year before and that the theological schools were able to conduct their work. Chung Chi College's relationship with the government had improved, and there was "a new hope for securing a better educated ministry for the Church in that area." Yet he admitted there was not much prospect of Chung Chi College having a department or college of theology or of entering into an agreement with a theological school to provide the equivalent of junior college preparation for those interested in the ministry, so it seemed unlikely it would be able to offer a B.Th. degree, even though there was a sufficient number of interested students to create a higher theological college. R. O. Hall, the Anglican bishop of Hong Kong whom Smith met briefly, was encouraging such a college in response to the Anglican Church's need for a better educated ministry. Smith reported that the Anglicans expected Chung Chi College and the University of Hong Kong to prepare potential candidates for ministry through the B.A. level. When Chung Chi College moved to its new site in the New Territories, the old site would be used for a higher grade

141 C. Stanley Smith to Principals of Theological Schools in Southeast Asia Receiving Grants from the BF, NTS, Singapore, February 18, 1955, ALW.

theological school. The Anglicans had begun the school relying heavily on tutorial instruction, private study, and reading for completion of the curricular syllabus. The Anglicans, through Hall, had approached the American Methodists and Presbyterians in Hong Kong about cooperation in an advanced theological school. The Methodist bishop had reacted very favorably, but Smith was uncertain whether this was an official reaction. The Presbyterians were more cautious, did not want to enter an already organized Anglican school, and were concerned that the planning had been done entirely by Anglicans and that the property was Anglican owned. Smith thought the curriculum was good but reflected Anglican needs and practices. Yet if there were the prospect of a school in Hong Kong, those there, especially the Presbyterians, were hesitant to send more students to Trinity College because of the expense involved and because the students might remain in churches in Singapore after living there for three years.[142]

In Taiwan Smith learned of plans to move the Taiwan Theological College to a suburb. Smith visited the site with James Dickson, head of the college, and thought the location was ideal except for its distance from the city. The Board of Directors asked Smith for a Board of Founders grant of $20,000 for a new dormitory. Relaying this request, Smith commented that he thought the move was not conditional upon receiving the grant and that, if it sold the city property, the school would have sufficient funds to purchase the new site and build there. He reported that the directors of the school wanted to move because, thanks to the presence of the American army, the area around the present campus had become a red-light district populated with bars and hostesses. Yet Smith noted that another area of the city was worse and commented that "these evidences of the moral degradation of the capital of [Taiwan] of which our American armed forces are such a large factor, makes one pause and consider the moral cost of a military occupation whether of a friendly or a conquered nation." Smith noted that some military officers attended Rotary meetings and some enlisted men frequented the Armed Forces Service Center that the Dicksons, who were Canadian Presbyterians, operated. He continued, "Maybe a theological college should stay in such an environment...witnessing to a higher conception of life and moral values, but it is probably asking too much to expect it to do so. One wonders how long a nearby Presbyterian church will survive in that neighborhood."[143]

[142] C. Stanley Smith, Report on Visit to Northern East Asia, July 31-August 20, 1955, ALW.

[143] Ibid.

Smith once again observed the interest in Bible schools in Taiwan. The Taiwan Theological College once had an affiliated Bible school, but the latter had separated from the theological school and was then being operated by the Presbyterian Church in the U.S. and the Canadian Presbyterians, who worked together in the Synod of North Taiwan. He likened this Bible school to the Bible Teachers' Training School in Nanjing, except that the Taiwan school was coeducational.[144]

Smith also presented the problem of finding qualified teachers for regional theological schools for consideration by the Board of Founders. He observed that there were fewer missionaries and few men interested in becoming ministers. Yet he also reported an increased interest in ministerial preparation for college graduates. The Southern Baptist mission offered courses in both Hong Kong and Taiwan for college graduates leading to a B.D. degree, and Smith believed that the awarding of this degree stimulated interest in the programs. Both Hong Kong and Taiwan had Christian colleges and universities offering B.A. degrees. He hoped these programs would produce an increasing number of candidates for the ministry but was somewhat skeptical since, on the Chinese mainland with thirteen Christian colleges, there had never been more than twenty-five college graduates in the whole of China seeking admission to ministerial training in a single year. He suspected the abundance of candidates in Taiwan just then might reflect the absence of alternative opportunities for college graduates. If true, then the pool of candidates would decrease in a few years. Therefore, Smith urged caution in granting funds for new buildings and equipment.[145]

Smith was critical of the Southern Baptist seminary in Taiwan in spite of its large enrollment of Bachelor of Divinity degree students because it offered "a B.D. degree which has no legal basis of incorporation but which rests only on the authority and reputation of the school granting it—like the old *Tao Hsieh Shih* degree Nanking offered before the Board of Founders incorporated to grant degrees...[and] the SBC was using English nomenclature, e.g., B.Th., B.R.E., B.D., which Nanking had never done." Smith also reported that, in both Hong Kong and Taiwan, college graduates who were studying for the B.D. degree were often in classes with undergraduate B.Th. students and were asked only to do additional reading or to write an extra paper.[146]

144 Ibid.
145 Ibid.
146 Ibid.

Smith also visited the new site of Tunghai University but did not speak with any officials of that school, which was supported by the United Board for Christian Higher Education in Asia and was designed to replace thirteen small Protestant colleges. The plan was of great interest on the island, but Smith wondered whether the new university would be able to retain the Christian character of the former colleges, especially since he learned that only two hundred of five thousand applicants would be accepted for the fall term. "With the ratio of Christians to non-Christians on the Island, one cannot but wonder how many of the two hundred accepted...will be Christians." Smith observed that many in the Taiwan churches with whom he talked were "fearful of the answer to this question as it affects the Christian character of the University."[147]

There were also concerns as to the extent to which this university would serve the Taiwanese constituency that had been represented in the older Christian colleges. Many had hoped that Tunghai University would be for the Taiwanese, but that hope was not fulfilled. There were no Taiwanese on the teaching and administrative staffs, although a few remained on the board. Smith also noted that there were no direct representatives of church bodies on the board, that the university would offer no theological education courses, and that it had planned no relationship with any theological colleges for the future. He had suggested the possibility of a building for theological courses near the university, but this idea did not receive an enthusiastic response. He did not see any hope of having a B.D. course related to the university nor a B.Th. course for which the university would offer two years of preparation in the arts.[148]

At Tainan Theological College, which the Board of Founders had generously supported, Smith was warmly welcomed and learned much in informal discussions. Regarding the continuing tension between the Taiwanese and the recently arrived Chinese Nationalists, Smith reported the general view that the Taiwanese would eventually prevail in their disputes because of their numbers.[149]

Smith visited a refurbished building at Tainan Theological College that had been funded by the Board of Founders and the foundation for a chapel where, with board agreement, the college wanted to erect a plaque recognizing Rebecca Wendel Swope and Ella Wendel. The school had a new dormitory for eighty-four men but still

147 Ibid.
148 Ibid.
149 Ibid.

needed space for fifty more. Despite this need, Smith recommended that their request for the next year be placed in the secondary category because granting special favor to any one school would inevitably provoke resentment among others. Since the college had housing for only five of its eight faculty members, Smith suggested that the Board of Founders consider a grant for two more faculty houses as a means of expressing its satisfaction with the work of the college.[150]

Smith cautioned those with whom he spoke in Tainan that the large number of candidates for ministry might be temporary, but they responded emphasizing the likely impact of the "Double the Number of Churches Movement," which was planned to increase the number of churches from 150 to 300. Smith wrote the Board of Founders that the optimism might be warranted. He observed that the local churches screened their candidates for ministry carefully, as did the local presbyteries. Applicants to the school also had to pass the entrance examinations, but still the number of students exceeded dormitory accommodations. Some Bible school students were resident in the dormitories, and the churches needed them for the time being, even though the Bible school course was to be phased out in the next two years. Smith reported that there were quite different views on Bible schools in the north and south of Taiwan. In Taipei, admission to Bible school was based on junior middle school preparation and offered no hope that graduates would be given church jobs, while Tainan Theological College "received mainly more mature men—women were so far not enrolled—who were already deacons or elders in the church and prepared them for definite service in the churches in connection with the Double the Number of Churches Movement, particularly in the training of new church members." Those at Tainan were also strongly in favor of a B.D. degree course being established somewhere on the island because, while at the moment the greatest need was for those with the B.Th. degree, they knew there was also a demand for better educated clergy.[151]

After his visits to schools in Taiwan, Smith concluded that there was a definite need for a B.D. course in Taiwan, and he reported that even Hwang of Tainan Theological College, who at the Williams Bay meeting had insisted that B.A. students could go abroad for this level of professional education, now thought this professional degree should be offered in Taiwan. Smith believed that the course would not be large, perhaps between six and fifteen students, and therefore did not believe

[150] Ibid.
[151] Ibid.

that a separate school should be built. He thought the faculty should be at least half Chinese and argued against offering such a course at Tunghai University, since the church had little connection there. He also commented that there was no interest in uniting the Taiwan Theological College with the Tainan Theological College but that there was interest in bringing the former school up to the latter's level.[152]

Smith also recommended that the Board of Founders assist Higher Theological College in Jakarta, where the principal, Peter Latuihamallo, requested funds to assist the college in employing a Chinese professor of biblical languages with a degree from the Netherlands. Smith thought that, if the Board of Founders were going to give special consideration to some schools, this was a worthy request. He also reported favoring aid for the Theological Academy in Jogjakarta, which had increased its enrollment of Chinese students from one in 1952 to the present twelve. He also recommended helping the new theological school that had moved from Timor to Makassar and had built a two-story building to house 150 students and had sixty-five currently enrolled. He suggested that the board grant $20,000 to build a residence for visiting faculty or to install electricity in all of the buildings.[153]

In a letter to Cartwright that accompanied his report, Smith said that, after his trip, he thought it was important to build up a B.D. course in every country, as there did "not seem to be much lessening in the difficulties of students, especially Chinese, going from one country to the other for study." He also remarked that he and the Board of Founders "have been thinking too much in terms of an advanced course in an institution of its own which would have to be built in some central place where students from several countries could come," but he noted the international difficulties presented to such a plan "seemed practically insurmountable." He also observed that "such a school would be expensive to operate, would have to have a special faculty of its own and would require a fairly large student body to justify its cost. We seem to have forgotten our experience in Nanking where we simply added a B.D. course to our already existing B.Th. course." Smith also suggested a religious studies degree be offered at an existing Christian college or university but observed that such a program would be difficult to implement. He thought it would be impossible in Taiwan but was a possibility at Chung Chi College in Hong Kong.[154]

152 Ibid.

153 "Excerpts, C. Stanley Smith, September 27, 1955, October 13, 1955, Liston Pope Papers, YDS (hereafter PopeP).

154 C. Stanley Smith to Frank T. Cartwright, Singapore, August 27, 1955 (?),

Smith wrote that some of the regional colleges had gradually emerged as preeminent. These were the Higher Theological College in Jakarta, Union Theological Seminary in Manila, and Tainan Theological College in Taiwan. Smith wished that his own school, Trinity College in Singapore, were among these but wrote that it was not because of conditions that "are extremely difficult to alter. In western faculty we are excellent, we have some first grade students, but we have too many of sub-standard, or only Bible school qualifications and our course is too short." He added that Trinity needed more Asian faculty and that the local churches needed to realize their need for qualified ministers.[155]

When Smith's recommendations for grants for the coming year reached the Board of Founders, some members of the board expressed concern that Smith had not given sufficient consideration to a request from the College of Theology at Silliman University for a grant to classify and catalogue its library. Smith, however, defended his recommendation to Cartwright stating that the amount asked was too large for the size of the library involved and that he did not favor spending so much money on this school, since Union Theological Seminary in Manila was more "representative of all the Christian work in the Philippines and had a much larger faculty and student body." Smith also questioned whether the board should make grants of this kind for libraries unless prepared to do the same for other schools. He concluded with the observation that he was sympathetic to the college's library needs but wanted to be fair to all.[156]

Late in 1955 in a major policy decision, the Board of Founders, by a unanimous vote, "in accordance with its amended charter," agreed to use the funds it had "in places of major need or strategic importance for the strengthening of Christian theological education in Asia, recognizing however special responsibilities for eastern and southeastern Asia." The board thought the terms of the Swope-Wendel Fund required it to give special consideration to Chinese communities and Chinese students, so it provided a continuing provision for the translation of the Christian classics, basic theological texts, and "other contemporary theological books of outstanding value" into Chinese. The board also agreed to

ALW. Smith's suggestion that there need not be a separate institution and separate campus in every country was an idea that would eventually develop into the South East Asia Graduate School of Theology, a cooperative venture of many of the schools that were assisted by BF during this period.

155 Ibid.

156 Ibid.

give aid to "qualified and approved students" to study outside their homelands. Grants-in-aid, which were to be nonrecurring in character, were to be given to union schools, first, then to denominationally sponsored schools that "because of special circumstances serve the churches generally of a given area." The board members wanted their program balanced among these priorities. Grants to institutions were to be in proportion to what their normal sponsoring institutions gave. Along with the IMC, the Board of Founders would continue to study the needs of theological education in South East Asia and to determine if it needed one or more theological colleges of university grade.[157]

Though the board saw no conflict between these policies and the recommendations of Smith, the latter indicated that he was confused by this action. He believed the board had approved his recommendation of the previous year that it support a few strong schools in three or four South East Asian countries with building grants and support for Asian faculty for three to five years, and that the board was now backing away from that decision. Smith continued to believe that a few institutions should receive special assistance in order to develop strong seminary programs. He added that he hoped such action would break the vicious cycle into which the Protestant churches of the region had fallen and that local churches would realize that more Asian teachers would have to come from them. While Smith thought that the board had been reluctant to proceed with support for only a few schools, he explained that his own intention was not to withdraw the small grants from the schools previously supported but to continue them while concentrating on a few really strong schools. He recommended that the Board of Founders have a few definite objectives but not have its own theological seminary in East or South East Asia unless a relationship could be reestablished with Nanjing. Specifically, he reiterated his conviction that the Board of Founders should concentrate resources on Tainan Theological College in Taiwan, urging it to become a union institution as its president hoped it would; Union Theological Seminary in Manila; Trinity College in Singapore; and Higher Theological College in Jakarta, and give only small grants to other institutions .[158]

In a private letter to Abbe Livingstone Warnshuis, a member of the Board of Founders, Smith wrote that he was disappointed that the board had not accepted his recommendation for helping four or five schools–one in each country. He assumed that perhaps the

157 Long Range Policy of the Board, September 21, 1955, ALW.

158 Excerpt, C. Stanley Smith, n.p., July 12, 1955; September 21, 1955, ALW.

board wanted to do this but did not want to establish it as policy. He hoped that no board members were still thinking in terms of a single theological school for South East Asia, for he believed there were simply too many political problems in the securing of visas and movement about the region.[159]

Recognizing the need of Asian churches for lay workers, Smith also submitted a request to the Board of Founders for grants to underwrite their training. He asked for $2,500 for refresher courses at Tainan Theological College, McGilvary Seminary in Thailand, Insein Seminary in Burma, and Union Theological Seminary in Manila. His earlier inquiry regarding lay training had been referred to a committee, and the charter of the Board of Founders stated that it could fund requests if for "ordained and unordained mininistry," but were lay people covered? Smith thought the wording might preclude such grants, but he also observed that both the British and American Methodist churches use lay preachers. Therefore, he thought such funding might be permissible under the terms of the charter.[160]

Concerning other institutions and their physical facilities, Smith wrote that Taiwan Theological College had sold its city property. However, this action had been taken without consulting its mission, and Smith believed this might lead to hard feelings. He also reported that in Indonesia, outside Jakarta, it was difficult to get students into theological schools. Frequently there were no senior middle schools available to potential students, and where such schools existed, those who attended them seldom seemed interested in ministry. The new school at Makassar was requesting funding, and Smith was supportive of its request even though, at that time, the school enrolled only one Chinese student. He noted that, though it had a library, it contained only old Dutch books, which few of the students could read.[161]

As Smith concluded his report to the board, he was aware that the forthcoming 1956 conference would likely change the course of theological education in South East Asia for many years to come. Planning for that conference was consuming much of Smith's time, and it would occupy even more in the months to come.

The Board of Founders was dealing with a variety of issues during this period, but foremost was planning for the Bangkok

159 C. Stanley Smith to A. L. Warnshuis, [Singapore], November 24, 1955, ALW.

160 C. Stanley Smith, Grants for Training of Lay Workers, September 21, 1955, ALW.

161 C. Stanley Smith to BF [Singapore], September 27, 30, October 4, 13, 1955, all ALW.

conference. Dean Liston Pope of Yale Divinity School spoke to the board in October 1955 and laid out his plans to visit seminaries in Asia as well as to participate in the Bangkok conference. On other matters, the board approved the appointment of H. P. Van Dusen and F. T. Cartwright as its representatives on the China Committee of the Far Eastern Joint Office, it addressed its pension obligations to Chinese members of the Nanjing Seminary faculty and to Miss Marguerite Rouse, and it accepted Dr. George Earle Owen as a successor to E. K. Higdon representing the Disciples on the board.[162] The board shared Smith's belief that the forthcoming conference would be critical to the development of theological education in South East Asia.

Already the Board of Founders' support of theological education throughout South East Asia was beginning to have a significant regional impact. Winburn Thomas of Higher Theological College in Jakarta praised the board's work in Indonesia, but his comments might well have been echoed by those in Tainan, Manila, or Singapore:

> The NTS contributions definitely are changing the character of Indonesian theological education. You have lifted the face of the Djakarta buildings, you have added valuable staff there, you have enabled additional students to study, and you have given us needed books. In time, the total impact of American gifts through personnel, equipment and books, will effect a transformation in Indonesian theology. We will be permanently indebted to NTS for having enlarged its operation to include Indonesia.[163]

[162] Minutes, BF, October 13, 1955, January 19, 1956, FTEA.
[163] Quoted in Frank T. Cartwright to BF, n.p., n.d. (probably 1955).

CHAPTER 5

The Foundation for Theological Education in South East Asia

Theological education in South East Asia took a dramatic stride forward in February and March 1956 when two simultaneous meetings were held in Bangkok. One was sponsored by the Board of Founders of Nanking Theological Seminary and the other by the World's Student Christian Federation.[1] The two meetings held joint sessions to hear their main speakers and then separate sessions to discuss issues of particular interest to a single group. With the convening of these conferences, not only was theological education in South East Asia elevated to a critical position among issues facing the church, but a major leadership shift also began to occur, with Asian Christians emerging to assume critical positions in theology and theological education in the institutions of South East Asia. The Board of Founders continued to grant significant support to theological education in the region with income from the Swope-Wendel fund, but after these conferences it was increasingly Asians who were determining the needs of the region and how these

1 The official name was changed in 1960 from World's Student Christian Federation to World Student Christian Federation.

funds were to be expended. Change was gradual; all members of the Board of Founders continued to be Americans for the time being, but their ideas were changing in response to the decolonization of the region. Even the name of the board would be changed to the Foundation for Theological Education in South East Asia (FTESEA).

In preparation for the 1956 conference, the Board of Founders appointed a planning committee composed of M. Searle Bates, R. Pierce Beaver, Frank T. Cartwright, and Luther A. Weigle. The committee wrote Rajah Manikam, bishop of Tranquebar and East Asian secretary for the World Council of Churches and the International Missionary Council, and C. Stanley Smith in February 1955 suggesting that, since this was to be the first Asian regional conference on theological education, it should be considered preliminary, establishing the ground work for subsequent deliberations. The committee thought it would be most fruitful if the conference approached its subject from "the perspective of the cultural situation, the experience, the resources, the insights, and the needs of the churches of the region, rather than from the viewpoint of administrative problems related to a system of education imported from the West."[2]

While the committee did not want methodological matters excluded, it wanted them to "appear in truer perspective" and as "they emerged out of a study of the needs, opportunities, and functions of the ministry in Southeast Asia." To the committee it appeared that the "recruiting, training, and support of an adequate ministry is the foremost problem confronting the churches in Southeast Asia." It believed that

> the root of the difficulty is not primarily the poverty of the people and their consequent inability to support the ministry. It is rather the unwillingness of the people to give their sons and substance for the maintenance of a clergy not recognized as relevant to the common life. The Christian ministry is alien to, and unappreciated by, peoples who have known nothing like it in their past cultural experience, excepting in the Philippines and parts of Indonesia where Christianity is in places very old but where the patterns of the ministry introduced from abroad have not always appealed to the people as being relevant to their situation. The ministry has, in fact, in some places appeared

2 M. S. Bates, R. P. Beaver, F. T. Cartwright, and L. A. Weigle, Committee; Memorandum for Rajah Manikam and C. Stanley Smith [New York], February 11, 1955, ALW.

> to be identified with colonial control. These peoples have for centuries and even millennia supported religious structures which have appeared relevant to their social needs. The Christian Church might not wish to employ the same methods, but the fact remains that any people will find the means to support religious institutions adapted to their situation and speaking to their spiritual and material needs.[3]

The committee continued with the observation that in South East Asia "the sense of Christian vocation is weak or lacking," citing the strength of the family, which meant that a whole family needed to give a son to the church; a church vocation was not simply an individual's decision. The conference therefore needed to consider "the universal elements in the concept of the Christian ministry, exploring its Biblical, theological, and historical foundations. It might then look at [ministry] from the perspective of the total experience of the Church across the ages. It might, and ought, next and in detail examine the actual ministry of the churches in Southeast Asia." The committee acknowledged that the time allotted for the conference was too short to accomplish this task, but it believed that at least a beginning was required. The committee also asked that the conference examine the patterns of clergy of the ethnic religions and Roman Catholicism:

> The similarities and the marked differences will appear, and some light may be shed on some of the functions, problems, and support of the ministry. The whole study of the ministry, its functions, its forms, its training, its support, and also the important question of vocation should be made against the background of the specific task of the Church in the specific cultural situation of the countries of Southeast Asia."[4]

The committee expressed the hope that out of such a study might come a sense of how to "stimulate a constant supply of recruits, how a pattern of ministry may be shaped to fit the cultural requirements as well as the inherent needs of the Church, and how this ministry may be adjusted in the matter of support to the economic base of the land." Further, the committee observed, "the relationship of the doctrine of the priesthood of all believers to the total ministry of the Church should be kept clearly in view during the conference." Laity needed to understand their role in ministry, an understanding that would

3 Ibid.
4 Ibid.

require guidance by the clergy.[5] The memorandum continued with the judgment that

> the first problem of any theological seminary is how to be the Church in microcosm....In lands where the concept of the Church is alien to spiritual experience, the seminary ought to offer that new experience in all fullness, so that pastors going forth into the congregations may know what it is that they seek to foster and of which they are expected to be exemplars. The most vital and fundamental experience to be gained by a seminarian is that of being part of a ministering community in Christ, corporately worshiping and interceding, enjoying fellowship and mutual love, witnessing to the lordship of Jesus Christ and the relevance of His Gospel to the local cultural situation.[6]

Whatever the institution or curriculum, the primary question needed to be "how may that institution become a ministering community producing effective servants of the larger community, the Church, mature in their faith and competent in their ministry?" Seminary training needed to take place within the larger church.

> The seminary through its total life and curriculum seeks these objectives: Fostering maturity of individual faith and corporate responsibility; imparting the heritage of the Christian past; opening the wellspring of spiritual vitality; guiding experience in the life and work of the Church in the neighborhood and in the world; facing the contemporary culture under the illumination of the Christian Gospel; and imparting the techniques of the ministry.[7]

In Asia Smith, Manikam, and others had been planning for the 1956 conference for months with Board of Founders support for preconference meetings in each of the South East Asian nations. After attending an audiovisual conference in Thailand in March 1955 and holding discussions there, Manikam went on to Burma, Hong Kong, and Taiwan. Smith attended the Indonesian conference and one in Malaya and met with a group from Chiang Mai while in Bangkok in March. They developed a list of people who should be invited to present papers at the national conferences whose deliberations would

5 Ibid.
6 Ibid.
7 Ibid.

be summarized and discussed at the 1956 meeting. Smith had earlier asked the Board of Founders to provide a small grant to cover some of Manikam's office expenses in Bangalore as preparations for the conference proceeded.[8] However, as preparations continued, Smith expressed personal reservations about the growing expenses and observed that the board had appropriated more for the 1956 conference than was required to operate Trinity College for a year, with salaries of seven missionary teachers included![9]

Kyaw Than, the associate general secretary of the World's Student Christian Federation, sent Smith the agenda for a proposed Asian Conference of Theological Students, which would have the general theme, "Theology in the Service of Evangelism." Smith forwarded this information to the Board of Founders with the observation that it might be wise if the student conference of thirty to forty-eight people could meet at the same time as the 1956 Conference on Theological Education, which anticipated an attendance of seventy participants in addition to instructors. Smith observed that the students' topics were very general, while those proposed for the educators' conference were quite technical and "of special interest to those actually engaged in Theological Education." If the conferences were held together, participants could attend some of the open sessions of each meeting. Smith also advised that local Christians should be given an opportunity to attend and thought the major problem would be finding a suitable place which could accommodate 110 to 120 people.[10]

At a meeting in Bangkok, Manikam and Smith agreed that the two conferences should meet together. The Board of Founders also hoped that the Conference on Theological Education might take up some of the more general topics proposed by the students for their meeting. The board saw this as an excellent opportunity to bring together students from theological colleges, most of whom were Asian, and the instructors, most of whom were Western. However, the size of the combined meeting made a gathering in Chiang Mai difficult, so they decided to hold the conferences at Wattana Presbyterian Girls' School in Bangkok and settled on the dates of February 21 to March 6, 1956. Smith and Manikam decided to limit the number of participants to three delegates from each of the seventeen schools, a representative

8 C. Stanley Smith to Frank T. Cartwright [Singapore], December 30, 1954, ALW.

9 C. Stanley Smith to Frank T. Cartwright, Singapore, February 19, 1955, ALW.

10 Ibid.

of the national council of churches or Christian council in each of the seven countries, two delegates from India, one from Pakistan, one from Korea, and one or two from Japan. They estimated the cost of the gathering at $12,000, with those from outside the area paying their own expenses or obtaining a special grant from the Board of Founders.[11]

Smith observed in his 1955 annual report to the Board of Founders that the Wattana School, selected as the site for the 1956 conferences, had also been the site of the 1948 South East Asia conference of the WCC and IMC in 1948. He reported having sent information concerning the forthcoming conference to all schools. Smith reported having received a great variety of replies. Some found such a conference either unrealistic or provocative, while others were enthusiastic and found the proposal excellent. Benjamin Guansing of Union Theological Seminary in Manila protested the date, which would conflict with his school's graduation and perhaps with that of other Philippine schools. However, Smith asked him to make adjustments, since only three delegates were required and one was to be from the Board of Directors. He pointed out that the date could not be changed without also changing the location. Smith also advised the Board of Founders that administrative costs not included in earlier budget figures would raise the total required from the board for the conference to $13,000.[12]

During the summer of 1955, Smith visited Bangkok to assure that preparations for the 1956 conference were progressing on schedule. He then went on to Taipei, where he talked with various people about the forthcoming conference and urged them to consider theoretical or academic items for the proposed agenda. However, Smith reported that "they always came back to the most pressing problems of their own situation." They focused on the six-year curriculum for senior middle school graduates. Smith admitted he did not know a great deal about many of their concerns and felt pleased that, at Nanjing Seminary, the faculty had spent more time on curriculum "to keep up with the changing fashions in theological education in the West."[13]

While in Taiwan, Smith held a two-day conference with people from both Taipei and Tainan. Again, he found that even in this more

11 Rajah Manikam and C. Stanley Smith to Frank T. Cartwright, Charles Ranson, Kyaw Than, Visser 't Hooft, Hong Kong, March 11, 1955, ALW.

12 C. Stanley Smith, Annual Report, Field Representative in Southeast Asia, 1954-55, ALW.

13 C. Stanley Smith, Report on Visit to Northern East Asia, July 31-August 20, 1955, ALW.

formal setting people did not want to discuss "the more general items on the nature of the church and the ministry" but preferred to consider "more concrete problems such as Bible schools, B.D. courses, lay training, and refresher courses. However, the more they discussed these practical subjects, the more it became evident that they were really facing the more theoretical issue of the nature of the church and its relevance to the present needs as well as the question of the nature of the ministry." As a result of this experience, Smith wrote the Board of Founders that he wondered if the order of the agenda for the 1956 conference should not be changed to employ "a more scientific approach from the particular and the concrete to the more general and theoretical," since he had found it "practically impossible to arouse interest in more general subjects until the consideration of particular problems opened the way for them."[14]

Smith and Manikam met again in Colombo in September to continue planning discussions for the Bangkok conference. They still needed to resolve the issue of who would coordinate and manage the conference. Smith indicated he would talk with Leck Tai Yong, general secretary of the Church of Christ in Thailand, concerning this matter. Smith also wanted Samuel Moffett, a Presbyterian educational missionary formerly at Nanjing Seminary and then working in Korea, assigned to help with the Bangkok conference.[15]

By October, Smith's reports to the Board of Founders indicated that he was sending funds to Taiwan and would soon send funds to Manila and Jakarta to underwrite pre-Bangkok conferences in each place. He also sent the tentative agenda for the Bangkok meeting. A quota of six people had been assigned to Hong Kong, two from the Lutheran Theological School, one from the Southern Baptist Theological School, and three from the churches. Timothy Chow had been asked to represent the Hong Kong Methodist churches. Smith noted that because of comity agreements entered into by the mission boards, the Methodists were strong in Malaya, the Baptists in Burma, and the Presbyterians in Thailand. Only in the Philippines were there denominational churches of equal strength. While there was an Anglican church in Malaya, it had only one-third the membership of the Methodist church there.[16]

From the pre-Bangkok conferences came a variety of suggestions for topics to be discussed in the larger meeting. These included:

14 Ibid.
15 Ibid.
16 C. Stanley Smith to BF [Singapore], October 25, 1955, ALW.

pretheological preparation, recruitment and maintenance of students, instruction and curriculum, textbooks and administration, faculty departmentalization and libraries, standardization, objectives of theological education, classification, Bible schools, extramural relations with the church and the ecumenical movement, maintenance of the clergy, and financing theological education and postgraduate theological education at home or abroad.[17]

Smith asked Liston Pope, dean of Yale Divinity School, to speak about trends of theological education and their relevance to South East Asia, noting that the Reverend Russell Chandran, principal of the Theological College of the Church of South India in Bangalore, would deal more precisely with trends in Asia and that Dr. Benjamin Guansing from Union Theological Seminary in Manila might also speak on the same subject. Smith had also suggested that Pope travel about South East Asia prior to the conference so that he could observe different trends in the region.[18]

As the date of the conference neared, people from the Philippines and Indonesia asked to be assigned additional delegates, arguing that if they traveled as a group they could receive reduced airfare. Smith, however, insisted on limiting the numbers to those originally specified, since the hall would not seat more. He did, however, permit McGilvary Theological College in Chiang Mai, as one of the host institutions, to send several faculty members as auditors. No sessions were designed to be open to the public because of limited space, but Smith agreed "to giv[ing] a few tickets of admission to some of the joint sessions for pastors and other church leaders in Bangkok.[19]

The Board of Founders' conference on theological education opened in Bangkok with fifty-one delegates from Burma, Hong Kong, Indonesia, Malaya, the Philippines, Sarawak, Taiwan, and Thailand representing theological schools, churches, or councils of churches. Nine fraternal delegates represented Ceylon, India, Japan, Korea, and Pakistan. Eight of the nine "speakers and official guests" were from Western countries and represented the leadership of the World Council of Churches, the International Missionary Council, and the National Council of Churches in the United States. Among the issues discussed at the conference were "Theology in the Service of Evangelism," "Theological Education and Its Environment in Southeast Asia,"

17 Rajah Manikam, "Excerpt, Circular Letter No. 5, Southeast Asia Theological Education Conference, PopeP.

18 Ibid.

19 C. Stanley Smith to Rajah Manikam [Singapore], January 2, 1956, ALW.

"Trends in Theological Education," "The Work of Seminaries in Southeast Asia," "The Ministry in Southeast Asia," "Recruitment and Maintenance of the Ministry," "Bible Schools and their Relation to Theological Education," and "Is an Ecumenical Theological Education Possible?" Participants also considered the need and possibility of creating a higher theological faculty for the region and an association of principals of South East Asian theological schools."[20]

Liston Pope wrote, as the conference commenced, that it was "off to a good start: attendance is superb and the spirit and content are excellent." He hoped some "tangible results" would flow from the meeting and was "convinced that representatives of the Great White Father should stay in the background."[21]

From the World Student Christian Federation meeting emerged a major theme that Asia after 1945 was in a period of transition and that it was the responsibility of theological institutions to recognize that old ideas imported from the West were no longer adequate and to prepare clergy to meet the demands of the new situation. Some of the Asians objected to using the term "relevancy," insisting that relevancy was not a biblical category, and preferred instead the term "emphasis," though they acknowledged that emphasis could change over time. The students wished to "guard against the graduate who knows the subtleties of Hebrew grammar, but who has not a clue as to the basic social and political tensions within his congregation, nor their actual ways of life and thought outside the religious hot-house atmosphere of the church, and who cannot speak really intelligibly and relevantly to the ordinary parish layman."[22]

Descriptive comments on the "ideological and cultural ferment" occurring in Asia included "a great passion for nationalism; a resurgence of non-Christian religions; a drive towards raising the standards of living and bringing about social justice; and a certain assimilation of Western culture and ideas." It was noted that "the Western impact [had] awakened the people into a sense of dignity and historical mission. Nationalism [was] the attempt to put economic and social content into this new concept. Faced with the breakup of the old patterns of social

20 WCC, "Bangkok Conference," YDS; also cited in "Editorial: Theological Education and Evangelistic Fervour," *SEAJT*, XV, 2 (1974), 1-9; Cartwright, *River*, 35-40.

21 Excerpt, Liston Pope Letter, February 23, 1956, ALW.

22 T. V. Philip, "Report and Interpretation of a Theological Students' Conference with a Statement by Participants," Theological Students' Conference, Bangkok, Thailand, February 21-March 6, 1956, 2-6, WSCF files, YDS.

living, people in Asia [were] searching for a new foundation upon which to build a new society."[23]

Another theme of the conference was an expressed need for Christians to relate to their communities and particularly to those of other faiths within their communities. Pope emphasized that the pastors were not merely chaplains but leaders of the community. He emphasized that Protestants interpret the world and the Bible in terms of their experiences and how they view the Bible's application to each situation. When dealing with non-Christian religions, Russell Chandran remarked that these other faiths should be studied "in their present manifestations and power and not merely in their classic form. There is a need to meet non-Christians on the level of philosophy and to study the sociology of religion."[24]

On the same topic, Mathew P. John, who had prepared a background paper for the meeting, stated that the relationship of Christians to people of other religions was crucial:

> All human representation of the Gospel must share in the human imperfection, but we have to be cautious not to make [it] even more imperfect than [is] unavoidable. Association of particular cultural forms with the Christian way of life and [an] attitude of superiority and condescension toward other religions is based on ignorance of the riches of other religions and false identification of the socio-historical entity of which we are a part with the Church as it is in God's plan, and a failure to bear the fruits of repentance and the spirit, have to be confessed by the churches and Christians.[25]

John also declared that the church in Asia was mainly a rural church and that theological education needed to be aware of that fact. Many rural communities had fallen apart under the influence of urbanization, and this critical problem needed to be addressed. One could not simply add courses in agricultural sciences to the curriculum. Rather, "the question is how we can develop in theological students a spirit of identification and sensitivity to the needs and feelings of others. Everywhere in Asia there is a search for a new community."[26]

23 Ibid., 6.
24 Ibid., 8.
25 Ibid., 9.
26 Ibid, 10.

Other speakers drew attention to the fact that Christians in Asia were criticized because they

> sometimes ha[d] a tendency to keep away from the culture and art, but very often make use of the foreign artistic forms imported from the West. Sometimes we identify the Gospel with Western culture. We are afraid of using indigenous forms of expression of art, music, worship, and customs. We want everything to be distinct from the Hindus, Buddhists, and Muslims. We often forget that the culture of a people is the carrier of the Gospel.[27]

The World Student Christian Federation meeting also considered how the ecumenical movement related to theological education. All the students at the conference agreed there was "the lack, in a proper sense, of community and devotional life in theological seminaries in Asia." Students and professors, they believed, were too focused on "grades and marks" rather than on the whole person. The students pointed out that in many seminaries there was no pastoral care, and they felt that too often churches sent to seminaries only students who were acceptable to the churches as they were. "Theological seminaries are only keen to produce students whom the churches will accept," but many students insisted that the church did not need to be conformed to but rather to be transformed.[28]

Many students at the meeting expressed the opinion that "our seminaries should be a model for all the world of Christian community, and a pointer to all educational authorities on how to run...institutional life." Some observed that what they termed "pious cliques" flourished on many seminary campuses, composed of people who felt that they were better than other students, and that some professors encouraged such groups. The students believed they needed to discover what "Christian piety" meant and stressed that the seminaries needed to be "communities of worship."[29]

Other students at the conference thought the seminaries did not need new classes or new admission standards but rather a "new theology [arising] out of the actual situation in Asia: 'In school and pulpit the task of theology today is not simply an affair of translating ancient ideas into modern language, but of wrestling with ultimate problems, as they arise in contemporary form.'" The problem, as these

27 Ibid.

28 Ibid., 12-14.

29 Ibid., 14.

students saw the matter, was in the way things are taught "so that the minister may develop a capacity to understand theologically the problems and tensions involved in the situation and to preach the word of God relevantly to that situation."[30]

Many argued that new teaching methods and new ways of evaluating students were required and that senior students should be consulted on what was to be taught. They also felt there was urgency to the matter of the devotional aspect of theological education, stating that many seminaries held frequent worship services but never communion.[31]

Tracy Jones, secretary of the Methodist Board of Overseas Mission and an alternate member of the Board of Founders, submitted a report of his observations to the Board of Founders following the Bangkok conferences. The conferences had been the first meetings of their kind in Asia, and most of the major Protestant theological schools were represented. As an interesting anecdote reflecting a common Asian approach to religion, Jones reported that the director general of the Thai Department of Religious Affairs, Ministry of Culture, Nai Fung Srivicharan, a devout Buddhist, attended the opening meeting of the conference and, when speaking to a group, declared, "All religions are the same. Our problem is similar to that of going to Singapore. You can go by train, by plane or by ship. Such is the road of religion."[32]

In this report Jones observed that "the power of religious syncretism is strong in Thailand," and that "after 128 years of Christian missionary work there are less than 20,000 Protestants in the country and only slightly more Roman Catholics." He noted that, among those attending the conference, some had "read of Buddhism, but many had not realized how strong it was. The classical religions of Hinduism, [and] Islam, as well as Buddhism are re-discovering their power over culture, politics, and family life." In view of this situation, those at the conferences had tried to determine "what kind of theological training would best prepare the student eager to enter the Christian ministry."[33]

Jones also observed that the conference participants represented nineteen theological schools, which had a total of 1,087 students enrolled, 875 of them men and 212 women. Of those students, 390—or

30 Ibid., 15.

31 Ibid., Appendix, 1-3.

32 Tracey Jones, "Some Remarks Concerning the Theological Conference Held in Bangkok, February 20-March 7, 1956," June 18, 1956, ALW.

33 Ibid.

36 percent—were Chinese, and only four of the nineteen institutions had no Chinese students enrolled. Five of the students who participated in or worked in these conferences had, by 1970, attained doctorates and become leaders in the Association of Theological Schools in South East Asia (ATSSEA), a group organized in 1956-57 and inspired by these Bangkok conferences.[34]

Reflections upon these meetings revealed serious problems facing Christianity and Christian education in Asia. Jones enumerated three of these:

"*First, theological education in Asia is an imitation of the West.*" Pope had visited many of the theological schools from Taiwan through Indonesia before the meeting and said, "I have found not a single new creative idea in any of the schools. They are all imitations of the West." Some of the schools followed the Continental pattern and emphasized Greek, Hebrew, German, French, and Latin as tools for understanding the Bible, while others followed the British pattern. Charles Ranson said, "The purpose of the British university is pragmatic. The goal is not so much the mastery of a particular subject...as to learn how to think....Other institutions imitated American schools and emphasized a balance between basic biblical courses and a whole variety of practical courses in religious education, field work, homiletics, and others," adding that the schools of Japan, Malaya, Taiwan, the Philippines, and some in India followed this form.[35]

Second, it was evident from some of the papers and discussions that were described as "thin" that a "more careful study of the questions that were up for discussion" was required. Jones reflected that

> certain issues were never touched at all. For example, there was no serious discussion of religious liberty, and certainly none regarding the philosophical basis of such liberty. There was a very inadequate analysis of contemporary political and social problems, and there was little indication that the problems of rapid social change had been thought through.[36]

Jones acknowledged that this weakness might have resulted from the wide geographical area represented and the diversity of cultures from which participants came. Many of the participants were using English

34 Ibid.; Alan C. Thomson, "A Note on the Development of the Association of Theological Schools in Southeast Asia," *SEAJT*, XVI (1975), 36-44.

35 Tracy Jones, "Some Remarks," emphasis appears in the original.

36 Ibid.

as a second language, and there was also the pressure of limited time as they tried to cover a wide range of topics in a few days.[37]

The third issue mentioned by Jones was the "frustration" that resulted from the fact that many could discern the problems but no one could offer a solution. He believed that they had not

> adequately...come to terms with the mind and the heart of the Asian people. The problem was that of relevance, of communication of the fundamental ideas of the Christian Faith in ways that would speak to the problems of the environment. It was realized that some of the Western ways were good. Certainly objective exegesis was essential to Asia. We cannot get Buddhists, Muslims, Hindus, to read critically their Scriptures as long as we refuse to do it with our own Bible.[38]

Conference participants believed that much of Western theology was inadequate for the Asian church. Indeed, the report on theology read, "The theology of the West should not be transplanted wholesale to the East." Tracey Jones believed that it was not clear what needed to be done. "About the only clear conviction was that the real encounter would have to come from Asian theological professors. Ultimately it would [require] men and women who had been nurtured in the soil of Asia, who had been caught up in the social and political changes, who could develop a theology that would be more relevant to the situation." He continued that most of the Asians had been trained in the West and knew more about its traditions than those of Asia. "Many of them knew little of the non-Christian religions, and the need for a stronger emphasis on such training in the schools was felt. Although no clear light was seen, out of the discussions some suggestions did come which over the course of time might profoundly help relate theological education more closely to the problems of Asia."[39]

In spite of the uncertainty and frustration, a few specific proposals were adopted for immediate implementation or for further consideration. First, a journal of theology was to be established and located at one of the theological schools to help Asian and missionary teachers exchange ideas. Second, the principals of the nineteen schools would join together as "an Association of Theological Principals" with the thought that this group might develop into "a Theological

37 Ibid.

38 Ibid.

39 Ibid.

Association for the Asian Schools, thereby making possible easy exchange of ideas, problems, personnel, planning and institutes for teachers." This proposal resulted in the formation of the Association of Theological Schools in South East Asia in 1959 after further action during the 1957 summer institute in Singapore. Third, there was discussion of organizing a "Higher Theological Faculty" of two to five individuals with the hope that advanced theological study at the Ph.D. level might become possible in Asia. Such a faculty could encourage scholarship toward the writing by Asians of the history of Asian churches and missions in Asia, subjects long treated almost exclusively by Westerners. Fourth, the conferees recognized the need for and endorsed holding a follow-up institute in 1957.[40]

With respect to Christian laity in Asia and its relationship to theological education, Tracey Jones summarized the thought of the conference:

> The urgent call to find new ways to train and enlist the laity was again and again emphasized. Here, the thorny question of the Bible schools came up, and the general feeling was that there was a real place for them, and consideration should be given to increase this type of training, thinking of the possibility of a growing number of ordained men in the Churches who might not have formal education, but who would be available for many of the pastoral jobs that better trained men simply [would] not assume. The danger of such schools undermining a well-trained ministry was recognized, but it was felt that the risk should be taken in light of the other needs. Fuller and more intensified training of church members through the theological schools was also recommended.[41]

The principals of the theological schools represented at the conference recommended that a Board of Founders' field representative reside in Asia to "give guidance in theological education" and to "screen financial requests" and make recommendations to the board. They expressed the belief that there was a growing sense of regionalism and of the need for cooperation in the area.[42]

Liston Pope met with the heads of the various Asian seminaries while in Bangkok and gave the following report to the Board of

40 Ibid; Cartwright, *River,* 17.
41 Ibid.
42 Ibid.

Founders: To his inquiry as to whether Smith's visits had been helpful, C. H. Hwang of Tainan Theological College responded, "tremendously." Hwang added that Smith's visits encouraged the church to do more and that the succession of visits was particularly helpful. Many believed that the visits had made them conscious of the Chinese and had encouraged leadership training. Peter Latuihamallo of Indonesia stated that the visits had "roused interest in Chinese students and in the employment of Chinese teachers." He also expressed gratitude that the Board of Founders had agreed to extend its aid to non-Chinese Christians and for the board's assistance with his school's library and reported that the current major problem he faced was housing for an increasing number of students.[43]

One delegate observed that there seemed to be a "divergence between what the New York Board would like and what East Asia needs" and argued that there needed to be more interpretation of the Board of Founders' policies. He believed there was "some uncertainty as to whether...Smith interprets New York's [policies] clearly." He cited specifically the issue of whether the Board of Founders was willing to make capital grants only to key institutions or to all regional theological institutions. A few told Pope they would prefer direct contact with those in New York.[44]

Recognizing some of the problems incident to Smith's long association with Nanjing Seminary and his present appointment half time as the Board of Founders' field representative and half time to the presidency of Trinity College, Pope made a note for himself that it would be best if Smith's successor were not the head of one of the institutions being supported by the board. The new person also needed to be "not so heavily oriented to Chinese" and to have a good relationship with Cartwright's successor.[45]

Those attending the session with Pope believed the Board of Founders had been very effective in supporting libraries and refresher courses for clergy, and they thought the board should support a theological journal in South East Asia. James Dickson of Taiwan Theological College stated that the Board of Founders' aid "had been of incalculable value," and he suggested that the board support a series of lectures, perhaps by the field representative, on specific topics like religious education or the rural church. He thought the location of

43 Liston Pope, "Seminary Heads–Handwritten Notes," February 28, 1956, Bangkok, PopeP.

44 Ibid.

45 Ibid.

the field representative's office was unimportant as long as it was in Asia. Several thought the board should work to coordinate the various institutions in matters such as standardization of programs. The group also discussed the relationship of the Board of Founders to the World Council of Churches and the International Missionary Council. Some thought the field representative could represent all of these groups, but others disagreed, since the Swope-Wendel fund came only from the United States. Again, Pope made a note to himself emphasizing the importance of this relationship. He believed the consensus of the meeting was that the field representative needed to live in South East Asia and act as a screening agent for the Board of Founders and that a theological journal should be established for the region.[46]

Following his meeting with a group of presidents of South East Asian theological institutions for discussion of the issue of summer institutes, Pope observed that most were in favor of a two-month, yearly seminar on a single topic, but the fact that institutions did not follow similar calendars presented a difficulty. They decided that participants in these institutes needed to be given a semester's leave to attend. The presidents generally expressed their unhappiness that the institutes would be limited to theological educators, for they believed lay people might also be interested. There was a general feeling that the person conducting the institute needed to travel through South East Asia prior to the meeting of the institute and also that those teaching at the institutes should include South East Asians. Pope wondered if the Board of Founders' mission could be extended to include training of the ministry as well as training for the ministry. Discussion also ranged about the question of whether the institutes should be limited to South East Asians or should be open also to Indians, Japanese, Koreans, and perhaps others. Rajah Manikam preferred the larger Asian concept, but others argued that South East Asians "got lost" among those from larger countries and that the other countries were more developed theologically than were the South East Asian countries. They did agree that there could be no institute in 1956 because there was not adequate time for planning.[47]

The Bangkok meeting on theological education was widely praised for the work it had done. Hwang wrote that it was "unique in [South East Asia] and memorable in its actual happenings and fruitful for the future." However, he also cautioned that it was premature to think of setting up a higher theological faculty for South East Asia. At

46 Ibid.

47 Liston Pope, "Presidents—Handwritten Notes," February 29, 1956, PopeP.

a special meeting of the Board of Founders in April 1956, Manikam declared that it had been "exhilarating to be with the able leaders of these theological institutions to discuss, plan, consult, and worship together."[48]

Post-Bangkok conferences were planned in several countries to discuss implementation of ideas presented in Bangkok. In Indonesia, for example, theological school leaders wanted to use the follow-up conference to work toward a unified curriculum for all their schools.[49]

Shortly after the Bangkok conference, the Board of Founders sponsored a regional workshop on degrees to consider the questions of whether it was desirable to standardize degrees throughout the area and whether such standardization could reasonably be expected to be achieved. The participants concluded that the "main desirability in the presentation of and possession of degrees lies in the respective national contexts, and not to any marked degree across the national borders within the area." They believed it was impossible at present to standardize degrees. In order to facilitate sending theological students abroad, particularly to the West, they thought it was "highly desirable" to have the ATSSEA, then in the process of formation as a result of Bangkok Conference recommendations, "evaluate the standards of existing schools." Such an evaluation should consider the academic study required for the degree, standards of the faculty, the quality of the library and other institutional facilities, rather than simply examine the number of years of education required for admission to a degree program and the number of years required to be spent in the institution in pursuance of the degree. Recognizing the different levels of schools in the area, the standards they set were:[50]

Classification	Entrance	Length and Content of Courses	Function/ Purpose of the School
1. Lay Training School	Determined according to local need	Short term instruction	According to the local need

48 Excerpts, C. H. Hwang to BF, n.p. [Tainan], April 16, 1956; Minutes, Special Meeting, BF, NTS, April 17, 1956, both ALW.

49 C. Stanley Smith to Frank T. Cartwright, Singapore, May 17, 1956, ALW.

50 Richard W. Bryant, "Report of the Workshop on Degrees," April 17, 1956, ALW.

2. Bible School	Primary education	2-3 years; emphasis on biblical knowledge and practical subjects	Training evangelists and Bible women
3. Theological School	Junior Middle School	4-5 years; training of pastors and workers	Theological course
4. Women's Training Schools	Senior Middle School	3-4 years; training of women workers	Training women workers
5. Theological College	Senior Middle School	(A) High school, 4-6 years; (B) Junior College, 3-4 years;(C) B.A. graduate, 3 years	Training of pastors and women workers

In March 1956 Cartwright confirmed to the Board of Founders that no summer institute could be held that year because there had been inadequate planning time following the Bangkok conference and because construction work on the Trinity College campus had been slow. However, he also confirmed that an institute would be held in 1957. Smith thought the 1957 study institute might focus on New Testament scholarship, for considerable interest had been shown in that topic in Bangkok. Alternately, he wrote, they might study non-Christian religions in the region, specifically Buddhism, Islam, Hinduism, the Confucian tradition, and "the underlying animism in all of these countries." Smith also suggested that the group working on plans for a regional association of theological schools could draft a constitution for discussion at the institute. He advised the board that requests were coming "thick and fast" for the Board of Founders to fund travel for American professors to lecture in South East Asia. He thought Western theologians lecturing in Asia should spend longer than a sabbatical leave in the area so they could come to understand the local situation.[51]

Participants in the Bangkok conference from the United States visited area schools prior to or following the conference and made a variety of recommendations to Smith based upon their observations. For example, Pope was troubled by the weak libraries of regional

[51] Frank T. Cartwright to BF, New York, March 30, 1956; C. Stanley Smith to Frank T. Cartwright, Singapore, May 17, 1956, both ALW.

theological schools and said that only Union Theological Seminary in Manila had a library that was "anywhere near" adequate. While the Higher Theological College in Jakarta had a fairly good collection, its books were in Dutch and German, languages which were "becoming largely unknown to post-revolution students." In reporting these observations to the Board of Founders, Smith noted that he had earlier been opposed to giving Silliman College of Theology in the Philippines money for cataloguing and other library work in part because he thought a systematic method of library organization for the entire region should be developed. He proposed two solutions. One was to ask a Western librarian with experience in Asia to spend at least two years in the region working with various libraries and training part-time people for each institution, since most schools could not afford full-time librarians. The other proposal was to offer a short-term course of perhaps three to six months to introduce staff members from the theological schools to the fundamentals of library work. Those staff members could then train students, possibly students receiving scholarship assistance in exchange for library work, to operate the libraries. Smith reflected that he had done this kind of work as a student at Auburn Theological Seminary and that his experience enabled him to train a library assistant at Nanjing Seminary. Smith favored the second proposal because it would be less expensive, and he recommended that the Board of Founders send a librarian to the region first to survey the libraries and then to offer the course. He believed the training should be offered in the region because "the more I see the results of sending immature men abroad for special training, the more I question the wisdom of it." He thought such students became accustomed to having equipment their own schools could not afford and then were unhappy with the situation after returning home. A training program in Asia would allow them to use the equipment that was available to them there. He urged that such a course provide some training in the use of audiovisual equipment.[52]

Following additional visits to various schools for consultation, Smith reported that agreement had been reached to have "Christianity and the Non-Christian Religions of Southeast Asia" as the primary subject for the 1957 study institute. There was interest in a theological examination of these religions, including animism, for

> the purpose of clarifying the essential differences in theological thought and religious practice as between the East and the

[52] C. Stanley Smith to Frank T. Cartwright, Singapore, July 2, 1956, ALW.

> West, or as between those religions which have grown out of the Semitic or Syriac background and those which have developed from an East Asian background, e.g., Taoism, Hinduism, and Buddhism. Special attention should be given to the phenomena [sic] of Animism which seems to be the primitive foundation upon which all the religions of East Asia have developed.[53]

The interest, Smith explained, was not in comparative religion but in the "basic theological ideas which underlie" these religions. Smith thought Hendrik Kraemer was the most knowledgeable person on these subjects, and he was asked to lecture on Islam and animism and the relationship of these religions to Christianity.[54] Paul Devanandan of Bangalore agreed to talk on the religions of India.[55] Smith reported there had been no consensus on a second topic, but the rural church and the relationship of the church to industrialization had been suggested. Smith believed that, because the Indonesians had the greatest number of students preparing for the ministry, they should have a larger say in the selection of institute subject matter. The only person Smith knew who had studied industrialization and Christianity in Asia was Henry Jones, who had conducted research on this topic in China, India, and Japan and was then living in Osaka. However, when asked to participate in the institute, Jones suggested instead his Philippine colleague, Fidel Galang, who held a Columbia University Ph.D. and was then the Methodist superintendent in Luzon. Galang specialized in the problems of the urban church and industrialization in Asia.[56]

Following the Bangkok conference, Smith continued working with regional theological schools in his role as field representative of the Board of Founders. The issues the schools faced were varied and complicated and included expanding cities and soaring land costs, selection of students to be supported for study abroad, ordained married couples whose job assignments were distant from one another,

53 C. Stanley Smith to Frank T. Cartwright, Singapore, October 10, 1956, ALW.

54 Kraemer, until recently the director of the WCC's Ecumenical Institute at Bossey and then a visiting professor at Union Theological Seminary in New York, had spent the years 1921-35 in Indonesia.

55 Devanandan held a Ph.D. in comparative religions from Yale University and headed the Center for the Study of Hinduism (later the Christian Institute for the Study of Religion and Society) in Bangalore.

56 Frank T. Cartwright to BF, New York, October 17, 1956, enclosing C. Stanley Smith to Frank T. Cartwright, Singapore, October 10, 1956, ALW; and C. Stanley Smith to Liston Pope, Singapore, March 5, 1957, PopeP.

and the status of Bible schools vis-a-vis theological seminaries. It was apparent that this postcolonial period was presenting new challenges and compelling the Asian schools to take new directions in their work as they sought to address the pressing issues of their changing societies. Circumstances in Asia were also compelling the Americans who constituted the Board of Founders in New York and controlled the Swope-Wendel fund to reassess their thinking regarding theological education in Asia.

The familiar Western model of ministerial preparation including a baccalaureate degree in liberal arts followed by a professional program of approximately three years and leading to a bachelor of divinity degree simply did not fit the realities of life in Asia, where many Christians lacked access even to secondary education. Furthermore, while few in Asia could afford the luxury of long years of education prior to ordination, the Christian church was growing so rapidly in some areas that many congregations would have been without any ministerial leadership had only those attaining a Western level of education been ordained. Thus the board came to recognize that Asian patterns of ministerial education could not, at least in the immediate postcolonial period, be structured on a Western model.

One of the critical problems of Asia, rapid urbanization, manifested itself in the problems of Union Theological Seminary in Manila. In 1955 this theological school had wanted to move from the city to the suburbs and needed funds to purchase land, the price of which was increasing weekly. Smith's response was sober but realistic. He wrote the Board of Founders that, because the Philippine government was developing land near the site the school had selected, land costs were likely to rise constantly. Recognizing the magnitude of the proposal, Smith wrote, "There is little doubt in my mind that in this project for moving [UTS in Manila] into the suburbs *they are embarking upon a plan which will not only involve even hundreds of thousands of dollars but will have to be supported almost entirely from abroad.*" Yet, while expressing caution regarding the move of the entire school, Smith recommended a grant of $50,000 for the purchase of land for a rural church experimental station. But E. K. Higdon, a board member with prior experience in the Philippines who was sent to assess the situation, was much more supportive of the proposed move. He recommended that Union Seminary purchase twice as much land as it needed, sell the half it did not need after a few years, and use the income from the sale to finance the whole project. Eventually, the seminary did purchase its new site and moved there, but the issue involved much of Smith's and the board's time for many months as they wrestled with determining an appropriate response.[57]

The question of church-state relations continued to present problems for Asian Christians and the Board of Founders. This was particularly true in Taiwan. A possible theological program at Tunghai University, a consolidation of several Christian colleges at Taichung, had been the subject of a meeting between Arthur L. Carson, an educational missionary of the Presbyterian Church, U.S.A., and Pope during the latter's visit to Taiwan prior to the Bangkok meeting. Carson reported that the president of the university had presented a proposal for a theological program there to Chiang Kai-shek, the president of the Republic of China, but that he had received no response. Accordingly, Carson urged that the Board of Founders "must move with caution and carefully think out each step. This is true not only because of the traditional governmental attitude against religion, but also because of the tangled church situation on Taiwan." Carson continued that the university was considering a religion department at Tunghai that would serve all students, not a professional program, though some might be led into the ministry. He also believed that the curriculum should be offered in Mandarin Chinese. After several years, if the existing seminaries did not object, Tunghai might start a three-year graduate curriculum in theology. In the meantime, university graduates seeking graduate study in religion could study abroad. However, once Tunghai University began offering two years of general education for theological students, the enrollment at Tainan Theological College declined.[58]

57 C. Stanley Smith, "New Site–Manila," September 21, 1955, emphasis in original; E. K. Higdon to Frank T. Cartwright, Quezon City, Philippines, December 16, 1955, both ALW; Minutes, Annual Meeting, BF, NTS, January 19, 1956, FTEA.

58 Arthur L. Carson to Frank T. Cartwright, January 17, 1956; Frank T. Cartwright to BF, TTC Requests and Recommendations for 1957-58 [1957?], both ALW. The Taiwan situation was tangled and complex because the nineteenth- and early twentieth-century foreign missionaries there had used the local vernacular, as had all early missionaries in China. However, when the Nationalist government retreated to Taiwan in 1949 following its defeat on the mainland, the Mandarin-speaking Nationalist mainlanders viewed the indigenous, Taiwan-speaking church members as opponents of their government. Hwang, the president of TTC and a native Taiwanese, was entangled in this situation and eventually fled the island for Britain. For an excellent account of the contemporary church situation in Taiwan see Murray A. Rubinstein, *The Protestant Community on Modern Taiwan: Mission, Seminary, and Church* (Armonk, N.Y.: Sharpe, 1991).

From Insein, Burma, Paul Clasper reported to Smith that during 1955 the seminary had acquired the religion section of the former Judson College Library but added that most of the books had been through two wars and needed rebinding. He also observed that the theological school in Insein offered a course that included a series on Buddhism. He commented that Burmese and Karen students were working together in his school and that this was an invaluable experience for both groups. The student body had tripled over the past year, and one-half of the students now were non-Karen. The Karen churches, however, did the best job of financing their students. Clasper also explained that because of the seminary's location ten miles from Rangoon, it was in need of housing for families since many married men were applying for admission. The school hoped to become interdenominational and had asked the Anglicans and Methodists to join it. It was also attempting to serve the Chinese Christians in Upper Burma and in the cities.[59]

> At the present time, there are many scattered Chinese congregations of an independent nature which have little or no contact with one another and struggle along with very little outside assistance. They have made some definite proposals which seem to indicate that there is strong interest in working together. In this our Divinity School Chinese students have taken the lead and are recognized as the most able Chinese leaders by these churches. It remains to be seen what direction this will take, but there is no doubt of the appreciation of the local Chinese churches for this interest and help coming from the Divinity School.[60]

Smith received a request from R. O. Hall of the Hong Kong Theological School in May 1956 asking for Board of Founders' support for a non-Asian dean for a period of five years. In his request, Hall indicated that the Methodists, Presbyterians, and Baptists had joined in supporting the college. Smith forwarded the request to the board

59 Paul Clasper to C. Stanley Smith, Insein, Burma, March 7, 1956, ALW. Many Karen converted to Christianity in the nineteenth century as a means of gaining foreign help against the ethnic Burmese, their traditional opponents, and also because the arrival of Western missionaries seemed to complement the Karen tradition that a younger white brother would one day return with their lost sacred book. See John F. Cady, *History of Modern Burma* (Ithaca: Cornell Univ. Press, 1958), 98-99.

60 Paul Clasper to C. Stanley Smith, Insein, Burma, March 7, 1956, ALW.

but indicated that he had talked with the school's representatives at the Bangkok meeting and had cautioned them not to expect help, since the Board of Founders supported only Asian or former missionary faculty from Nanjing Seminary. He had also told them that a union college was not a denominationally founded school that other groups later joined, but rather one established on an interdenominational basis from the beginning.[61]

Indonesia remained an area of primary concern for Board of Founders members following the Bangkok meeting because of the very large number of Protestant Christians in that country. D. S. Simon Marantika, general secretary of the National Christian Council in Indonesia, wrote Cartwright that there were 3,100,000 Protestants in Indonesia and that this number represented more than half the membership of all the national Christian communities represented in the Bangkok conference. Additionally, almost half the students enrolled in the nineteen theological seminaries represented at the conference were enrolled in Indonesian schools. Marantika estimated that four thousand Indonesian congregations were then in need of pastors and added that only the Higher Theological College in Jakarta educated Indonesia's future professors and theologians.[62]

Yet less developed institutions in Indonesia also sought the Board of Founders' assistance in strengthening their programs. As a result of having attended the Bangkok conference, T. S. Sihombing of the Nommensen Theological School in Siantar, Indonesia, wrote to Smith that Pope had suggested it might be possible for the board to support his school with a grant for library books.[63]

Smith returned to Indonesia in August 1956 for a five-week visit to the institutions being supported by the Board of Founders. His impression of conditions there was generally positive. At the end of his journey, Smith wrote the board that it was his

> conviction that the organization of theological education in Indonesia is sound and generally effective; that the advance of theological education has been unusually rapid especially during the past four or five years; that it is constantly advancing

[61] R. O. Hall to C. Stanley Smith, Request from Hong Kong Theological School, May 8, 1956, ALW.

[62] D. S. Simon Marantika to Frank T. Cartwright, Jakarta, May 15, 1956, ALW.

[63] T. S. Sihombing to C. Stanley Smith, Siantar, Indonesia, May 31, 1956, PopeP.

> and that the leaders of theological education, both missionary and Indonesians, are alive to the need for thorough theological training of the ministry and are doing their best to bring this about.[64]

Smith continued that he found "sound biblical and theological instruction" in Indonesia and that he had "found the church in all parts of Indonesia freer from the often disrupting effects of passing evangelists and religious fanaticism than in some other countries." He also found "a general open mindedness and eagerness for new methods and new approaches to the problems of theological education among both missionaries and Indonesian pastors, teachers and administrators." Smith wrote that this was especially true among the younger men and women. He suggested the need for a thorough study of the curricula of the various schools and expressed the opinion that admission standards were too low in some of them. He singled out Higher Theological College in Jakarta for praise with respect to its "effective work." Because of the rural nature of the church in Indonesia, Smith believed the schools should concentrate on rural issues, and he also urged better instruction in homiletics. He noted the acute need for adequate libraries and for better instruction in how to make use of the libraries they had. He wrote that the board's policy of making only small grants over the past four years had been wise in that it did not impair the independence of the schools. He also noted the unanimous praise heard in Indonesia for the board's Bangkok conference.[65]

In a letter to Cartwright concerning this trip, Smith wrote that he had traveled from Semarang to Jogjakarta by taxi and had seen a "large number of Communist symbols along the way," but he added that the Christians, both Roman Catholic and Protestant, had "political parties of their own with their own signs and symbols." The seminary at Jogjakarta was headed by S. P. Poerbowijogo, a young Indonesian whose competence Smith praised and whom he described as "quite a scholar in his own right...." Smith also noted that D. C. Mulder, a missionary faculty member there, was often sought out as a lecturer by universities and higher middle schools because of his understanding of Islam. Smith reported that the church in central Java had sixty thousand members, that the Chinese were well integrated into the community and considered themselves Indonesian, and that Chinese pastors preached in Indonesian. He reported that the leaders of the

64 C. Stanley Smith, "Conclusions and Suggestions Arising from the Visit to Indonesia, August 13-October 7, 1956," ALW.

65 Ibid.

Jogjakarta school were interested in raising their standards and that, because of inadequate dormitory space, they were currently accepting a new class only biennially.[66]

Smith described religious ceremonies he had witnessed at the temples: "Bali is one place in which to study the development of primitive animism as it has been influenced by Hinduism. It is also a living demonstration of the inability of even a higher religion such as Hinduism to banish the basic animism which permeates the religious life of the whole area of Southeast Asia."[67]

At Makassar local Christians who were government officials assisted Smith in obtaining the required permission to visit Ambon. The theological school at Ambon had been nearly destroyed by U.S. bombing during World War II and had had no lights for the dormitory the previous year. However, Smith found that its current problem was water. The wells at the school were dry in the hot season, and the students took water from the professors' homes. The town also lacked adequate water, and many people blamed the problem on the nuclear tests conducted in the Pacific. Smith wrote that in Ambon 50 percent of the population was Christian and that there was a large Muslim population as well. He reported that the two groups got along well, each following its own laws as well as an older traditional law which was applied to everyone. "On the whole so far as I could learn there was fairly good feeling between Christian and Moslem with cooperation and a live and let live spirit." Smith added that members of the two groups were distinguished only by the women's clothing.[68]

Smith commented that the Christian community in Ambon suffered from the loss of Kita Manuputti, who had transferred to Makassar. He confirmed that she was "an extremely capable woman, well trained, a good teacher, and a vigorous personality." He added there was some indication that she might be asked to become the director of the Makassar school but also reported some opposition to such a move. Smith had "some very interesting and valuable conversations with this couple." Samuel Manupitti was knowledgeable concerning the animistic religions of the island south of Ambon. He had been assigned as a superintendent of a local church, and Smith noted that situations in which both husband and wife are ordained pastors create "some very interesting questions."

66 C. Stanley Smith to Frank T. Cartwright, Singapore, October 11, 1956, ALW.

67 Smith, "Conclusions," 7, 9.

68 Ibid., 12, 18.

At a meeting of the synod of churches of the Moluccas, Smith was asked to answer questions, one of which was what the synod should do in the case of couples who were both ordained clergy. Smith commented that this brought up a problem that the Indonesian church had not previously faced and that he doubted if many Western churches had adequately addressed. He wrote that he had responded that most of the ordained women he knew in the West were single, but he could not state that as an actual fact. He noted that his own Presbyterian church had recently granted permission to presbyteries to ordain women to the ministry if they chose to do so. He tried to identify some of the principles involved in addressing the problem and ruled out requiring ordained women to remain single, since he thought that was contrary to Protestant principles and practice. He believed the primary problems were related to assignment of an ordained woman to a place where her husband did not live and providing women clergy time for child rearing, since ordained women had every right to raise families if they so desired. Smith suggested the possibility of an inactive status for ordained women while their children were too young to permit full-time work in the church. He also said that, in discussing the matter in small groups, he found that most agreed with this proposal. However, Smith thought problems such as the one raised by the transfer of Mrs. Manuputti from the theological school in Ambon to that in Makassar could not be solved by a universal rule and should be worked out individually. As an aside to this issue, Smith observed that linking the schools at Ambon and Makassar would be problematic because of their different histories.[69]

At Bandjermasin Smith learned that, in spite of long contact with Christianity, many Dyaks had returned to their old religion. Also distressing was the fact that most of the fifty-nine students at the theological school there had chosen to enter that school only after failing their senior middle school graduation examinations. The Basel Mission worked in the area and emphasized rural work. Its attitude was reflected in a statement at a recent conference of the church of Indonesia where it was declared

> that the cutting edge of the church was not the men trained in schools like the [HTC] or even those based upon junior middle school, but was the men and women who were going out of the lower grade Bible schools who were willing to go back to the

[69] Ibid., 13, 21, 22.

> villages and rural areas and minister, not only to the Christians, but also to try to evangelize the non-Christians.[70]

Smith questioned whether this was an entirely accurate picture of the situation in Indonesia but granted a good deal of truth in the statement. Yet he recognized that, even if this judgment were accurate, the higher schools were essential to provide the teaching staffs for the lower schools. He also reported that the school at Bandjermasin, like those at Ambon and Malang, lacked library facilities.[71]

Several months after his lengthy visit to Indonesia, Smith received a request from the Evangelical Church of Kalimantan for a Board of Founders grant to assist the church in opening a Bible school at Bandjarmasin to train clergy for rural work. Smith forwarded the request with the observation that he was uncertain how this school was connected to the theological school at Bandjarmasin, but that it was to have twenty-five students in a four-year course and that he recommended a grant of $1,000 to assist in initiation of the project.[72]

Turning his attention again to Taiwan in 1957, Smith reported yet another problem in relations between the theological schools and the government, a problem that had not arisen elsewhere. Students attending Taiwan theological colleges had the same legal standing as students attending universities, but theological students were under the Department of Interior, which handled religious matters, rather than the Department of Education, which had responsibility for university students. Consequently, their military service responsibilities were not the same. Students at universities were exempt from military service until graduation, but those at theological colleges could be and were called up at any time. The students "may have had part of a term, or one year, or some other period and no regard is paid to the fact that if they are called up in the midst of a term, they lose credits for the work already done. The students are arbitrarily called and have no recourse," Smith wrote. He indicated that forty men from the Tainan Theological College were serving in the military when he visited there the previous November and that this obviously decreased the college's enrollment.[73]

70 Ibid., 23, 29, 30.

71 Ibid.

72 C. Stanley Smith, "Theological Training School of the Evangelical Church of Kalimantan," Singapore, February 18, 1957, ALW.

73 Frank T. Cartwright to BF, "TTC, Requests and Recommendations for 1957-58" [1957?], ALW.

Tainan Theological College had asked the Board of Founders for salary to employ a Taiwanese faculty member in the field of Christian and social ethics, but Smith thought the school or the local churches needed to assume the costs of employing nationals as professors. For the Taiwan Theological College, Smith forwarded to the board a request for $20,000 for a new chapel. Smith remarked that this institution was making more progress in integrating mainlanders and Taiwanese than any other in Taiwan, and he also indicated the Canadian mission was taking greater interest in the college.[74]

During this period the board also had to deal with issues related to Smith's retirement and selection of its field representative.[75] In May 1955 Smith had asked the board for a scholarship for John R. Fleming, a missionary of the Church of Scotland. Fleming had been in Manchuria in the 1930s and had transferred to Malaya, where he was then secretary of the Malayan Christian Council. Fleming was also teaching at Trinity College and had been suggested as Smith's successor as president of the college. However, Hubert Sone became president of Trinity, and Fleming became the Board of Founders' representative in South East Asia. Smith had earlier expressed the hope that an Asian could follow him, and it was clear that others in New York shared this hope. However, no Asian candidate was available, and Smith was convinced Fleming was well qualified to do a fine job for the Board of Founders and the Asian schools. When in 1958 the board asked Fleming to be its field representative in South East Asia, he was told he would need to work toward the establishment of a secretariat for the East Asia Christian Council and to plan for the "world-wide advance in ministerial training under the leadership of the IMC." The board hoped that the Malayan Christian Council would be able to find someone to replace Fleming within six months and that it would allow him to begin work immediately on preparations for the 1959 study institute and for the projected theological journal. After joining the Board of Founders' staff in July 1958, Fleming continued to teach one course each semester at Trinity College but devoted the remainder of his time to the board. The board appropriated $10,000 for Fleming's living quarters in the new building at Trinity. Fleming subsequently also succeeded Cartwright upon the latter's retirement to become executive secretary of the Board

74 Ibid.

75 Smith was born in 1890, and the BF first considered the selection of a replacement as field representative in 1956 when Smith reached the age of sixty-six. Minutes, Annual Meeting, BF, June 4, 1956, FTEA.

of Founders in 1961. Smith, who had arrived in China in 1917 and joined the Nanjing Theological Seminary faculty a year later, returned to the United States and resumed work under the Methodist Board training outgoing missionaries and doing research at the Missionary Research Library at Union Theological Seminary in New York.[76]

The Board of Founders responded to problems related to physical facilities at Trinity College at this time as well. In November 1957 the Board of Governors of the college voted to ask the Board of Founders for $60,000 for two dormitories, one for men and one for married couples. The Anglicans had promised another $33,000 to help finance these buildings. Three years earlier, while in the United States, Smith had made a request for $30,000 for a men's residence to replace the old one, which he described as "termite-ridden and dilapidated, without suitable bathing and toilet facilities...[and] dark and mosquito-infested with, in most cases, study and sleeping arrangements that offered little privacy either for study or living....[The facility was] nearly, if not actually, a century old." Smith told the board that he "never took visitors to see it except at a distance when the trees covered it up fairly well." He also expressed the fear that, if the city engineer ever appeared to inspect the building, it would be condemned. When Trinity was asked to host a study institute, it could do so only because the eighteen participants could be housed in the women's dormitory on the fourth floor of a new building.[77]

Trinity's housing problems posed especially difficult questions for the Board of Founders. Anglican students traditionally had a warden and a subwarden living with them, but the college had only provided housing for its Asian faculty. A larger issue concerned property rights. The property on which Trinity College had been built belonged to the Women's Board of the Methodist Church in the United States, and the question of who would own the buildings erected with non-Methodist

76 C. Stanley Smith to Frank T. Cartwright, Singapore, May 13, 1955; "Memo Concerning Possible Future Plans for Field Representative of BF in Southeast Asia," April 17, 1956; Minutes, Annual Meeting, BF, NTS, January 20, 1958; A note of Cartwright's dated February 3, 1958, indicated Fleming had resigned from the MCC effective June 30 and would begin work for the BF on July 1, 1958, Cartwright Note, February 3, 1958, all ALW. Frank T. Cartwright to James Duffin, New York, June 29, 1961; and John R. Fleming to All Seminary Presidents in Southeast Asia Receiving Grants from BF/NTS, New York, July 7, 1961, both FTEA.

77 Minutes, Annual Meeting, BF, NTS, June 3, 1958, FTEA; C. Stanley Smith, "A Report to the BF on the Request of Trinity College, Singapore, for a Grant for New Student Hostels," January 17, 1958, ALW.

funds was difficult to resolve, as the college then had only a thirty-year lease on the property. The Board of Founders approved $30,000 to build a men's dormitory to house twenty-five to thirty men, with the stipulation that the building should be used for this purpose as long as Trinity remained a union institution.[78]

With expulsion of Western missions from the People's Republic of China, the Literature Production Program, translating Christian classics into Chinese, took on added significance as a tool for continuing support of the Chinese Christian community. This program, under the direction of Francis P. Jones, continued to work on the translation of Christian classics into Chinese from its office at Drew University in Madison, New Jersey. Jones reported to the Board of Founders in 1955 that because of the backlog of manuscripts awaiting editing and revision, translation work would be reduced in the forthcoming year in order to enable the editors to catch up. Three years later, at the time of the 1958 Board of Founders annual meeting, Jones reported that the program's budget for the year was $26,100 and that Drew University had begun charging rent of $50 per month for office space. N. Z. Zia, a Nanking Theological Seminary faculty member in the late 1940s, had come from Hong Kong and joined the staff in April.[79] Jones also reported that three volumes had been printed in Hong Kong: Calvin, volume 2; Luther, volume 1; and Newman. Two manuscripts, Calvin, volume 3, and the Latin Church, had recently been sent to Hong Kong for printing. Two more, Luther, volume 2, and Niebuhr, were in the final stages of preparation. Sales for the years 1956 and 1957 were: 494 copies of Calvin, volume 1; 238 copies of William Temple; 400 copies of Wesley; 161 copies of Rauschenbusch; 178 copies of Calvin, volume 2; 167 copies of Creeds; and 149 copies of Luther, volume 1. No figures were available on sales of the Newman volume.[80]

Jones reported that fourteen volumes were in various stages of translation and editing but that the Catholics, who had planned to provide five volumes in this series, indicated they were unable to continue

78 Ibid.; Minutes, Annual Meeting, BF, NTS, January 20, 1958, FTEA. Cartwright wrote to the BF concerning these issues and a meeting held by representatives of groups involved in an attempt to resolve them. See Frank T. Cartwright to BF, New York, May 26, 1958, ALW.

79 Zia Nai-zing or Hsieh Fu-ya (1892-1991) was a prominent Christian scholar in China prior to 1949, when he left Nanjing for Hong Kong. From 1958 until his retirement, he was engaged in the Christian classics translation project.

80 Francis Jones, "LPP of the NTS Report," May 28, 1959, ALW.

with the project. Jones wanted to have sixteen volumes of the first twenty-six done before he retired in 1960. He expressed a willingness to work part time after retirement if he could have one Chinese coworker and if the Board of Founders would continue to publish the works. He also advised the board that he had been subscribing to various theological journals for the Nanjing Seminary library, but, as they were piling up in his office and he thought it unlikely they would ever reach the seminary, he asked to terminate the subscriptions and give those journals already received to the field representative in South East Asia for distribution to whatever regional library wanted them.[81]

As of May 1958, Jones was able to give an overall summary of the work accomplished on translations since the program was begun: Among the Christian classics, volumes on the Post-Apostolic age, Tertullian, Eusebius, the Arian controversy, Augustine's *Confessions,* two translations of Augustine's *City of God,* a volume of medieval devotional literature, and volumes of writings of Ritschl and Harnack were in manuscript in Nanjing. Other works in process were the later Ante-Nicene writers, the Christian school of Alexandria, the Eastern church, medieval thought, patristic and medieval sermons, one volume of Luther and Melanchthon, British Presbyterianism and Puritanism, seventeenth- and eighteenth-century rationalism, Kant, eighteenth- and nineteenth-century idealism, Jonathan Edwards, Ernst Troeltsch, Soren Kierkegaard, and Reinhold Niebuhr. Works planned but not yet begun included Augustine's further works, Thomas Aquinas, a devotional anthology, the Quakers, Anglican thought, pietism and devotional literature, Schleiermacher, Protestant sermons, and a volume on Barth and Brunner.[82]

In the following year, the Literature Production Program report indicated that more books had been sold but that none were circulating to any extent in China. A copy of each book had been sent to Nanjing Union Theological Seminary, but the seminary had not acknowledged receipt. Yet books had reached China's central repository:

> Copies have also been sent to the National Library in Peking, and those have been acknowledged with a cordial letter of thanks, and the hope that we will continue to send succeeding volumes to them. [Moses] Hsu has sent the Wesley volume and Vol. I of Calvin to his father in Amoy [now Xiamen], and a letter in reply has said that the Wesley volume was being passed around from

81 Ibid.
82 Ibid.

> hand to hand among preachers of Amoy and eagerly read. The Calvin volume, the letter said, was in the hands of Rev. Chou Ching-tseh, whom readers of the *China Bulletin* will recognize as the Amoy pastor denounced as a rightist in last year's report.[83]

Later that year Searle Bates prepared a report on the Literature Production Program for the Board of Founders in consideration of Francis Jones's planned retirement in 1960 and the fact that his Chinese collaborator, N. Z. Zia, was then sixty-six years old and nearing retirement. Bates thought it possible that a large number of the forty-six volumes in the Early, Medieval, Reform, and Post-Reformation series would be done, "assuming a future life for the nine volumes now in manuscript in Nanking." He proposed suspending the contemporary series, since only the volumes of William Temple and Reinhold Niebuhr were completed and some of the selections made in the 1940s no longer appeared as important in the 1960s. He asked board to continue funding the program at the rate of $16,000 per year until 1964, when the program was scheduled to end.[84]

By mid-1960, the Literature Production Program had published the second volume of Luther's work, the third volume of Calvin's, a volume on the Latin Church, and Reinhold Niebuhr's *Nature and Destiny of Man.* Other translations were in Hong Kong awaiting printing, including a volume on the Age of Reason, Kant, Ernst Troeltsch's *Social Teaching of the Christian Churches*, patristic and medieval sermons, Jonathan Edwards, and the Quakers. At the Board of Founders' annual meeting that year, program issues were discussed in light of the retirement of Jones and Zia. Both were willing to continue working part time, and the program was therefore reduced but not ended. Board minutes indicate that in 1960 just over $10,000 had been expended on the project, more than half for salaries. In 1964 it was reported that more than ten thousand volumes of the Christian Classics Library in Chinese translation had been sold.[85] *The Age of Reason in Religion*, *Kant's Moral Philosophy*, *Sermons*, *Quaker Classics*, and *Works of Jonathan Edwards* had been published by the following year.[86]

83 Francis Jones, "LPP of the NTS Report," May 28, 1959, ALW; and Minutes, Annual Meeting, BF, NTS, May 28, 1959, FTEA.

84 M. Searle Bates, "LPP Report," October 29, 1959, ALW. Bates had taught history at the University of Nanking and was then teaching at Union Theological Seminary in New York and a member of the BF.

85 Minutes, Annual Meeting, BF, NTS, May 27, 1960; May 28, 1962; June 2, 1964; all FTEA; "LPP of the NTS Report," May 27, 1960, ALW.

86 Minutes, Annual Meeting, BF, NTS, June 7, 1961, FTEA.

Cartwright, who made periodic trips to visit South East Asian theological institutions in his capacity as executive secretary of the Board of Founders, made a three-month trip with John Fleming in late 1958 to acquaint Fleming with the schools and to introduce him to their staffs. The two visited eleven countries and thirteen of the fifteen theological schools then receiving aid from the Board of Founders. They also held discussions with people in Hong Kong and in Hualien, Taiwan, concerning the possibility of establishing new training centers in each place. Cartwright later wrote that Fleming looked at the schools as a Scottish Presbyterian with classroom and faculty experience, whereas he viewed them as an American Methodist with no firsthand knowledge of theological instruction. He also commented that Fleming, who was selected to become the first executive director of the Association of Theological Schools in South East Asia upon its founding in 1959 while retaining his position with the Board of Founders, viewed himself as the servant of the Association of Theological Schools in South East Asia while being responsible to the Board of Founders. He also reported to the board that Fleming was attempting to commence publication of the proposed regional theological journal.[87]

Fleming spent eleven days in Taiwan, usually accompanied by Cartwright, visiting Taiwan Theological Seminary, Tainan Theological College, Tunghai University in Taichung, and some of the tribal churches in the mountains. He then went on to Hong Kong, where he spent a week with the Union Theological College, the Lutheran Seminary, and Chung Chi Christian College. Afterward he briefly visited McGilvary Theological Seminary in Thailand. Cartwright and he then visited the seminary in Insein, Burma, and then went on to Indonesia via Singapore. In Indonesia they visited the Methodist Theological School in Sibu, Borneo, a Methodist Agricultural Center in Nangamujong, and the churches of the Dyaks. They visited the Nommensen University at Siantar in Sumatra but were unable to travel further in that area because of unsettled conditions in the region. The two visited Higher Theological College in Jakarta and then a teachers' training college and the beginnings of a Christian university in Salatiga. They also made visits to the theological schools in Jogjakarta and at Makassar. Back in Jakarta they met with Indonesian National Christian Council and Higher Theological College personnel before leaving Indonesia. In the Philippines they visited Union Theological

87 Frank T. Cartwright, Report to Mid-Year Meeting, New York, January 5, 1959, ALW.

Seminary in Manila and St. Andrew's Theological Seminary in Manila, the College of Theology, Central University of the Philippines at Iloilo, and the College of Theology, Silliman University at Dumaguete City.[88]

During this extensive journey, Cartwright and Fleming observed how much the Bangkok conference and the subsequent creation of ATSSEA had done to build unity among the Christians of South East Asia. They accepted few requests for funding during this trip, but Cartwright reported they made a commitment of $1,000 on behalf of the Board of Founders to fund a meeting in Manila of the Filipino and missionary members of the Federation of Churches Committee on Theological Survey. Jose Yap, chair of the federation, had called the conference and asked for five representatives from the two major denominations, the United Christian Church of the Philippines and the Methodists, two from the Baptists, and one each from other cooperating churches. Each of the four theological colleges was asked to send an official representative. Fleming was asked to give the opening address.[89]

Cartwright reported to the Board of Founders that he and Fleming had spent three strenuous days on Taiwan visiting congregations among the aborigines on the east coast in the company of Dickson, a Canadian Presbyterian and principal of Taipei Theological School, who had worked for many years with representatives of the mountain tribes, and Edward Currie of the Presbyterian Church in the U.S., and several Taiwanese. During the latter years of the Japanese occupation of the island during World War II, there had been reports of an underground Christian movement inspired by an elderly woman who had studied briefly with the Dicksons before disappearing into the rugged mountains. After the war, a few Christian congregations were discovered there. Encouraged by other Taiwanese Christians, these congregations developed with largely untrained lay leadership until, at the time of the visit, there were said to be "more than 450 congregations...made up for the most part of illiterate people."[90]

Cartwright reported to the Board of Founders that those acting as pastors to these congregations were poorly educated, but that a few trained Taiwanese pastors had been assigned by the General Assembly of the Presbyterian Church of Taiwan to help them. Recognizing the scope of the problem of preparing leaders from these tribes, the General Assembly had established a theological training center near Hualien, the

88 Ibid.
89 Ibid.
90 Ibid.

largest city of the mountain area, to serve them. Cartwright indicated that the center had flimsy buildings that were entirely too small for the fifty-three students then enrolled. Thirty-three students were in the regular three-year course, to which admission required only six years of elementary study, though a few students had completed junior middle school. Twenty students were enrolled in a one-year course. Cartwright commented:

> Rarely indeed has my heart been stirred more deeply than by meeting some of the heroes of this church, people who defied Japanese police force, who often met secretly and with sentries posted, some of their leaders having been imprisoned, beaten savagely, not once but often—and then having gone on as modern apostles preaching the Gospel.[91]

Cartwright further observed that he wholeheartedly joined with Fleming in recommending that the Board of Founders make an exception to its policy of aiding only institutions that qualified as theological colleges and grant a sizeable amount of funding, to be matched by the Christians on Taiwan and by the cooperating Presbyterian Boards of Foreign Missions, to meet the needs of this school. "The need is overwhelmingly clear, and the opportunity is just ahead of us, an opportunity that may fade with passing years," he wrote. In justification of his recommendation, Cartwright observed that

> when we discussed this project, we realized that such a request would create some problems for the BF in view of their general policy regarding the minimum standards for theological institutions. This training school accepted students who have had a primary education only, but my own opinion is that in a case like this, where a whole church of 350 congregations and 70,000 members is in dire need of a trained ministry, we have to accept the situation as it is, and begin training the ministry at the highest point of education [they have attained]....They have many more applications for entrance than they can take.[92]

Cartwright indicated some urgency about this matter and reported that other groups were showing signs of aggressive work among the aborigines. He mentioned that aboriginal students were

[91] Ibid.

[92] Ibid. In September 1958 this training school accepted a class of 39 from 140 applicants.

being admitted into the mission schools and that a new Canadian missionary with a Ph.D. degree from Edinburgh was beginning work among them. On the basis of this recommendation, the board gave $30,000 to the General Assembly of the Presbyterian Church in Taiwan's Committee on Mountain Work for the cost of buildings. This grant was supplemented by $15,000 from the Canadian Presbyterian Church and $7,500 each from the English Presbyterian Church and the Taiwan Presbyterian Church. The school also received $18,000 from Inter-Church Aid to purchase thirty-five acres of land.[93]

These aboriginal Christians suffered disastrous losses from a typhoon in the fall following Cartwright's visit. Cartwright reported information from John Whitehorn, who was working with the tribes, that fifty churches had collapsed during the typhoon and another forty-seven were damaged. One church member had been killed and more than sixty injured, and the houses of more than one thousand church members had collapsed or were damaged. Whitehorn estimated the losses of these tribal Christians at $10,600.[94]

The ability of the Board of Founders to support programming throughout South East Asia depended on income from the Swope-Wendel grant. At its annual meeting in 1958, the board took note of the fact that much of the Swope-Wendel fund was held in government bonds, and it requested that the Investment Committee of the Division of World Missions of the Methodist Church, which held and managed the funds, reconsider this arrangement with the objective of diversifying investments to receive a higher rate of income from the fund. In continuation of its scholarship support, the Board of Founders also voted at this meeting to grant funds to E. Y. Cheng to attend the WCC Ecumenical Institute in Bossey, Switzerland; to H. Y. Liu, for travel and study in England; to C. S. Cheng, a pastor in Taiwan, for study in the United States; to T. S. Chang for travel to New York, where he had been granted a scholarship at Union Theological Seminary; and to Samuel Chu-san Ting, who had been studying in the United States at his own expense, to travel to Singapore, where he was to divide his time between teaching church music and offering private lessons at Trinity College.[95]

93 Ibid. and Minutes, Annual Meeting, BF, NTS, January 16, 1959, FTEA. The city near which the training school was located is referred to as Auliang in the report, but Hualien is likely the site meant.

94 Frank T. Cartwright to BF, New York, October 29, 1959, ALW.

95 Ibid.; Minutes, Annual Meeting, BF, NTS, June 3, 1958, FTEA.

The Reverend Peter Latuihamallo, from the theological school in Jakarta, made a presentation to the Board of Founders on Christianity in Indonesia. He stated that the first real theological college had begun classes in 1934 and that its first class of seventeen graduates was therefore available to lead the church when World War II began and the Dutch were evacuated or interned. He also explained to the board that the lower level theological schools educated people as evangelists, while the higher schools such as Higher Theological College in Jakarta and the college at Nommensen prepared people for the ordained clergy.[96]

This meeting also adopted a memorial to Abbe Livingstone Warnshuis, a long-time member of the board. It received John Fleming's formal acceptance of the position of regional representative of the Board of Founders in South East Asia and expressed its appreciation to Stanley Smith upon his retirement. The board also voted to fund preparation of a basic list of theological books and periodicals and a list of books in simple English appropriate for use in Asian theological schools. The work was to be done by the Yale Divinity School library and the Missionary Research Library in New York.[97] A little more than a year later, the board memorialized Smith, who had died in retirement.[98]

An analysis of appropriations by the Board of Founders from January 1, 1937, to June 30, 1959, was prepared for and presented to the board in early 1960. This report revealed that during this period the board had expended $1,801,011. Of this amount, $508,304 went directly to Nanjing Union Theological Seminary between 1937 and 1950. Other expenditures included $425,091 for buildings and repair; $248,600 for the Literature Production Program; $170,307 for the support of missionaries in the field and in translation work; $123,925 for seminaries other than Nanjing; and lesser amounts for refresher courses, classroom equipment, scholarships for study abroad, books, institutes, and conference.[99]

A financial analysis prepared for the same meeting indicated that the Board of Founders' income was derived from two primary sources. The first was an investment account supervised by Morgan Guaranty Trust Company, an account then containing $305,522.35 and earning annual income of about $9,000. This fund had been created from surplus working capital and contingency reserves which

96 Ibid.
97 Minutes, Annual Meeting, BF, NTS, June 3, 1958.
98 Minutes, Special Meeting, BF, NTS, November 19, 1959, FTEA.
99 "Analysis of Appropriations of the BF, January 1, 1937, to June 30, 1959," April 30, 1960, ALW.

might be required for operations. The major source of income was the Swope-Wendel Permanent Fund, which was carried in the portfolio of the Division of World Missions of the Methodist Church and then had a balance of $2,531,695.80, on which a minimum of 3.5 percent per annum was being received. In recent years the actual payment had exceeded 4 percent for an annual income of $101,267.85 for the most recent period. Thus the total annual income available to the Board of Founders was about $110,000. The restricted reserve contained $99,215.01, and the board wished to reduce this to $50,000 by transferring the excess to unexpended income, which would then be termed unappropriated surplus. Additionally, the board's pension reserve was $38,279.15. Appropriations amounted to $46,551.32, and administrative expenses were $870.98. The budget for the Singapore office was $6,840 for 1958-59 and $7,170 for 1959-60.[100]

Fleming's budget recommendations for regional work in 1960-61 were forwarded to the Board of Founders by Cartwright in 1960. They included $20,000 for the recurring theological study institute; $1,500 for the *South East Asia Journal of Theology*; $5,720 or $7,720 for the Singapore office, depending on whether the automobile was replaced; and $3,500 for the Church of Scotland to cover the portion of Fleming's time devoted to the board. Cartwright, who would be retiring from the position of executive secretary in 1961, proposed additionally $8,000 for that position and the New York office; $750 for the executive secretary's overseas travel; $6,800 for management, accounting, and auditing expenses in New York; and $10,000 for the Literature Production Program operations exclusive of Francis Jones's salary.[101] These recommendations from the executive director and the regional representative were approved. Such recommendations from either the executive director or the regional representative were generally approved by the board if funds were available and if the recommendations fell within the guidelines earlier adopted.

The Board of Founders awarded a number of fellowships annually for Asian faculty members to study abroad. Typical of these grants were those given for 1960-61, which included awards to Levi V. Oracion, Union Theological Seminary in Manila, to work with Raymond Morris

[100] "Financial Analysis, April 30, 1960," in Minutes, Annual Meeting, BF, NTS, May 27, 1960, and John Fleming, "Singapore Office Budget," May 2, 1959, in Frank T. Cartwright to BF, New York, May 15, 1960, both ALW.

[101] Minutes, Annual Meeting, BF, New York, May 27, 1960, FTEA; "Field Representative's Recommendations, 1960-61," in Frank T. Cartwright to BF, New York, April 27, 1960, ALW.

at the Yale Divinity School library so that he could manage the Manila library upon his return; Samuel Johannes Manuputti, Theological School, Makassar, for travel to study rural evangelism, contingent on his obtaining other assistance; Nico Radjawane, Malang, a young part-time teacher whose abilities had impressed both Fleming and his teachers and whose study was judged likely to benefit the whole church; and Ivy Su-teng Chou, Ed.D., Methodist Theological School, Sibu, Sarawak, for completion of a B.D. degree at Union Theological Seminary in New York. Ivy Chou would later serve as executive director of the Foundation for Theological Education in South East Asia and of the Theological Education Fund of the World Council of Churches from 1972 to 1977. Several others received smaller awards.[102]

Fleming's other recommendations that year included a request for assistance for Tainan Theological College, which continued to experience rapid growth in enrollment and where most of the students were on scholarship. He wrote that the local churches were unable to support all of these students. The college then had 50 new students, 7 of them university graduates, and a total enrollment of 182. Fleming believed that a grant of $2,000 for scholarship aid would be very helpful. He also recommended $1,200 for a scholarship at Tunghai University, $1,000 for a refresher course, and $1,500 for library grants. For Taiwan Theological College in Taipei, Fleming recommended $2,000 for scholarship assistance, reported that this school had 35 new students and a total enrollment of 115, and that it had two new Chinese teachers with master's degrees from Princeton Theological Seminary. He also recommended $1,000 for a refresher course and $1,000 for the library there.[103]

Fleming included extensive comments on the Mount Morrison Theological Institute in Taiwan, the training center for mountain tribes that had so impressed Cartwright on his visit to the island. Fleming reported that from the General Assembly of the Presbyterian Church in Taiwan he had learned that this center offered a two-year preparatory course for elementary school graduates, a four-year main course, and a one-year practical work course. For junior middle school graduates it offered three years of high school as well as the main course and practical work course. The school served ten different tribes and had moved seven times in thirteen years. Everyone at the school, including

102 Minutes, Annual Meeting, BF, NTS, May 27, 1960, FTEA; Cartwright, *River*, 34.

103 "Field Representative's Recommendations, 1960-61," in Frank T. Cartwright to BF, New York, April 27, 1960, ALW.

two seventy-five-year-old men and nine women with children strapped to their backs, engaged in twelve hours of manual work weekly. They had planted nearly 100,000 fruit trees, azaleas, pines, and other plants on the mountain sides. They had also constructed four bamboo buildings and a five hundred-yard road and were helping the Honghui church establish a farm for self-support. They also sent students to preach at twenty-five tribal churches on Sundays. Fleming had not visited during the past year and found this request difficult to evaluate, but he recommended $2,250 for scholarships, $2,300 for audiovisual equipment and materials, $500 for a refresher course, and $500 for the library.[104]

Most of the requests from regional schools that Fleming forwarded to the Board of Founders in 1960 were for such usual things as libraries, scholarships, and refresher courses, but some were extraordinary. For example, the rector of Higher Theological College in Jakarta expressed concern over the board's decision of the previous November to decrease support for Asian faculty over a period of five years. Higher Theological was concerned about how this policy might affect its ability to replace Pouw Le-gan, their only ethnic Chinese faculty member. Pouw was eager to pursue further study or to leave Indonesia, whose government policies were discriminatory toward Chinese people even if, as in the case of Pouw, the individuals held Indonesian citizenship. If Pouw left, under the board's new policy, the college would not be eligible for Board of Founders' support for a replacement, since the only possible replacements were Indonesian. Fleming observed that it was going to be difficult to apply this new policy regarding support of Asian faculty, particularly because of the financial and economic difficulties in Indonesia. He recommended a grant of $1,500 for Pouw's salary, to go with him if he should leave Higher Theological College for another board-supported school. Fleming also suggested that, if Pouw were able to get a scholarship for study in the United States, the board give him supplemental support with the understanding that he would return to teach at a theological school in South East Asia. Fleming added: "He is an exceptionally able man; was Rector of [Higher Theological College] before Soedarmo; teaches in the field of practical theology and non-Christian faiths; has excellent English and could teach in it, though his language is Indonesian." Fleming recognized that his recommendation was not consonant with current board policy, but he added that this case was an exceptional circumstance.[105]

[104] Ibid.
[105] Ibid.

For the theological school in Jogjakarta, Fleming recommended $2,000 for Asian faculty support for two Chinese professors and the family of Oey Siauw Hian, who was studying in Scotland, along with funds for the library, a refresher course for clergy, and student scholarships, ten of which went to Chinese and four to Javanese.[106]

Later in the year, D. C. Mulder wrote from the Theological Academy at Jogjakarta that this school was considering a union with the school in Malang and raising its admission standard to require senior high school graduation. He believed the combined institution would emphasize pastoral and evangelistic work, while the Higher Theological College in Jakarta would stress practical theology and the missionary approach to non-Christian religions and movements on Java. The only problem he could foresee to the union might be disagreement over locating the new school.[107]

For the theological college in Malang, Fleming forwarded a request from A. de Kuiper, the librarian, who wrote, "When there is a librarian, there should be a library! But alas, this is scarcely the case." Fleming had visited the school in January and February 1960 and reported that the library was in the rector's house and consisted of "about four hundred books, mostly in Dutch, and a few in German and English. According to de Kuiper, 'Most...[were] written well before World War I, if not before the Franco-German war----!'" Fleming supported the request for funds for books and reported that English language facility at the school was "remarkably good, and being very systematically taught by Mrs. Van Akkeren." He thought this school should join the one at Jogjakarta and expressed doubt as to whether the Dutch teachers, currently due for furlough, would be allowed to re-enter the country. Fleming also supported a request from the Christian Literature Society in Jakarta for a grant to assist its translation project.[108]

Philippine schools had submitted a number of requests to the Board of Founders, which Fleming forwarded with his other recommendations. Guansing at Union Theological Seminary in Manila requested a grant for non-Chinese scholarships, the library, and a refresher course. Silliman University's College of Theology sought funds for scholarships including one for George Po Ba, a student from Burma, and a stipend for the editor of the college quarterly.

106 Ibid.

107 Excerpt, D. C. Mulder to [John R. Fleming?], [Jogjakarta?], December 18, 1960, ALW.

108 "Field Representative's Recommendations, 1960-61," in Frank T. Cartwright to BF, New York, April 27, 1960, ALW.

The College of Theology of Central Philippines University asked for $1,150 to employ a Filipino staff member, if a suitable person could be found. Kenneth Losh had written, "This is the most critical need of our Seminary." Although the school theoretically had three full-time American teachers, because of furloughs and study leaves there were never three on campus at one time. Losh also expressed concern that a disproportionate number of students were women and that the majority of their instruction was offered by women.[109]

John Hamlin, principal of the McGilvary Theological Seminary in Chiang Mai, was on furlough at Union Theological Seminary in New York in 1960 working on the translation of Christian texts into Thai. Fleming asked the Board of Founders to support this project. He observed that there were almost no theological textbooks in Thai and that Hamlin had found a Columbia University student in the Ed.D. program to assist him. She was a Buddhist but was interested in Christianity and had taken courses at Union Theological Seminary in New York, was an author, and had experience as a translator. Their first project was a translation, a scholarly study of the New Testament, and they were requesting that the board provide publication costs.[110]

In the hope that the Board of Founders would be able to provide funding for building projects, Fleming forwarded several requests. Tainan Theological College asked for $25,000 for an auditorium and music rooms, as its president wrote that

> we are repeatedly admonished that the church in Asia must be presented on a broad front, that it might be aware of its social setting and produce an indigenous culture. Fair enough; but where is this to be produced? In a registered University or High School where religious activities are forbidden by the Minister of Education? In a local congregation with limited resources? In [Taiwan], at least, I doubt if there is any place which has half the opportunity of a theological college, engaged as it is in thinking through the relation of its faith to its surrounding society, with a staff for mutual discussion and stimulus and a body of students large enough to experiment with and who will be taking the results of experiments into all the churches.[111]

The president extended his plea by observing that the choir had taken the lead in choral services and other religious music programs

109 Ibid.
110 Ibid.
111 Ibid.

and had produced three religious plays. The college hoped to have three trained music teachers by the summer of 1960, and the president reported that "there is a baby organ in every classroom and several more in the corridors, all in constant use once the 'all clear' sounds at the end of lectures." The college needed a large hall for concerts, twelve small practice rooms, and one or two classrooms which could be used for audiovisual presentations. Fleming supported this request and added that Tainan Theological College is "doing one of the best jobs in the area."[112]

The Theological School in Bandjermasin requested $4,000 to rebuild the school. Fleming supported this request as well as one for $15,000 from McGilvary Theological Seminary in Chiang Mai. The latter request was for a portion of the cost of a faculty house and a music building. If the board could not support both projects, Fleming gave priority to $5,000 for the faculty residence.[113]

Concerned about the range of Christian literature available in Chinese translation, Fleming had asked all schools teaching in Chinese to recommend ten works they would like to see translated into Chinese and proposed a meeting in Hong Kong in 1961 for discussion of this issue. He asked the Board of Founders to earmark $5,000 for that purpose. He also thought the board needed to consider the question of English language for students whose first language was not English and the related issue of how English was being taught in South East Asia and the kinds of basic theological texts that were needed in simple English. He also recommended $20,000 for ATSSEA for a study institute to be held in 1960 and for costs related to its accreditation program for the regional schools.[114]

Later in the fall, Cartwright advised the Board of Founders that the World Council of Churches' Theological Education Fund had granted funds for Tainan Theological College's auditorium and music rooms. He therefore recommended that the board grant $4,500 to the Theological School in Bandjarmasin and $15,000 to McGilvary Theological Seminary for a faculty house and either a building for music and religious education or a men's dormitory, together with remodeling of the main building.[115]

The meeting Fleming had proposed on theological tools and texts in Chinese was held in Hong Kong in November 1960 under

112 Ibid. One of these music teachers was Dr. I-to Loh, a major contributor to hymns for the Asian churches.

113 Ibid.

114 Ibid.

115 Frank T. Cartwright to BF, New York, October 28, 1960, ALW.

the joint sponsorship of the Board of Founders and the Theological Education Fund. Eighteen people attended; five of them were Chinese. Preliminary conferences had been held in Singapore, Hong Kong, and Taiwan, and representatives of twenty different theological colleges had attended one of those. Fleming served as chair of the Hong Kong meeting, which agreed on a Greek-Chinese dictionary, a grammar and syntax, a Bible dictionary, a Bible commentary, and a handbook of biblical and theological terms (which would have to be written), a Bible atlas, and a dictionary of the church for inclusion in the category of basic tools. Among essential texts, participants agreed to include theological studies, histories, and commentaries on the Old and New Testaments. They also wanted a new church history, works on doctrine and ecumenics, studies of religion, the philosophy of religion, ethics and moral teaching, practical theology, and world religions.[116]

With the expansion of its role into South East Asia, by 1961 the Board of Founders had spent all of the funds that had accumulated during the years when it could not send funds to China and prior to the court ruling granting the board a legal basis for expanding into South East Asia. Most board expenditures had been for buildings, summer institutes, and support of faculty members and libraries.[117]

The year 1961 marked the retirement of Frank T. Cartwright, who had served as executive secretary of the Board of Founders from its inception. A decision was reached to make John R. Fleming the executive secretary of the board as well as regional representative, thereby combining the positions that had hitherto been separate. Fleming thus became executive secretary effective with the 1961 annual meeting, and Tracey Jones, Jr., became the assistant secretary with responsibility for those board functions in the United States that could no longer conveniently be cared for by the executive secretary in Singapore. Ivy Chou, a faculty member of the Methodist Theological School in Sarawak whose U.S. study had been supported by the Board of Founders, spoke at this meeting. Memorials were introduced for Handel Lee, the first Chinese president of Nanjing Union Theological Seminary, who had recently died in Beijing, and for E. K. Higdon, who had represented the Disciples on the board for many years.[118]

116 "Field Representative's Recommendations, 1960-61"; Minutes, ATSSEA Meeting on Theological Tools and Texts in Chinese, Hong Kong, November 16-18, 1960, both ALW.

117 Frank T. Cartwright to Kalimantan Theological School, New York, June 28, 1961, MA/RO.

118 Minutes, Annual Meeting, BF, NTS, June 7, 1961, FTEA.

At the 1959 request of Charles Ranson of the Theological Education Fund, the Board of Founders' secretary, Cartwright at that time, began serving as a consultant to the Theological Education Fund and Ranson, as the fund's representative, began attending meetings of the Board of Founders as a consultant. This arrangement opened new avenues for the Board of Founders in its work for the strengthening of theological education in South East Asia, and the practice continued under Fleming.[119]

It had become increasingly apparent that the legal name, Board of Founders of Nanking Theological Seminary, no longer reflected the work of the board, and, at the 1962 annual meeting, board members discussed the name. A memorandum circulated by Cartwright and Fleming in preparation for the meeting had provided a relevant legal opinion, and the Board of Founders agreed to make application to change the name to the Foundation for Theological Education in South East Asia (FTESEA). A resolution to that effect was adopted at the 1963 annual meeting.[120]

With the new name came new emphases. For example, in 1963 and 1964 the Association of Theological Schools in South East Asia had moved to establish a regional graduate faculty in theological studies, which came to be named the South East Asia Graduate School of Theology (SEAGST). This faculty included members of the faculties of cooperating seminaries, and students enrolled for graduate study were to reside at the seminary where appropriate research advisers were available for their chosen fields of study. In response to this development, the FTESEA at its 1964 annual meeting agreed to support the graduate school on a two-year experimental basis though, in doing so, it was compelled to decrease the amount of aid it could direct to individual theological schools. The foundation also expressed a desire to decrease grants for libraries and indicated that future library grants would be contingent upon the various schools "designating a substantial amount of their budget for book purchases." It authorized the executive secretary, Fleming, to make such grants only if he were satisfied that the schools had met this requirement.[121]

119 Frank T. Cartwright, "Report of the Mid-Year Meeting," January 5, 1959, MA/RO.

120 Minutes, Annual Meeting, BF, NTS, May 28, 1962; May 28, 1963, both FTEA. No copy of the preparatory memorandum of 1962 appears to have survived.

121 Minutes, Annual Meeting, FTESEA, June 2, 1964, FTEA.

By constitutional revision the FTESEA expanded its membership in 1966. Representatives were added from the Board of World Missions of the Lutheran Church in America, the National Council of the Episcopal Church, the Division of World Missions of the Evangelical United Brethren Church, and the United Church Board for World Ministries. The Board of World Mission of the United Church of Canada and the General Board of Missions of the Presbyterian Church of Canada were also invited to join the foundation, and they did so the following year.[122]

At the same annual meeting, the FTESEA voted to appropriate $5,000 for the Chinese Theological Texts Translation Program, which it was then conducting in cooperation with ATSSEA and the Theological Education Fund, and an additional $5,000 for a workshop for translators and writers to be held in Hong Kong or Taiwan or perhaps in both these locations under the leadership of Francis Jones and Moses Hsu.[123]

A partnership between the FTESEA and the WCC's Programme for Theological Education (PTE/WCC) was reaffirmed in 1977, with Charles Forman and Marvin Hoff representing the FTESEA. It was agreed that the foundation would provide a financial grant to the PTE/WCC for an Asian staff person to act as a resource on theological education in Asia. The foundation provided support annually with the exception of 1994 and twice made grants of $100,000 for theological education in India and the Pacific.[124] By 1990 the FTESEA envisioned its work as involving relationships with ATESEA, with the PTE/WCC, and in China with Nanjing Union Theological Seminary and, through the China Christian Council, with other Chinese seminaries.[125]

122 Minutes, Annual Meeting, FTESEA, June 3, 1966, FTEA.

123 Ibid.

124 Marvin D. Hoff to John Pobee, n. p., November 25, 1994, FTEA.

125 Marvin D. Hoff to Yeow Choo Lak, n. p., January 2, 1991. In 1994 the FTESEA directors voted to allocate 20 percent of the budget of the executive director's office to ATESEA administration, 60 percent to China projects including publications, and 6 percent to the PTE/WCC work. See Marvin D. Hoff to White and Ching-fen Hsiao, n.p., December 17, 1994, FTEA.

CHAPTER 6

Adjusting to a Postcolonial Era in South East Asia

In the years following World War II, the rise of nationalism and the collapse of colonialism in Asia led quickly to demands that churches free themselves from control by missions based in Europe or America and begin to develop an indigenous Asian Christianity. By the mid-1950s, members of the Board of Founders were well aware of and sympathetic toward these changes taking place within the Christian communities in South East Asia. Frank Cartwright reported that the 1956 Bangkok conference, the 1957 institute, and subsequent meetings of the presidents of theological schools had fostered a "growing, and now striking, feeling of oneness among Asian Christians [that] is not limited to the theological schools." Cartwright cited the meetings of Christian college presidents initiated and sponsored by the United Board for Christian Higher Education in Asia and the East Asia Christian Conference, held at Prapat in 1957, as further evidence of this development. Reviewing their previous work in the region, he asserted that the Board of Founders and its regional representative, C. Stanley

Smith, had envisioned "the trend and [were] contributing toward its strengthening."[1]

One manifestation of this change was the creation of the Association of Theological Schools in South East Asia (ATSSEA), which grew directly out of the Bangkok conference and which later was transformed into the Association for Theological Education in South East Asia (ATESEA). Indeed, in terms of long-ranging consequences for Christianity in South East Asia, this was the single most important development from that meeting. At the conference the need for an association of theological schools and colleges in the region was recognized, and, as a preliminary step to its creation, participants organized an Association of Principals of Theological Schools and Colleges in South East Asia. Benjamin I. Guansing, president of Union Theological Seminary in Manila, was elected head of the group, which held its first meeting before the conference adjourned and accepted the assignment of drafting a constitution. This group also agreed to work for the establishment of a higher theological school faculty in Asia composed of outstanding scholars well versed in various theological fields.[2]

The constitutional committee met in Manila in 1956, but the constitution had then been approved by only eight of the eighteen schools. Therefore another meeting of principals or their representatives was called to follow the Singapore Study Institute in 1957, since thirteen of the people involved would also attend the institute. This meeting, which occurred from August 31 to September 3, 1957, was chaired by Guansing, while Ivy Chou, a Methodist theologian leading the Sarawak Theological School, served as secretary. The earlier draft constitution had been modeled on the constitution of the American Association of Theological Schools, but it was revised to reflect conditions in South East Asia. Once approved by a majority of the schools, ATSSEA automatically came into being and established its headquarters in Singapore.[3] The history of these two associations, ATSSEA and ATESEA, is the subject of another chapter.

As a result of concerns raised on numerous occasions but most recently at the 1956 conference in Bangkok, the Foundation for

1 Frank T. Cartwright, Report to Mid-Year Meeting, New York, January 5, 1959, ALW.

2 C. Stanley Smith, "Report to the BF on the Conference of Principals of Theological Schools in Southeast Asia," 1958, FTEA; Benjamin Guansing to [Frank T. Cartwright?], excerpt, March 14, 1956, ALW.

3 Smith, "Report to the BF on the Conference of Principals."

Theological Education (FTESEA) directed special attention to the needs of libraries at the various institutions it supported. One result of this attention was the organization and convening of a workshop on theological libraries, which offered significant assistance to the participating institutions and also brought into sharp focus some of the problems of theological education too closely tied to Western missions.

The state of the libraries at these schools in many ways reflected the distinctive problems of theological education in South East Asia. Smith had long been concerned about libraries and had periodically reported his concerns to the Board of Founders. Those attending one of the first meetings of the newly created ATSSEA discussed the library situation and created a Committee on Aid to Theological Libraries in South East Asia, which recommended conducting a "short-term intensive course in library science for the persons in charge of the libraries and [have prepared] a basic list of books to guide them in building their collections." Smith had proposed that duplicate books in American libraries be sent to the Asian seminaries, but the librarians present opposed that idea, arguing that such books were rarely of value and their libraries were then stocked with books of marginal use.

Preparing a list of essential books for the libraries was a difficult task, but Raymond P. Morris of the Yale Divinity School Library agreed to accept this assignment. The Board of Founders granted him $250 to assist with the costs of the project. Frank Price, with his long experience teaching at Nanjing Union Theological Seminary, agreed to undertake creation of a list of "books of stature in very simple English." Books were categorized into volumes appropriate for specialists, those appropriate for mature students, those appropriate for persons with limited English proficiency, and books of unusual value. It was recommended that the Board of Founders print both lists and make them available to interested people and institutions as well as to theological colleges in South East Asia. Participants in the ATSSEA committee meeting wanted their training session held in February and March of 1959 or in the summer of that year in connection with the study institute. They recommended that the library training session be six weeks long and that its emphasis be on training people who would serve as librarians for some time in the future.[4]

The committee recommended that the library training session be staffed by one person from a South East Asian country and

[4] Committee on Aid to Theological Libraries in Southeast Asia, "Report to BF" [1958?), ALW.

one American. The Asian would be expected to address the special problems of preserving books in the tropics and using local materials and homemade equipment as substitutes for many items that would be too expensive to import from the West. The American was to provide information on theological literature and "the role of the library as a teaching and learning tool and as a research resource for professors." The objectives of the session were to be:

> (a) the training of the present librarians (mostly nationals, it is hoped) in essential library techniques in special relation to conditions in the region; (b) to enable these librarians to train their assistants and in some instances their successors; (c) to acquaint themselves better with the whole range of theological literature (especially in English) and the sources of bibliographical information; and (d) to provide more effective uses of the library as a teaching and learning resource.[5]

The committee believed that the two best qualified Americans were members of their committee: Morris and Robert F. Beach, "both of whom are extremely interested in this project."[6]

This committee also recommended that the people conducting the training session visit all the seminary libraries before the meeting. The committee therefore requested that six months' salary be provided prior to the training session for the American's travel, and a bit less for the Asian's. The committee also wanted a manual of library service prepared for students. While acknowledging that the Indonesians followed Dutch library practices and that some others followed British practices, the committee believed the problems presented by these differences could be overcome.[7]

Cartwright presented the problems of the libraries to the January meeting of the Board of Founders in 1959. Only one institution had a librarian whose major assignment was to the library. All the others had added library work to the teaching duties of faculty members. The meeting of librarians was approved and scheduled for Dumaguete in February 1959, but, as three of the institutions were in session at that time, Cartwright suggested the Board of Founders provide them with funds to hire substitute instructors. Morris had agreed to conduct the workshop and thought it would be one of the best investments of income from the Swope-Wendel fund, commenting that "potentially,

5 Ibid.
6 Ibid.
7 Ibid.

it ranks close to the program of advanced training for qualified and experienced faculty members."[8]

In preparing for the workshop, each librarian was expected to consider his institution's book holdings and compare them to Morris's list. Generally, the basic holdings of the libraries were inadequate because of losses during wartime, because of limited financial resources, or because some of the schools were new. The need for designated grants to the schools for libraries became apparent. The importance of books that were written in simple English and that would help students bridge the language barrier and cope with standard works in English was underscored by the workshop.[9]

It was acknowledged in this workshop that all the libraries were very weak in periodicals and needed jobbers in the United States and the United Kingdom to assist them in securing out-of-print books. Faculty members usually could not afford books, so libraries were even more important than in the West, and mission boards that supported theological colleges needed to be made aware of the importance of libraries. National churches in the region also needed to be made aware of the need, and participants in the workshop suggested that national faculty members should receive a monthly allowance for books, as was the practice at the Higher Theological College in Jakarta.[10]

While English was the language of communication in these schools, some books were available in Chinese. "In general, however, the situation is that students have to depend on (a) lectures; (b) an inadequate number of books in their own language; (c) an insufficient number of 'B Class' books in English; and (d) standard books in English inadequately understood, at least in the earlier years of theological education." To remedy the situation, workshop participants suggested that authors be encouraged to write in their native languages and that improvement in the teaching of English either in pretheological education or in the first two years of theological education be given higher priority. There was no unanimity of opinion concerning the issue of instruction in the biblical languages. While desirable, such

8 Frank T. Cartwright, Report to Mid-Year Meeting, New York, January 5, 1959, ALW.

9 "Report of Southeast Asia Theological Schools Librarians' Workshop at Silliman University, Dumaguete City, Philippines, February 9-27, 1959, Under the Auspices of the ATSSEA and the Nanking BF," ALW. See also Raymond P. Morris to BF, n.p., May 20, 1959, R. P. Morris Papers, YDS (hereafter MP).

10 Ibid.

instruction would greatly increase the time committed to language study. In the case of Indonesia, for example, that would mean students would have to learn their vernacular, Indonesian, English, Greek, and Hebrew, which would leave little time for biblical or other theological studies.[11]

Those attending the librarians' workshop came with extremely diverse preparation and experience, suggesting the difficulties of dealing with libraries and librarians in the ATSSEA member theological schools. The participants ranged from the dean of McGilvary Theological Seminary to current undergraduate theological students. Their educational backgrounds ran the gamut from a D.Th. degree from the University of Zurich and Oxford University undergraduate degrees to those holding no university degrees.[12]

It was recommended at the workshop that each library have a collection including the Bible in the original languages, concordances, Bible dictionaries, and at least one Bible commentary based on the original languages. It was also recommended that each library hold books, periodicals, and documents on the history of the church in its own area. Additionally, the libraries might have special collections of books of local and regional interest:

> For example, Siantar might aim to have a complete collection of books in the Batak language; Jakarta might have a special collection for Islamic studies; and in the Philippines, a school might aim to have a complete collection of all Protestant Christian literature of Philippine origin. Churches should be informed about the archive facilities of the libraries, and encouraged to preserve materials of historical value.[13]

All libraries also needed a complete collection of theological books in the regional and national languages and linguistic tools for the study of these languages. Scholarly journals were needed for the disciplines taught.[14]

When the workshop considered physical facilities for libraries, those attending were urged, as they planned construction, to keep in mind potential growth over a thirty-year period. The ideal was a library that could be the center of a student's study, with open access to books.

11 Ibid. "B Class" was a reference to books written in simpler English for those with limited English language proficiency.

12 Ibid.

13 Ibid.

14 Ibid.

"The library fails of its purpose if the student feels he is barred from direct access to the books," Morris observed. The librarian needed adequate training in library science and should be knowledgeable concerning the courses taught at the school. "An effective library cannot be run by a part-time clerk, let alone built up that way," he wrote.[15]

It was recommended that theological schools' budgets include at least $100 per annum for each full-time faculty member for book acquisition and a pro-rated amount for part-time faculty. Alternatively, a school might allocate 7 to 12 percent of its budget for the library. Establishment of extension services to serve graduates was also recommended, since the books they needed were seldom available to them elsewhere.[16]

Shortly after the workshop ended, Morris observed that he believed the participants accepted the philosophy of the library "without a feeling that it was imposed on them by America." He had misgivings about his list of books recommended for the libraries but reported that it had been very well received and that he thought it "could very well exercise a pronounced influence in the development of the book collections of these libraries. At least it proved an invaluable approach to these institutions which, by and large and for reason, feel that Americans have little other than money to offer in theological education." He added that his basic approach had been bibliographical, stressing the matter of substance, which he thought had been wise. Morris reported that the library needs of the institutions had been identified at the workshop, a statement of standards had been prepared for submission to ATSSEA, a library manual had been prepared, and a rough outline of book classification suitable to South East Asia had been developed. He would finish the classification system upon his return to the United States but thought it "(a) convey[ed] to them that essentially it is their thinking and not a foreign imposition and (b) gave them real insight into the meaning of book classification." He added that he had found there was

> in the East an almost complete misunderstanding of the nature and the meaning of organization. Only three or four of those present, for instance, knew what the book budgets of their institutions were. Organization and system are largely alien to their mode of thinking and living. When they attempt

15 Ibid.
16 Ibid.

organization, they often misjudge its purpose and frequently they over-organize, or organize "blindly" and by rote.[17]

Morris reported the workshop had spent considerable time on this issue but added that while in Burma he had met two other Americans working on library problems, one sent to the University of Rangoon by the Ford Foundation and one from Queens College in New York who was on a Fulbright grant. Both remarked about this lack of understanding of organization. "These two men have been most helpful to me. It comes as a surprise how little is known about the more fundamental library problems in these parts. For instance, books deteriorate rapidly and surely there are things one can do to retard" the process.[18]

Morris visited Japan, Taiwan, Hong Kong, the Philippines, Singapore, Indonesia, Thailand, Burma, and India while in Asia. He went on to Egypt and then visited the Vatican, the WCC headquarters in Geneva, UNESCO in Paris, and professors in Utrecht, Hamburg, and Britain. Prior to the workshop, he visited Taiwan Theological College and Tainan Theological College in Taiwan; Union Theological College and Lutheran Theological Seminary in Hong Kong; Union Theological Seminary and St. Andrew's Seminary in Manila and the College of Theology, Silliman University, Dumaguete, in the Philippines; Trinity Theological College in Singapore; and Nommensen University in Siantar and the Higher Theological School in Jakarta, Indonesia. After the workshop he visited in Bangkok and at the Insein Theological Seminary in Burma and various schools in India and Egypt. He also visited other Christian institutions and libraries and reported he had seen a total of fifty libraries and met with about four hundred people. He served as a consultant for twelve libraries, seven of them members of ATSSEA. His work for them ranged from reviewing architectural plans for new buildings to recommending equipment and classification and cataloguing of books as well as training personnel.[19]

Morris's approach was designed to elicit as much information as possible regarding theological libraries in the region. At each school visited, he met with the president, dean, or principal and asked for that individual's perception of the library. He then met the one or two people most knowledgeable concerning the library and then with ten

17 Raymond P. Morris, "Brief Appraisal of the Librarians' Workshop at Dumaguete, Philippines," Insein, Burma, March 11, 1959, ALW.
18 Ibid.
19 Raymond P. Morris to BF, n.p., May 20, 1959, MP.

to fifteen students. He also spent considerable time in the libraries and met with faculty, mature students, and pastors. Yet he cautioned that "even so, four months is a short period to assess the complexities of Christian theological education in Southeast Asia. For this reason my conclusions must be tentative. I frankly do not know what to make of some of the things I have heard and seen." The great range in educational backgrounds of the participants made the workshop difficult, and Morris thought he should have had twelve months preparation, not five. "The morale of the participants held to the end. Those who were in attendance were very kind, and I appreciate[d] their cooperation and support. As a result of this Workshop, we are in a position to do something fundamental for their libraries and teaching situations which would have been difficult if not impossible otherwise."[20]

Morris cautioned that there were great differences among the cultures of South East Asia and that it was impossible to consider the role of the library unless one considered the "entire process of theological education as it is carried on in this area of Christendom." He wrote that "a library...reflected educational methodology and social processes; its place, use, and nature are highly conditioned by cultural factors and traditions." In general terms, he had found libraries were not used by the students. Morris wrote, "Hendrik Kraemer is undoubtedly right when he is quoted as saying that 'theological students in Southeast Asia do not read books.' Granted that, as with any generalization, exceptions must be made, I found this to be true. At least there are great differences between the use of books in the educational process as followed throughout this area and that in the West." Morris continued that this did not mean libraries were not needed; they were, and native preachers had few books and no resources with which to buy them. He believed the institutional collection was the only way to meet their needs but noted that it might be beyond the Board of Founders' ability to supply. If library needs were not met, he believed it would lead "to some unfortunate, if not disastrous, results for the Christian community."[21]

Morris explained that an inability of students to use English, even in India, was a major factor affecting library use. Students learned about books through the lectures of their teachers, and since there was so much emphasis on examinations, learning by rote was stressed. He believed the system did not teach students to use books in a mature way, "creatively or in dialogue or in developing [the] ability to relate

20 Ibid.
21 Ibid.

information found at one place to new situations. It lays stress on information at the expense of insight. The result is a very restrictive kind of education." He continued that South East Asia was emerging from an oral tradition where there was no emphasis on books and that this problem was reinforced by the additional one that since pastors could not afford books, they did not use them in their work.

> In light of this, we can understand the deep concern of Hwang when he says: "Something is radically wrong with the whole process of our theological education." Indeed something is wrong with Christian theological education in Southeast Asia. Foremost among the things that are wrong is the superimposing of Western institutions and educational patterns on this area of the world. What we have imposed is not a replica, but a caricature of Western education and it is producing different results than we should expect to find in the Netherlands, in Britain, or in America.[22]

Morris was particularly critical of the American effort to impose its pattern of theological education, which he described as "the least effective." He lamented that "this has deepened the general distrust of American understanding of education and its methodology....By and large, we have not given sufficient thought as to what constitutes effective theological education for cultures which are devoid of, and are limited in, matters of book tradition, or which possess an ancient educational tradition like that of the Chinese." He thought the conferences sponsored by the Board of Founders for theological educators of the region were most helpful and "probably one of the most important things that the Nanking Board can do for theological education in this area at this time." He described the problem as one of how to develop "a theological education methodology which will be effective in this area." He believed the solution was to be found neither in sending Asian leaders to the West for advanced education nor in sending out able and well-trained missionaries as teachers, for "the day of the evangelist-teacher who is pressed into theological teaching against his will and better judgment is and should be over." Rather, wrote Morris,

> the problem will be met when all who are engaged in theological education in this area become more informed and sensitive to the cultural, theological, psychological, and societal factors involved in education. They must focus their attention not upon Western

[22] Ibid.

> institutions but upon themselves, their people, and their needs. The situation demands leadership willing to experiment and to see things in new relationships.[23]

Morris offered the criticism that the discussions of "standards, degrees, methodology, etc." which took place at the Bangkok conference occurred within the context of Western thinking. In Asia, he observed

> there is a further tendency (which may not be limited to this area of the world) to regard a degree as a symbol of office rather than as a beginning of a process which will be lifelong in nature. The use of books as a habit of work for the task of the ministry is something which, in general, is imperfectly understood and is rarely followed. We can begin to get at the problem only when we are prepared to do experimental thinking which is at once incisive and radical enough to view things in contexts of other than Western terms.[24]

Morris thought Asian Christians could not address the issue of the "mature use of the book" until there was Christian literature which is "linguistically simple, culturally oriented to the situation, and suitable in subject matter for purposes of instruction." He thought World Christian Books and the Christian Students' Library were "only meager beginnings. The task seems almost overwhelming in its proportions." He observed that each of the various institutions he had visited viewed this as the primary problem of theological education. Students always asked for recommendations of books they could read and understand, and faculty also needed books.

> It would be almost impossible for us in the West to be fully sensitive to the problem of the intellectual and spiritual isolation from the world of learning in Christendom on the part of leaders, teachers, and students engaged in theological education in the East. This is contributing to some unfortunate consequences. It is well known that theology throughout this area is prevailingly conservative, which is, of course, a defensible position. But it is not a defensible position if the theologian is unable to explain his conservatism or if he is inadequately informed as to the currents of thought in Christendom. These limitations have bearing upon the ecumenical movement of the world Christian community.

[23] Ibid.
[24] Ibid.

> Doubtless this isolation has contributed to the emergence of a narrow biblicism with its tendency to ignore or to overlook two thousand years of Christian experience.[25]

Morris expressed the opinion that there was also too heavy an emphasis on "sacred languages" and a "general reluctance to broaden the curriculum," which "results in failure to examine or to understand the relationship of religion to culture and...encourages too-quick conclusions concerning the relation of Christianity to other faiths." He believed libraries needed to be broader in subject area than they were in Western theological libraries. He urged that Christians in Asia understand themselves in perspective. He emphasized the need for better education and training of leaders and acknowledged that missionary teachers would be needed for some time to come, while insisting they must have "the best qualifications in training, strength of personality and character." Observing that he had heard a great deal of criticism of the process of training Asian leaders in the West, Morris thought there needed to be a place in the East for them to obtain higher theological education. As to the legitimacy of the complaints he heard, Morris wrote that criticism of educating Asians in the West "originated in 1) human self-interest; 2) it maintained that training of native leadership in the West was excessively expensive; and 3) that frequently Western training unfitted the candidate for work when he returned. The latter could be both good and bad. This whole question needs to be carefully examined and there is no simple answer."[26]

Morris also recognized and commented upon the problem of recruiting good students for theological education in the region:

> Christianity in Southeast Asia suffers in this respect because it is a minority movement and is correspondingly limited in the range of talent and resources it can attract to its leadership. Throughout this area there is a great desire on the part of young people for an education. There is evidence that students attend theological schools because they cannot avail themselves of other kinds of formal education. The implications of this for Christian vocations are obvious.[27]

Additionally, the low salaries offered to ministers in the region inhibited recruits. Morris commented on his observation of the result:

25 Ibid.
26 Ibid.
27 Ibid.

> The concept of the role and place of the ministry, as this has been affected by the institutional framework imported from the West, altogether too frequently has adversely affected recruiting to the ministry. For these and other reasons the quality of students frequently appears to be far from satisfactory. Certainly, the initial impression one gains of the theological student in this area is that he does not compare favorably with students in the government schools and universities.[28]

Morris thought that support from the West would have to continue for some time for providing physical equipment; operating budgets for instruction, libraries, and books; for conferences; and for fellowships for a select few to study abroad. Churches in the area needed to be encouraged to support theological education, and support from the West should "advance the whole Protestant community in this area. The...Protestant Church has...too many schools with a resulting loss of efficiency." Morris doubted if every school could be supported. "An initial impression of the Protestant mission effort at the point of theological education is that it is lacking in a grand strategy, that there has been too much improvisation, and that the shortcomings resulting from these too frequently are perpetuated." He advocated closer scrutiny of the use of grants, for "the plain facts are that the Nanking Board has not and is not in all instances securing the desired benefits which they can reasonably expect from their contributions."[29]

Morris discerned a major problem in the "transfer of the control of theological education to indigenous auspices. This involves the question of native leadership and teachers versus the missionary and a re-examination of the meaning of indigenous church work." He wrote that it was not simply a matter of turning institutions over to local leaders who had not been trained to operate them or of "assuming the commendable position that we in the West are 'partners' with those in the East in a world mission enterprise." He quoted one leader who declared, "'We know who holds the purse strings.' Quite clearly, the Church and the mission bodies have failed to anticipate fully the dynamic nature of the change on the mission field and have not, in this respect, prepared for it."[30]

Morris also believed that the church had not properly assessed the role of theological educational leadership in the life of the community.

28 Ibid.
29 Ibid.
30 Ibid.

Whatever the reasons for this, he believed they were reaping the results of miscalculation. He wrote that he could cite examples where the transfer of administration from missionaries to indigenous leadership seemed to set the course for the institution's financial and educational ruin. He believed that the term "'indigenous church' needed to mean something more than the accident of birth and nationality. It should mean a certain perspective, understanding, temperament, empathy, frame of mind and spirit which is truly a part of and belongs to a situation." Saying that he had heard the term, "Asian revolution," frequently from young churchmen, Morris wrote, "My quick impression is that in some respects neither we nor they fully understand what this means. It could mean that the future involves far greater and more radical changes in the younger churches in their relationship with the West than is now envisaged." Westerners would have to reckon with younger and more radical church leaders. "This could have profound influence upon the development of Christianity in this area. It could result ultimately in the growth and the development of a new kind of Christianity oriented to Asia. To a degree that this may be so, much that we are and have been doing in our mission effort would be running against the tides of time." Morris granted that he was making his assessment on the basis of "incomplete information" but also cautioned that "in a period of world revolution we must be alert lest time and opportunity pass us by because we have been too focused on salvaging something that must be shaken."[31]

Fleming reported to the Board of Founders that one participant had stated that the library workshop had "opened new windows" and "served to emphasize how very far we are from attainable goals and even from 'minimum standards.'"[32]

Influenced by the impact of the librarians' workshop, a proposal was made in 1960 to offer a M.Th. degree in theological librarianship in the region based on the experience of librarians at St. Andrew's Theological Seminary in Manila, which had been cooperating for five years with the Department of Library Science at the University of the Philippines by having the latter's students work as interns at St. Andrew's. The proposed graduate program would require a college degree for admission, including courses in history, sociology, and culture of the applicant's country and one year's experience in a

[31] Raymond P. Morris to BF, n.p., May 20, 1959, MP.

[32] "Field Representative's Recommendations, 1960-61," in Frank T. Cartwright to BF, New York, April 27, 1960, ALW.

theological library, preferably the one where the applicant would work after graduation.[33]

With the formation of the Association of Theological Schools of South East Asia in 1959, John R. Fleming became the association's first executive director while continuing to serve as field representative of the Board of Founders, a position he had assumed in 1958. The relationship of the two institutions remained close, with the Board of Founders encouraging development of the association while devoting considerable attention to the translation into Chinese and publication of classics of Christian thought.[34]

In his 1961 report to the Board of Founders as its field representative, Fleming wrote:

> Regarding the schools and their faculties [in South East Asia], I would say quite definitely that the support of [the BF] and the existence of ATSSEA is providing a valuable impetus to the work of theological education in the area. Standards are being raised, libraries are improving, faculties are being better trained—and though much is still to be done in these and other directions (e.g. texts production and writing, curriculum revision, practical training, etc.) all this is providing a background of helpfulness and new vision that is a real stimulus. Most encouraging of all, one can discover in some quarters a readiness to ask radical questions about theological education and the training of the Ministry in Asia that means a questioning of traditional and accepted (and mainly Western) patterns. This is encouraged by our Study Institutes and through meetings of Presidents/Deans in the [ATSSEA], so that these should continue, I believe, to be important parts of our program and policy.[35]

Fleming hoped to encourage the theological schools in Hong Kong to organize themselves into a more ecumenical group. He observed that "denominational evangelism is keen in Hong Kong, but genuine ecumenicity is in shorter supply," noting that the Board of

33 Ibid.

34 Minutes, Annual Meeting, BF, NTS, May 28, 1959; May 27, 1960; June 7, 1961, FTEA. Upon the death of C. Stanley Smith, a special meeting of the BF adopted a memorial; Minutes, Special Meeting, BF, NTS, November 19, 1959, FTEA; Cartwright, *River*, 44-47.

35 "Field Representative's Report, 1960-61," in Agenda, Meeting, BF, NTS, June 7, 1961, ALW.

Founders was supporting four distinct denominational programs in the city.[36]

Fleming reported that the ATSSEA executive committee meeting in July 1960 focused on raising standards of accreditation and accepted seventeen schools into membership in one of three categories.[37] The committee also discussed a closer relationship with the theological school in Serampore, India, as some South East Asian students sought either Serampore or London B.D. degrees. Fleming did not regard the establishment of such a relationship as a solution to the problem of academic standards in South East Asia but reported he was watching developments.[38]

At its meeting of June 7, 1961, as earlier noted, the Board of Founders took formal action to elect Fleming to replace retiring Frank Cartwright as executive secretary of the board, a position he filled in addition to his field work and work with the ATSSEA. Ivy Chou of the Methodist Theological School in Sibu, Sarawak, who would later serve as executive director of the Foundation for Theological Education in South East Asia, addressed this meeting.[39]

In 1963, in cooperation with the Theological Education Fund of the World Council of Churches and the World Mission Boards of the United Presbyterian Church, U.S.A., the Presbyterian Church in the U.S., and the Methodist Church, the Foundation for Theological Education dispatched Frank Price to Asia to conduct a survey of the rural churches and the training of clergy for rural ministry, issues which were critical for the churches in Asia. In his report, Price stated that he and his wife traveled for 444 days, staying in 110 different places. Their longest period in any country was six months in India. They visited seventy-one senior grade theological schools: twenty-six in India, three in Thailand, one in Singapore-Malaya, seven in the Philippines, one in Sarawak, seven in Indonesia, four in Hong Kong, four in Taiwan, eight in Japan, and nine in Korea. Some of the institutions they visited were not associated with their national councils of churches, and they did not include a listing of the numerous junior-grade Bible schools that they also visited. According to Price's survey and the additional information he received from Burma, Ceylon, and Pakistan, there were then 4,740 students in 105 theological schools in the region: 900 in

36 Ibid.

37 ATSSEA maintained three levels of accreditation: full accreditation at the B.D. degree level, associate membership, and affiliate membership.

38 Ibid.

39 Minutes, Annual Meeting, BF, NTS, June 7, 1961, FTEA. The BF changed its name to the FTESEA in 1963.

Japan; 800 each in India, Indonesia, and Korea; 400 in Taiwan; 300 in the Philippines; 120 in Burma; 100 in Hong Kong; 50 each in Malaya-Singapore, Pakistan, and Thailand; 40 in Sarawak; 20 in Ceylon; with about another 4,000 students enrolled in the Bible schools of these countries.[40]

Price's objective had been to study the rural situation and village needs in each country and the rural reconstruction and community development programs of governments and nongovernmental agencies. He also visited rural churches, Christian service stations, Christian agricultural schools, and colleges with courses on rural life and service. He held consultations, joint studies, and seminars with theological faculties and talked to students about the Christian rural mission and opportunities for rural service. He attended regional and national consultations on rural issues with theological and church leaders in India, Japan, Korea, Malaya, Sarawak, and Taiwan; and he exchanged follow-up correspondence with many of those whom he had met. In his general observations, Price noted that in all the countries he visited except Taiwan and Japan the populations were more than two-thirds rural. "Modern technology, industrialization, and urbanization are affecting rural life, but also creat[ing] new social problems for rural people moving to the cities." He wrote that "Christian churches and groups face a challenging opportunity in the rural areas if they can do something to raise standards of living—physical, economic, intellectual, cultural, religious, and carry out a comprehensive program of witness, worship, education and service." He stressed that strong rural churches needed to become "independent and self-sustaining." If the churches were to play a role in rural reconstruction and regeneration, then the theological schools needed to train clergy to relate to conditions in the countryside. In order for them to do this, Price advocated that all seminaries should have a rural orientation and specialized courses for rural church majors. He also thought the programs of specialized rural seminaries such as existed in Japan and Korea needed to be replicated elsewhere, and he noted that some schools were moving in that direction. He also encouraged internships as an essential part of preparation for rural ministry.[41]

Participation in FTESEA programs became increasingly difficult for schools and personnel in Burma after 1963, when restrictions were

40 Frank W. Price, "Report on Study Tour of Asian Countries—On the Rural Church and Training of Rural Ministers," Minutes, Annual Meeting, FTESEA, June 2, 1964, Appendix IX, FTEA.

41 Ibid.

placed on travel abroad from that country. On May 31, 1966, all foreign missionaries were forced to leave that country. Subsequently members of the Foundation for Theological Education in South East Asia occasionally visited seminaries in Burma on tourist visas, but by the mid-1970s even that was becoming difficult.[42]

Strengthening theological institutions and improving their academic standards was regarded as critical by the FTESEA. The foundation therefore was supportive of efforts by ATSSEA to establish an accreditation program for these schools.

In 1965 the FTESEA dispatched H. P. Van Dusen, then chair of its board, to South East Asia to assist the ATSSEA in its accreditation of schools and to evaluate the development of the accreditation program. He presented a lengthy report to the foundation at its annual meeting in 1965 summing up his work with the ATSSEA accreditation advisory team. With this team he had visited seven countries over a period of two and a half months. He stressed that the work of the team was advisory to ATSSEA's Accreditation Commission, although the team believed that to limit itself only to the technical details of accreditation was an "unjustifiable expenditure of time and funds" and therefore discussed "every major aspect of the preparation of the Ministry and the life and problems of the Churches." Originally, the team was planned to include the ATSSEA director and Van Dusen, along with an "outstanding Asian theological educator." However, no educator was able to spend the entire time with the team. Raden Soedarmo of Higher Theological Seminary, Jakarta, accompanied the team to Thailand and the Philippines; Ivy Chou, president of the Methodist Theological School, Sibu, Sarawak, joined it in Malaysia; and Wu-Tong Hwang joined it in Taiwan. Van Dusen noted that the team visited fifteen schools and made informal visits to two or three others, but travel difficulties made it impossible to visit two or three others in Indonesia.[43]

Van Dusen cited as a major problem of theological education in the region the fact that it had been neglected during the early twentieth century. Specifically, he noted that between the Edinburgh Conference of 1910 and the Tambaram Conference of 1938, the topic was not even mentioned at world church gatherings. In 1938 when the topic was broached, theological education was described as "the weakest single

[42] Alan C. Thomson, "A Note on the Development of the Association of Theological Schools in Southeast Asia," *SEAJT,* XVI (1975): 36.

[43] Minutes, Annual Meeting, FTESEA, June 1, 1965; H. P. Van Dusen, Report to ATSSEA, March 17, 1965, 1, both FTEA.

element in the entire enterprise of Christian Missions." Van Dusen continued that, as far as he knew, this

> startling admission has...never been challenged. The typical, though not uniform, picture then was: tiny, poorly equipped, inadequately staffed institutions, mainly Bible schools in character, not infrequently situated alongside strong, vigorous Christian Universities, often, however, at remote locations far removed from the teeming centers of life and thought, in which devout young men, principally from village and small-town backgrounds, were prepared for a predominantly rural pastorate under the guidance of a small group of meagerly-trained missionary teachers.[44]

Van Dusen observed that the reasons for this neglect were the assumptions that elementary, secondary, and collegiate education deserved priority in resources and attention; only missionaries were competent to lead the church; all theological education institutions needed to be denominational, while few denominations had the resources to build and staff them; piety rather than learning was the chief requisite for village ministry; and, specifically in South East Asia, the denominational seminaries were copies of ones in the West which themselves were "woefully inadequate." Thus the weak starting point of many of the seminaries contributed to the current problems."[45]

Van Dusen thought the Asian revolution was the largest issue the seminaries were then facing. By revolution he meant not only independence, but also the swirling flood-tide of change about which no one could predict the outcome. He saw emerging a new Asian leadership brought about by the tremendous increase in higher education and the new Asian society with its "novelty, fluidity, complexity, [and] unpredictability."[46]

On the positive side, Van Dusen declared that the one conclusion which stood out sharply in his mind was:

> There is hardly a single school, whatever its size, however remote its location and meager its resources, which does not embrace within its total program at least one element which is distinctive, if not unique, which surpasses in quality if not in character similar elements in any sister school in the area, and which merits

44 Van Dusen, Report to ATSSEA, 2.
45 Ibid.
46 Ibid., 3.

> serious study by every other school and consideration for possible emulation. Many of the most imaginative, original and effective experiments and improvements are to be found, not in the larger and more favored schools of long-established reputations—sad to relate, several of these exhibit some of the weakest features in the whole range of theological education in Southeast Asia—but in some of the smaller, less well known and less well furnished institutions.[47]

Accordingly, Van Dusen recommended that within the next two years the heads of all schools visit sister schools in the area with the aim of improving their own schools. Following those visits he recommended longer visits between schools for those seeking to implement improvements and a system of visiting scholars between the institutions. He also recommended that ATSSEA establish a series of workshops, in addition to the study institutes, centered on specific needs like English and biblical languages, audiovisual education, and broadcasting.[48]

Van Dusen also found that many schools, including some of the larger ones, did not have well established and functioning boards of trustees or directors. Accordingly, he recommended that the ATSSEA Accreditation Commission set guidelines that required such boards to have fifteen to twenty-five members, so they would represent all Christian groups that the schools served. The boards needed to have men and women members, many lay people, and they needed to be rotating to allow for broad membership. He also encouraged attendance at board meetings by faculty members and board members' presence at student final examinations.[49]

Considering faculties, Van Dusen found that most included 50 percent or more nationals from the country of location, but he favored increasing this figure to at least two-thirds. There was a very favorable ratio of faculty to students ranging from thirteen to one to three to one, with the average being eight to one. He noted this was a much better ratio than found in the schools in the West. He recommended using visiting and exchange professorships to broaden the experience of the faculty, noting that each school needed to have at least one visiting professor in residence at all times. He also favored a program of tutors, both to allow professors a lighter teaching load and to permit

47 Ibid.
48 Ibid., 4.
49 Ibid., 5.

younger scholars to experience teaching with a view that they might later become professors.[50]

Van Dusen found the libraries at each institution vastly improved when compared with conditions he had observed twenty-six years earlier, but he cautioned that the libraries alone did not mean the schools had improved. He emphasized that students needed to improve their ability to use English and then needed to be taught how to read and use the books in the libraries.[51]

Van Dusen found little agreement among the schools of the region as to the structure of theological education. Some of their programs were based on European models and others on American models. The European-based schools tended to emphasize biblical languages and historic theological disciplines, while the American-influenced ones concentrated on "practical theology." However, he did note that some of the Indonesian schools, generally committed to the European model, had recently added courses in Christian education and one had added a course on church music. Overall, however, he found all the schools to have an imbalance one way or the other. He believed that those schooled in Greek and Hebrew did not benefit from the languages per se, which he thought graduates only infrequently used, but rather from the "discipline in clear thinking, precise discrimination and careful statement effected by Biblical language drill." He also found the students of schools which emphasized biblical languages "more mature intellectually" than those from the American-influenced schools. Yet, he also found a "grave inadequacy" in language teaching at all the schools. He found this to be true even of English, which he said "for better or worse...seems destined to be the theological *lingua franca* for East Asia."[52]

Van Dusen found an almost unanimous recognition that two or three semesters were not enough to prepare students for the ministry. Therefore, he made several recommendations, including weekend field work, summer appointments with churches, and semester or full-year internships with churches. He also favored three types of training: rural, urban, and clinical; the latter to be conducted in hospitals, prisons, or as chaplains at other institutions.[53] He also suggested that, in light of the popularity of the Bible schools, which had lower or no academic requirements for admission, and of the apparent preference of some

50 Ibid.
51 Ibid., 6.
52 Ibid., 7-8.
53 Ibid., 8-9.

congregations for people trained in them, the ATSSEA institutions should consider establishing programs to meet the needs of ministerial candidates unable to qualify for admission to their regular programs.[54]

The most "flagrant and shocking inadequacy" of the schools, Van Dusen found, was their near total dependence on foreign financing. He noted that the South East Asian churches had, since independence, assumed the costs of hospitals, higher education, etc., but that the theological schools still seemed to depend on foreign sources for 80 to 90 percent of their budgets. He believed it was time for the Asian churches to assume responsibility for educating their clergy.[55]

In summary, Van Dusen concluded that the theological schools were in much better condition than he had anticipated and that he could not term any of them "weak." Not one was "lacking in vigorous leadership, admirable faculty-student rapport, and eagerness for advancement." He asserted that many of them were in advance of some theological institutions in the West.[56]

The issue of recruiting and maintaining national faculty for the theological schools continued to be a concern of the FTESEA. Fleming wrote in 1967 that it was "rapidly becoming a serious problem." He noted that some schools that had national faculty candidates available did not appoint them. Those schools preferred to accept a Western missionary as a faculty member, since that person's salary, housing, and transportation were all paid from abroad. This factor was having an impact on requests to FTESEA for support of Asian faculty members for their first five years, and, because of the economic situation, the foundation was unable to stick to the five-year limit in some cases. Fleming cited the example of Tainan Theological College, where the foundation had been supporting three Asian faculty members for the past six years, adding that, if the FTESEA ceased its support, the college would be in difficulty. The same was true at the Higher Theological School in Jakarta and the Theological School at Jogjakarta, where the foundation had supported faculty members for six years. It was also supporting Asian faculty members at Trinity College in Singapore, Union Theological Seminary in Manila, and McGilvary Theological Seminary in Thailand. Fleming thought the mission boards supporting the FTESEA could appropriate funds for these salaries and channel them through the foundation.[57]

54 Ibid., 9.
55 Ibid., 10.
56 Ibid., 11.
57 John Fleming to Representatives of Member Boards of FTESEA, June 23,

As ATSSEA developed into a strong association, FTESEA continued to support it, while increasingly turning to its leadership for advice regarding its work in the region. At its 1967 meeting, for example, the foundation continued its fiscal support for ATSSEA in the appropriation of funds for the *South East Asia Journal of Theology (SEAJT)*, for the "Societies of Scholars" or institutes, one of which, for church historians, teachers of ecumenics and missions, and probably theologians, was to be organized by Kosuke Koyama, the newly appointed executive director of ATSSEA.[58]

John Fleming had served as executive for both the FTESEA and ATSSEA but was resigning these posts to assume a faculty position at St. Andrew's University in his native Scotland. In his executive director's report to the FTESEA for 1966-67, Fleming indicated that, on the way home from the foundation's 1966 annual meeting in New York, he had visited Union Theological Seminary in Manila for discussions regarding his replacement as ATSSEA director and the establishment of a South East Asia Graduate School of Theology. During the year he had attended various meetings and workshops and traveled to many of the schools in South East Asia. In the Philippines in November 1966, he observed that it was difficult to increase the percentage of nationals and decrease the percentage of Western missionaries on seminary faculties. First, increasing national faculty members meant stretching the budgets of the institutions unless funding increased greatly. He thought FTESEA would have to help schools reach these goals. He also observed that the urban-industrial and rural training institutes for students that had been established the previous year were a success at Union Theological Seminary's campus in Dasmarinas. In Burma there was concern that the government might limit funding for theological schools from outside the country, but Fleming reported that the schools there had seventy-three students enrolled, with six full-time and eight part-time faculty members.[59]

The fifth biennial meeting of ATSSEA was held November 15-18, 1967, in Singapore, with Ivy Chou serving as chair. At that meeting Fleming resigned as executive director and was succeeded by

---

1967, in Minutes, Annual Meeting, FTESEA, May 31, 1969, Appendix II, FTEA.

58 Minutes, Annual Meeting, FTESEA, June 2, 1967, FTEA. Koyama was then a Japanese missionary in Thailand.

59 Minutes, Annual Meeting, FTESEA, June 2, 1967; Executive Secretary's Report, Appendix II, FTEA.

Kosuke Koyama.[60] Koyama also became editor of the *South East Asia Journal of Theology* and dean of the South East Asia Graduate School of Theology. As executive director of FTESEA, Fleming was succeeded by Alan C. Thomson, an American Presbyterian missionary in Indonesia. Thomson and Koyama shared an office in Singapore for four years, and close cooperation between ATSSEA and FTESEA continued, even though the two organizations had separate directors. Koyama was invited to attend the FTESEA annual meeting in New York in 1969 along with Shoki Coe from Taiwan, who represented the Theological Education Fund of the World Council of Churches.[61]

Both Fleming's final report and Thomson's first were presented at this 1969 meeting, and in their statements and in actions taken by the foundation are reflected continuing efforts to adapt the work of FTESEA to the new realities in South East Asia. Fleming declared:

> Turning now to the direct question of FTE's contribution in the past ten years, as a factor in FTE's re-thinking of its task in the next ten years, I would say this contribution can be understood as contributing (a) to a *self-awareness* of the South East Asia theological schools in their relationships to one another in the region and in relation to the Asian churches' theological task at this stage of their history; and (b) to a raising of standards in the schools' own functions of theological education in terms of academic standards, sociological relevance and vocational commitment. There is a third area, namely (c) FTE's contribution to the North American Mission Boards in relation to their responsibility–and privilege–in helping to strengthen Asian churches at the vital point of leadership training and theological education.[62]

Looking forward after a few months on the job, Thompson urged:

> I believe, and this is the chief thing I would like to urge in this annual report, that from now on, the Association [i.e. ATSSEA]

[60] "Minutes, Biennial Meeting, ATSSEA, 1967," *SEAJT*, IX (1968): 70-99; John R. Fleming to Representatives of Member Boards of FTESEA, June 23, 1967, in Minutes, Annual Meeting, FTESEA, May 31, 1969, Appendix II, FTEA.

[61] Minutes, Meeting, FTESEA, June 12, 1969, FTEA.

[62] J. R. Fleming, "Memorandum on the Contribution of FTE 1957-1968," May 30, 1969, in ibid., Appendix VI.

> must be permitted to play the dominant role in setting policy and mak[ing] proposals for theological education in the region....I see the role of the Foundation director as that of liaison between the Association and in part the schools on one hand and the North American members of the Foundation on the other.[63]

This 1969 meeting, chaired by H. P. Van Dusen, took a number of actions reflecting both its historic obligations and its vision of new working relationships in Asia. Annual pensions were voted for Mrs. Handel Lee, the widow of the first Chinese president of Nanjing Union Theological Seminary, and for Margaret Rouse, a retired staff member of that seminary. A desire was expressed for continued cooperation with the World Council's Theological Education Fund in South East Asia, and the consultative relationship with that body held formerly by Fleming was approved for Thomson. Responsibilities for literature were sorted out, with FTESEA maintaining responsibility for the long-standing Christian Classics [Translation] Program then in its final stage but referring the Chinese Theological Literature Project to ATSSEA.[64]

The FTESEA voted a budget for support of ATSSEA and its journal, *SEAJT,* as well as its own Christian Classics Program. It provided a grant for a consultation on theological education to be convened at Chung Chi College in Hong Kong and voted scholarship assistance for several Asian students matriculating abroad. However, it encouraged Asian schools to seek training for their teachers in a wider variety of countries and recommended that American theological schools encourage Asian applicants to receive as much education as possible in South East Asia before commencing their studies abroad.[65]

After receiving the reports and recommendations of Fleming and Thomson, the foundation identified critical challenges requiring its attention. Board members discussed "the very difficult problem" of spiritual nurture in theological schools in a secular age. Though they believed this was a problem shared by theological schools in East and West, they expressed the opinion that Asian Christians faced unique problems in defining and shaping ministry:

> The problem of an economically viable pattern of ministry and the related question of whether Asian theological schools are taking this question seriously enough and not just continuing a tradition adopted from the West [requires urgent attention].

63 Minutes, Annual Meeting, FTESEA. June 12, 1969, FTEA.
64 Ibid.
65 Ibid.

> Here, Asian religious patterns of "priesthood" and the economic-sociological basis need to be studied, though these Asian cultural patterns are changing rapidly.[66]

A particularly valuable contribution to the development of theological education in the region was made through a series of study institutes. C. Stanley Smith had suggested study institutes on topics of interest to Asian educators from his first involvement in South East Asia. The Board of Founders had endorsed the idea, and the first was planned for 1956. However, planning for the Bangkok meeting became so time consuming that the first institute was not held until 1957. Initiated and funded by the Board of Founders, the institutes received strong support from ATSSEA participants as well. The institutes proved invaluable in strengthening both the knowledge base and morale among faculty members of participating institutions. Originally it had been planned to hold the institutes in conjunction with the ATSSEA biennial meetings, but, by 1961, all agreed that this arrangement had become too cumbersome. Subsequent institutes were held in the alternate years, when the ATSSEA general meeting was not held.

The themes of the first study institute held in Singapore in 1957 and directed by Smith were "Urbanization in Asia" and "Approach to Men of Other Faiths." Hendrik Kraemer of the Netherlands and Paul Devanandan of India were the primary leaders. Other leaders included Fidel Galang of the Philippines, Donald V. Wade of Canada, and G. Reichelt of Hong Kong. A critique of this first study institute was sent to Cartwright by C. H. Hwang of Tainan Theological College, who had served as dean of the institute. He provided a summary of the views and recommendations of participants. Those who had attended it urged the Board of Founders to continue the program annually, with one major theme and closely related minor themes each year. The participants particularly appreciated the fellowship of other theological educators, noting that, while many considered it a holiday, they had read more books than they would have had they stayed at home. Overall, they believed two months was too long for the institute, as only one of the lecturers was able to remain for the entire time, so they recommended that future institutes be scheduled for only six weeks. They recommended that only those who taught the subjects to be discussed at the institutes should be invited to attend, noting that, while the topics were interesting, if one did not teach the subject of the institute, the program did not particularly help one become a better

66 Ibid.

teacher. All the participants thought they needed more time to prepare for the institute, as most arrived in Singapore not having read the two textbooks sent, in many cases because they had arrived rather late or at the end of the semester. They preferred to have the study institute be the climax of a year or at least six months of study. Participants suggested a five-year program be established for the institutes, perhaps on topics of the Bible, doctrine, history, practical matters, and religious education. Participants recommended that the dean of the institution where the institute was to be held serve as the dean of the institute, but they believed that a full-time director was also needed. On a more critical note, they found the Bible study at the institute was not directly related to the topics discussed and seemed an "afterthought."[67]

The proposed second institute in 1959 was to focus on the theme of biblical theology, and participants in the 1957 institute thought it would be helpful if some of the lectures covered related topics such as the religious background of New Testament times, evangelism, the missionary, or the ecumenical movement in South East Asia. This study institute was held in Singapore July 15 to August 28, 1959, following a three-day meeting of the ATSSEA. Fleming was the institute's director, and its topic was "The People of God in the World." The faculty included Hidenobu Kuwada, president of Union Theological Seminary, Tokyo, who spoke on the relation of biblical theology to theology in Japan; James Muilenburg of Union Theological Seminary in New York, who discussed the Old Testament; and Paul Minear, of Yale Divinity School, who discussed the New Testament. Forty delegates, twenty-eight of whom normally taught Old or New Testament as their primary courses, attended the institute. Ten others taught theology, and two taught history of religion, missions, and practical theology. They represented twenty-six theological schools in nineteen countries.[68]

In a critique of the second study institute penned for *SEAJT,* participant Ivy Chou, principal of the Methodist Theological School in Sarawak, stated that

> we hear much talk about "indigenous Asian theology," and the need to promote theological insight which is not a mere reflection of Western theological thinking, but is an interpretation of the

[67] C. H. Hwang to Frank T. Cartwright, Tainan, Taiwan, October 11, 1957, MA/RO. Hwang is also known as Ng Chiong Hui and as Shoki Coe.

[68] "ATSSEA, Meeting, July 13-15, 1959," *SEAJT,* I (1959): 8; "Second Theological Study Institute, Singapore," *SEAJT,* I (1959): 4-6; "Editorial, Missiology in South East Asia," *SEAJT,* X (1968-1969): 3.

> faith in terms of Asian thought-forms and cultural backgrounds. I know of no way more constructively effective for the promotion of such thinking than the Study Institutes such as we are having. Here, probably for the first time, theologians of the Asian lands are able to meet together in an Asian land, looking at the Biblical truths as a group of Asian theologians, discovering their implications in the Asian setting, and testing them against the Asian church life. This is the way the so-called indigenous Asian theology will be slowly produced.[69]

Chou also found the composition of the institute, which included fraternal delegates from Ceylon, India, Japan, Korea, and Pakistan, "quite ideal," and thought the teaching was "top quality."[70]

The third study institute had as its theme, "Christ and Culture–The Encounter in East Asia," and was again held in Singapore from July 20 to August 31, 1960, with Fleming again serving as director. Its lecturers included Daniel Day Williams, Union Theological Seminary in New York, and C. L. van Doorn, Netherlands Missionary Council, both of whom gave daily lectures, and R. P. Kramers, Institute for the Study of Chinese Religion, Tao Fong Shan, Hong Kong, who lectured weekly. Twenty-five delegates attended the entire meeting, and they represented sixteen theological schools and four Bible schools in South East Asia. Others came from theological schools outside Southeast Asia, one was from the International Christian University in Tokyo. Topics discussed ranged from Christ and culture in the Bible and in Christian experience to Christ and contemporary faiths, including Marxism, scientific humanism, and existential humanism.[71]

In commenting on the study institute for the Board of Founders in New York, Williams wrote that he thought the institutes could be improved in several ways. For example, those who attended were extremely busy people with heavy teaching loads and so were not prepared to do the work required in preparation for the institute. He proposed that, in the future, participants submit in advance a plan for their research at the institute, with the assurance that these plans could be flexible. He also thought that the lectures that Van Doorn,

69 "Some Impressions of the Theological Study Institute, 1959," *SEAJT*, I (1959): 19.

70 Ibid.

71 "The 1960 Theological Study Institute Held at Trinity Theological College, Singapore," *SEAJT*, I (1960): 27-32; "Editorial, Missiology in South East Asia," *SEAJT*, X (1968-1969): 3.

Kramers, and he had given would have been more valuable if they had related directly to the situation in the Asian churches at that time. He recommended that a part of the institute be "devoted to concrete analysis of the present cultural and political situation [in South East Asia] and its bearing on the Christian task." He also suggested that some of the seminars be reorganized as small discussion groups, that there be fewer hours devoted to formal lectures and more time for group discussion and recreation, and that future meetings discuss "fundamental theological themes" including a "radical examination of the curricula and teaching content and methods of the various schools." He insisted that "anything which will encourage such fundamental analysis of the Christian faith and its meaning for Asia today, the modes of its communication, and the challenges which it faces, should be done."[72]

The fourth study institute was held in Singapore in August 1962 with Fleming again serving as director. Its topic was "Christian Ethics and Decision in the Rapidly Changing Society Situation of South East Asia." Participants were from Borneo, Burma, Ceylon, India, Indonesia, Japan, Korea, Pakistan, Philippines, Singapore, Taiwan, and Thailand. The major speakers at the meeting were John C. Bennett, dean of Union Theological Seminary in New York, and D. T. Niles, a prominent Asian theologian then serving as general secretary of the East Asia Christian Conference.[73]

Held in Singapore from July 29 to September 6, 1963, again with Fleming as director, the fifth study institute's topic was "Church History, Teaching, and Writing." The major speakers were James Hastings Nichols of Princeton Theological Seminary and Stephen Neill, who was currently professor of missions at the University of Hamburg. Nichols's lectures, "Challenges to Christianity in the Modern West," dealt with issues of modern science, nationalism, agrarian reform, industrialization, and Marxism. Participants in the institute considered the issues of nationalism and religious liberty. Reporting on this institute, Gerald Anderson, United Methodist Church missionary faculty member at Union Theological Seminary in Manila, noted that the conference found parallels between the secularization and pluralization of society in seventeenth- and eighteenth-century Europe

[72] Daniel D. Williams, "Reflections on the Singapore Institute, 1960," n.p., January 17, 1961, MA/RO.

[73] "Editorial: Importance of Social Ethics," *SEAJT*, IV (1962): 4-6; "Editorial, Missiology in South East Asia," *SEAJT*, X (1968-1969): 3; "Retrospective Evaluation of the 4th Institute," *SEAJT*, IV (1963): frontispiece.

and the contemporary issues facing Burma, Malaysia, and Vietnam. According to Anderson, participants also saw commonalities between the ideas of nineteenth-century Danish nationalist N. F. S. Grundtvig, who sought to develop "human and national self-consciousness as preparation for the gospel in his country," and those of "Asians who are concerned that Christianity belong to, identify itself with, and participate in the vocation of nation-building in Asia today." Anderson reported that the conference also saw that "the failure of the church effectively to reach the working class that emerged from the industrial revolution [stood] as a lesson and a challenge to the churches in Asia as they race to keep up with rapid social change on all sides."[74]

Neill's lectures identified "three problems for church history studies in the younger churches: (1) the general lack of a historical consciousness, (2) a dominating Western orientation in church history, and (3) too little literature and leisure for scholarship." He continued that seminary students "show little interest in historical studies and do not readily see the significance of history for the Christian faith," adding that many of the non-Christian faiths of the region denied history and that attitude, deeply embedded in the culture, influenced Asian Christians and was not easy to overcome. He insisted upon the need for an Asian perspective on church history. There was also a discussion about writing church history from an Asian viewpoint. When did a national church history begin: when the first missionaries arrived or when the first convert was made or when the first clergy were ordained? When did church history separate from mission history? Participants also discussed the problems created by the fact that so many church and mission archives were located in Western countries and inaccessible to many Asian scholars searching for source materials. As a result, most of the histories of the younger churches were, at that time, still being written by missionaries, who frequently did research when at home on furlough. It was suggested that the problem could be lessened by the establishment of a center for church history at one of the stronger seminaries in the area.[75]

The sixth study institute examined the theme, "Worship and Music in the Asian Churches Today," and it was held in Hong Kong from July 19 to August 20, 1965, with Fleming as director. Thirty-eight people from twelve countries participated. Fleming reported it was most

[74] Gerald Anderson, "Asian Studies in Church History," *Christian Century*, October 23, 1963: 1306; "Editorial, Missiology in South East Asia," *SEAJT*, X (1968-1969): 3.

[75] Anderson, "Asian Studies," 1306.

successful and "fulfilled its main objective in bringing together leading church musicians and a number of people concerned about better and more indigenous worship forms in Asia." Those at the institute produced a seventy-page booklet, *Some Asian Orders of Worship,* which included an experimental liturgy and some original Asian musical compositions.[76] Interest developed at this institute contributed to the establishment of the Asian Institute of Liturgy and Music in Manila.

The seventh study institute was held at Chung Chi College in Hong Kong July 28 to August 29, 1966, and dealt with the topic, "Church and Society." The chief lecturer was Robert Lee of San Francisco Theological Seminary, and other lecturers were Kenyon Wright from India, Richard Poethig from Manila, and Paul Webb from Hong Kong.[77]

The eighth study institute considered "Missiology, Ecumenics, and Church History" and was again held at Chung Chi College from June 23 to July 19, 1968, with thirty participants. Lecturers included R. Pierce Beaver, University of Chicago; Elmer Douglas, Hartford Seminary; and William Hackett, formerly of Burma and then at Chung Chi College. Out of this meeting was organized the South East Asia Society of Church History and Ecumenics, which had as its aims promoting fellowship among scholars in the fields of church history, ecumenics, mission, and world religions; encouraging productive scholarship in these disciplines; and seeking the improvement of teaching in the theological schools in South East Asia.[78]

The ninth study institute on the topic, "Christian Education," was held July 15 to August 12, 1970, with Randolph C. Miller of Yale Divinity School as the main lecturer. Thirty-one papers were presented at this institute, with Miller concluding

> that cultural differences are significant. There is a tremendous need to make Christianity intelligible in the languages and thought forms of Asia, and this cannot be done by Westerners.

76 Minutes, Annual Meeting, FTESEA, June 3, 1966, FTEA. The January 1966 issue of *SEAJT* was devoted to music and liturgy. The institute had been planned for Singapore but was moved when political conflict between Malaysia and Indonesia threatened that site. The seventh and eighth institutes were held in Hong Kong as well, but in 1972 they returned to Singapore.

77 Ibid.

78 Minutes, Annual Meeting, FTESEA, May 31, 1968, Executive Secretary's Report, Appendix III, FTEF; "Editorial: Missiology in South East Asia," *SEAJT*, X (1968-1969): 3-8; "The Birth of a New Society," *SEAJT*, X (1968-1969): 194-95.

> There is a Western cultural overlay to almost all Asian Christianity, and some Asian Christians are unconsciously so Westernized that they reject the attempt to use their own cultural resources (music, dance, art) in the churches.[79]

Reflecting upon the complexities of the situation in which Asian Christians lived, Miller insisted that, in spite of the cultural differences and issues of cultural communication, there is a "common humanity under God by whatever name (or no name) he may be called."[80]

"Order, Revolution, and Covenant" was the theme of the tenth study institute, held in Singapore July 19 to August 15, 1972. Professor Charles C. West of Princeton Theological Seminary was the leader. Nineteen representatives from eight South East Asian countries, as well as representatives from four other countries, attended. Among the topics discussed were varieties of power, political power, and God's ultimate power. Recognizing that South East Asians live amidst traditional structures and customs, the participants considered the limitations of such structures, emphasized the theme of covenant, insisted that responsible development of Asian economic power has a high priority, and declared that promoting Asians' "quest for self-identity" is the task of the church.[81]

The 1972 study institute was the last of its kind, though in 1977 ATSSEA decided to resume offering study institutes every two years under the title, "Colloquia on Asian Perspectives in Christian Thought." Each colloquium was to consider a topic of "specific relevance and urgency in the Asian situation," and Asian scholars from diverse disciplines were invited to research the topic in order to participate. Sponsored from this point by ATSSEA, these colloquia nonetheless continued to receive the support of FTESEA.

The *South East Asia Journal of Theology* was another major contribution to the development of Christian theological education that grew out of the Bangkok meeting with the enthusiastic support both of the Board of Founders (later FTESEA) and the ATSSEA (later ATESEA). The journal was inaugurated by Fleming in 1959. Published quarterly, its early issues contained brief minutes of the ATTSEA meetings as well as notes reporting FTESEA meetings. Reports of various other Christian meetings, primarily those held in Asia, were

79 "Editorial, Reorganization of Theology," *SEAJT*, XI (1970): vi; Randolph C. Miller, "Some Asian Contributions to Christian Education," *SEAJT*, XI (1970): 12-13.

80 Ibid.

81 "Theology of Power for Social Justice and Liberation in South East Asia," *SEAJT*, XIV (1972): 81.

also published. Comments on the study institutes, as well as papers by many of those who gave presentations at the institutes, appeared in the journal, as did lists of books to be read by participants in forthcoming institutes. Other articles by Westerners and by Asians addressed a wide variety of theological topics as well as specific issues, such as the teaching methods used in various schools. For example, the journal published an address to the American Theological Library Association by Morris, in which he discussed the library institute he had conducted for the region.[82]

The journal also included brief book reviews, as well as notes on the various member schools, their programs, and admission standards. Occasionally an issue was devoted almost exclusively to one topic; for example, the July 1961 issue contained four articles on Buddhism and its relation to Christianity; the October 1967 issue was devoted to the Philippines; and the January 1968 issue was devoted to Indonesia. By 1964 the journal had attained a circulation of 978, and by 1967 its circulation had risen to 1,400.[83]

In 1983 the *North East Asia Journal of Theology* and *SEAJT* merged to form the *East Asia Journal of Theology.* The new periodical was the organ of the North East Asia Association for Theological Schools and ATESEA and was established "to encourage Asian theological thinking; to relate the Gospel to our cultural, historical, and religious situation in East Asia; to study problems related to the teaching of theology and aims of theological education in East Asia; to share news about member schools of the Associations; and to maintain contact with theology and ministry beyond the region of East Asia.[84] A further consolidation in 1987 resulted in the creation of the *Asia Journal of Theology*, the organ of these two regional associations as well as the Board of Theological Education of the Senate of Serampore College.[85]

From its earliest work in Nanjing, the Board of Founders supported translation of theological texts into the Chinese language. After 1951, when ties with China were broken, this work became increasingly important. Following the FTESEA decision to ask ATSSEA to assume

82 Raymond P. Morris, "Some Impressions of the Libraries in Protestant Theological Educational Institutions in Southeast Asia and the Implications for the Christian Church," *SEAJT*, II (1960): 8-16.

83 Minutes, Annual Meeting, FTESEA, June 2, 1967, Executive Secretary's Report, FTEA.

84 Yeow Choo Lak, Circular Letter 1983/60, Singapore, April 12, 1983; ATESEA Handbook, 1984, both ATESEAF.

85 *Asia Journal of Theology*, I (1987): 1.

responsibility for the Chinese Theological Literature Program, ATSSEA accepted this assignment with continued fiscal support from the foundation for the project.[86] The Board of Founders and FTESEA had experienced a variety of challenges during the 1960s, especially difficult was locating suitably qualified Chinese people with the linguistic and theological expertise required. Efforts to share costs with other groups, such as the Council for Christian Literature for Overseas Chinese, also proved difficult. Nonetheless, by 1964 a significant number of volumes had been published.[87] At its 1966 meeting the FTESEA voted $5,000 for this program, now termed the Chinese Theological Texts Translation Program, and another $5,000 for a workshop for translators and writers to be held in Hong Kong or Taiwan (or both places) under the leadership of Francis Jones and Moses Hsu.[88] At the time of the 1967 FTESEA annual meeting, Fleming reported that thirty-four volumes in the series had been published and a number of others were being translated or written. Choan-Seng Song of Tainan Theological College, an associate director of ATSSEA, was assuming more responsibility for this work at that time.[89] A related Chinese Theological Education Series translated and published books under ATSSEA auspices, and another program was engaged in collecting materials on the history and mission of the churches in China. These materials eventually were housed in the Chung Chi College library in Hong Kong. All of these efforts enjoyed the approval and direct or indirect fiscal support of FTESEA.[90]

The foundation's commitment to improvement of theological education in Asia had also led to the establishment of the South East Asia Graduate School of Theology (SEAGST) in 1966. Although the FTESEA had been supporting Asians engaged in graduate work in the United States for many years, by the 1960s foundation members were beginning to express some dissatisfaction with that arrangement,

86 Minutes, Annual Meeting, FTESEA, June 12, 1969, FTEA.

87 "Field Representative's Report, 1960-61," in Agenda, Meeting, BF, June 7, 1961, ALW; Minutes, Annual Meeting, FTESEA, June 2, 1964, "Executive Secretary's Report," Appendix II, FTEA.

88 Minutes, Annual Meeting, FTESEA, June 3, 1966, FTEA. Jones had been responsible for this program since it was begun in wartime China, and Hsu was one of his assistants.

89 Minutes, Annual Meeting, FTESEA, June 2, 1967, Executive Secretary's Report, FTEA.

90 "Commission on Non-Traditional Study, October 3-5, 1975," in Minutes, Annual Meeting, FTESEA, May 31, 1969, Appendix II, FTEA; Emerito Nacpil, Circular Letter 1980/2. [Manila?], January 21, 1980, ATESEAF; Minutes of the Graduate School of Theology Senate Meeting, Manila, October 13, 1978, MA/RO.

since it did not always serve the educational needs of Asian students. In 1961 Cartwright wrote that Kuo Te-lien was studying at the University of Chicago Divinity School, where three-fourths of the students were enrolled in a doctoral program. Cartwright believed that Chicago was an "ivory tower, and [was] not suitable to a candidate from our part of the world." Kuo then moved to Princeton Theological Seminary. Pinsu Akkapin of Thailand, who was preparing to teach at McGilvary and was then a student at Union Theological Seminary in New York, was at the 1961 Board of Founders' meeting where these matters were discussed and suggested that "there should be more cross fertilization of students for the ministry in Asia. That is, of students going to Manila, Singapore, India, and other places where high grade instruction can be given in a language that the student himself is qualified to use."[91]

At its annual meeting in 1964, the FTESEA strongly endorsed the proposal for a South East Asia Graduate School of Theology, which was anticipated to be a cooperative venture of the member schools of ATSSEA permitting graduates of approved theological schools in the region to engage in graduate study with the regional scholar or scholars best qualified in the student's chosen field of study. The foundation recommended that ATSSEA move gradually, with an initial program at the master's degree level with the following suggestions: "1) The program be tried on an experimental basis for two years. 2) Only two theological disciplines be offered at the start, and these should be Social Ethics and the History of Religions. 3) The work be centered at schools having the most strength in faculty and library in these fields, distinguished scholars be invited to participate, and consideration be given to the ease of entry and communications when sites were selected. 4) The advice of the [Theological Education Fund] be sought for the project." The FTESEA approved an initial allocation of $40,000 for the project.[92]

By 1966 the FTESEA board noted that progress had been made toward creating the South East Asian Graduate School of Theology and gave its assent to Fleming becoming its dean along with his other responsibilities to FTESEA and ATSSEA. The foundation viewed with favor the idea of broad interregional representation on the school's board and suggested that an external team of examiners be created with members from Europe, North America, and North East Asia.[93]

91 Frank T. Cartwright to J. R. Fleming, New York, September 29, 1961, MA/RO.

92 Minutes, Annual Meeting, FTESEA, June 2, 1964, FTEA.

93 Minutes, Annual Meeting, FTESEA, June 3, 1966, FTEA.

The graduate school commenced its operation in 1966 with four students: two in Taiwan, one in Singapore, and one in the Philippines. The 1967 entrance examination was to be held in May, and twelve people were expected to take it. The accredited schools in Indonesia planned to join the graduate school in 1968. By then there were eight students enrolled and another eight preparing to take the entrance examinations. The FTESEA and Western church boards generally encouraged Asian church workers to do their graduate work in Asia. South East Asia Graduate School of Theology gave its first two degrees in the Philippines in 1969. In 1974 there were fifty-eight graduate students in the program.[94] After Fleming's return to Scotland, the primary responsibility for the school's oversight shifted from FTESEA to ATSSEA, with Kosuke Koyama serving as dean of the school as well as executive director of the association. Yet FTESEA continued to take a vital interest in the development of the graduate school and to provide fiscal support for its program.

The phrase "critical Asian principle" was first used at a meeting of the graduate school in Bangkok in 1972. It is understood to describe seven traits summarizing the characteristics of Asia:

1) There is a plurality and diversity in races, peoples, cultures, social institutions, religions, ideologies, etc.
2) Most of the Asian countries have had a colonial experience.
3) Most of the Asian countries are striving for modernization, social justice, economic growth, and self-reliance.
4) People are searching for an authentic identity and cultural integrity.
5) Asia is the home of living religions.
6) There is a longing for social order beyond the current alternatives, and
7) The Christian community is a minority in the vast Asian complex situation.[95]

According to Emerito Nacpil, at a 1972 discussion of the feasibility of a doctoral degree in theology, among the points made was the one that the degree "should be a doctor of theology, a professional

[94] Ibid.; Minutes, Annual Meeting, FTESEA, May 31, 1968, Appendix II, Executive Secretary's Report; Thomson, "A Note on the Development," 38.

[95] Emanuel Gerrit Singgih, "Critical Asian Principle," in Sientje, Merentek-Abram and A. Wati Longchar. *Partnership in Training God's Servants for Asia: Essays in Honor of Marvin D. Hoff* (Jorhat, Assam, India: ATESEA and FTESEA, 2006), 136.

degree with a distinctly Asian orientation," and the senate of the South East Asia Graduate School of Theology made this understanding "a critical principle of the whole program." Subsequently this phrase has been used not only for graduate work, but for all the work of the church in the region.[96] Its many facets are reflected in the 1988-89 Handbook of ATESEA, SEAGST, wherein the critical Asian principle is described as including situational, hermeneutical, and missiological as well as educational elements.[97]

By 1978 there were twenty-one students studying for SEAGST's master of theology degree in the Philippines: five at the Divinity School, Silliman University; six at St. Andrew's; and ten at Union Theological Seminary. From the Burma/Malay/Singapore area an enrollment of eighteen students was reported. Workshops on nation building and theology were planned in Rangoon and Chiang Mai. The Taiwan area reported that seven students graduated in 1978 and four new ones were admitted. In addition, ten other students were pursuing the program. In the Hong Kong area there were three students at Concordia Theological Seminary, with several new students expected. The Indonesia area reported eleven students then in the program, with another two expected in the fall. A doctoral program was inaugurated in 1974 with the enrollment of the first student at that level. Though smaller than the master's degree program, it extended the level of theological education available to faculty members in the region.[98]

In 1978 a proposal was advanced to expand the graduate school by creating an Eastern Indonesia Area. The Theological School at Ujung had the only accredited B.D. program in the area and was therefore suggested as the center for the graduate school in the region.[99] A year later at the annual meeting of ATSSEA, creation of an Institute of Advanced Pastoral Studies was recommended. Existing SEAGST programs were focused on academic leadership. Even though the master of theology program offered leadership training in pastoral work, its "style and ethos [were] characteristically academic." A need was discerned for continuing theological education for those who worked primarily in parishes. The program had been discussed previously, and by 1979

96 Emerito Nacpil, "A Historical Footnote," n.d.; Yeow Choo Lak, *The ATESEA The SEAGST,* n.d., both ATESEAF.

97 Handbook of ATESEA, SEAGST, 1988-89, ATESEAF.

98 Report of SEAGST, 1978, ATESEAF; Thomson, "A Note on the Development," 40.

99 Report of the Executive Director of ATSSEA and Dean of SEAGST, 1978, ATESEAF.

it was felt to be time to begin this nondegree program for the clergy, which would concentrate on "retraining and continuing theological education for clergy,...provide...specialized training in the various forms of pastoral ministry and in Christian leadership, [and]...develop a body of contextual literature in pastoral theology." For admission the applicant was to hold a "basic theological degree," have three years' full-time experience in the ministry, hold a position as a pastor or church administrator, live and work near the program, and be able to devote the necessary time to study. It was proposed that the program begin in Taipei, Manila, and Jakarta, with two-hour meetings once a week, under the supervision of a faculty member of SEAGST. Each class was to identify problems it would research and study, and each student was to write a thesis in his or her field of study. It was hoped that the program would be of thirty months' duration. Graduates of the program were to be given a Graduate Diploma in Pastoralia, which would be regarded as the equivalent of a professional doctorate in practical ministry.[100]

The graduate school established a research program for individual faculty members or teams of faculty to fulfill that part of the charter which called for research on the Christian faith as it related to non-Christian religions. The purpose of the research program was to

> identify the major theological issues arising out of the variety of contexts and situations in Asia; encourage constructive theological reflection in relation to these characteristically Asian theological issues, produce theological writings which will be used as a source-material for teaching and to promote contextual theological construction; and to provide opportunity for theological scholars to engage in research and reflection... addressing themselves constructively to the prospects and problems of theology and theological education in Asia.[101]

By 1988 the purpose of the doctoral program at South East Asia Graduate School of Theology was defined as "the promotion of theological research and reflection; faculty development and academic careers in theological education; [and] encounter and theological dialogue with societies and cultures and religions in Asia." The doctoral program was open to members of faculties of seminaries in the region and "the study program of the applicant [needed to] be a part of the

[100] Institute of Advanced Pastoral Studies in Minutes, Annual Meeting, ATSSEA, Manila, October 1979, ATESEAF.

[101] Handbook of ATESEA, SEAGST, 1988-89, ATESEAF.

faculty development plan or program of the school in which he [was] teaching or which [was] sponsoring him." Each student needed to be partially supported by the sponsoring seminary if a study fellowship from the graduate school was requested. Applicants were required to hold a master of theology degree or an equivalent degree, such as the master of sacred theology or master of arts degree. The research of each student was expected to be "fundamentally Asia-oriented."[102]

In the 1990s, South East Asia Graduate School of Theology was offering the degrees Master of Theology (M.Theol.), Doctor of Pastoral Studies (D.P.S.), and Doctor of Theology (D.Theol.). The resources of all the accredited schools in the region were available to all students. The school's main purpose was to provide South East Asians an opportunity to receive advanced education in the area without having to study in Europe or North America. The specific aims as then defined were:

> 1) to assist in the intellectual and spiritual development of Asian theologians so that their Christian ministry will be enriched and more effective; 2) to contribute to the emergence of a contextual and Asia-oriented theology by providing the facilities, and opportunities for research into, and reflection upon, the Christian faith as it relates to the non-Christian religions, cultures, and traditions of Asia, and to contemporary Asian society and its problems; 3) to further the training of competent teachers for the theological faculties of the region and of leaders for Christian ministry in church and society; 4) to promote opportunities for the interchange of graduate students and faculty members between the different participating institutions with a view to enhancing both a regional consciousness and Christian fellowship across the barriers of race, cultures, and nations.[103]

The work of FTESEA and ATSSEA became more clearly distinct from 1967. John Fleming's dual responsibilities for both organizations were separated with his departure from Singapore. As previously noted, Alan C. Thomson became executive director of FTESEA and Kosuke Koyama headed ATSSEA. Yet both maintained their offices in Singapore, and FTESEA funding decisions reflected discussions among the two directors as well as with representatives of Asian schools and deliberations of the foundation's board in New York. However, with

102 Ibid.
103 Yeow, *The ATESEA The SEAGST.*

Thomson's departure, Ivy Chou became executive director of FTESEA in 1972. Because she combined her half-time appointment to the foundation with another half-time appointment as the executive director of the Joint South East Asia office of the Theological Education Fund of the World Council of Churches, she occupied the education fund's office in Bromley, England (greater London). The removal of the FTESEA's executive director from the region and from direct day-to-day contact with ATSSEA's director argued for new planning and resource allocation procedures. Equally important was the growing maturity of the churches and theological schools of South East Asia and of ATSSEA, a factor which encouraged further devolution of decision making regarding grants from the foundation's board to a responsible body in the region. These factors led first to the creation of a Joint Regional Planning Commission (JRPC) and subsequently to its reorganization into a Resource Commission.

Initiated by the FTESEA board in 1972, preparations began shortly after Chou joined the foundation as its executive director. The board voted

> to initiate a cooperative process involving consultation with the churches, institutions and associations, through which joint North American-Southeast Asian efforts in theological education can be coordinated and evaluated on a broad ecumenical base which more adequately expresses the fundamental purpose and full potential of the Foundation....[104]

At its 1973 meeting, the FTESEA voted to hold a consultation of Asian church leaders in conjunction with ATSSEA's meeting in April 1974 in order to explore the matter more fully. After discussions with board members, Chou met in Singapore with Koyama to determine the interest of ATSSEA. Chou then sent a memorandum to the heads of FTESEA-related institutions reporting decisions made at the 1973 annual meeting of the foundation. She indicated that the foundation had agreed to a new structural model and had asked ATSSEA members "to consider organizing a working committee in South East Asia to make recommendations on the disposition of FTE funds for grants." She noted that FTESEA wished for the involvement of representatives of related churches and of the Christian Conference of Asia as well as of the member schools of ATSSEA. The foundation proposed that

[104] Quoted in "How did the Joint Regional Planning Commission Come About?" *SEAJT,* XVI (1975): 64.

the new model be introduced on an experimental basis for three years (1975-1977).[105]

Further negotiations followed regarding the extent to which various constituencies should be involved in the decision-making process, and Charles Forman, chair of the foundation, Paul Gregory, first vice-chair, and Chou represented the FTESEA at the 1974 ATSSEA meeting. On April 12, 1974, ATSSEA accepted the FTESEA proposal and adopted "Regulations and Procedures for the Joint Regional Planning Commission" to be established by joint action of FTESEA and the association. Guidelines indicated that the commission would include representatives of the foundation and the association, the church, an Asian theological educator from outside South East Asia, and a staff member of the Christian Conference of Asia.[106]

FTESEA anticipated that the Joint Regional Planning Commission would have enormous benefits for the foundation itself. Paul Gregory, who became the FTESEA representative to the commission, indicated that the foundation anticipated that the commission would "secure more sharply articulated Southeast Asian goals, priorities, and strategy for theological education, as a framework for decision making." The foundation also hoped that it might "make available to North American boards related to FTESEA the insights which emerge from [Commission deliberations]...." The commission might also "enable FTESEA to play a more potent catalytic and enabling role in a continual process of exchange and mutual stimulation between theological thinking and theological training in South East Asia and North America." Additionally, the commission might "develop a model for ecumenical cooperation" that would contribute to "mature partnership and celebration of the unity of the Church."[107]

When the first meeting of the Joint Regional Planning Commission convened in Taipei on October 6, 1975, members reaffirmed that the commission was the creation of the FTESEA and ATSSEA and that it would report its actions to both bodies. The JPRC believed it was its task to "encourage the advancement of theological education in the theological schools and regional coordination," but left the actual work of carrying out programs and projects to ATSSEA.

105 Ivy Chou to Heads of FTESEA-related Institutions, Bromley, England, December 14, 1973, Ivy Chou correspondence, FTEA; Thomson, "A Note on the Development," 42-43.

106 Ibid.

107 Paul R. Gregory, "Significance of the Commission for FTESEA and the Related North American Boards," *SEAJT*, XVI (1975): 64-67.

In considering funding requests, it sought to "encourage growth and coordination in the region" and to "seek understanding of the situations and needs from which the requests have arisen." Commission members expressed their belief that theological education was advancing where it considered a "mutually creative relationship" between the churches and the schools, where it entered into a dialogue with other religions, and involved itself in the whole life of the community which it served. The commission also declared that it would regard self-reliance, critical self-evaluation, and contextualization in theological reflection as evidences of advancement.[108]

The planning commission then studied the reports of the team that had recently visited institutions in the Philippines and Taiwan. Four major issues were listed in the team's report: women in theological schools, viability of the schools, field education, and church representation on the planning commission.[109]

On the issue of women in theological schools, the visiting team noted that women formed the majority of the students at some of the schools, and the question was "whether the church is ready to give women a place in its ministry, and whether the theological schools are adequately prepared to offer them the kind of training that would fit them for the church's expectations." The team wondered if some women attended theological schools to obtain degrees in order to engage in some other kinds of work, and also if some women who were qualified both in kindergarten teaching and theology were pressed by the church to work to the point of near exploitation. The team observed that many churches expect women workers to have administrative, typing, music, and educational skills."[110]

The team had found the question of viability to be one with which they believed the churches, seminaries, and ATSSEA had to struggle. It feared that the issue was not being taken seriously enough. On the topic of field education, the team found that students were demanding more faculty involvement in this aspect of their education. The students believed they needed "help to bridge the gap between what they learn at a theological school and what they face in the churches, and the gap between modern theological understanding and their traditional religious views." They were also concerned that representatives of the churches on the planning commission might feel as though they were

108 Minutes, Annual Meeting, JRPC, October 6-8, 1975, ATESEAF.

109 Ibid.

110 Ibid.; Resource Commission for Theological Education in Southeast Asia, [1978], ATESEAF.

outsiders, since other members were professionally linked through the theological institutions.

Members found the concept of the team itself to be useful because they believed that "such teams encouraged self-study," and, as they were made up of those who knew the "historical, cultural and ecclesiastical contexts in which member schools operate," they would be less likely to make decisions from the perspective of a single school or region. They proposed that in the future the teams arriving at a school needed to meet immediately with the faculty to clear up issues that were not clear in the advance materials and then to meet with students, church representatives, and university administrators, if relevant, without faculty in attendance. They also recommended that two days be allotted to each school visit, even though they knew this was not always possible. Accordingly, they thought the teams should not be scheduled so tightly that team members never had a free day to talk with each other or to compensate for travel problems.[111]

At this first meeting, the Joint Regional Planning Commission received requests for funds from sixteen institutions that the FTESEA had previously supported, for a total of $86,264, and the commission forwarded as approved requests with a total cost of $67,657. Other requests for faculty development, an interseminary program of field education in the Philippines, the ATSSEA office, the SEAGST, the *SEAJT*, a workshop on management, and a Pan-Asian Consultation to be held in 1977 amounted to $183,484. Of these, requests with a cost of $153,707 were approved.[112]

The planning commission was authorized to review requests and make grant recommendations to FTESEA for a three-year period. During those years, though the commission worked effectively, a variety of issues arose that led the foundation and other participants to reconsider its structure and function. While it had no desire to return to unilateral decision making, the FTESEA was concerned to protect its own integrity and tax exempt status and to remain engaged with the theological programs of the region. Additionally, the Theological Education Fund, with which FTESEA had shared its director and worked so closely, ended its mandate, and the WCC initiated a new Programme on Theological Education in 1977.

[111] ATSSEA/FTE JRPC, Summary Comments and Recommendations of the Philippine-Taiwan Visiting Team [1975]; Minutes, Annual Meeting, JRPC, October 6-8, 1975; both ATESEAF.

[112] Ibid.

The FTESEA also experienced a change in executive leadership at the end of 1976, as Ivy Chou retired and was replaced as executive director by Marvin D. Hoff, the secretary for operations and finance of the Reformed Church in America and the Reformed Church's representative on the FTESEA board.[113]

Hoff envisaged a broader role both for FTESEA and for the regional commission. To a meeting of the foundation's executive committee in early 1977 Hoff proposed that the FTESEA regard as its major guidelines the strengthening and advancement of theological education in South East Asia and assisting the churches of that region in furthering the cause of theological education. He also urged maximizing Asian input in determining priorities and in decision-making processes and suggested that the foundation might serve as a link between boards and agencies in the United States and the churches in Asia in the cause of theological education. Critical to Hoff's view was the possibility that FTESEA could promote support for these efforts beyond its own resources.[114]

The proposal for a new Resource Commission to replace the Joint Resource Planning Commission was received and approved by the FTESEA board in December 1977.[115] At an executive committee meeting of ATSSEA in Kaohsiung, Taiwan, in February, 1978, plans for the Resource Commission were established, and its committee met as part of the ATESEA meeting in Manila that October. Committee members discussed the weaknesses of the JRPC that had been considered in planning for the Resource Commission. First, the JRPC could recommend funding requests only to FTESEA, whereas the Resource Commission could recommend requests to other agencies as well. Second, the JRPC had been composed almost exclusively of theological educators, whereas the Resource Commission would also include a significant representation of church men and women. Third, the JRPC had been jointly sponsored by FTESEA and ATSSEA, whereas the Resource Commission was established by ATSSEA, although the FTESEA had been consulted in the planning, had endorsed the proposal, and was prepared to use the Resource Commission's mechanism for decision-making.

113 Minutes, Annual Meeting, FTESEA November 14, 1975; Minutes, Executive Committee Meeting, FTESEA, September 8, 1976; both FTEA.

114 Marvin D. Hoff, "Staffing the Foundation for Theological Education in South East Asia—A Working Paper," an enclosure in Minutes, Executive Committee Meeting, FTESEA, January 26, 1977, FTEA.

115 Minutes, Annual Meeting, FTESEA, December 2, 1977, FTEA.

The Resource Commission's members also discussed the nature and task of a theological vocation, the implications of contextualizing theology, and the resources available to the commission. They conceived their task to be securing for Christianity a hearing among the many faith options available in South East Asia. As a minority religion, they believed Christianity was "required to validate itself." They expressed a concern to avoid allowing yesterday's vision to become tomorrow's repetition. For example, they asked how the expansion and improvement of libraries could be included in the priorities and thrusts instead of just adding more books, even those written by Asians. Could church members who were professionals be trained to be "doers of theology?" They emphasized that, in order to be effective, the Resource Commission required the close cooperation of the ATSSEA and the FTESEA. Yet the commission expected to work with various institutions to obtain funding for its many needs. When it was established, the commission had as its members six churchmen—one each from Hong Kong, the Philippines, Taiwan, Singapore, and two from Indonesia; six heads of schools—one each from Hong Kong, the Philippines, Taiwan, Thailand, and two from Indonesia; two members at large from India and Korea, and consultants from the WCC's Programme on Theological Education and the FTESEA.[116]

Though the FTESEA approved these first Resource Commission requests for ATSSEA, for seminaries, and for the commission's visits at its December 1978 meeting, the board's discussion and questions concerning these items suggested the need for further clarification. Hoff wrote to the Resource Commission following this meeting and offered both a critique of the October 1978 requests and suggestions for future submissions.[117] Over successive years mutual confidence was established, along with a better understanding of the operating procedures and expectations of each group. For several years, commencing in 1979, the FTESEA voted to fund all requests presented by the Resource Commission.[118]

At the 1982 meeting of the Resource Commission, more specific guidelines for awarding grants were set forth. Priority was to be given to operation and ongoing program categories; grants were to be given

[116] Minutes, Resource Commission Meeting, Manila, October 16-17, 1978, ATESEAF.

[117] Marvin D. Hoff to Resource Commission, New York, January 12, 1979, FTEA.

[118] Minutes, Annual Meeting, FTESEA, December 7, 1979; December 12, 1980; December 11, 1981; December 10, 1982; December 15, 1983; all FTEA.

to encourage continuing theological education programs and various forms of theological education by extension; grants were generally not to be made for undergraduate level programs, which were held to be the responsibility of the churches; post-B.D. scholarships were generally to be awarded only for fields of study which were not offered by SEAGST; grants to cover new, unexpected faculty salaries were to be considered but to be reduced annually by 20 percent; "in making judgment on requests, comparative levels of national economy, situation, and potential of the individual school's program" were to be considered. Grants could be for two years, but would be paid on an annual basis as funds were available.[119]

Upon renewal of contacts with China, the FTESEA reaffirmed "its continuing commitment to carry out the original, and amended, purposes of...the Board of Founders of Nanking Theological Seminary." It therefore invited requests for assistance from Nanjing Union Theological Seminary.[120] While this resumption of support for theological education in China created some concern that the FTESEA might be unable to fund its ongoing programs in South East Asia at an adequate level, this concern initially proved to be largely unnecessary. Though on several occasions reductions were made in grants recommended by the Resource Commission, in most instances funding was at or very near the level of commission requests even as the FTESEA grants to China increased.[121] Indeed, in early 1991 Hoff informed Yeow Choo Lak that the cuts in programs in South East Asia that the foundation had expected as requests from China increased did not occur, and there were actually increases in grants to South East Asia and more increases were expected in 1992 and 1993.[122]

This benign situation changed quickly and dramatically, however. A drop of $100,000 in income from the Swope-Wendel fund was reported in 1993, and the FTESEA ran deficits in both 1992 and 1993.[123] At the 1993 annual meeting, Hoff reported that the foundation had been using accumulated undesignated funds for the renewal of programs in China, but that these funds were now exhausted. With the

[119] Marvin D. Hoff, "1982 Meeting of RC of ATESEA," 1982; and Yeow Choo Lak to Marvin D. Hoff, n.p., November 8, 1982, both ATESEAF.

[120] Minutes, Executive Committee, FTESEA, May 3, 1982, FTEA.

[121] Minutes, Executive Committee, FTESEA, October 14, 1980; Minutes, Annual Meeting, FTESEA, December 12, 1980; December 11, 1981; December 10, 1982; December 15, 1983; December 20, 1984; December 19, 1985; December 18, 1986; December 17, 1987; all FTEA.

[122] Marvin D. Hoff to Yeow Choo Lak, n.p., January 2, 1991, FTEA.

[123] Minutes, Executive Committee, FTESEA, December 15, 1993, FTEA.

further reduction in interest being received on the Swope-Wendel fund, only $50,000 was allocated for Resource Commission grants, and funds for ATESEA and SEAGST were completely eliminated.[124]

Both ATESEA and the FTESEA were mindful of the changing fiscal situation and sought to adjust to it. By this time, ATESEA had a significant endowment, and some of its operating funds came from sources other than the foundation. Hoff discussed the implications of these changes with Yeow and conveyed the FTESEA board's view that some adjustments would be required.[125] After further consideration by the foundation, and with a desire to focus its limited funding more directly on theological education, Hoff advised Yeow in March 1996 that the foundation could no longer be the primary supporter of ATESEA's administrative functions.[126] Fortunately, the fiscal difficulties of this period abated, and FTESEA again was able to provide significant funding for ATESEA.[127]

The foundation's fiscal problems could not be resolved, however, simply by eliminating the grant for ATESEA's administrative operations. The executive committee met in September 1994 and noted that earned income from the Swope-Wendel fund had dropped from 11.81 percent of principal in 1982 to 5.76 percent in 1993. The committee endorsed a fundraising program to permit the FTESEA's continuation of effective support of Asian theological education.[128] As Ching-fen Hsiao, chair of the board, explained to members, this decision represented a major shift in the long range direction of the foundation. "Rather than just disburse the funds that come to it from the Swope-Wendel Fund, the directors have decided to engage in fund raising, especially through Foundations, for theological education in China and South East Asia."[129] A special meeting of the entire FTESEA board followed, and this body endorsed the proposal. Full consultation with partners prior to commencement of the program and cooperation with the denominations involved with FTESEA were recognized as essential.[130] Hsiao advised the foundation's directors and consultants

124 Minutes, Annual Meeting, FTESEA, December 16, 1993, FTEA.

125 Marvin D. Hoff to Yeow Choo Lak, n.p., January 14, 1995, FTEA.

126 Marvin D. Hoff to Yeow Choo Lak, n.p., March 5, 1996, FTEA.

127 Marvin D. Hoff, "Brief History of the FTESEA from the Search Document" [2006], FTEA.

128 Minutes, Executive Committee, FTESEA, September 8, 1994, FTEA.

129 Ching-fen Hsiao, Memorandum to Trustees of the FTESEA, New York, September 19, 1994, FTEA.

130 Minutes, Special Meeting, FTESEA, October 13, 1994, FTEA.

in January of 1995 that Hoff, the executive director, would commit a significant portion of his time to this advancement program.[131]

Later that year ATESEA asked Hoff to seek major grants from the Luce Foundation and other sources for a variety of projects ranging from endowment support for the SEAGST and ATESEA to support for doctoral students.[132] By August of the following year, the advancement program efforts had produced commitments of $895,000 for various projects, including a $270,000 grant from the Luce Foundation for books for Chinese pastors.[133] Two years later the effort had commitments of $1,276,000.[134] At the end of 1999, the total had reached $1,421,000.[135]

Concerned that the FTESEA not simply fund the same or similar programs year after year, the board asked the Resource Commission in 1999 for "new creative proposals." Proposals were forthcoming, and the first of these were approved for ATESEA and SEAGST at the 1999 annual meeting, along with grants to the Commission on Theological Education of China Christian Council and the World Council of Churches' Ecumenical Institute.[136] In 2000, similar grants were again made.[137]

In another new and creative initiative the FTESEA, along with ATESEA, reached out to support the Association for Theological Education in Myanmar (ATEM), which was experiencing great difficulties.[138] Problems encountered by students from Myanmar studying abroad had been the subject of a conference in Yangon in February 1999. The ATEM schools selected their candidates and forwarded their names to ATESEA. If the students were to study in Singapore, they needed to take entrance examinations, but those who went to Hong Kong or Korea did not. Those who studied in Hong Kong or Korea were given scholarships by the seminaries, and

131 Ching-fen Hsiao to FTESEA Directors, Alternates and Consultants, n.p., February 7, 1995, FTEA.

132 Marvin D. Hoff to Charles Forman and Ching-fen Hsiao, n.p., June 8, 1995, FTEA.

133 Marvin D. Hoff to FTESEA Executive Committee, Holland, Mich., August 19, 1996; FTEA.

134 Minutes, Executive Committee, FTESEA, December 17, 1998, FTEA.

135 Minutes, Annual Meeting, FTESEA, December 16, 1999, FTEA.

136 Ibid.; "New, Creative Proposals from the RC of ATESEA" [1999], FTEA.

137 Minutes, Annual Meeting, FTESEA, December 14, 2000, FTEA.

138 All earlier references to the country of Myanmar use the traditional name Burma. However, because the ATEM uses the name Myanmar, it appears appropriate to use that name in this context.

SEAGST paid for their travel. Two Myanmar students had studied at Western Seminary in Holland, Michigan, with no support from ATEM, although that association endorsed their studies. Other problems concerned the decline in educational standards and English language proficiency in Myanmar, factors which made it extremely difficult for students to study at foreign universities. Students frequently had difficulty obtaining passports and visas, which sometimes resulted in their arriving too late to enroll for the term for which they had applied and incurring additional expense while waiting for a subsequent term to begin.[139]

As sensitivity to feminism generally and specifically to women's roles in the church increased during these years, the membership and activities of the FTESEA reflected this change. It is interesting that in spite of the general paternalism characteristic of Asian cultures, women have consistently played a significant role both in churches and in church schools in that region. Women theologians were frequently recipients of Board of Founders' scholarships for overseas study from as early as 1938, but, with the appointment of Ivy Chou as executive director in 1972, the FTESEA became identified visibly with concerns focusing on women in the church.[140] Three members-at-large of the FTESEA in 1975 were women, and, from 1984 when Laura Luz Bacerra joined the board representing the Christian Church (Disciples of Christ), participating denominations more often chose women as their representatives. Letty Russell, a distinguished professor of theology in the Yale Divinity School with an international reputation for her interest in feminist issues, became a member-at-large on the foundation's board in the same year and provided effective leadership within the board thereafter.[141]

When a group of Asian women theologians first asked the FTESEA for travel funds in 1984, the board demurred because it had been provided no evidence that the recipients intended to return to

139 Marvin D. Hoff to Dawn Boelkins, n.p., December 18, 1995; Eh Wah, "Meeting Among ATESEA, ATEM, UBCHEA," Yangoon, February 11-12, 1999, both FTEA.

140 A list of recipients of BF scholarships from 1936 through 1962 is found in Cartwright, *River*, 33-34. The first women recipients were Huang Su-chen and Marcia Wang.

141 Minutes, Annual Meeting, FTESEA, November 14, 1975: Minutes, Annual Meeting, FTESEA, December 20, 1984, both FTEA. Sallie Lou MacKinnon was a charter member of the BF representing the Board of Foreign Missions of the Methodist Episcopal Church, South; Cartwright, *River*, 22.

Asia. However, when provided with such assurance, the foundation made a grant to this group in 1985 and frequently thereafter. By 1990, this group was known as the Asian/Asian-American Women in Theology and Ministry. The FTESEA support continued through the remainder of the 1990s.[142]

The FTESEA sponsored an event, called "Dialogue among Theologically Trained Women of Asia," in the summer of 1990. This event brought together ten Asian women theologians from various countries, nine of whom were then living in the United States and one in Sweden, to visit Christian women's groups in China. After their visits, the ten were joined by another twelve women for a consultation, "Feminist Theology in Cross-Cultural Perspective," in Hong Kong. Together, this group represented fifteen countries and twenty-two churches. Among the topics discussed were feminist theology; sexual exploitation; racial, cultural, and ethnic oppression; and violation of human rights and militarization.

They also discussed worship, Bible study, theological reflection, and biblical and church traditions as seen from women's perspectives in order "to develop our own insights as Christian women." The group defined feminist theology as women's theology or women doing theology or "the affirmation of God's intention for the full humanity of women together with men," adding that "we are practicing this affirmation of women within and outside our theological seminaries and churches. We are celebrating the gifts of women as preachers, teachers, musicians, organizers, mothers, and so much more."[143]

A subgroup of this consultation that studied sexual exploitation named itself "Not for Sale" and developed strategies for sharing information on church agencies working to oppose the global sex industry. With regard to racial, cultural, and ethnic oppression, the group called for sharing information and resources and opposing such oppression. It pledged to make this theme a permanent part of the feminist theology agenda. The subgroup on violation of human rights and militarization called for an end of church cooperation with groups using oppressive force and pledged to "strengthen women and

142 Minutes, Annual Meeting, FTESEA, December 20, 1984; Minutes, Annual Meeting, FTESEA, December 19, 1985; Minutes, Annual Meeting, FTESEA, December 12, 1990; Minutes, Annual Meeting, FTESEA, December 19, 1991; Minutes, Annual Meeting, FTESEA, December 16, 1999, all FTEA.

143 Letty Russell and Kwok Pui-lan to Marvin D. Hoff, New Haven, Conn., July 5, 1990; "Hong Kong Consultation Among Theologically Trained Women in Asia, Sweden and the USA," 1990, both MA/RO.

the church in the nurture of justice and peace, and solidarity with the people's struggles for life.[144]

These issues were also reflected in one of the new and creative proposals endorsed by the Resource Commission at the end of that decade. That proposal, called Women in Theology, was designed to address such issues as the feminization of poverty, which sometimes led to women being forced into prostitution, and overseas migration of women for employment to support families. The proponents of this program hoped to strengthen church communities to work for a fair and just society.[145]

In 1997 ninety Asian theologians from Australia, Bangladesh, Hong Kong, India, Indonesia, Japan, Korea, Laos, Malaysia, Myanmar, the Philippines, Singapore, Sri Lanka, Taiwan, and Thailand met in Suwon, Korea, to discuss the agenda for the church in Asia in the new century. ATESEA representatives were involved in this group, which was composed of Protestant, Orthodox, and Roman Catholic Christians. They expressed their commitment to ecumenism. They identified their challenges as coming from "globalization, new information technology, poverty, religious and ethnic revival and conflicts, the meeting of religions, the ecological crisis, women's movements, and other movements of the marginalized." Noting that churches had grown rapidly over the previous decades "especially among Pentecostal, fundamentalist and evangelical congregations," they believed they needed to respond to this new situation and "old paradigms of theological construction and old patterns of ministry [needed to] be changed and transformed...to respond creatively to this new situation." Among the statements they adopted was the affirmation, "Theology for us is not a systematic explication of timeless truths nor is it a matter of imposing a pre-fabricated system of ideas on a situation. Its object is to help people in their struggle for justice, freedom and community, as well as to serve the churches in their articulation and practice of faith."[146]

Many of the FTESEA and ATESEA objectives were shared by this larger and more ecumenical group, as its statement of future tasks suggests:

1) to deepen and broaden networks of Asian theologians through the sharing of Asian resources for doing theology, exchanges

[144] Ibid.
[145] "New, Creative Proposals from the RC of ATESEA" [1999?], FTEA.
[146] "Asian Theologians Setting Agenda for the 21st Century," *SEAJT*, XI (1997): 402-03.

among students and theological educators and inter-regional dialogues;

2) to investigate and seek resolution for the spiritual dimensions of communal conflicts;
3) to analyze the dynamics and the destruction of war so that the viability of war-making as a social institution can be theologically assessed and to promote peace with justice;
4) to explore ways of relating positively to other spiritual and religious traditions, in order to refine and strengthen our Christian commitment and faith;
5) to discern ways of drawing on indigenous spiritual traditions in Christian theology and worship;
6) to deepen the emerging dialogue between contextual theologies;
7) to integrate feminist insights and perspectives on reality, in the language of theology and all theological disciplines;
8) to continue to explore ways of articulating the meaning of Christ especially in the area of inter-faith dialogue and ecological concerns;
9) to articulate a "third generation" of missiology that goes beyond the paradigms of mission bequeathed to us by the ecumenical movement and Vatican II;
10) to commit ourselves to the formation of church leadership and theological educators by developing new theological curricula and pedagogies.[147]

As the twenty-first century began, the Foundation for Theological Education in South East Asia continued to work together with ATESEA, the Ecumenical Theological Education program of the WCC, and an ever widening group of ecumenical partners toward the development of the Christian church and theological education in South East Asia. The foundation was involved in a variety of programs and initiatives, all aimed at increasing the level of education and leadership ability for members of the Christian clergy and laity in South East Asia and the wider Asian world.[148]

[147] Ibid., 404.

[148] In 1997 Ching-fen Hsiao proposed and the FTESEA voted to "plan a process of setting up priorities for the first decade of the new century and millennium. This process should include our partners in South East Asia and China," Minutes, Annual Meeting, FTESEA, December 18, 1997, FTEA.

CHAPTER 7

Relationships with Nanjing Union Theological Seminary and China after Liberation

The sense of identity with and concern for Nanking Theological Seminary and its faculty remained strong among the members of the Board of Founders after the termination of formal relationships in 1951. The United States failed to recognize the new government in Beijing. Without diplomatic relations between the United States and the People's Republic of China, the transfer of funds to China was prohibited by the U.S. government and condemned in China as evidence of Western imperialism. Yet the Board of Founders sought information about Nanking Seminary and the churches in China wherever it could be found.

Hubert Sone, the last of the missionary teachers to leave the seminary, advised the Board of Founders in March 1951 that "...the Seminary, like all other church bodies and groups in China, has subscribed to the plan of full and complete 'self-control, self-support, and self-propagation.' This means they will carry on without funds from abroad." Yet he also expressed concern that the churches in China appeared "unable to give immediate help to the seminary." The seminary constitution was being revised, the supporting denominations limited to the Church of Christ in China, the Disciples, the Methodists, and the Baptists. All references to the Board of Founders were being eliminated, and there were to be no foreign members of the Board of Managers, while a Seminary Council composed of teachers, staff, and students, was replacing the governing faculty.[1]

Two years later Frank W. Price wrote Cartwright with information he had received in a letter from China. Twelve seminaries and Bible schools had been consolidated into Nanjing Union Theological Seminary. A twenty-seven-person board of directors had been selected, including many who had been associated with the old Nanking Theological Seminary such as Li Tien-lu, Handel Lee, Dr. Luther Shao, and the Reverend T. C. Bau. This board, meeting December 10-12, 1952, in Shanghai had elected K. H. Ting as president and Dr. Andrew C. Y. Cheng and the Reverend Ting Yu-chang as vice presidents.[2]

Following the 1956 Bangkok conference, Rajah Manikam made a trip to China and visited all the union theological seminaries in the country. To Frank Cartwright he reported what he had learned:

> I may pass on to you, and through you to your Board, the very strong feeling expressed to me by the President [Bishop K. H. Ting][3] and staff of the Union Nanking Theological Seminary that your Board of Founders should not any longer use the name of "Nanking Theological Seminary." I pointed out to them the legal problems involved in any change of name. They hold, however, that facts must be faced as they are and a Board in America has no right to use any more the name of a Seminary in China, with which it has absolutely no connections. They suggested that however difficult the legal process may be, your Board should take steps to have its name changed. I am passing on this information for what it is worth for consideration of your Board.[4]

1 Hubert L. Sone to Frank T. Cartwright, Nanjing, March 7, 1951, ALW.

2 Frank W. Price to Frank T. Cartwright, Richmond, Vir., January 24, 1953, ALW. The discrepancy in number of schools merged into Nanjing Union Seminary (11 or 12) results from the fact that the NTS-BTTS merger had already occurred. Some include both schools, some only one. Dr. Y. T. Wu and K. H. Ting were also members of the new board, and Ting Yu-chang (identified as Ting Yu-san by Manikam) was formerly associated with North China Theological Seminary.

3 All subsequent references to Ting refer to K. H. Ting unless another name is specified. The pinyin spelling which is commonly seen in China is Ding Guangxun.

4 Rajah B. Manikam to Frank T. Cartwright, Coimbatore, India, May 16, 1956, ALW. The proposal was not immediately implemented. However, as

Manikam also prepared an extensive report on the seminaries in China at this time, several years after the founding of the People's Republic and a decade prior to the Cultural Revolution which would, once more, transform the religious landscape there. Manikam wrote that representatives of various seminaries in China had held a conference at Nanjing Union Theological Seminary March 30, 1956. He described the seminary as "a union of eleven theological institutions, formerly scattered around China. Since the separate existence of all eleven institutions could not be justified after liberation, the union was effected in the autumn of 1952."[5] Y. T. Wu, who had been a YMCA secretary prior to 1949, became a prominent leader of the independent Chinese church following liberation. As head of the Three-Self Patriotic Movement, Wu suggested this consolidation in Nanjing. There Nanjing Seminary and the (Women's) Bible Teachers' Training School close by had already become one institution and were located on the Bible school's campus.[6] When Nanjing Seminary was opened as a union institution in the autumn of 1952, K. H. Ting was appointed principal and Chen Zemin[7] vice dean. To balance differing theological views, two vice principals were appointed– Ting Yu-chang, a conservative, and Andrew C. Y. Cheng, a liberal–and parallel curricula were offered. Four years later, at the time of Manikam's visit, the seminary enrolled 183 students representing nineteen denominations: Church of Christ in China, Anglican Church, Baptist Church, Methodist Church, English Methodist Church, China Inland Mission, China Evangelical Church, Self-supporting Church, the Little Flock, Pentecostal Church, Faith of the Apostles Church, Spiritual Work, Quaker Church, China Preaching Church, Seventh Day Adventist Church, Lutheran Church, Bethel Church, Disciples Church, and an independent local church. About thirty of the students were women. Manikam reported three levels of

the BF became more deeply involved with theological education outside of China and the possibility of a return to Nanjing became remote, the name was changed in 1963.

5 The term liberation was apparently used by Manikam as it is generally used in the People's Republic of China today as a reference to the Communist victory of 1949 and the expulsion of the Nationalist government. I have also adopted this common PRC usage.

6 The Bible Teachers' Training School was known by this title prior to 1950, though it was a women's school. Manikam uses the title Women's Bible Teachers' Training School, which must have been the usage in Nanjing in 1956.

7 All subsequent references to Chen are to Chen Zemin unless another person is specified.

instruction: a three-year program for university graduates leading to a B.D. degree; a four-year program for senior middle school graduates; and a four-to-five-year program for junior middle school graduates. He reported that most of the students from rural areas were enrolled in the second program. The union work appeared to be going well, and the seminary expected to enroll about one hundred new students a year. There was no lack of applicants, only the problem of selection. Of the graduates, 95 percent engaged in church work.[8]

Having been formed from the merger of so many small seminaries, Nanjing Union had a large faculty of thirty people, half of whom were women. All staff members were reported to engage in research. The principal subjects taught were New Testament, Old Testament, theology, and church history. Biblical theology, pastoral theology, and church music were also taught. Though Manikam was told there was no study of Marxism at Nanjing Union, a "course on current events was given once a week and the Constitution of China was studied carefully and the love of the motherland inculcated." Manikam remarked that "it was surprising to me to find no courses in Comparative Religions, [but] I understand from Bishop Ting that the study of Comparative Religions has never has never been popular in China. The school is expecting to publish a quarterly of Western and Chinese folk songs and hymns."[9]

In the report of his discussions, Manikam commented that, in addition to objecting to its use of the Nanjing Theological Seminary name, some in Nanjing also "were inclined to question the legitimacy of the use of funds earmarked for their institution [by the Board of Founders] on seminaries outside China.[10]

Manikam's report ranged beyond Nanjing to several other seminaries in China. Yenching (later Yanjing in pinyin) Union Theological Seminary in Beijing had also been formed by a union of eleven institutions. Newton Chiang was a research professor here. Fundamentalists, Assemblies of God, and Holiness churches cooperated in the seminary, and parallel courses were offered in dogmatics by

8 Rajah B. Manikam, "Report on China Theological Seminaries by Bishop Rajah B. Manikam to Division of Foreign Missions, NCCUSA, China Committee (Wallace C. Merwin, secretary)," July 10, 1956, ALW. NTS remains on the old BTTS campus in 2008. Its older buildings have been designated for historical preservation. At least one of the older NTS buildings survives on the campus of a large hospital to the immediate southwest of the BTTS.

9 Ibid.

10 Ibid.

Baptist, Methodist, and Presbyterian faculty. Yenching had seventy-six students representing ten to twelve denominations from fifteen provinces. It had been united in 1952 and had no connection with the former Yenching University that had become part of Beijing University. In the previous year, thirty students were admitted from an applicant pool of 186.[11]

Canton (later Guangzhou) Theological College was operated by three churches but had students from other denominations as well. The Reverend Lee Tin Oi, an Anglican who had been ordained in Macao during the Japanese occupation, was teaching there and was one of the few ordained women in China at that time.[12] Twenty-six students were enrolled, and six of these were doing practical work outside the seminary. The college admitted high school graduates to a four-year course and also offered a three-year course for junior high school graduates. It offered a refresher course for pastors as well.[13]

Chungking (later Chongqing) Theological Seminary was not on Manikam's itinerary, but he talked with the president and vice president of that school. It had been founded in 1944 by Marcus Chen and was operated by the China Inland Mission. It had been reorganized in 1950 and currently had seven professors from Methodist, Lutheran, China Inland Mission, and Anglican denominational backgrounds. It was fundamentalist in theology and currently enrolled thirteen students. During the previous year, it had accepted eight students from fifty to sixty applicants.[14]

Though the presence of other seminaries in China at the time of Manikam's visit attests to the survival of several Protestant theological institutions in addition to those merged into Nanjing Union Theological Seminary, that institution remained the strongest of the Protestant seminaries in China. Yet it suffered along with the weaker schools and the churches themselves as the new Chinese government struggled with its religious policies. All Protestant denominations in China were unified under the Three-Self Movement in 1954, and Nanjing Union received students from all Protestant traditions, but the seminary was closed for a time during the antirightist campaign in 1957-58. Nanjing Union reopened in 1961 following the third national meeting of the Three-Self Movement, and the Beijing seminary was absorbed and most of its library brought to Nanjing. However, Nanjing Union was

11 Ibid.

12 Li was also known as Florence Tim Oi Li.

13 Manikam, "Report on China Theological Seminaries."

14 Ibid.

closed once more in August 1966 with the coming of the Cultural Revolution and the arrival of Red Guards on campus. Faculty members were classified according to their perceived politics. Some were isolated and sent to hard labor in the countryside, others judged less hostile to Chinese socialism were sent to a rural reformatory to work for self-education for about six years, and those judged most sympathetic to the new society were allowed to remain in their homes.[15]

Following the end of the Cultural Revolution, conditions for the church in China began to improve. Chinese Protestants were permitted to send a delegation to the World Peace Conference in Montreal in 1979, an event which marked the conclusion of a long period of isolation and a renewal, albeit rather hesitant, of contacts between Chinese Christians and those of other lands. At the fourth national meeting of the Three-Self Movement, a decision was reached to reopen Nanjing Union Theological Seminary once again, and work to that end commenced in early 1981, with classes resuming in the fall of that year. At that time Nanjing Seminary had been designated as the Center for Religious Studies of Nanjing University, the latter an institution formed by the merger of Central University, a state university from the Nationalist period, and the University of Nanking, a missionary college. For a time the seminary envisioned its role as one of preparing Chinese intellectuals to understand Christianity.[16]

The tragic personal cost of these years of isolation for Christians both in China and the West was underscored by contact between the son of Handel Lee, long time president of Nanking Seminary, and the Board of Founders. As members of the board were directing their attention to the future of theological education in South East Asia, a letter arrived in 1961 from Richard Wen-han Lee, the son of Handel Lee. The son was resident in the United States, but Handel Lee was then within eight days of his death in Beijing. The son contacted the board out of concern for his father. Richard Lee indicated that he had talked with Price and enclosed a copy of a letter he had written to the latter with his letter to Cartwright. Richard Lee wrote that the Board of Founders had promised his father a pension, but that it had not been paid since 1949:

> Over the past years many thoughts have bothered me tremendously which may have altered considerably my views toward today's Christianity and its workers. I kept asking myself:

[15] Chen Zemin, interview with Samuel C. Pearson, Nanjing, July 1, 2005.
[16] Ibid.

> where are the free, unafraid Christian spirits and the independent Christian consciousness which have never been known to be subject to the dictate of any man-made restrictions. Were not these the very things that gave birth to Protestantism, to the spreading of Christianity all over the world, to the foundation of this good U.S.A., and to the establishment of the early Christian church itself?[17]

Richard Lee continued that he wanted to know when the church had "passed up the opportunity or obligation to rescue a person from distress, or knowingly let a person, let alone a good colleague and faithful fellow servant of God, be hungry and destitute and do nothing...hiding behind the excuse 'I was told not to'? How could they claim a clean and clear conscious [sic]?" He reminded the addressees that his father was incapacitated when he retired in 1949 and had lived the twelve years since without the pension he had been promised. Richard Lee had twice asked the Board of Founders for his father's pension and twice been refused. "What right does the [Board of Founders] have to deny the living of a fellow worker or to give him what's due him? Complacency, conformity, apathy...seem to me, to have taken over love, missionary zeal, Christian spirit and Christian conscious [sic]." He wondered how those who denied his parents their pension would react if the situation were reversed. He told Price, whom he had known since childhood, that he was indeed bitter. "How many tears have I shed and how many prayers have I said over my parents' miseries." He observed that his father was then seventy-five and his mother seventy-three, and, even if the Board of Founders acted, "it is already too late to compensate for all my parents ha[ve] suffered in the past, but it may serve to correct the situation at the present and in the future so that they may be comforted with the very thought they are not forgotten nor forsaken, and that God's love still prevails in this troubled world." Richard Lee concluded that his father was then in an oxygen tent at the Peking Union Medical College after having suffered another heart attack.[18]

Cartwright responded that he had known Lee's father "from the 1920s until the time when the changed international situation led my friends in China to ask that we no longer try to write them or send money to them." He indicated the Board of Founders knew there had been correspondence between Richard Lee and Francis Jones in 1955

17 Richard Lee to Frank W. Price, Hyattsville, Md., May 16, 1961; Richard Lee to Frank T. Cartwright, Hyattsville, Md., May 16, 1961, both ALW.

18 Ibid.

and several times since, and that they had tried to secure a license from the U.S. government to permit them to pay pensions in China. At the 1955 annual meeting, the Committee on Pensions had requested that Smith and Cartwright "be alert with regard to opportunities to give financial aid to the four Chinese professors: Handel Lee, Li Tien-lu, Chu Bao-hui, and Tao Chung-ling."[19]

Cartwright wrote Richard Lee that he had discussed Lee's letter concerning his father with Francis Jones, Price, and H. P. Van Dusen, chair of the Board of Founders. They had concluded that the U.S. government's prohibition on direct and indirect money transfers to China did "not stand in the way of our making a grant to help you of the Lee family in helping your parents." He enclosed a check for $500 from the Board of Founders to cover Lee's emergency medical needs and added that if this were insufficient to cover what Mrs. Lee had paid to the hospital, Richard Lee should advise Cartwright so that he could take the matter to the board. He also wrote: "To show you that the Nanking Board has real concern for your father and the three other Chinese faculty members of the earlier years, let me state that in the autumn of 1955 we set up in a special account a sum of money to be held until governmental restrictions should be lifted."[20]

Price also responded to his letter from Richard Lee and reminded Lee that many Christian organizations had asked the U.S. government over the years for permission to send money to former colleagues in China or to the Christian institutions there, but "the replies have generally been a stiff negative prohibition." He also reminded Lee that in 1951 the Christian institutions in China had to promise they would receive no funds from the United States. Price continued, "There is no lack of Christian understanding and sympathy here for the many families in China who need help..." but, if the situation were to be resolved, there were "formidable obstacles that must somehow be surmounted, without jeopardizing all funds of the Christian agencies in this country and the safety of Christians in China in relations with their government."[21]

19 Minutes, Annual Meeting, BF, NTS, January 13, 1955, FTEA. Cartwright had received a request from Cheng through Sone in 1951 requesting that "their American friends stop sending them any money and stop writing to them—completely, for a considerable period. Otherwise, the most innocent kind of letter may be taken to indicate some kind of secret connection and that cause grave danger," Frank T. Cartwright to BF, New York, April 18, 1951, ALW.

20 Frank T. Cartwright to Richard Lee, New York, May 19, 1961, ALW.

21 Frank W. Price to Richard Lee, New York, May 21 [1961], PP.

A few days later on May 24, Handel Lee died in Beijing at the age of seventy-five. The memorial minute of the Board of Founders noted that he had been an ordained Methodist minister and the first Chinese person elected president of Nanking Seminary, a post he held for eighteen years. He was born in Kiangningchen, a large market town between Nanjing and Wuhu, March 15, 1886. His primary and secondary education was in new Christian schools, and he then attended the University of Nanking, where he was graduated in 1912. "Answering the call of God to service in the Church," he entered the new Nanking School of Theology, later Nanking Theological Seminary, and completed the course in 1916. He served the Second Street Methodist Church in Wuhu and was ordained a deacon in 1918 and an elder in 1920. Sent to the United States in 1921, he earned the S.T.B. degree from Boston University in 1922 and the Th.M. degree from Drew Theological Seminary in 1923. Returning to China, he was pastor of Kuilang Church, the largest Methodist Church in Nanjing, and in 1927 became district superintendent of the Methodist Conference. He served as a member of the Board of Managers of Nanking Theological Seminary. In 1931, when it was decided to elect a Chinese president to replace Harry F. Rowe, Lee was one of two people recommended and was chosen by a majority vote. Before assuming this post, Lee returned to the United States for study and to confer with the mission boards supporting Nanking Seminary, especially with respect to the newly announced Swope-Wendel bequest. He received a Ph.D. degree from Drew University in 1933 with a thesis entitled, "The Adaptation of the American Rural Church Administration to the Rural Church in China." Boston University granted him an honorary doctor of divinity degree in the same year. Lee returned to China and his seminary post in 1933. In 1937 he moved the seminary to Shanghai and visited Sichuan Province to help set up the seminary branch in Free China. At war's end he returned with the seminary to Nanjing. Ill health forced him to resign in 1949, and he was succeeded in the presidency of the seminary by Andrew C. Y. Cheng.[22] Lee was a strong Methodist and committed to ecumenical efforts. In retirement he lived first in Nanjing and later in Beijing, where he died.[23]

22 All subsequent references to Cheng refer to Andrew C. Y. Cheng unless another person is specified.

23 Memorial, Handel Lee, written by Frank W. Price, June 15, 1961, Minutes, Annual Meeting, BF, NTS, June 7, 1961, Appendix, ALW. See also Frank T. Cartwright to Friends, New York, July 17, 1961, YDS. When Mrs. Handel Lee died in September 1978, the BF sent the Lee family $800 to assist with

More than a decade later, Richard Lee was able to secure a visa to visit his widowed mother in China. Ivy Chou reported to FTESEA directors, "Mr. Richard Lee, son of Mrs. Hendel [sic] Lee was finally granted visa to visit China, and he is now on his way. The visit will be about four weeks. He is taking to his mother her pension from the FTE for this year. I have asked him to convey our warm greetings and to find out as much as possible about Nanking Theological Seminary."[24]

President Richard Nixon's dramatic visit to China in 1972 and the admission of the People's Republic of China to the United Nations a year earlier gradually produced a new climate for U.S.-China relations and the opportunity for a renewed relationship between the FTESEA and Nanjing Union Theological Seminary. Learning in 1972 that John Fleming was planning a visit to China, Ivy Chou wrote him asking that he "bear in mind the special interest of the FTE as you visit." She added that "the interest in China of the FTE is very much alive" and that "I am sure that the FTE will be keenly interested in what you might observe as future trends in theological education in China."[25]

From retirement in Scotland, Fleming wrote to Tracey Jones in 1979 concerning the changed situation in China. Fleming reported that he had met with Ting in 1975 during a period when Nanjing Seminary was not operating. However, now the seminary was regarded as part of Nanjing University and was again enrolling students. Ting had recently written that he was happy about this development and the "new opportunities for witness." Fleming asked if the FTESEA had discussed this changed situation, since he knew that in the past the foundation had believed that if "it were ever possible to use the funds in relation to Nanking and China we would be under a moral obligation to do so." Fleming thought that a face-to-face conversation with Ting and others at that point would be in order.[26] Jones, no longer associated with the FTESEA, forwarded the letter to Marvin Hoff, who almost simultaneously received a handwritten note from Hunter Griffin, an FTESEA director and treasurer of the foundation, concerning the changing situation in China:

---

funeral expenses, Charles Forman to Marvin D. Hoff, New Haven, CT, September 27, 1978, FTEA.

24 Ivy Chou to Dr. Paul R. Gregory and Dr. Robert C. Lodwick, n.p., July 24, 1974, Ivy Chou correspondence, FTEA.

25 Ivy Chou to Rev. Dr. John R. Fleming, n.p., August 16, 1972, Ivy Chou correspondence, FTEA.

26 John R. Fleming to Tracey K. Jones, St. Andrews, Scotland, April 12, 1979, FTEA.

> If the leaders in China are "getting Nanking going" again then I think it *must* have implications for our basic resource funds that were *originally for* that purpose fully. You may want to do some investigating and hold some conversations and/or correspondence re thus—then undoubtedly it should be a matter for our full *Executive Committee* to discuss. It *could* affect our future policy and program substantially dependent on how we move.[27]

Andrew K. H. Hsiao, president of the Lutheran Theological Seminary in Hong Kong and a vice president of the Lutheran World Federation, was able to enter China in 1979 to visit his elderly and ailing mother. He was asked to explore the situation regarding theological education in China on behalf of the FTESEA and the ATESEA while there. Upon returning to Hong Kong, Hsiao prepared a report on conditions in China for the *Asian Lutheran News*. He reported that there was a general loosening of restrictions in China and that churches were beginning to open, but there was no interest in missionaries.[28] Hsiao subsequently prepared a more extensive report of his three-week trip to China, which was included in the minutes of the FTESEA's 1979 annual meeting. Hsiao had attempted to learn as much as possible about the churches that were then functioning, as well as those whose buildings were being used for other purposes. He met with about forty church members in the Hunan and Henan areas, of whom approximately two-thirds had been members of Lutheran churches in the past. The forty included four pastors, a Bible woman, and a church executive. He also met with church leaders in Nanjing, Shanghai, and Beijing. Interviewees included Chao Fusan, formerly principal of Yenching Seminary prior to its merger into Nanjing Union Theological Seminary and then deputy director of the Beijing Research Institute of World Religions of the Chinese Academy of Social Sciences, as well as Bishop K. H. Ting, then vice chancellor of Nanjing University and director of the Institute of Religious Studies at the university. With these individuals Hsiao discussed the past and present religious policies of the Chinese government, the present situation and future prospects of the church in China, and the needs and forms of future theological education, as well as the responsibilities and possible contributions of Christians outside China. Hsiao indicated that responses of those with whom he

27 Hunter Griffin to Marvin D. Hoff, n. p., April 24, 1979, FTEA. Emphasis in original.

28 *Asian Lutheran News*, 1979, 2, included in a letter, Marvin D. Hoff to FTESEA, New York, August 16, 1979, FTEA.

spoke ranged from tearful accounts of past suffering of Christians to restatements of the government's official policies toward the church.[29]

Hsiao reported that the Chinese government had recently changed the implementation of its policy toward religion and that the reopening of the Religious Affairs Bureau was an indication of the change. He reported that the church in China had suffered greatly during the 1950s and again during the Cultural Revolution but that Christian belief had survived even as the church became "invisible." Hsiao was told that, when the Tamishih Church was reopened in Beijing in 1972 to meet the needs of foreign diplomats and visitors, only ten to twelve people attended, including three Chinese pastors and their wives. However, by 1979 the church was overflowing on Sundays, and many people attended Thursday night Bible study services. There was a great shortage of Bibles and hymnals, but Ting had informed Hsiao that a new translation of the Bible was being made at Nanjing Seminary. Hsiao thought the Chinese would need Bibles from outside China for two or three years until this new version became available.[30]

Neither Chao nor Ting indicated any immediate plans to reopen seminaries but were considering the possible curricular structure to be instituted when reopening eventually occurred. They were considering three possible forms: intensive training, condensing the former four-year theological education program into two years; offering theological education courses by extension; and a higher level of education offered through the Religious Study Institute of Nanjing University, which Ting termed "a Christian body in a secular institution." This institute had begun recruiting its first students; most were Christian, but this was not an admission requirement. Hsiao also reported that many faculty members were engaged in research, writing, and translation, but that few had attended international conferences. Hsiao visited the Jade Buddha Temple in Shanghai and reported that its 7,240 volumes of the classical Buddhist Sutras, edited in 1735, had survived the Cultural Revolution.[31]

29 Andrew K. H. Hsiao, Report on Trip to China, July 25, 1979, in Minutes, Annual Meeting, FTESEA, December 7, 1979; Emerito Nacpil to Marvin D. Hoff, n. p., March 28, 1979; Marvin D. Hoff to Emerito Nacpil, n. p., August 14, 1979, both FTEA.

30 Ibid. The Bible translation referred to apparently was of the English New Testament known as *Good News for Modern Man*. It was not completed at the seminary, but a Chinese language translation was later made and published.

31 Ibid.

Regarding the church and mission situation in China, Hsiao reported that under the present situation it would be impossible to "send a large number of missionaries to China," to hold a large evangelistic campaign in Shanghai, or to stand on street corners to sell or hand out Bibles. However, Hsiao reported having told Ting that "preaching of the Gospel to mainland China is not only the responsibility of Christians in China, but also of every Christian, especially every Chinese Christian in the world. The Christians in Hong Kong have as great a responsibility in this mission as you have and have as much a right to do so as you do." Realistically, however, Hsiao cautioned that "we must understand the true condition in China and the actual situation of the church there so that we will not make unwarranted demands of the Chinese Church nor draft unrealistic plans." He wrote that one Chinese Christian leader had laughed at some Western perceptions of China in recent years. Hsiao declared that communism had brought many changes to China but "has not changed the spiritual condition of China's people." He described China as still "the largest mission field in the world." All Chinese Christian leaders had stressed in their discussions with Hsiao that any help from outside the country "should not hurt the [Three-Self] principles of self-support, self-administration, or self-propagation." Chao Fusan had indicated a need for information concerning overseas churches, especially those in Hong Kong, Taiwan, and South East Asia. Both Chao and Ting advised Hsiao of an urgent need for theological books, Bibles, hymnals, and cassettes of religious music. They also urged that more Christians visit China so that they might better understand the situation there. Hsiao observed that "visits by other Christians to China will not only promote mutual understanding, but will bring untold comfort and encouragement to Chinese Christians who have suffered so much, assuring them that they are not forgotten or alone." Christians in China also were eager for invitations to church meetings outside China. Hsiao had invited Ting to attend the ATSSEA meeting scheduled for the fall, and Ting had accepted.[32]

Ting then wrote to the FTESEA requesting approximately five thousand books for the Nanjing Seminary library, and two foundation directors, Paul Gregory and Newton Thurber, visited China in 1980 and returned with requests from local pastors for library materials. In response to these requests, the FTESEA undertook a book project for China.[33] Hoff contacted John A. Bollier, the librarian at Yale Divinity

32 Ibid.

33 Minutes, Executive Committee, FTESEA, October 14, 1980, FTEA.

School. Bollier assigned a Chinese student, Daniel C. S. Hsu, to compile a theological bibliography for Nanjing Union as part of a class project. This became the basis for what was called the China Library Project.[34] Frank Cooley, a furloughed Presbyterian missionary, initially coordinated the program. Later Hoff and his wife, Joan Hoff, assumed this responsibility. Shortly thereafter, Hoff wrote to the libraries of Lutheran Theological School and McCormick Theological Seminary in Chicago asking if they had duplicate volumes of theological works that they could send to Nanjing. He noted that the FTESEA had sent five thousand volumes and that the Catholic Theological Union in Chicago had sent another fifty-five hundred. The foundation also learned that the Three-Self Movement had begun reprinting the 1919 Chinese union version of the New Testament; the following year Dr. Franklin Woo, director of the China program for the National Council of Churches in the United States (NCC/USA), requested $4,000 from the FTESEA in order to provide printing equipment for Nanjing Union.[35] This grant was made in December 1981.[36]

Recognizing the sensitivity of renewed relationships with the Chinese Christian community and the need to respect the Three-Self principles, FTESEA deferred to the Chinese. With regard to the Nanjing library project, the foundation declared that it would "leave the initiative for any assistance to be provided, both as to its specific content and the matter of its delivery, with persons in China." It sought a low key and sensitive cultivation of relationships.[37]

Throughout the 1970s, the FTESEA had made discreet inquiries regarding the situation at Nanjing Union. Toward the end of that decade, as the seminary moved toward reopening, the foundation reserved $75,000 in a China Projects fund to respond to requests from Nanjing. In December 1980, the foundation received a report on a visit to China by Bishop Yap Kim Hao of Malaysia. Yap traveled on an invitation from Ting and reported that fifty to sixty churches were then open and that

[34] John A. Bollier to Mrs. Frank Cooley, New Haven, Conn., September 24, 1980; Marvin D. Hoff to Mrs. Frank Cooley, n. p., October 8, 1980, both FTEA. Frank Cooley had done some work on this project, but he went to Indonesia in July 1980, hence the letters to Mrs. Cooley.

[35] Marvin D. Hoff to Paul Gregory, n. p., August 17, 1981; Marvin D. Hoff to Earl Hilgert, n. p., November 5, 1980; Marvin D. Hoff to Robert J. Schreiter, n. p., February 29, 1980, all FTEA; Minutes, Executive Committee, FTESEA, December 11, 1980, FTEA.

[36] Minutes, Executive Committee, FTESEA, December 10, 1981, FTEA.

[37] Minutes, Annual Meeting, December 12, 1980, Appendix A, FTEA.

Nanjing Union would receive students beginning in February 1981.[38] In October 1981, after the seminary had begun its fall term, foundation representatives met with the seminary's president, Bishop K. H. Ting, and its dean, the Reverend Chen Zemin. Ting and Chen were urged to advise FTESEA of the seminary's needs. Hoff indicated that the foundation would respond to such requests and that it was looking forward to a continuing relationship with Nanjing Union Theological Seminary. Following this visit, the first of many that he would make over the following years, Hoff wrote to Richard L. Vreeland, treasurer of the World Division of the United Methodist Church, which held the Swope-Wendel fund, that the FTESEA remained "sensitive to their responsibilities for relationships with [NTUS]" and had three accounts totaling $150,000 to meet any "new, emerging needs" there.[39]

The resumption of operations at Nanjing Union and the increasing ability for people in the United States to communicate with the seminary inevitably raised questions concerning the current use of the Swope-Wendel fund, which had originally been designated for the specific support of that seminary. Roger M. Whiteman, the attorney for the World Division of the General Board of Global Ministries of the United Methodist Church, the successor of the Board of Foreign Missions of the Methodist Episcopal Church to which the Swope-Wendel funds had been bequeathed, expressed concern regarding the extent of Nanjing Seminary's potential claim on the income from the Swope-Wendel fund and drafted a letter to be sent to Ting seeking clarification. Some members of the mission staff of the Methodist General Board of Global Ministries were troubled by this letter, which ignored the complexities of the Three-Self principles under which the Chinese church relates to others and did not address the issue of the role of the FTESEA as the board authorized by the Surrogate's Court of New York County to receive and disburse the income from the Swope-Wendel fund. Consequently, this draft document was shared with FTESEA staff and reviewed by the Executive Committee at a meeting conducted by telephone on August. 20. A "Statement of Affirmation" was approved at this time regarding the foundation's work with Nanjing Union Theological Seminary for presentation to the World Division of the Board of Global Ministries of the United Methodist Church. The statement affirms FTESEA's

> continuing commitment to carry out the original, and amended, purposes of its predecessor, the Board of Founders of Nanking

38 Minutes, Executive Committee, December 11, 1980, FTEA.

39 Marvin D. Hoff to Richard L. Vreeland, n. p., January 4, 1982, FTEA.

> Theological Seminary. In carrying out the original, and amended purposes, the F.T.E. will consider in the spirit of the original bequests requests for assistance and financial support received from Nanjing Union Theological Seminary.[40]

Hoff was planning a visit to China, and he was instructed to present a copy of the "Statement of Affirmation" to Ting during his forthcoming visit to the seminary should he think it advisable. Since Ting was not in Nanjing during the time of Hoff's visit, he summarized the statement verbally in a meeting with vice principal Chen Zemin and librarian Xu Rulei. After consultation, they asked Hoff to give them the statement, and he did so. He also sent the document to Ting with a covering note.[41]

In response to this statement concerning the foundation-seminary relationship, Xu Rulei subsequently wrote that he, Ting, and Chen had "talked over the matter in Beijing and felt that we would prefer at this stage to refrain from either giving an endorsement or voicing an opposition to the transactions as described in the statement." He indicated that, at that time, the only existing relationship between FTESEA and Nanjing Union Theological Seminary was the exchange of books for the library, and the seminary leaders did not wish to discuss financial matters. Xu expressed the feeling that they were "grateful to the FTE for what it generously does to provide us with books. But we do not feel we can commit ourselves now to anything further. I hope this does not make things unnecessarily hard for you."[42]

Clearly the seminary's leaders were reluctant to give the sort of definitive response that some in the United States would have preferred. Both political circumstances and cultural differences were involved. In the hope of avoiding any misunderstanding, members of the FTESEA board solicited advice from Chinese colleagues. After receiving a copy of the letter, Yeow Choo Lak, executive director of ATESEA, wrote to Hoff that he could see from his familiarity with "Chinese psychology, custom and way of expression" that those in Nanjing were happy with the present arrangements and, as they had stated, "would prefer at this stage to refrain from either giving an endorsement or voicing an

40 Minutes, Executive Committee, FTESEA, August 20, 1982, FTEA.

41 Minutes, Executive Committee, FTESEA, October 4, 1982, FTEA.

42 Xu Rulei to Marvin D. Hoff, Nanjing, October 5, 1982, MA/RO and FTEA. In this letter Xu also asked about the cost of a microfilm reader and microfilms of nineteenth-century books that were available from Princeton.

opposition to the transactions as described in the statement." Yeow cautioned that it would be unwise to press for any further statement.[43] While the FTESEA believed that the issue had been satisfactorily resolved, Whiteman did not. In November he again drafted a letter to Ting. This letter reviewed the origin of the Swope-Wendel fund and stated that, because various mission boards had cooperated in support of Nanjing Seminary, a Board of Founders had been organized to allocate the funds in a more "formal manner." When "political and ecclesiastical changes" occurred in the 1940s and 1950s, the World Division petitioned the Surrogate's Court in New York County "stating that because of the change in events it had become impossible to continue to use the money for the maintenance of the Seminary" and requesting permission for the use of income from the Swope-Wendel fund by the Board of Founders for purposes "contributing to Christian theological education in areas of Asia and the Western Pacific beyond the confines of China and for educational assistance to Chinese and other Far Eastern students preparing in other lands for the ministry as well as for the purposes of contributing to Christian theological education in China itself." The court had approved this new purpose.[44]

Nanjing Seminary having resumed its work, Whiteman thought the FTESEA and the World Division needed a definitive answer from seminary officials to the question of the permissibility of sending funds to the People's Republic of China for the maintenance of the seminary. The United States now permitted such payments, but the position of the Chinese government required clarification. While Whiteman believed that, if the answer were negative, the current court order would remain in effect, the seminary should be asked to advise the FTESEA if the situation changed in the future.[45]

This letter was considered at an Executive Committee meeting of the FTESEA at which Whiteman was present, December 9, 1982.[46] When the matter was not resolved at that meeting, the foundation consulted with its legal counsel and then advised Xu that "the [FTESEA] lawyer has concluded that [Xu's statement] should be adequate to meet all the legal requirements within the United States." Hoff further affirmed to Xu that it would now be possible for the FTESEA "to meet [its] responsibilities"..."and still respond appropriately to requests

43 Yeow Choo Lak to Marvin D. Hoff, n. p., December 16, 1982, MA/RO.

44 Draft, Roger M. Whiteman to K. H. Ting, New York, November 1982, FTEA. This letter was never sent to Ting.

45 Ibid.

46 Minutes, Executive Committee, FTESEA, December 9, 1982, FTEA.

from Nanjing Union Theological Seminary and the China Christian Council." The issues that had been raised appeared to have been resolved with respect to the relationship between FTESEA and Nanjing Union Theological Seminary.[47]

These issues remained unresolved for a time, however, between the FTESEA and the World Division of the General Board of Global Ministries of the United Methodist Church, which managed the Swope-Wendel Fund. The Reverend Edwin Fisher, Jr., the World Division staff person assigned responsibility for relationships with the China Christian Council (CCC), convened a meeting October 31, 1984, to "consult on matters relating to the Swope-Wendel Trust." The World Division was represented at the meeting by Michael Hahm; Richard Vreeland, the World Division treasurer; Roger Whiteman, legal counsel to the division; and Fisher. The FTESEA was represented by Charles Forman, the foundation's chair; Paul Gregory, vice chair; Newton Thurber, a member of the United Presbyterian Church mission staff and FTESEA director; William O'Shea, the foundation's counsel; and Hoff. O'Shea had prepared a legal opinion in preparation for this meeting, and from the outset "there was unanimous agreement with [that opinion]." After a wide-ranging discussion of the origins and history of the Swope-Wendel Fund, the group arrived at agreement on three items:

> (1) The present procedure of the World Division disbursing the income from the Swope-Wendel Fund to the Foundation for Theological Education in South East Asia meets the legal requirements of the State of New York, and the moral responsibility to carry out the wishes of the donors. (2) The Foundation for Theological Education in South East Asia will continue to give the highest priority to requests for assistance from Nanjing Union Theological Seminary, Nanjing, China and will encourage the leadership of Nanjing Union Theological Seminary to request assistance from the FTE through correspondence and periodic visits by its Executive Director. (3) The Foundation for Theological Education in South East Asia will provide the Treasurer of the World Division with regular documentation on its programs, including those related to Nanjing Union Theological Seminary, through program reports, agendas, minutes and financial statements.

[47] Marvin D. Hoff to Xu Rulei, n. p., December 16, 1982, FTEA.

With these agreements, the questions raised by Whiteman from 1982 to 1984 and included in his draft letter to Ting in November 1982 had been answered to the satisfaction of all parties.[48]

While the legal status of the Swope-Wendel bequest was being reconsidered in light of normalization of diplomatic relationships with China and renewed contact with Nanjing Seminary, the FTESEA was also increasing its activities in support of the seminary and the China Christian Council. In addition to making the grant of $4,000 for the printing press at Nanjing Union Theological Seminary, a large gift of duplicate books was received from Catholic Theological Union in Chicago and shipped to Nanjing, and the library of Dr. Donald Stine was received and shipped. The board initiated discussion regarding assistance for erection of a new library building at the seminary in 1982.[49] The issue of pension obligations incurred at Nanking Seminary prior to 1950 was revisited by the Executive Committee in 1983, and the executive director asked for names of people "who are believed should be receiving pension funds for their years of service at Nanking."[50] On behalf of the China Christian Council, of which he was president, Ting in 1983 asked the FTESEA to support publication of two periodicals, a request to which the foundation responded positively, though not immediately. One, the *Nanjing Theological Review*, contained articles from Nanjing seminary's quarterly review, converted into traditional Chinese characters for the Chinese diaspora. The other, the *Chinese Theological Review*, was an English-language journal containing articles, statements, and sermons of the CCC translated from their original Chinese.[51]

For a consultation in Hong Kong in 1981, Ting penned an article entitled, "Theological Education in New China," which subsequently was included in a WCC study of theological education by extension. In this English-language document, Ting wrote that the two goals

48 Minutes, Executive Committee, FTESEA, December 19, 1984; Minutes, Annual Meeting, FTESEA, December 20, 1984; William J. O'Shea to Hoff, New York, August 28, 1984; "Record of Meeting" of October 31, 1984, signed by Edwin O. Fisher, Jr., FTEA.

49 Minutes, Annual Meeting, FTESEA, December 12, 1980; Minutes, Executive Committee, FTESEA, December 10, 1981; Minutes, Executive Committee, FTESEA, May 3, 1982, all FTEA.

50 Minutes, Executive Committee, FTESEA, November 8, 1983, FTEA.

51 Basic information on the *CTR*, [1999], FTEA. The publication of the *CTR* was announced in the *International Review of Missions (IRM)*, LXXV (1986), 167; and a review of the first issue by Robbins Strong, "Missions in China: Different Perspectives," appeared in *IRM*, LXXVI (1987), 125-28. In 1999 the circulation of the *CTR* was six hundred.

of theological education in contemporary China were to "elevate the theological level of our membership, and...popularize theological knowledge." He affirmed that the Chinese people were seeking answers to questions concerning the meaning of life and the nature of the good and cited as evidence the fact that the periodical *Youth in China* received some sixty thousand letters in response to an article on the subject. Ting added that many of the problems with which Western Christianity was struggling, such as homosexuality or feminism, were not then regarded as problems in the Chinese church.[52]

Hoff had commenced his frequent visits to China on behalf of the FTESEA to survey conditions at Nanjing Seminary, in the churches, and in the work of the China Christian Council, and he submitted reports on these visits to the foundation on the occasion of its annual meetings. His report for 1982, entitled "Training for Ministry in China," reported that about six hundred churches were then open in China, that Nanjing Union Theological Seminary had formally reopened as a seminary in 1981 after having been designated as the Center for Religious Studies in 1979, and had accepted fifty-two students from an applicant pool of more than three hundred. Hoff sketched the curriculum and faculty and noted that the vast majority of the seminary's books had been destroyed by the Red Guards during the Cultural Revolution, that the need to rebuild the library collection was critical, and that, as of late 1982, the FTESEA had provided the seminary with more than four thousand titles for its library. Hoff observed that several local or regional Christian councils had conducted training for leaders and that some of these were beginning to develop more formal schools.[53]

Hoff reported to the Executive Committee early in 1984 and to the entire board in December of that year on another trip to China. This delegation included Henry S. Wilson, director of the Board of Theological Education in Serampore, India; Peter D. Latuihamallo, chair of ATESEA and a professor in Jakarta; Andrew Chiu, president of Concordia Theological Seminary in Hong Kong; Yeow Choo Lak, executive director of ATESEA; and Samuel Amirtham, director of the Programme on Theological Education of the WCC, as well as Hoff. They visited churches in Shanghai, Guangzhou, Beijing, and Hangzhou and found them open and busy. The Hangzhou congregation in

52 K. H. Ting, "Nanking Union Theological Seminary: Theological Education in New China: Part I: New Beginnings," *Ministry by the People: Theological Education by Extension*, ed. F. Ross Kinsler (Geneva: WCC Publications, 1983), 265, 269, 271.

53 Marvin D. Hoff, "Training for Ministry in China," Minutes, Annual Meeting, FTESEA, December 10, 1982, Appendix A, FTEA.

particular had experienced a revival, and the church was packed. Hoff reported that Nanjing Union had 185 enrolled students, including 71 women, and that the average age of students was twenty-four. Of the faculty of twenty, six were women. Regional Protestant seminaries were open or planned at Fuzhou, Shenyang, Beijing, Shanghai, Hangzhou, Wuhan, and Chongqing, and six or seven Catholic seminaries were open, including the national seminary in Shanghai.[54]

At this annual meeting, FTESEA provided travel assistance for a visit to Chinese theological institutions arranged by the Christian Conference of Asia. The foundation also reached out to assist Catholic seminaries in China. Hoff had reported the desperate need of Catholic seminaries for books. Ting had arranged for a meeting between Hoff and Father Aloysius Jin Lu-Xin, principal of the national Catholic seminary in Shanghai, to discuss the possibility that the foundation could provide books for the seminary library. In response to this need, the FTESEA authorized its executive director

> to expand the project for providing library books and student text books at Nanjing Union Theological Seminary to Theological Seminaries endorsed by Nanjing Union Theological Seminary or the China Christian Council, including Catholic Seminaries, and charge the expenses to the Nanjing Project Account.[55]

At the same meeting, having found that there were no longer any valid claims on the pension fund established for Nanjing Seminary faculty and staff, the foundation transferred the balance in that fund to an account for Nanjing publications. It also voted to increase funds available to the Nanjing projects and Nanjing publications accounts by transfer of a 1984 surplus in excess of $76,000.[56]

An interesting perspective on the Chinese Protestant church at the time was provided in a lecture by Bishop Ting, which Hoff circulated with his own report at the 1984 annual meeting. Ting's lecture, entitled "A Chinese Christian Selfhood," had been delivered in Tokyo in September of that year. Ting spoke of selfhood "in the making" in the period from 1949 to 1966, though he traced the three-self idea back to a statement by Henry Venn of the Church Missionary Society in London in 1850. "Selfhood in trial" covered the difficult

54 Marvin D. Hoff, "Report on Trip to China," attached to Minutes, Executive Committee, FTESEA, January 17, 1984; Minutes, Annual Meeting, FTESEA, December 20, 1984, FTEA. Wilson became executive director of FTESEA in 2006.

55 Ibid.

56 Ibid.

years of the Cultural Revolution, 1966 to 1976, in which Nanjing Seminary became the headquarters of the Red Guards of Nanking and "we were all driven out of the compound." Finally, Ting described the years since 1976 as a period of "selfhood in thanksgiving and in action." He affirmed that the church in China enjoyed "a reasonable amount of religious freedom," that 1.3 million Bibles had been printed in China, and that the church was experiencing a resurrection.[57]

Nanjing '86, an international gathering in Nanjing at which American and third world theologians spoke, was provided FTESEA support in response to the request of Franklin Woo of the China Program of the National Council of Churches. Charles Forman, chair of the FTESEA and professor of missions at Yale Divinity School, joined Hoff in representing the foundation at that gathering. Additionally, Forman and Hoff visited churches and church leaders in Shanghai, Xi'an, and Beijing.[58]

In 1987 the FTESEA made a major commitment to support Chinese theological students studying in Canada. Again, this initiative came in response to a request from China. Ting had requested assistance from the FTESEA, the Canada China Programme, and the National Council of Churches in the United States for support of Chinese theological students in North America as the Chinese church sought to develop young leaders. The China Programme developed plans to receive five students and asked for FTESEA's assistance. The board, which had already been assisting a Chinese graduate student at Yale and a woman theologian from Hong Kong then writing her dissertation at Harvard, endorsed granting aid to a maximum of $95,950.[59] At this time the principal of the Swope-Wendel fund had reached $4,404,114, and the income projection for 1988 was $450,000, with $318,000 available for immediate expenditure. With funds thus available, an additional $75,000 was transferred to the Nanjing/China theological projects account and $40,000 to the Nanjing/China publications account.[60]

57 K. H. Ting, "A Chinese Christian Selfhood," in ibid.

58 Minutes, Annual Meeting, FTESEA, December 19, 1985, FTEA. Hoff reported on Nanjing '86 and the meetings with Chinese church leaders at the annual meeting in 1986, Minutes, Annual Meeting, FTESEA, December 17-18, 1986, FTEA.

59 Minutes, Executive Committee, FTESEA, May 27, 1987; K. H. Ting to Marvin D. Hoff, Nanjing, January 22, 1987; Minutes, Annual Meeting, FTESEA, December 19, 1985; all FTEA.

60 Minutes, Annual Meeting, FTESEA, December 17, 1987, FTEA.

In 1988, Hoff traveled to China along with Ching-fen Hsiao, a representative of the United Church of Christ to the FTESEA and the newly elected vice-chair of that body. They learned that twenty-three Shanghai churches were then open and that Shanghai's East China Theological Seminary, opened in 1985 and offering a three-year program, currently enrolled ninety-one students. They also visited Chengdu churches and the Sichuan Theological Seminary in that city, as well as Anhui Seminary in Hefei. In Nanjing they were introduced to the work of Amity Press and met with Ting, who encouraged them to begin plans for translation of significant theological works into Chinese. While those meeting with the bishop agreed that the China Program of the NCC/USA administered by Franklin Woo would provide leadership for such a project, they also agreed that FTESEA would provide funding. They learned that the Commission on Theological Education of the CCC had a membership of nineteen from various seminaries and was engaged in preparing syllabi and textbooks for the theological schools. At the annual meeting that year, the FTESEA voted additional funds for books for Chinese theological libraries, authorized $12,311.76 toward NCC/USA support of Chinese students in the United States, and provided $25,000 for research into Chinese church history in the United States and the United Kingdom by Xu Rulei, the librarian at Nanjing Union, and his assistant, Liu Jing. Hoff later noted in a letter to Xu that this was the first such travel grant made by FTESEA since 1950.[61]

Based on action taken at the 1988 annual meeting, Hoff confirmed to Ting in early 1989 that the FTESEA would help sponsor both the *Nanjing Theological Review* and the *Chinese Theological Review*, since the Commission on Theological Education of the CCC indicated that they were important. However, he indicated that the foundation did not believe it should provide scholarships either for students enrolled at Nanjing Union or for graduates serving in the ministry, since the directors believed that their mission lay elsewhere.[62]

With the opening of many Protestant seminaries in China in addition to Nanjing Union Theological Seminary, the FTESEA sought to determine how it might deal with requests for assistance from these various schools. After Hoff's report on his recent meetings with church leaders in China, the foundation at its 1988 annual meeting

61 Minutes, Executive Committee, FTESEA, April 22, 1988; Minutes, Annual Meeting, FTESEA, December 15, 1988, Marvin D. Hoff to Xu Rulei, n.p., January 3, 1989, all FTEA.

62 Marvin D. Hoff to K. H. Ting, n. p., January 2, 1989, FTEA.

considered working more closely with the Commission on Theological Education of the CCC and asking that commission to coordinate and review requests to the foundation from seminaries other than Nanjing. Members of the FTESEA Executive Committee then met with Bishop Shen Yifan, senior pastor of Shanghai's International Church and chair of the Commission on Theological Education; Bishop Sun Yanli, senior pastor of Shanghai's Muen Church and principal of the Huadong Theological Seminary; and Wu Gaozi, vice-president of the CCC and former general secretary of China's preliberation National Christian Council, in New Haven in April 1989 and agreed on this arrangement. At the same meeting they appropriated an additional $15,350 for aid to two Chinese students in Canada.[63]

Receiving a request from Willie W. W. Wong of the Chinese Christian Literature Council for three hundred copies of the *Daily Study Bible* by William Barclay for distribution to pastors and students in China, Hoff wrote to Ting and Shen, asking if this grant were advisable. Shen responded in the affirmative. In February 1990, the FTESEA purchased the books at a cost of $17,000, and in the following year the foundation purchased additional books at a cost of $60,000 for thirteen seminaries in China.[64]

Evidence of the changes occurring not only in Asia but in the FTESEA as well was provided at the 1989 annual meeting, when Charles Forman, after a lengthy chairmanship, retired from that position. He was replaced by Ching-fen Hsiao, a member of the board representing the United Church of Christ and an immigrant to the United States from Taiwan, where he had served as president of Tainan Theological College, one of the seminaries outside China with which the Board of Founders and the FTESEA had enjoyed a long and close relationship. Forman was returned to the board as an at-large member.[65]

The FTESEA 1990 annual meeting was the occasion for another report from Hoff on his observations during a visit in September of that year. He visited Shanghai, Hangzhou, and Nanjing and was present for celebration of the fortieth anniversary of the Three-Self Patriotic Movement. Hoff noted that the East China Theological Seminary had

63 Minutes, Executive Committee, FTESEA, April 2, 1989, FTEA; Marvin D. Hoff to Rhea M. Whitehead, n. p., January 2, 1991, FTEA.

64 Marvin D. Hoff to Directors, Alternates and Consultants, FTESEA, Holland, Mich., March 26, 1991; Marvin D. Hoff to K. H. Ting, n. p., January 3, 1990; Marvin D. Hoff to Ching-fen Hsiao, n. p., February 10, 1990; all FTEA.

65 Minutes, Annual Meeting, FTESEA, December 14, 1989, FTEA.

moved to a new campus, that the Zhejiang Seminary in Hangzhou had graduated more than 150 students, 40 percent of them women, over the past four years, and that Nanjing Union had a current enrollment of 227 students and a library of more than 50,000 volumes, more than half of which had been provided by the FTESEA. The newest Protestant seminary had recently opened in Kunming.[66]

The Chinese Protestant Church took another major step toward greater involvement in world Christianity in 1991 when the China Christian Council joined the World Council of Churches at the latter's meeting in Canberra, Australia.[67] The Chinese church's increased visibility brought additional interest and offers of assistance. Yet the critical importance of the Three-Self principles both to the church and to the Chinese government complicated many relationships. The FTESEA which, through its executive director, had considerable experience in dealing with such matters, sought to encourage greater cooperation and lessen misunderstandings. For example, in 1991 a Christian charitable organization in Britain sought to aid the Chinese seminaries but insisted that they comply with the foundation's policies and procedures for grant applications. Hoff, indicating he hoped the foundation would find a way to grant its assistance to the Chinese seminaries, explained the sensitivity of the Chinese with regard to these matters:

> The Chinese desire to promote "self support" has kept them from requesting grants and filling out formal applications in the past and will no doubt do so in the future. A great many positive reasons lie behind their stance on this matter...at this point in their ecclesiastical and political development, [but] they do desperately need financial help to publish theological works for pastors, lay leaders and theological students....[68]

Significant FTESEA capital and operating grants were made to the Chinese seminaries and to the Commission on Theological Education (CTE) of the China Christian Council in the early 1990s. Grants of $25,000 for the CTE and $20,000 for Nanjing Union were made in 1990. On the recommendation of the CTE, a grant of $20,000 was made to the seminary in Chengdu, Sichuan Province, for assistance

66 Minutes, Annual Meeting, FTESEA, December 12, 1990, Appendix A, FTEA.

67 K. H. Ting, "Speech on the Admission of the CCC to the WCC," Canberra, February 18, 1991, FTEA.

68 Marvin D. Hoff to Alec Gilmore, n. p., January 2, 1991, FTEF.

in constructing a new building in 1991. A similar grant was made to Nanjing Union, which was planning a new library building, and the CTE grant was renewed. The FTESEA asked for additional information and authorized its Executive Committee to appropriate up to $200,000 for the Nanjing Union library "on condition of receipt of acceptable vision statement."[69] Hoff was authorized by the Executive Committee to advise Nanjing Union that the foundation would make a $200,000 grant toward the library building and seek an additional $50,000 from member denominations. When denominational support was not received, the foundation granted an additional $50,000 from its own funds in 1992. Five years later FTESEA voted an additional $100,000 grant to provide furnishings and computers for the new library. Again, operating grants of $25,000 for the Commission on Theological Education and of $20,000 for Nanjing Union Theological Seminary were authorized.[70]

Hoff's report to the 1991 FTESEA meeting indicated he had assisted the China Christian Council in its preparation of an application for admission to the World Council of Churches, had consulted with Nanjing Union Theological Seminary regarding its proposed new library, and had provided assistance to Chinese students in the United States and Canada. This meeting also received a report that N. Z. Zia, the sole surviving pensioner from the old Nanjing Seminary pension program, had died in Guangzhou at the age of one hundred.[71] At its 1992 annual meeting, the FTESEA received both Hoff's report on the fifth national conference of the China Christian Council and a report from the chair, Ching-fen Hsiao, on his recent visit to several theological schools in China. Hoff sketched the actions taken at the fifth national conference of the CCC, where congregations were authorized to choose baptismal and Communion rituals of their preference and the authority of bishops was described as pastoral but not administrative. Forty-five younger pastors were ordained at this meeting. Hsiao described his visits to Zhongnan Theological Seminary

[69] Marvin D. Hoff to Directors, Alternates, and Consultants, Holland, Mich., March 26, 1991; Minutes, Annual Meeting, FTESEA, December 12, 1990; December 19, 1991, all FTEA.

[70] Minutes, Executive Committee, FTESEA, June 22, 1992; Minutes, Annual Meeting, FTESEA, December 17, 1992; Minutes, Executive Committee, FTESEA, December 17, 1997, all FTEA.

[71] Minutes, Annual Meeting, FTESEA, December 19, 1991, and Appendix A, FTEA.

in Wuhan, Shaanxi Bible School near Xi'an, and Guangdong Union Theological Seminary.[72]

Increasing engagement in China both with Nanjing Union and with the Commission on Theological Education of the China Christian Council placed new demands on FTESEA resources and compelled the foundation to review its strategy both in China and in South East Asia. Though the Swope-Wendel fund had grown to $5,120,339 by the end of 1989, investment income had not grown so rapidly. The income projection for the year 1990 was only $390,000. To meet China commitments, the FTESEA was forced to cut Resource Commission requests for South East Asia schools in 1991 and 1992.[73]

The Executive Committee of the FTESEA convened in June 1993 to explore a variety of questions that had arisen with the foundation's increasing activity in China. The committee considered whether "representatives from China [should] participate in allocating the resources of the FTE." It also asked, "Should new decision making processes be developed for the new context...[and] are the present use [sic] of the FTE funds the most meaningful and creative?" Since the Chinese seemed more interested in contacts with Western churches than with those in Asia, members of the FTESEA wondered as to the appropriate role of the ATESEA's Resource Commission in determining allocation of funds for China. The committee wondered if the foundation should play a more active role in raising funds for China and if the Resource Commission should have a role in establishing the percentage of foundation funds disbursed in China. As Bishop Shen was scheduled to visit the United States and Canada in the fall of 1993, these questions were to be discussed with him.[74] A few months later at the annual meeting, the FTESEA directors faced a decline of $100,000 in the annual earned income from the Swope-Wendel fund occasioned by a decline in interest rates in the United States. This fact gave new urgency to "the new directions for the FTE" that had been advanced by the Executive Committee at its June meeting and convinced the directors to vote in December "to become proactive in seeking funds for projects in China."[75]

72 Minutes, Annual Meeting, FTESEA, December 17, 1992, Appendices A and B, FTEA.

73 Minutes, Annual Meeting, FTESEA, December 14, 1989; December 12, 1990; December 19, 1951; December 17, 1992, all FTEA.

74 Minutes, Executive Committee, FTESEA, June 23, 1993, FTEA.

75 Minutes, Executive Committee, FTESEA, December 15, 1993; Minutes, Annual Meeting, FTESEA, December 16, 1993, both FTEA.

Ching-fen Hsiao, chair of the FTESEA, had made specific recommendations for a fundraising program, had presented this proposal and, with its acceptance, appointed a committee of Charles Forman (the prior chair), himself, and Marvin Hoff (executive director), to design an advancement program for the FTESEA.[76] The committee reported to the Executive Committee in September 1994. This meeting became a brain-storming session in which the committee endorsed the importance of the FTESEA entering into an advancement program for theological education both in China and in South East Asia. It also affirmed the importance of consulting with partners prior to beginning a program and of conducting the program in cooperation with the denominations and their representatives on the FTESEA. The committee proposed a three-year program commencing in 1994 as the primary focus of foundation attention, to be followed by evaluation and further planning.[77] At a meeting in the following month, the FTESEA

> voted to endorse the advancement sections of the long range planning document for sharing with the Resource Commission of ATESEA, Nanjing Theological Seminary, and the Commission on Theological Education of the China Christian Council, and further to request reports from these partners on their reactions to the possibility of the FTE initiating a three year advancement program for discussion at the annual meeting in December, and further to make a decision on the advancement aspects of the long range plan at the December 1994 meeting.[78]

The committee then consulted with Nanjing Union Seminary, the Commission on Theological Education of the CCC, and ATESEA before drafting the final report. In their responses, the three Asian partners indicated their priorities. The FTESEA voted at its annual meeting to establish an "advancement program for ATESEA, the Commission on Theological Education, CCC, and Nanjing Theological Seminary...." The program was to seek new funding to underwrite the programs that the Asian partners had identified.[79] Hoff reported at this meeting with regard to the ATESEA accreditation program for member schools, which he described as "one of encouragement and guidance rather than

[76] Minutes, Annual Meeting, FTESEA, December 16, 1993; Ching-fen Hsiao to Directors, New York, September 19, 1994, attached to Minutes, Executive Committee, FTESEA, September 8, 1994, both FTEA.

[77] Minutes, Executive Committee, FTESEA, September 8, 1994, FTEA.

[78] Minutes, Special Meeting, FTESEA, October 13, 1994, FTEA.

[79] Minutes, Annual Meeting, FTESEA, December 15, 1994, FTEA.

a strict enforcement of the standards," and he also described his visit to China and Nanjing Seminary.[80]

As China became more open to the West and as the Chinese church found more freedom of expression, the FTESEA took great interest in understanding the Chinese church and the social and political context in which it ministered. Concern for developments in China was expressed in foundation meetings as frequently as concern about strengthening its ability to fund important programs. The directors followed church pronouncements regarding the student demonstrations in Beijing during the spring of 1989 that culminated in the Tiananmen Square affair of June 4.[81] At a consultation on Chinese Theological Education in Stony Point, New York, April 4–6, 1990, K. H. Ting reported that after June 4 there had been "extra tension, but no heavy pressure upon the church....The attitude toward religion is more favorable than at any time in the past."[82] This relatively positive assessment was reinforced the following year when the China Christian Council joined the World Council of Churches.[83]

A speech by Ting before the Chinese People's Political Consultative Conference in March 1993 was included with materials for the FTESEA annual meeting later that year. Entitled, "Religious Work Should Reflect Reform and Openness," Ting's speech advocated a role for religious institutions in "creating a favorable environment for economic construction, reform and openness, while at the same time bringing into play the initiative of citizens who hold religious beliefs to involve themselves in socialist construction." Ting declared that

> the only scientific way to deal with religion is to respect it, not to aggravate it. The best approach to religion is to allow it to be self-regulating; not to make vain attempts to control and attack it. To blindly oppose religion, or to strengthen control over it will certainly give rise to a frenzy, which will be good for neither the nation nor the church.[84]

80 Ibid., Appendix A.

81 A press release dated May 23, 1989, indicating that Bishop Ting's support for the student demonstrations was circulated among members of the FTESEA Executive Committee; Minutes, Executive Committee, FTESEA, December 13, 1989, FTEA.

82 Joan Hoff to Executive Committee, FTESEA, n.p., April 20, 1990, in Minutes, Executive Committee, FTESEA, December 12, 1990, FTEA.

83 Marvin D. Hoff to Directors, Alternates and Consultants, Holland, Mich., March 26, 1991, FTEA.

84 K. H. Ting, "Religious Work Should Reflect Reform and Openness," in Minutes, Annual Meeting, FTESEA, December 16, 1993.

K. H. Ting and his son, Stephen (Yanren) Ting, spoke to a special meeting of the FTESEA in October 1994. Yanren Ting, a professor at Nanjing University and member of the Board of Directors of Amity Foundation, spoke on the work of that foundation. Amity had been established by Chinese Christians in 1985 to promote education, social services, health, and rural development in China. Its press is responsible for printing and distributing Bibles in China. Ting reported that the press had printed more than eight million Bibles and that these were being distributed to the churches of China and, through the churches, to individuals. He estimated that a third of the Bibles were distributed to members of house churches.[85]

K. H. Ting reported on the China Christian Council and addressed the new registration procedures imposed on religious groups in China. Regulations stipulated that registration of a church (or temple or mosque) requires having a name, a fixed address, a significant number of participants, legitimate sources of income, a person or persons providing leadership, etc. Local cadres are required to register groups meeting these criteria. Ting indicated that the distinction between CCC churches and unregistered house churches was blurring. Many registered churches had meeting points distant from the sanctuary, sometimes in houses. With regard to the many new seminaries, Ting indicated that most were dependent on local clergy and had no full-time faculty members. However, more than sixty graduates of Nanjing Union Seminary were serving provincial or regional seminaries as full-time teachers. *Tian Feng*, the Protestant journal, was described as becoming more evangelical and less political. Ting also reported on five Chinese students approved by the CCC for study in the United States.[86]

It was at this meeting that the foundation voted "to establish a four year FTE advancement program for ATESEA, the Commission on Theological Education, CCC, and Nanjing Theological Seminary."[87] This fundraising program became a major responsibility of the executive director as Hoff approached charitable foundations in the United States and Europe on behalf of the foundation and its Asian partners. Gradually the FTESEA became an informal mediator between its partners and charitable groups that wished to grant assistance but had less experience working in the region or were less knowledgeable of the needs. The hunger program of Church World Service, for example,

85 Minutes, Special Meeting, FTESEA, October 13, 1994, FTEA.
86 Ibid.
87 Ibid.

agreed in 1996 to provide a grant for a food subsidy for the students at Nanjing Union Seminary.[88]

In his approach to other funding sources, Hoff emphasized that the Asian partners were also contributing to their priority programs. In correspondence with a German church foundation in 1996, Hoff noted that the Chinese had provided some funds for most of the projects for which he was seeking additional grants. They had already produced fourteen volumes in the textbook series and had distributed more than two hundred sets of tool books. The FTESEA had made a grant of $250,000 for the construction of the Nanjing Seminary library. He indicated that the foundation was buying new furniture and a computer system with both English and Chinese software for the library as well. Hoff also assured the foundation of the reliability of Nanjing Seminary while explaining its reluctance to submit formal applications for assistance and project descriptions. He wrote that FTESEA had been cooperating with the seminary since 1980 and observed that the foundation had

> not expected formal budgets and reports, but have carried out the accountability through personal visits and correspondence. Although our colleagues in China have not developed formal budgets and project descriptions in English, they have proven to be reliable partners. Since they have limited personnel, to my knowledge they have not been developing formal priorities, budget, etc. They do this more informally, and then devote their resources to the programs they have intended to implement. Yes, the principle of "self-support" has great meaning for our colleagues in Chinese theological education. They do not see themselves developing lists of projects for international support. They are ready to receive gifts from colleagues who know about their programs and wish to support them. The reports that are needed by mission boards will probably have to be written by one of the ecumenical staff members after a visit to China and shared with other donors.[89]

Further explicating the situation in China with respect to theological education, Hoff indicated that the Commission on Theological Education of the CCC had ties to all of the seminaries. The FTESEA had provided some funds for regional and provincial

88 Marvin D. Hoff to Grystin Granberg, n. p., February 29, 1996, FTEA.
89 Marvin D. Hoff to Inken Woehlbrand, n. p., March 12, 1996, FTEA.

seminaries in the past, but only when the commission had requested it. In the future, he anticipated that the commission might again make requests for these seminaries, and he observed that some FTESEA funded projects benefited all seminaries in China. Hoff observed that lay training projects were generally conducted by regional and provincial Christian councils and that he did not know of any conducted by the CTE. He thought these were carried out with "limited local resources" and knew of none which had sought external funding.[90]

Hoff made plans to share information regarding the needs of theological education in China with the Scandinavian China office during a visit to Oslo in August, and he also approached all the mission boards in the United States and Canada with China programs and contacted American foundations with interest in China that were not church affiliated. He maintained communication with the Ecumenical Theological Education program of the WCC with regard to these matters. Hoff urged interested groups to send someone to China and observe the projects that the Chinese church was undertaking and assured them that "the FTE has no desire to stand between Chinese theological education and potential donors. We merely want to facilitate the communication in the best way possible." As to varied reports and perceptions of the church situation in China, Hoff added the caveat that "everything is true somewhere in China, but nothing is true everywhere."[91]

A Dutch mission organization advised Hoff in March that it would grant $45,000 to the Chinese for the theological textbook and tool book projects. The tool book project was designed to provide basic Christian books to 2,500 to 3,000 clergymen and women at nominal cost. Hoff observed that "although the FTE has become the communicator for these projects, we expect that the mission boards will be in direct contact with our colleagues in China." He explained that seminaries in remote areas were included in the projects and that all the principals of Protestant seminaries were represented in the CTE/CCC. Hoff also indicated that, in addition to this Dutch contribution, a German group was considering a grant of $200,000 to $300,000. The Board of Missions of the Netherlands Reformed Church had given a $56,015 grant to Nanjing Union Theological Seminary; and, in his letter of acknowledgment, Hoff mentioned that the sixteenth book

90 Ibid.

91 Ibid.; and Marvin D. Hoff to Inken Woehlbrand, n. p., March 19, 1996, FTEA. The Ecumenical Theological Education program was created by a merger of the Programme on Theological Education and the Ecumenical Institute.

in the religion series, *A History and Theory of Sacred Music,* had just been published and noted the Luce Foundation's interest in supporting publication of these books. Hoff also contacted both the Swedish Mission Council and the Danish Missionary Society in April 1996 to request their support for projects in China. He reported to the FTESEA in August that these several advancement efforts had produced commitments of $895,000, including the Luce Foundation's $270,000 for various projects.[92]

The FTESEA's fundraising efforts continued to produce an outpouring of support for theological education in China: a $100,000 annuity from a Chinese-American woman for the Nanjing Union Seminary library; $75,000 from the Reformed Church Women's Ministries; $6,000 from the Evangelical Lutheran Church in America for the *Nanjing Theological Review*; the equivalent of $480,000 for sixteen two-year scholarships for Chinese seminary professors from various American seminaries; $55,000 from the Reformed Church of the Netherlands for textbooks; and $66,750 from the Evangelische Missionwerk in Hamburg for textbooks. In May 1997 an anonymous donor gave $10,000 for food for students at Nanjing Seminary. Through December 31, 1999, a total of $1,421,000 had been committed either to China programs or to ATESEA programs.

In enumerating these gifts, Hoff observed that many people around the world were interested in Chinese theological education but that foundations in the United States remained reluctant to grant funds for use in China, though they were willing to fund Chinese students at American institutions. He also informed the Chinese that other groups were interested in their projects and that, even though a group might not fund one specific project, it sometimes made other gifts because of its interest in those projects. He reiterated that organizations in the West wanted detailed information about requests, including budgets, and that he stood ready to do whatever he could to assist them in meeting these expectations. Hoff also reported that some European seminaries seemed ready to assist needy regional or provincial seminaries if those schools were willing to share their needs with the ecumenical community.[93]

92 Marvin D. Hoff to A. E. Hoekema-Norel, n. p., March 12, 1996, December 14, 1996; Marvin D. Hoff to Hsiao Ching-fen and Charles Forman, n.p., August 30, 1996, March 12, 1996; Marvin D. Hoff to Calvin Ratcliff, n. p., October 3, 1996; Marvin D. Hoff to Lars Hofgren; Marvin D. Hoff to Jorgen Skov Sorensen, both n.p., April 4, 1996, all FTEA; Hoff to Executive Committee, FTE, Holland, Mich., August 19, 1996, FTEA.

93 Marvin D. Hoff to Peng Cuian, n. p., May 30, 1997; Marvin D. Hoff to Peng

To Su Deci, general secretary of the China Christian Council, Hoff wrote regarding his contacts with potential European supporters and expressing the hope that they would provide assistance to the Chinese church. He reported to Su that he had been able to secure eleven or twelve full financial aid packages for two years each in order to enable Chinese theological students to study in the United States and estimated the total value of these scholarships at $330,000 to $360,000. Hoff also indicated that the Luce Foundation and Mustard Seed continued to be interested in China projects and asked the Chinese to send the Luce Foundation one copy of each of the books they had published in the Chinese Theological Series.[94]

When, in the spring of 1996, Hoff learned that the Council on World Mission had sold its Hong Kong property, he wrote to the council encouraging the use of some of the income from the sale to support theological education in China. He observed that the Hong Kong property had originally been designed to serve the Chinese people and that "theological education in China is one of the most needy mission situations in the world."[95]

Communication between the Chinese Christian community and Western communities continued to be characterized by difficulties and misunderstandings, and the FTESEA sought to use its experience with the Chinese church to build confidence among other Christian communities. When some in Europe expressed concern regarding the use of their funds in China, Hoff wrote explaining causes of some of the problems. Except for him, all with whom they were in correspondence were using English as their second language, and Hoff stated that those in China had very limited experience in using formal written English. "They are not accustomed to writing proposals, sharing plans, or providing financial reports in English," he observed. He also noted that the Chinese did not translate the notes of their Theological Commission into English and that his inability to communicate in Chinese was a great handicap to them.

Hoff granted that Westerners were accustomed to "planning, financial reporting, accountability structures, etc.," but noted that their Chinese colleagues found it difficult to adapt to Western cultural

---

Cuian and Kan Baoping, n. p., August 29, 1997; Hoff to CTE/CCC and NTS, n. p., March 3, 1997; Minutes, Annual Meeting, December 16, 1999, all FTEA.

94 Marvin D. Hoff to Su Deci, n. p., April 17, 1996; Marvin D. Hoff to Kan Baoping, n. p., August 17, 1996, both FTEA.

95 Marvin D. Hoff to Lucy Dulfer-Luyendijk, n. p., April 4, 1996, FTEA.

expectations and experiences. He also pointed out that he had found the process of "communicating and relating" in China quite different from that elsewhere. Everything in China regarding Christianity was new, Hoff wrote, and the people involved were new to their leadership positions. He recalled that eighteen years earlier there had been no open churches, church structures, nor seminaries, but that currently there were 2,000 churches, more than 2,500 "meeting points," between ten and twelve million Protestant Christians, and thirteen seminaries. He also observed that the China Christian Council at that time had ten commissions, of which the Commission for Theological Education was one.[96]

Hoff described the difficulties resulting from the scarcity of leadership within the Christian community in China and the consequent assignment of multiple responsibilities to a single individual. As examples, he explained that Kan Baoping was a professor of systematic theology at Nanjing Union Theological Seminary, also its librarian, pastor of St. Paul's Church in Nanjing, and executive secretary of the CTE/CCC. Su was associate secretary-general of the CCC, chair of the CTE/CCC, president of East China Theological Seminary, vice chair of the Shanghai Christian Council, and minister of the Shanghai Community Church. He added that these individuals did not have adequate support staff and so were required to do all of the work themselves.[97]

Hoff also observed that the forty to fifty members of the CTE/CCC received financial reports and that he therefore believed that the actual use of these funds in China was a matter of general knowledge among Protestant leaders. The Chinese had also offered to send a financial report to any board of missions which asked for one. However, Hoff again emphasized that the FTESEA monitored the use of its funds by his visits to China and the visits of other members of the foundation. He offered to provide this kind of on-site monitoring of grants for the European organizations if they desired that the foundation do so. Hoff reiterated that "the [CCC] has desperate needs for financial support for their work" but that because each person had so many jobs and because of Chinese Christian

> commitment to "self-support," it is more difficult for Western agencies to relate to them than many other places in the world.... [Yet] China is the most rapidly expanding Christian population

96 Marvin D. Hoff to A. E. Hoekema-Norel, n. p., August 30, 1996, FTEA.

97 Ibid.

> in the world. It would be very sad if we could not find ways to stand beside them with spiritual and financial support in this their time of great need. Previous generations devoted a great deal to mission in China, and we now have the possibility of doing something in our time–a possibility that did not exist for thirty years.[98]

Hoff concluded with the expressed hope that European Christians could find a way to help those in China while maintaining a sense of accountability for their grants.[99]

The FTESEA found additional effective means of aiding Nanjing Union during the 1990s. With respect to the new library building, Hoff wrote librarians in the United States seeking guidelines and suggestions for this building designed to serve about 150 theological students and to house a collection of 50,000 volumes. In response he received numerous ideas and questions, which were forwarded to Nanjing for the seminary's consideration.[100]

Travel grants both for study and for attendance at international meetings became an important tool for the FTESEA in strengthening ties between the Chinese church and Christian communities elsewhere. A grant was made to Liu Miechun of Nanjing Union Seminary for study in Canada in 1993, and similar grants were made directly to the Canada China Program in 1994 and 1995. In 1996 the grant was renewed and increased. A report was received in 1994 on five Chinese students in the United States on grants secured by the FTESEA. The International Association for Mission Studies was also granted $5,000 for use by Asians in travel to their conference in Argentina with the understanding that of four grants anticipated, two would go to women and at least one to a Chinese person. When the Ecumenical Theological Education program of the WCC through the CCC invited Su Deci, principal of the East China Theological Seminary at Shanghai who held a M. Th. degree from Wesley Theological Seminary in Washington, D. C., and Peng Cuian, a member of the Nanjing Union faculty who had studied Old Testament in England and had visited the United States to attend a meeting in Oslo, the FTESEA agreed to pay the travel expenses for them.[101] The foundation also sought funds from other sources to underwrite Chinese attendance at international Christian meetings and

98 Ibid.

99 Ibid.

100 Marvin D. Hoff to Norman Kansfield, Steven Peterson, and Robert Grant, all n. p., January 2, 1991; Marvin D. Hoff to K. H. Ting, n. p., January 28, 1991, all FTEA.

101 Minutes, Special Meeting, FTESEA, October 13, 1994; Minutes, Annual

visits to the United States for some of the leaders of the CCC, as well as funds to permit leaders of various provincial and regional Christian councils in China to meet with one another.[102]

While seeking U.S. seminary support for Chinese students, Hoff consulted with Ting and with members of the FTESEA board regarding the problems presented by the fact that many of the first such students would have been denied study in secondary or even primary schools because of the Cultural Revolution and would have to compensate for this severe educational handicap. From Ting he learned that many of these students required two years to finish courses at theological colleges, and he wrote to correspondents in the States that the Chinese would have suggested "exposure" time in the West rather than a formal degree program were it not for new requirements of the national and provincial departments of education that post-secondary teachers must hold degrees. Those consulted in China thought the M.Th. degree program would be more appropriate for such students than the D.Min. and M.A. degrees. It was also understood that many of the students would probably be unable to pass the standard English language examinations and would need special help with language.[103]

In his appeal to U.S. seminaries to sponsor Chinese students by covering their expenses for two years of study, Hoff wrote that there were only about 700,000 Protestant Christians in China in 1949 but that their numbers had grown to perhaps eight million in 1994. He had "attended worship services in every area of China on every day of the week, and the sanctuaries have always been filled to overflowing. BUT, there are only 1,200 ordained pastors to serve more than 8,000 churches and more than 20,000 meeting points in this vast Christian community." Hoff continued that China had only very old or very young professors because of the disruption of the nation's educational system during the Cultural Revolution. All of the students being

Meeting, FTESEA, December 15, 1994; December 14, 1995; December 12, 1996; Marvin D. Hoff to John Pobee and Judo Poerwowidagdo, n. p., May 15, 1995; Marvin D. Hoff to Kan Baoping, n. p., October 4, 1995, all FTEA.

102 Ching-fen Hsiao to Robert Carl (draft), n. p., September 21, 1994; Marvin D. Hoff to Cynthia McLean, n. p., November 17, 1995, both FTEA.

103 Marvin D. Hoff to Carnegie Samuel Calian, Marvin D. Hoff to Donald W. McCullough, and Marvin D. Hoff to Robin Lovin, all n. p., October 10, 1994; Marvin D. Hoff to Dawn Boekins, n. p., November 9, 1994, all FTEA.

recommended for study in the United States were Nanjing Union graduates who were teaching in other seminaries in China.[104]

Ting retired from his positions heading the China Christian Council and the Three-Self Patriotic Movement in 1997, though he retained the presidency of Nanjing Union Theological Seminary. Han Wenzao was elected president of the CCC to succeed Ting. Su Deci became the general secretary, and Bao Jiayuan became an associate general secretary. Hoff immediately contacted these new leaders to maintain relationship and assure them of continuing FTESEA support.[105]

Even as the Chinese church was experiencing a change in leadership in 1997, FTESEA faced its own imminent changes with the anticipated retirements of its long-time executive director and its board chair. Seeking to sustain the momentum that had developed with the successful programs of the 1990s, Ching-fen Hsiao challenged the board in 1997 to "plan a process of setting up priorities for the first decade of the new century and millennium" and to "include our partners in South East Asia and China" in this planning process. His proposal was immediately endorsed by the board.[106]

The FTESEA continued to serve in its role as interpreter of the situation of the Chinese Protestant community to Americans and Europeans. Responding to a 1997 inquiry from a Reformed Church in America clergyman in New York concerning religious conditions in China, Hoff gave an assessment of the situation from an American perspective. He wrote that there were then between twelve and fifteen million Protestant Christians in China and the seventeen seminaries were able to accept only one in six applicants. He added that Amity Press, in a joint venture with the United Bible Societies, had printed fifteen million Bibles in China in recent years. In 1996 alone they had printed three million copies, more than the American Bible Society had printed. He also reported that the Religious Affairs Bureau required every church to register, giving its name, fixed address, number of participants, legitimate sources of income, and names of its leaders. He acknowledged that some Protestants refused to comply with this requirement and had suffered persecution as a result. Hoff noted that some members of registered churches had been oppressed and persecuted as some Communist cadres "try to block all Christian

104 Marvin D. Hoff to Dawn Boelkins, n. p., October 3, 1994, FTEA.

105 Marvin D. Hoff to K. H. Ting, Han Wenzao, Bao Jiayuan, Su Deci, all n. p., January 27, 1997; Marvin D. Hoff to Su Deci and Kan Baoping, n. p., March 3, 1997, both FTEA.

106 Minutes, Annual Meeting, FTESEA, December 18, 1997, FTEA.

worship." He explained that the Chinese government was very sensitive to connections between Christians and international groups and that Chinese Christians were compelled to be careful about such relationships. He also observed that the Chinese government was well aware of the role that churches had played in the overthrow of communism in Eastern Europe and that this was another source of governmental concern about the churches.[107]

The FTESEA also sought to acquaint Chinese Christians more fully with its work. Huibing He Kennedy and Peng Yaqian, two Chinese teachers studying at Columbia Theological Seminary in Georgia, were invited to New York for the December 1997 meeting of the FTESEA.[108] Similarly, Hoff invited Sun Xipei, whom he had met in Hangzhou in 1996, to visit the United States to attend the FTESEA's annual meeting in 1998 and to visit several Protestant churches. Hoff assured Sun that the foundation would pay his expenses.[109]

At the December 1998 meeting, the FTESEA was able to approve a special grant of $40,000 to remodel and upgrade the music building at Nanjing Union and $7,500 to purchase a minibus for transportation of students. The foundation also set aside $15,000 for computers for the seminaries in Beijing, Hangzhou, Shanghai, and Nanjing and asked the Commission on Theological Education of the CCC to establish priorities for distribution of the computer funds to the four institutions, while adding that it hoped to provide an additional $15,000 over the next three years. At the same meeting, $15,000 was voted for the commission, both for its annual meeting and for a seminar for faculty members of CCC seminaries. Grants of $3,000 for the Chinese theological textbook series and $10,000 for a program to train librarians at the CCC seminaries were approved, and another $5,600 was committed for theological books in English and in Chinese.[110] During 1999, Philip Wickeri agreed to select fourteen to eighteen English language theological books to be sent to the seminaries at Nanjing, Shanghai, Beijing, Hangzhou, Wuhan, Fuzhou, Shenyang, Chengdu, and Guangzhou, and six to eight books to be sent to the other CCC seminaries in China.[111]

107 Marvin D. Hoff to Peter Paulsen, n. p., September 17, 1997, FTEA.

108 Marvin D. Hoff to Huibing He Kennedy, Peng Yaquian, both n. p., July 15, 1997, FTEA.

109 Marvin D. Hoff to Sun Xipei, n. p., October 9, 1997, FTEA.

110 Marvin D. Hoff to Chen Zemin; Marvin D. Hoff to Sun Xipei and Su Deci, both n. p., January 8, 1999, FTEA.

111 Minutes, Annual Meeting, FTESEA, December 17, 1998, FTEA; Marvin D.

An extensive report on the seminaries and churches of China was presented by Hoff at this meeting. He noted that there had been "great changes since 1982." Nanjing Union had a total annual enrollment of about 160 students in B.Th. and M.Th. degree programs combined. It also offered correspondence courses for church workers in the field. More than seventy Nanjing graduates were then teaching in other CCC seminaries. The Yanjing Seminary in Beijing had moved to a new campus with facilities for accommodating up to 400 students, though the current enrollment was 73. East China Seminary in Shanghai was preparing for a move to a new suburban campus and currently enrolled 90 full-time and 25 part-time students. Zhejiang Seminary in Hangzhou had broken ground for a new campus able to accommodate 250 students, with a current enrollment of 64 and a new sacred music department. Hsiao reported on discussions with the United Board for Christian Higher Education in Asia looking toward cooperation between the two organizations in support of religious studies programs in secular universities.[112]

At the 1999 annual meeting, the FTESEA again discussed Hsiao's proposal for planning and scheduled a retreat to focus on mission and vision statements for the foundation in the forthcoming decade. It also voted to develop proposals for cooperation with the United Board and approved funds for the Commission on Theological Education and for the CCC as well as for ATESEA and the WCC's Ecumenical Institute, based upon the institute's response to FTESEA requests for "new and creative proposals."[113]

Hoff reported on his visits to several of the seminaries in China and particularly on his visit to the city of Harbin and the Harbin Bible School. Harbin then had twenty-seven churches in the central city. Its Bible school had opened in 1996 and then enrolled sixty students, including twenty-five in a music program. Responding to this report, the FTESEA granted the Harbin Christian Council $6,000, half for a lay training center and half for a new church building.[114]

The foundation asked the newly elected CCC president, Han Wenzao, and general secretary, Su Deci, to evaluate the importance

---

Hoff to Sun Xipei, Su Deci, Chen Zemin, and Kan Baoping, n. p., January 25, 1999, and September 25, 1999, all FTEA.

112 Minutes, Annual Meeting, FTESEA, December 17, 1998, Appendices A and B.

113 Minutes, Annual Meeting, FTESEA, December 16, 1999, FTEA.

114 Ibid., Appendices A and B; Marvin D. Hoff to Lu Dezhi, n. p., September 25, 1999, FTEA.

of the *Chinese Theological Review* for the Chinese church in December 1998. Han responded in December 1999 that they believed that this publication was one of their "musts," as it was their means of sharing Chinese theological thought with friends abroad. At the same time, Janice Wickeri, who was editing the *Review*, reported having received a grant of $40,000 to cover costs for a three-year period.[115]

Su Deci wrote in 1996 that China had, in the past two decades, become "reconnected with the world through the policy of openness and reform....This makes it possible for the Christian Church in China to share with churches overseas on a broader and more profound basis."[116] Evidence of this openness and sharing with Western Christians was seen in the return of Western teachers to Nanjing Seminary after an absence of nearly fifty years. China had welcomed foreign teachers into its universities from the late 1970s, particularly those in fields like foreign language, engineering, and economics. However, Nanjing, as a religious school, was under the cognizance of the State Administration of Religious Affairs (formerly Religious Affairs Bureau), rather than the Ministry of Education, as was the case for universities. Concerns both in the Religious Affairs Bureau and the CCC itself regarding the Three-Self principles delayed return of foreign teachers to the seminary. Nevertheless, Faye Pearson, a Southern Baptist with long experience in Hong Kong and Taiwan, was invited to work with the CCC in 1998 and began teaching English language courses at Nanjing Union Seminary in 1999. She was a first, and formal approval from the Religious Affairs Bureau of Beijing for her appointment came only in December of that year. Subsequently, two Americans joined the faculty in 2001. Anne Wire from the Presbyterian Church (USA) and San Francisco Theological Seminary, taught New Testament, and Carolyn Higginbotham, from the Christian Church (Disciples of Christ) and then at Muskingum College, taught New Testament. Ray and Rhea Whitehead of the United Church of Canada began an extended period of part-time teaching in theology and ethics in 2002. Samuel Pearson of the Christian Church (Disciples of Christ) also joined the faculty in the field of church history in 2002. When Pearson left Nanjing Union for Renmin University's Institute for the Study of Christian Culture in 2004, Miikka Ruokanen of the Finnish Church and the University of Helsinki moved from Renmin's Institute to Nanjing, where he taught

[115] Han Wenzao to Marvin D. Hoff, e-mail, December 5, 1999; J. K. Wickeri to Marvin D. Hoff, e-mail, December 13, 1999, both FTEA.

[116] Su Deci, "Theological Education in China," *CTR*, XI (1996), 45.

theology. The FTESEA generously supported these new arrivals and the window on the world they brought to Nanjing Union and its students with textbooks and other instructional materials.[117]

As the twentieth century came to a close and Nanjing Union Theological Seminary celebrated the fiftieth anniversary of its reorganization in 2002, the relationship between the FTESEA and the seminary, which had begun some sixty years earlier, and between the FTESEA and the CTE/CCC, a relationship established in the 1980s, were strong and obviously would continue in the new century. The FTESEA would continue to support faculty members' advanced study abroad, the libraries of Nanjing Union and other CCC seminaries, publications, and a variety of other projects recommended either by the Commission on Theological Education or by seminary leaders.[118] Aware of the rapid development of China and the Chinese church, Ching-fen Hsiao had called upon FTESEA in 1997 to establish "priorities for the first decade of the new century and millennium." After consultation with partners in China and South East Asia, a retreat was held in 2000 to review the foundation's mission and vision. With respect to China, the foundation committed itself to encourage the development of Chinese theology; to strengthen the educational experiences of the Chinese theological faculty members; to assist in strengthening seminary libraries in developing schools; to participate in the development of an ecumenical forum in North America for relating to the Christian communities in China; and to continue to nourish relationships with Nanjing Theological Seminary and the Commission on Theological Education of the China Christian Council. This statement was approved by the FTESEA board at its annual meeting in 2000.[119]

Two years later, with the retirement of Hsiao, Gerald H. Anderson, director of the Overseas Ministry Study Center in New Haven, became the new board chair. In 2006 Dr. H. S. Wilson, then the H. George Anderson Professor of Mission and Culture and Director of the Multicultural Mission Resource Center of the Lutheran Theological

[117] E.g., when I joined the NTS faculty, the FTESEA provided textbooks for my classes, a generous expression for which both I and my students offer gratitude.

[118] For an account of the fiftieth anniversary celebration see *NTR*, 2002, 4 (no. 53). Marvin Hoff represented the FTESEA at the anniversary celebration.

[119] Minutes, Annual Meeting, FTESEA, December 18, 1997; Marvin D. Hoff, "Significant Stages in the Mission of the Foundation for Theological Education in South East Asia"; Minutes, Annual Meeting, FTESEA, December 14, 2000, FTEA.

Seminary of Philadelphia, became executive director of FTESEA upon the retirement of Hoff.[120] With new leadership and a newly refocused mission statement, the Foundation for Theological Education in South East Asia anticipated continuing its work in support of Christian theological education in China and South East Asia in an age profoundly different from that in which the Board of Founders of Nanking Theological Seminary had been established.

120 Minutes, Annual Meeting, FTESEA, December 12, 2002; Invitation to FTESEA banquet honoring the Rev. Dr. Marvin D. Hoff and Joan B. Hoff and introducing the Rev. Dr. Henry S. Wilson, December 8, 2006, both FTEA.

CHAPTER 8

The Association for Theological Education in South East Asia, 1959-2002: A Pilgrimage in Theological Education

Michael Nai Chiu Poon

The Association for Theological Education in South East Asia (ATESEA) was founded in response to the radically altered political situation in China in the post Pacific War years. Four successive executive directors led the association from 1959 to 2001: John Fleming (1959-1967), Kosuke Koyama (1968-1974), Emerito Nacpil (1974-1981), and Yeow Choo Lak (1981-2002). Those four decades spanned a remarkable time of transitions in world history and in world Christianity. Tumultuous events took place in the region and in the wider world. South East Asia was in the heart of the "Asian Revolution," which transformed a cluster of newly established and hesitant nation-states into an influential geopolitical and economic bloc. At the same time, nation building and identity politics also gave rise to ethnonationalist conflicts: the unrest in Kalimantan, Sulawesi, and Maluku in Indonesia; the Malaysia-Indonesia conflict over Borneo; the Mindanao conflicts in the Philippines; Myanmar's state policies towards ethnic minorities; and the Thailand-Malaysia disputes over southern Thailand are cases in point. In the world of religion, Christianity did not merely shift southwards, but also developed newer forms that were still in gestation.

Martin Marty rightly underscored the wider centripetal and centrifugal historical forces that shaped the modern ecumenical movement in the second half of the twentieth century.[1] My aims are to interpret ATESEA's rise and development against these powerful currents, apart from which ATESEA's history cannot be properly understood. (See Appendix 1: Timeline of the Association.)

ATESEA was established in 1959 under the name, "The Association of Theological Schools in South East Asia" (ATSSEA). The present name, "The Association for Theological Education in South East Asia," was adopted in 1981. The association was arguably the embodiment of an ecumenical resolve for theological education in South East Asia. It spearheaded an ambitious experiment in contextualization amid complex geopolitical and ethnoreligious realities in South East Asia after the Pacific War. What follows is a portrait of the association's rise and development, to shed light on an institutional narrative that has appeared elsewhere.[2]

Williams Bay Consultation, 1954

The consultation regarding theological education in South East Asia convened by the Board of Founders of Nanking Theological Seminary, held August 9-10, 1954, in Williams Bay, Wisconsin, was pivotal to the development of theological education in South East Asia.[3] Thirteen representatives from South East Asia (Taiwan, Indonesia, Hong Kong, the Philippines, and Thailand) met with fifteen members of the Board of Founders and ecumenical leaders to discuss the situation of theological education in South East Asia. H. P. van Dusen, chair of the Board of Founders, convened the meeting. Three key people were in the meeting: C. Stanley Smith, Board of Founders' field representative in South East Asia, former vice-president of Nanking Theological Seminary, and principal of Trinity College, Singapore, from 1954 to

1 Martin Marty, "The Global Context of Ecumenism 1968-2000," in *A History of the Ecumenical Movement. Volume 3, 1968-2000*, ed. J. H. Y. Briggs, M. A. Oduyoye, and G. Tsetses (Geneva: World Council of Churches, 2004), 3-26.

2 See Choo Lak Yeow, *ATESEA Celebrates its Golden Jubilee: A Story of ATESEA in 50 Years (1957-2007)* (Quezon City, Philippines: ATESEA, 2007).

3 Consultation Regarding Theological Education in Southeast Asia, Williams Bay, Wisconsin, August 9-10 1954, Records of the Nanking Theological Seminary, Board of Founders, 1940-1963, Special Collections HR1340, Folder 2, Yale University Divinity School Library, New Haven. See also Cartwright, *River*, 11, 26.

1956; Rajah Manikam, Joint East Asia secretary of the International Missionary Council and the World Council of Churches; and Charles Ranson, who in 1957 would become the first director of the World Council of Churches' Theological Education Fund (TEF). The Williams Bay meeting was arguably the first ecumenical gathering on theological education in South East Asia, among clusters of nation-states linked by the waters from the East side of Bengal Bay through Malacca Straits, Java Sea, and China Sea, that would assume a regional identity by the end of the century.

The consultation took place against two immediate contexts. First, the Communist victory in China in 1949 and the withdrawal of foreign missionary personnel at the height of the Korean War left the Board of Founders of Nanking Theological Seminary uncertain of its directions. C. S. Smith posed the question, "What part of the Seminary's program could practically be carried out *outside* of China?" in his report to the Board of Founders of March 19, 1951.[4] Acting on this report, the board commissioned him and Sydney R. Anderson to make a survey of theological education in South East Asia, "where there were Chinese churches and large Chinese populations, to see whether, within the legal limits of its income, it could help in the training of ministers and church workers in that area."[5] Anderson and Smith toured South East Asia in early 1952. Their subsequent report underscored the urgency of preparing Christian leaders to meet "the infiltration and development of Communist influence and ideas" in the region.[6] The board held a special meeting September 12, 1952, to receive the report, and it resolved to amend the charter of the Nanking Theological Seminary, in light of existing conditions in China, to allow for the distribution of funds "in areas of Asia and of the western pacific beyond the confines of China" and "for educational assistance to Chinese and other Far Eastern students preparing in these or other lands for the ministry or other services in the Christian Church."[7]

4 C. S. Smith, The Program of the Nanking Theological Seminary with Relation to World Outside of China, March 19, 1951, Records of the Nanking Theological Seminary, Board of Founders, 1940-1963, Special Collections HR1340, Folder 1, Yale University Divinity School Library, New Haven.

5 Anderson and Smith, *Report*, iii.

6 Ibid., 97-98.

7 Minutes of the Meeting of the Board of Founders of the Nanking Theological Seminary, September 12, 1952, New York City, Records of the Nanking Theological Seminary, Board of Founders, 1940-1963, Special Collections HR1340, Folder 1, Yale University Divinity School Library, New Haven.

Second, quite apart from the Communist threat and China focus, the question of Christian responsibility in the independent nations loomed large on the horizon. Japan's "liberation" of Eastern Asia from its four Western colonial powers (American, Dutch, British, and French) raised new possibilities and aspirations among indigenous peoples and brought about new sets of relations among ethnic groups. Social and national revolutions followed. Indonesia set the pace in proclaiming independence on the heels of the Japanese surrender. The Philippines and Burma followed by the end of the 1940s. The hard-earned independence not only signaled liberation from the immediate Western colonial powers. More significantly, it offered opportunities for the "younger churches" in the newly established nation-states to work out ways by which a sense of interdependence might be developed. In the 1949 East Asia Christian Conference held in Bangkok, Rajah Manikam expressed the common problem in these terms:

> The multitudes which inhabit East Asia are today caught in the terrific maelstrom of a gigantic revolution....A dynamic and militant communism challenges the Christian Church in most parts of East Asia. Contending crusading forces of revitalized old religions shout their slogans, and engage in violent conflict with Christianity. A great void, a moral vacuum, has been formed by bleak disappointment with life, and consequent despair which finds life empty of meaning. It is against this background that we, representatives of our churches and Christian councils, are meeting here today....However, all this darkness and the troubled conditions of life in East Asia offer an unprecedented opportunity to Christian forces. The situation calls for Christian light and Christian witness. [8]

The "Eastern Asia" conference consisted of church representatives from Burma, Ceylon, India and Pakistan, Indonesia, Japan, Korea, Malaya, the Philippines, and Thailand, spread over subregions that the United Nations Statistics Division would later classify as "Eastern Asia," "Southern Asia," and "Southeastern Asia" in its geoscheme. But Manikam and the conference participants were untroubled by the "Eastern Asian" and "East Asian" signifiers. The "gigantic revolution"

[8] Rajah B. Manikam, "The Task of the Bangkok Conference," in *The Christian Prospect in Eastern Asia: Papers and Minutes of the Eastern Asia Christian Conference, Bangkok, December 3-11, 1949* (New York: Friendship Press, 1950), 4.

in the post Pacific War years demanded common strategies and close collaborations. Subregional identity politics and interests had not yet surfaced.

Manikam followed the crusading theme of his Protestant missionary forebears; the difference was that the call was sounded by an emerging "East Asian" leader rather than a Western missionary. Eastern Asia was undergoing fundamental political, social, and religious changes brought about by urbanization and secularization. And perhaps for the first time in over a century, Christians in the region found themselves no longer at the forefront of these changes. In fact, Christian churches were marginalized and by and large existed as small minorities in the new nation-states. Churches then faced huge tasks: Not merely did they need to rebuild their infrastructures from the ruins of the Pacific War. They had to start from scratch, for hardly any infrastructure was in place in politically realigned South East Asia. After all, China, Japan, and Korea had been the main focus of Protestant missionary activities by mid nineteenth century. The footholds in South East Asia were no longer needed for the China mission. The 1952 report of the East Asia study conference organized by the World Council of Churches held in Lucknow, India, echoed this sense of crisis:

> A social revolution is taking place in East Asia. This involves fundamental changes in the structure and conception of every aspect of social life. What is our responsibility as Christians in this situation?
>
> We are concerned with social justice, that is to say with the development of social conditions in which human dignity and freedom can find their expression as befits the nature and destiny of man as a child of God. Communism has awakened and challenged our conscience to see the need for action. It is not, however, primarily the fear of Communism but our concern for our brother for whom Christ died, that should impel us to fulfil our social obligations. But a positive programme for social justice will help to meet the challenge of Communism.[9]

Far from a retreat into hiding:

> There is need [for the church] to develop techniques and programmes of social service and action which will make a

9 "The Responsible Society in East Asia," *Ecumenical Review* 5, no. 3 (1953): 298.

> contribution towards humanizing the social and technical revolution which is taking place in all the social groups. This requires re-thinking the nature and structure of the Church's life in a changing society. The Church's aim should be to build up cells of true community-living as a means of humanizing the impersonal relationships of modern large societies.[10]

The "church" should then take the lead in this humanizing crusade; by this the conference participants meant those who joined the ecumenical movement. There was an air of confidence that the ecumenical movement was the future for world Christianity and the vanguard for social development in the postcolonial age. These "ecumenical churches" needed to be equipped for the long-term intellectual tasks in Asia; so the need for higher theological education. These Christian leaders were deeply suspicious of the Bible schools. In C. S. Smith's earlier estimates in 1952, these schools were ecclesiastically divisive and theologically fundamentalist. The 1956 Bangkok Conference on Theological Education would offer a warmer assessment: "We all agree that there is a need which the Bible Schools may meet for lay training of pioneer rural workers, and the training of women for Christian service, or even the training of regular church workers where there is no seminary."[11]

In other words, members of the Board of Founders and the national church leaders came together at the Williams Bay meeting with two common concerns: the Communist threat and Christian responsibilities (and survival) amid seismic changes in South East Asia. They quickly recognized they had to start from a low baseline. C. S. Smith made this observation: entering students in theological studies did not come with adequate educational preparation, there were few qualified Asian teachers available and little money to pay their salaries, and academic standards among theological schools were too diverse. The priority then, Van Dusen concluded, was "to strengthen existing schools." One decade later, Van Dusen described the situation in the early 1950s in these words: "The overarching fact from the *past,* the baseline, which furnishes the starting-point for all our thinking is: the palpable and lamentable *neglect* of Theological Education [in Christian

10 Ibid., 303.

11 Anderson and Smith, *Report*, 88; Ralph B. Manikam and C. Stanley Smith, eds., *Conference on Theological Education in Southeast Asia, Bangkok, Thailand, Feb. 21 - Mar. 8, 1956: Record of Proceedings* (Singapore: Malaya Pub., 1956), 29.

Mission] through the half century prior to World War II." It was regarded as a peripheral concern: "The normative Ministry for which candidates were to be prepared was the village pastorate, for which piety rather than learning was the prime, if not the only requisite." He further singled out one specific factor for the Asian scene: "Theological Schools in Southeast Asia were projections of denominational Seminaries in the West which, at that period, were similarly neglected and woefully inadequate."[12]

But how could the existing theological schools be strengthened? Here participants at Williams Bay wrestled with two sets of concerns that would remain with ATESEA in the following years. The first had to do with the material basis for theological education. Funding had to come from somewhere, and the Board of Founders was the obvious benefactor. The South East Asian members at Williams Bay included eight representatives of theological schools who were already receiving grants from the board. But how could funds designated for the training of Chinese be diverted to the general support for theological education in South East Asia? And how could theological schools in South East Asia, whose primary responsibilities were for their respective nations, be limited by the board's Chinese focus? Manikam raised this issue:

> If the Board was helping Chinese in Nanking, there would be no objection; but now, since that is closed, can it just barge in on the whole area saying our primary responsibility is for Chinese?...At a time when we want to pull together, this creates a picture we don't want to see, and it doesn't take into account the history of theological education in East Asia.

The board members' responses to Manikam's remark were significant:

> E. L. Smith: [I support] the policy as broadening the responsibility of the Board, and at the same time, *it must make sure the Chinese are not neglected.*

> J. W. Decker: The Board's policy is for having a general responsibility for Asia, and specifically for SE Asia. What we do want are suggestions as to what to do *if present commitments don't take all the available funds.*

12 H. P. van Dusen, "An informal report to the Association of Theological Schools in South-East Asia," *SEAJT* 6, no. 4 (1965): 46-47.

> Van Dusen: The Board finds itself with an inner tension, not between members of the Board, but between a concern for all these larger issues, and *for the Christian Church in China and Chinese Christians* [emphasis mine].

The rationale for the board's funding of theological education in South East Asia, and the wider funding issues in the region, would persist in ATESEA's story. To anticipate a later chapter in the story, when China re-entered the world stage in the 1980s, the board's basis of support to South East Asia would become problematic. South East Asian theological schools would find themselves competing with their Chinese counterparts for funds from the West. After all, China is a huge geopolitical reality no one could ignore. Back in 1954, the board had to engage two fronts: first, general responsibility for theological education in South East Asia; and second, special focus for the training of Chinese. C. S. Smith used the occasion of the Williams Bay meeting to approach the board independently to provide Trinity College, Singapore, with a US$50,000 grant for the construction of a new school building.[13] The reasons were clear. In his earlier report Smith had ruled out Manila and Jakarta as centers for higher theological education for Chinese. Singapore with its stable political situation and high concentration of ethnic Chinese would become such a base.[14]

This led to the second set of concerns, which focused on whether theological education in South East Asia should be centralized. Pierce Beaver of the Board of Founders expressed this well in the meeting: "If we want standardization, and more than that, to achieve the goals of theological education, one of these institutions has to become an advanced center in close and intimate relation to all the others." C. H. Hwang's response to Beaver was immediate:

> It is only within the church that we consider SE Asia as a group. The international situation is such that a center would not be available to all of that area. All theological training needs to follow the needs of church and lead it in the right direction.

Hwang (Shoki Coe), principal of Tainan Theological College, could not be clearer on his priorities. He regarded Taiwan as the

13 C. S. Smith to Frank Cartwright, December 30, 1954, Records of the Nanking Theological Seminary, Board of Founders, 1940-1963, Special Collections HR1340, Folder 2, Yale University Divinity School Library, New Haven.

14 Anderson and Smith, *Report*, 23-30.

concrete context of theological education and engagement; theological schools across South East Asia should do the same in their locations. Too much centralization was "premature." Ralph Ward from Hong Kong responded to Hwang's comment: "The next step is to encourage interpretation from the stand-point of the people of Asia." How then to raise standards in a geopolitically diverse region when all theological schools had to attend to their immediate contexts? Instead of establishing one center to resource the region, the strategy was to find ways to develop existing schools across the region and raise them to higher standards. The Williams Bay meeting came up with the suggestion of a "summer institute of theology," "bringing top leadership from SE Asia, Europe, [United] States [of America], for high level study....This might be financed by the Board of Founders, for say two months a year, for a trial period of five years." The summer Study Institute would become a centerpiece in the early years of ATESEA's development.

The Williams Bay meeting resulted in the "Conference on Theological Education in Southeast Asia," held February 21 to March 8, 1956, in Bangkok, with Manikam and Smith as codirectors. The eighty-four participants included the codirectors, fifty-one South East Asian delegates [Burma (4), Taiwan (6), Hong Kong (5), Indonesia (14), Malaya (3), Philippines (13), Sarawak (1), Thailand (5)], thirteen "special visitors," nine "fraternal delegates from other Asian countries" (India, Pakistan, Ceylon, Korea and Japan), and nine "speakers and distinguished guests."[15] Twenty-one theological schools were represented. The conference agreed to two concrete projects:

(1) Organizing a higher theological faculty to serve the whole of East Asia, based preferably in Bangalore, "to provide facilities for advanced theological studies in Asia." "Such a faculty will help the churches to train Asian theological teachers required for the existing theological institutions";[16] and, of more immediate relevance to South East Asia,

(2) Organizing an association of theological school principals for South East Asia. Such an association would help (i) in matters of accreditation; (ii) improve standards of all theological schools to meet the requirements for accreditation; (iii) interchange teachers and students; (iv) towards an understanding of common needs and problems of theological colleges; and (v) voice appeals to ecumenical bodies for the needs of theological education in South East Asia. This

15 Manikam and Smith, eds., *Conference on Theological Education*, 71-74.
16 Ibid., 37-39.

association of school principals should take steps to turn itself into an Association of Theological Schools and Colleges in South East Asia.[17]

Joint Action for Theological Education

Representatives from sixteen schools in Taiwan, Hong Kong, the Philippines, Malaya, Sarawak, Indonesia, Thailand, and Burma came together at Trinity Theological College, Singapore, August 31-September 2, 1957, to follow up the Bangkok decisions and draft the constitution of the new association. The sixteen founding schools were Baptist Divinity School in Burma; Tainan Theological College and Taiwan Theological College in Taiwan; Lutheran Theological Seminary and Union Theological College in Hong Kong; Trinity Theological College in Malaya; Sarawak Bible School in Sarawak; Saint Andrew's Theological Seminary, College of Theology (Silliman University), Union Theological Seminary, and the College of Theology (Central Philippine University) in the Philippines; Djakarta Theological College, Faculty of Theology (Nommensen), Jogjakarta Theological Seminary, Makassar Theological School in Indonesia; and McGilvary Theological Seminary in Thailand.[18]

The Association of Theological Schools in South East Asia (ATSSEA) held its first full meeting in Singapore July 13-15, 1959. At that meeting, the constitution was accepted, and the association was no longer provisional. Henceforth, the offices of chair and executive director gave the association a public presence. The interlude between 1957 and 1959 was significant. Not only did the theological schools

17 Ibid., 55.

18 The list of founding members has never appeared in official publications of the association, nor been identified in previous histories, including the reports on the 1957 and 1959 meetings in Singapore in its official journal, the *South East Asia Journal of Theology*: ATSSEA, "Association of Theological Schools in South East Asia: First regular meeting scheduled for July 13-15 1959 at Trinity Theological College, Singapore," *SEAJT* 1, no. 1 (1959): 5-7; ATSSEA, "Association of Theological Schools, South East Asia: Some findings of the July 1959 meeting," *SEAJT* 1, no. 3 (1960): 67-68. The list here is pieced together from the 1952 Anderson-Smith *Report*, participants at the 1954 Williams Bay meeting and the 1957 Bangkok conference, the list of institutions Raymond Morris visited in his South East Asian tour of 1959 [Report of Raymond Morris to the Board of Founders, May 20, 1959, Records of the Nanking Theological Seminary, Board of Founders, 1940-1963, Special Collections HR1340, Folder 10, Yale University Divinity School Library, New Haven], and the names of individuals and institutions that appeared in the first issues of the *South East Asia Journal of Theology*.

need time to ratify the provisional constitution; more importantly, as we shall see, the founding of the Theological Education Fund in 1958 made the association financially viable.

The constitution listed four purposes:

1. To provide facilities for its members to confer concerning matters of common interest related to theological schools;
2. To consider any problems that may arise as to the relations of such institutions to one another or other educational institutions;
3. To recommend standards of theological education and maintain a list of members institutions on the basis of such standards;
4. To promote the improvement of theological education in such ways as it may deem appropriate.

The membership consisted of institutions engaged in education and training for the Christian ministry in South East Asia. There were from the beginning three types of members: accredited, associate (for those institutions that were not yet accredited by the Commission on Accreditation), and affiliated. The last category was for those institutions "for fraternal purposes by the Executive Committee without reference to procedures of Accreditation."[19] Bible schools were excluded from membership at that time. The category, "affiliated," was dropped by the end of 1960s. In 1974, the membership structure was changed to offer "regular" membership for those institutions "regularly engaged in training for the Christian ministry in South East Asia" and "affiliate" membership for institutions "involved in or concerned with theological education in South East Asia, such as study centres, lay training institutes or church bodies." This classification remains to the present.

The association's institutional history tells an impressive story of theological education in South East Asia. From its beginnings with sixteen founding schools in 1957, membership swelled to eighty-one by the end of 2001. It was arguably the most recognized accreditation body for theological education in South East Asia. It pioneered region-wide cooperation in theological education and research, setting standards of excellence through its consortial advanced degree programs, publications, seminar-workshops, and experiments in nontraditional

[19] ATSSEA, "Association of Theological Schools in South East Asia: First regular meeting scheduled for July 13-15 1959 at Trinity Theological College, Singapore," 7.

forms of theological education. The association's journal, the *South East Asia Journal of Theology*, chronicled developments in theological education and thinking from 1959 to 1982; it remained the unrivalled source for understanding post colonial theology in South East Asia.[20] The *East Asia Journal of Theology* succeeded the *South East Asia Journal* in 1983. From 1985, the *Asia Journal of Theology* became the organ of the Association for Theological Education in South East Asia, the North East Asia Association of Theological Schools, and the Board of Theological Education of the Senate of Serampore College.

The association's history divides conveniently into two parts: the Fleming and Koyama years to the mid 1970s, and the Nacpil and Yeow years from the mid 1970s to the turn of the century. Both Fleming and Koyama took up their office with considerable firsthand regional and missionary exposure. Koyama was a powerful intellectual in his own right. His unique credentials as a Japanese missionary to Thailand in the post Pacific War era made him an ideal successor to Fleming. Nacpil's and Yeow's experiences were in the main limited to their immediate surroundings before they assumed office. More importantly, huge geopolitical changes took place in the mid 1970s that aggravated the already vast economic differences among South East Asian countries. Places like Hong Kong and Singapore launched out to become world financial centers, while others like the Philippines and Indonesia would become mired in constant political unrest and social instability. Unexamined suppositions on the nature of regional and international partnerships began to surface. The Gross Domestic Product (GDP) of South East Asian countries underscored this plight. From 1960 to 2000, Singapore's GDP per capita (constant 2000 US$) jumped from 2,250 (1960), to 6,417 (1975), to 23,019 (2000). Corresponding figures for Indonesia were 196, 303, and 800; for Malaysia: 784, 1,378, and 3,881; for the Philippines: 612, 843, and 996.[21] For instance, Singapore's GDP per capita was nearly thirty times that of its neighbor Indonesia; implications for the material basis of theological education cannot be highlighted more clearly.

20 Cumulative index of *SEAJT* and *EAJT* is available at the Centre for the Study of Christianity in Asia, "The South East Asia Journal of Theology (*SEAJT*) and The East Asia Journal of Theology (*EAJT*) Cumulative Index," CSCA Trinity Theological College, http://www.ttc.edu.sg/csca/epub/seajt.htm.

21 Source: World development Indicators, World Bank, WDI Online, http://ddp-ext.worldbank.org (accessed December 1, 2008).

Pilgrim's Progress: Early Developments to The Mid 1970s

To Kosuke Koyama, the experience of violence rather than confident nation building marked the twentieth century. "It is violence... that has defined my life in this century." Speaking of his wartime experience in Japan, he recalled that "the idea that our life, personally and collectively, must be a movement toward God....I sensed...a great contrast between pilgrim progress and the 'demon progress,' as it were, of the cult of emperor worship. I concluded that Japan became a heap of ruins because it engaged in the cult of a false god–in idolatry...."[22] Violence, of course, did not end with the Pacific War. Asia was embroiled in endless ethno-nationalistic wars that came with nation building. To Koyama, theological education amid violent Asian revolutions in the postwar years must then be a matter of adopting, like Saint Francis of Assisi, a lifestyle of the holy stigmata of Christ. It must be a "pilgrim progress" towards this end. This insight underlined the association's first developments.

Fleming and Koyama arguably laid the foundations of ecumenical theological education in South East Asia. The mid 1970s was a turning point: Saigon fell to the Communists in 1975; the Cultural Revolution in China ended a year later. By the end of the 1970s, China had re-entered the world stage with its market liberalization policies. TEF programs would have concluded by 1977. Fittingly, Alan Thomson and Peter Gowing in 1975 took stock of ATSSEA's history.[23] Their perceptive assessments came at the end of a golden period in the history of ecumenical theological education in South East Asia.

ATSSEA's formation coincided with the birth of two ecumenical bodies. The East Asia Christian Conference (EACC) was formed under the joint support of the World Council of Churches and the International Missionary Council. The first conference took place in Prapat, Indonesia, in 1957; the inaugural assembly was held in 1959 in Kuala Lumpur, two months before ATSSEA's first full meeting.[24]

22 Kosuke Koyama, "My Pilgrimage in Mission," *International Bulletin of Missionary Research* 21, no. 2 (1997): 55.

23 Peter G. Gowing, "The South East Asia Graduate School of Theology: Advanced Theological Education by Consortium," *SEAJT* 45, no. 1 (1975); Alan Thomson, "A Note on the Development of the Association of Theological Schools in South East Asia," *SEAJT* 16, no. 1 (1975). See also *A Brief Look at the Association of Theological Schools in South East Asia* (Singapore: Association of Theological Schools in South East Asia, 1969).

24 East Asia Christian Conference, *The Common Evangelistic Task of the Churches in East Asia: Papers and Minutes of the East Asia Christian Conference: Prapat,*

The Theological Education Fund was founded in the World Council of Churches Ghana Conference at the turn of 1958. TEF was asked "to maintain liaison with the Board of Founders of Nanking Theological Seminary (New York), or other bodies with a similar programme, with a view to achieving reasonable co-ordination of programme."[25] Indeed, the Board of Founders (renamed Foundation for Theological Education in South East Asia [FTESEA] from 1962), EACC (renamed the Christian Conference of Asia [CCA] in 1973), and TEF would become ATESEA's three staunch ecumenical partners in a bold venture in theological education.

ATSSEA and TEF policies were closely coordinated. Leadership in both organizations overlapped and shared wide knowledge and experience in the region: Charles Ranson participated in the earliest discussions in theological education in South East Asia; Charles W. Forman, Ranson's TEF assistant and later chair, was a missionary in India; Shoki Coe had a long association with TEF, first serving from 1961 in the WCC Commission on World Mission and Evangelism (CWME) Advisory Group to evaluate TEF's First Mandate, then as the fund's associate director in 1965, and eventually as director in 1970; Ivy Chou of Sarawak, who was in ATSSEA's leadership from its beginning, was on TEF's staff in the 1970s.

The Theological Education Fund's funding policy was governed by three successive mandates: the First Mandate from 1958 to 1965; the Second Mandate from 1965 to 1970; and the Third and final Mandate from 1970 to 1977. Christine Lienemann-Perrim gave this astute assessment of TEF's work. Her depiction arguably applied equally to ATSSEA in the corresponding period:

> Whereas during its First Mandate the working emphasis was on strengthening the academic quality, the Second Mandate stressed the search for a relevant theology and the Third Mandate focused on the contextualization of theological education. In the course of all three mandates, the image of the pastor as the good shepherd taking care of his flock was speedily replaced by the concept of "a ministry of the people of God." The notion of the

---

Indonesia, March 17-26, 1957 (Rangoon: EACC, 1957); U. Kyaw Than, *Witnesses Together: Being the Official Report of the Inaugural Assembly of the East Asia Christian Conference, Held at Kuala Lumpur, Malaya, May 14-24, 1959* (Rangoon: EACC, 1959).

25 C. W. Ranson, "The Theological Education Fund," *International Review of Mission* 47, no. 188 (1958): 434.

> local church as a one-man show came under increasing criticism, while the perspective of a "ministry with the poor" (not "for" the poor) was recognized as an appropriate one for the Younger Churches....Within the context of this search all the traditional forms of theological education soon came into question, and people became uncertain as to the appropriate shape of theological education, the Christian ministry and the Church in general....In spite of this general uncertainty of its proper aims and methodology, the TEF forced itself to formulate concrete goals and take the first steps towards their realization.[26]

The First Mandate had two components: Major Grant and Text Programme. Major Grants were designated for selected seminaries "on the basis of their strategic location, the excellence of their present work, and their plans for development, offer the greatest possibilities for qualitative growth in the future." The Text Programme had a wider application "in the improvement of the libraries of theological schools and the preparation and translation of suitable theological texts."[27] Of the six seminaries that received Major Grants, two belonged to the association: STT Djakarta (US$100,000), and Tainan Theological College (US$85,000). The other four were Doshisha University Kyoto (US$138,000), Tokyo Union Theological Seminary (US$119,500), Yonsei University, Seoul (US$110,000), and Pacific Theological College, Fiji (US$100,000).[28] Concurrently, the Board of Founders commissioned Raymond Morris (Yale Divinity School librarian and president of the American Theological Library Association) to draft a *Preliminary and Tentative Listing of Books for the Libraries of Christian Theological Institutions in South-Asia.* Morris then conducted a South East Asian tour in early 1959, culminating in a region-wide librarians' workshop at Silliman University.[29]

The first meeting of ATSSEA in 1959 took place in such a climate. Faculty and library "strengthening" was one key emphasis, "the opportunity to meet, think, plan, and work together" in building

26 Christine Lienemann-Perrin, *Training for a Relevant Ministry: A Study of the Contribution of the Theological Education Fund* (Madras: Christian Literature Society, 1981), 230-31.

27 Ranson: "Theological Education Fund," 433.

28 Lienemann-Perrin, *Training*, 34.

29 On Morris's tour, see his May 13-20, 1959, Report to the Board of Founders, and Raymond Morris, "Some Impressions on the Libraries in Protestant Theological Educational Institutions in Southeast Asia and their Implications for the Christian Church," *SEAJT* 1, no. 3 (1960): 8-16.

up infrastructures from scratch was another.[30] An accreditation commission was formed to offer members suggested forms of standards. Morris's 1958 *Preliminary and Tentative Listing of Books* and the TEF book lists in the 1960s provided the basis for seminary library acquisition in South East Asia.[31] More importantly, four major programs underpinned ATSSEA's developments during the Fleming years: (1) the summer theological study institutes that began in 1957; (2) the *South East Asia Journal of Theology* launched in 1959; (3) from 1960 the Theological Texts: Translation and Writing Programme, with particular reference to Chinese and Indonesian settings; and (4) the founding of the South East Asia Graduate School of Theology (SEAGST) in 1966, as an experiment in decentralized graduate education leading to the M.Theo. degree.

The early 1960s was a time of self-assessment on the initial steps taken to raise the baseline. One of the earliest tasks of the WCC Commission on World Mission and Evangelism was to evaluate TEF's First Mandate as it drew to a close. The advisory group recommended that the fund abandon "Major Grants" in the future, because it perpetrated western forms of theological training as the final criterion for funding. The group also noted the growing opposition of the developing countries to neocolonialism in the world economy as well as in world mission and in education. TEF formulated the Second Mandate (1965-1970). The new emphasis was on the search for relevance in the local situations. Graduate study and faculty research, curriculum reform, and association of theological institutions became important considerations.[32]

Correspondingly in 1963, the East Asia Christian Conference conducted three Situation Conferences in Madras, Amagisano, and Singapore, in which Fleming and C. H. Hwang played important roles. The theme was "The Common Life and Mission of God's People in Asia today." To Hwang, Christians "must seek to discover concretely and realistically what Christ's revolution means in Asia's revolution."

30 ATSSEA, "Association of Theological Schools, South East Asia: Some findings of the July 1959 meeting," 68.

31 Arthur Marcus Ward and Raymond P. Morris, *A Theological Book List of Works in English, French, German, Portuguese, Spanish* (London: Theological Education Fund, 1963); Raymond P. Morris and Arthur Marcus Ward, *A Theological Book List, 1968; in Four Sections: English* (London: Theological Education Fund, 1968). See also Gerald Anderson, *Christianity in Southeast Asia: A Bibliographical Guide* (New York: Missionary Research Library, 1966).

32 Lienemann-Perrin, *Training*, 125-70.

It was a time when Indonesia, the Federation of Malaya, Singapore, Sarawak, and North Borneo were embroiled in political conflict and social unrest. Burma had come under military rule a year earlier. Hwang pointed out three areas for joint action among churches in Asia: unity, witness, and service. He was apprehensive about the resurgence of world-confessionalism, stagnating numerical growth among churches, and their inability to move outside secure institutional confines to new frontiers of service.[33] The 1963 discussions culminated in the EACC Consultation on Theological Education in South East Asia, held at Tao Fong Shan, Hong Kong, March 17-25, 1965, with the release of the Statement on Joint Action for Theological Education:

> Nine years of experience [since the 1956 Bangkok Conference] have clearly shown us that the time has now come to broaden the framework of theological education beyond national bases and interests so as to make effective witness to the Lord in this turbulent and divided area of the world. Joint action for Theological Education is therefore a test of loyalty and obedience to Jesus Christ on the part of seminaries and churches in South East Asia, and on the part of related mission boards in North America, Continental Europe and Britain. [34]

Accordingly ATSSEA in 1963 appointed a three-member accreditation commission to advise on necessary changes in the existing accreditation system and to explore the possibility of setting up a regional faculty and regional degrees. Van Dusen, chair of the commission, reiterated Hwang's words in his 1965 report: "A strictly academic programme is no longer adequate to prepare the Church's Ministry within the ASIAN REVOLUTION." There was a need for "carefully planned and supervised diversified exposure to contemporary ASIAN SOCIETY in its major aspects and experience in the Church's relation with the SOCIETY."[35]

Fleming underscored these same concerns in his addresses at the EACC Second Assembly in 1964 and the 1965 Hong Kong

[33] C. H. Hwang, "God's People in Asia Today," in *One People - One Mission. The Situation Conferences of the East Asia Christian Conference 1963*, ed. John Fleming (Singapore: EACC, 1963), 5-17.

[34] "A Statement on Joint Action for Theological Education by the Consultation on Theological Education in South East Asia," *SEAJT* 6, no. 4 (1965): 138-39.

[35] Van Dusen, "An Informal Report," 54.

consultation. While marking the advances in theological education in the decade of infrastructural development, he spelled out four issues facing theological education:

> We are concerned to find a pattern of theological education that will be Asian and contemporary, and at the same time be an educational process that will train men to think, and think on the basis of a solid grounding on the biblical, historical, and theological disciplines....Secondly, we have to think out our curricula more clearly than we have done before. This means in terms of the academic excellence and sociological relevance...and also in terms of the spiritual discipline in individual prayer and community worship....Thirdly, there is the relation between theological education and the renewal of the Church....Basic to this renewal is the renewed understanding on the part of the congregations of their missionary nature. This in turn raised a question of the varieties of ministries needed today...if there is to be a real "missionary" penetration of society and if "the ministry" is to be in a position to equip and train "the laity" for ministry in the world...engaging themselves in various forms of "pioneer ministry."...Fourthly, there is the issue of an ecumenical approach to all this. We are from different churches and different confessions but we have a common task and a common mission.[36]

These perceptions became programmatic to ATSSEA's future developments. Clearly the founding of SEAGST in 1966 was to be the concrete expression of joint action for theological education.

In 1968 Kosuke Koyama succeeded Fleming as the first Asian executive director of the association, now with the added responsibility as SEAGST dean. He came to his tasks with an acute sense of mission responsibility and spiritual humility in relation to his fellow Asians. His Thailand years in the early 1960s were the occasion of his initiation: "The realization that many of my EACC friends also knew the war, but as the victims of Japanese imperialism, was important for my new theological orientation."[37] His term straddled TEF's Second and Third mandates. Shoki Coe and Koyama were arguably the two most

[36] John Fleming, "'Then and Now,' in Theological Education in South East Asia," *SEAJT* 6, no. 6 (1965): 65-66. See also John Fleming, "A Survey of Theological Education in East Asia: Address given at the EACC Second Assembly, Bangkok, March 1964," *SEAJT* 6, no. 6 (1964):7-15.

[37] Koyama, "My Pilgrimage," 56.

outstanding Asian theologians who were able to provide intellectual leadership among the emerging national churches in the post Pacific War era. With Shoki Coe at TEF and Koyama at ATSSEA, ecumenical theological education in South East Asia entered a golden period. It was, in Koyama's words, a time of "decolonization of theology." His energy was devoted to building up SEAGST programs. His departure in 1974, and the concluding of the TEF program in 1977, marked the end of this golden period.

ATSSEA formulated the Critical Asian Principle in the early 1970s. Its oft-quoted "Historical Footnote" states:

> The phrase "critical Asian principle" has its genesis at the meeting of the Senate of the South East Asia Graduate school of Theology in Bangkok, 1972. In this meeting, a report on the feasibility of a theology doctoral program in the region was submitted for consideration and action.[38]

ATSSEA leaders had TEF's Third Mandate before them as they formulated the Critical Asian Principle. The Third Mandate crystallized the convictions Shoki Coe and his colleagues set at the end of a two-year policy review.[39] The new mandate carried the decolonization of theological education to the next stage: theological education moved from Western forms (still implicit in the First Mandate), through indigenization (still supposed in the Second Mandate), to contextualization (under the Third Mandate).

> The third mandate's strong emphasis on renewal and reform in theological education appears to focus upon a central concept, contextuality, the capacity to respond meaningfully to the Gospel within the framework of one's own situation. Contextualization is not simply a fad or catch-word but a theological necessity demanded by the incarnational nature of the Word. What does the term imply?... *It means all that is implied in the familiar term "indigenization" and yet seeks to press beyond.* Contextualization has to do with how we assess the peculiarity of third world contexts.

38 Emerito Nacpil, "Editorial: The Critical Asian Principle," *SEAJT* 17, no. 1 (1976): iii.

39 Theological Education Fund, "A Working Policy for the Implementation of the Third Mandate of the Theological Education Fund," *SEAJT* 14, no. 1 (1972): 64-71; Theological Education Fund, *Ministry in Context: The Third Mandate Programme of the Theological Education Fund (1970-77)* (London: Theological Education Fund, 1972).

> Indigenization tends to be used in the sense of responding to the Gospel in terms of a traditional culture. Contextualization, while not ignoring this, takes into account the process of secularity, technology, and the struggle for human justice, which characterize the historical moment of nations in the Third World....*Contextualization does not imply the fragmented isolation of peoples and cultures.* While within each diverse cultural situation people must struggle to regain their own identity and to become subjects of their own history, there remains an inter-dependence of contexts. Contextualization thereby means that the possibilities for renewal must first of all be sensed locally and situationally, yet always within the framework of contemporary inter-dependence which binds both the problems of the past and present and to the possibilities for the future....If, then, contextualization becomes a chief characteristic of authentic theological reflection, a request for support submitted to the T.E.F. will be judged to have potential for renewal when:
>
> 1. There is evidence of contextualization in *mission*.
> 2. There is evidence of contextualization in *theological approach*.
> 3. There is evidence of contextualization in *educational method*.
> 4. There is evidence of contextualization in *structure*.[40]

TEF's new emphases were evident in the fourfold Critical Asian Principle:

> 1. As a *situational* principle, by which we seek to locate where we are and thereby indicate our area of responsibility and concern, namely, the varieties and dynamics of Asian realities.
> 2. As a *hermeneutical* principle, suggesting that we are to understand the Gospel and the Christian tradition with these realities. Accordingly we must approach and interpret the Gospel and its traditions in relation to the needs and issues peculiar to the Asian situation. Alternatively, we must approach and understand Asian realities not only through variety of academic disciplines available in study and research, but also in the light of the Gospel and its traditions.
> 3. As a *missiological* principle, which aims at the responsibility of equipping people with a missionary theology capable not only of illuminating Asian realities with the flood-light of the Gospel, but also of helping manage and direct the changes now

40 Theological Education Fund, "A working policy," 66-67.

taking place in the region along lines more consonant with the Gospel and its vision for human life in God.
4. And finally as an *educational* principle which should give shape, content, direction, and criteria to our educational task in our member-schools and in the South East Asia Graduate School of Theology.

> From what has been said above, it can be seen that the critical Asian principle is a way of doing theological contextualization. It is primarily a method, and a method is judged by how well it works. [41]
>
> Clearly, the Critical Asian Principle was drafted with the Third Mandate in mind.

In 1973, TEF gave US$100,000 towards the SEAGST faculty development program.[42] To Koyama, the principle was not meant to be construed in abstract terms. It should carry practical outcomes in all aspects of theological education. Koyama insisted that the Critical Asian Principle should be translated in concrete terms:

> I have taken TEF's contextualization primarily as an insight not as a programme. But "programming of the insight" in the region is our responsibility in South East Asia. Insight can be formed in a flash of a moment. Programming and implementation of programmes cannot be done in one second magic. It takes time.[43]

Koyama underscored this point in his farewell report to the ATSSEA assembly in 1974.[44] Looking back to ATSSEA's developments over nearly two decades, he reflected on its two central aims: "to improve the standards of all the theological schools" and "towards an understanding of common needs and problems of theological education." Koyama then scrutinized every aspect of seminary life with the yardsticks of contextualization and the Critical Asian Principle. For instance:

> [On alternative patterns in theological education] What are the alternative patterns in theological education? They must be of a kind which South East Asian resources can support. What is the

41 Nacpil, "Editorial," ii-iii.
42 Lienemann-Perrin, *Training*, 181.
43 Kosuke Koyama, "Reflections on Association of Theological Schools in South East Asia," *SEAJT* 15, no. 2 (1974): 29.
44 Ibid., 10-35.

basic principle by which this search for alternative patterns can develop? What is such a critical Asian principle?

[On accreditation service of the association] I think that the Association's accreditation standards and notations are in character "ontological-structural" rather than "existential-functional-mobile." This is to say, they ask questions relating to institution rather than performance (products) or movement....By virtue of being such, accreditation may effect an inhibiting influence upon experiments which context may demand....The institution must remain a servant for the higher purpose (renewal-principle, protestant-principle, Christological Johannine principle" – "I decrease-he-increase"). When institution is a *pilgrim-institution* it is valuable.

[On endowment funds] Faculty development entails an ever growing financial need to support national faculty members. Endowment drives have been conducted in some of our schools....Within our region I think no "professor" must have an "eternity-arrangement" with regards to receiving of the benefits of an endowment....We cannot afford out-of-context security given to a few individuals in the life of the church. The benefit of endowment must be shared professionally and chronologically. The entire yield must be sued for the benefit of the group of Asian theologians who engage in different disciplines, and it must be reviewed every five or seven years. Endowment must not create a special class of people "on chairs," but it must serve to create "community benches" for Asian theologians.

[On dependence on financial support from abroad] ...Critical Asian principle is a principle of our responsibility. Theology must be responsibly constructed. Finance must be responsibly constructed....Critical Asian principle, then, is against paternalism.[45]

Asian Journeys: Scandal of Dependency

Koyama resigned in 1974, too soon to see his vision for the Critical Asian Principle come to realization in theological education programs. The years under Nacpil and Yeow were punctuated by transitions and relocations. During the Fleming and Kyama years, Trinity Theological College Singapore served as the home of the association. When Nacpil

[45] Ibid., 17, 19, 33-34.

took office in 1974, he moved the head office to Manila. Yeow moved it back to Singapore when he became the association's executive director in 1981. In 1998, Yeow moved the headquarters again to Manila, where it has remained since.

Wider ecclesiastical and political forces affected the association's fortunes. The early 1970s saw Singapore swept by renewal and charismatic movements.[46] By the 1980s, charismatic forms of Christianity had taken hold of mainline denominational churches and the fast-growing independent churches. These newer forms of Christianity by and large commanded local and popular support and were able to offer new approaches to Christianity.[47] Megachurches and congregation-based training centers began to emerge that would give an alternative (and seemingly more relevant) form of training than traditional seminaries could offer. The City Harvest Bible Training Center in Singapore was a case in point. So the association no longer merely had to contend with its traditional theologically conservative detractors. Megachurches began to assert themselves, providing a new base and interpretation for Christianity. The association's ecumenical cause suffered a further blow when Trinity Theological College came under evangelical leadership in 1982, depriving the association of a concrete base for theological education experimentation.

Political forces were also at work. In 1985 the Communion of Churches in Indonesia withdrew from membership in the Christian Conference of Asia (CCA) at its Seoul conference, in protest of the conference stance on East Timor. This situation continued until 1989. In 1987 Singapore authorities invoked the Internal Security Act to detain those involved in the "Marxist Plot."[48] On December 30, the government closed the CCA head office in Singapore and deported the staff. In 1989 the National Council of Churches Singapore terminated its CCA membership. In Yap Kim Hao's words:

46 Ban It Chiu, "Revive Thy Church, Beginning with Me," *New Covenant* 5, no. 11 (1976): 36-37; Manik Corea, "What really happened at ACS in 1972," *Impact* 23, no. 3 (1999): 22-25; Lorna Khoo, "A Brief Study of the Charismatic Movement in Singapore" (B.Th., Trinity Theological College, 1979); James Wong, "The Church Renewed for Mission: A Study of the Anglican Church in Singapore" (Oral Roberts Univ., 1986).

47 Daniel P. S. Goh, "Rethinking Resurgent Christianity in Singapore," *Southeast Asian Journal of Social Science* 27, no. 1 (1999): 89-112; Mayling Tan-Chow, *Pentecostal Theology for the Twenty-first Century: Engaging with Multi-Faith Singapore* (Aldershot: Ashgate, 2007), 15-28.

48 Ron O'Grady, *Banished* (Hong Kong: Christian Conference of Asia, 1990).

> When the CCA was sent out, the critics of the ecumenical movement in the churches took advantage of it to attack the CCA and the WCC. The ecumenical-minded people in the churches were helpless and the task of building up support for the ecumenical cause had to begin all over again.[49]

So ATESEA and the ecumenical movement became increasingly remote from church and seminary life in Singapore, the association's birthplace and home for nearly two decades.

But more practical issues and internal conflicts loomed large on the horizon. The 1977 correspondences between Nacpil and Ivy Chou at the TEF South East Asia desk in London highlighted these concerns. In April 1977 Nacpil wrote to Ivy Chou about the disposal of the remaining money TEF had allocated to ATSSEA in 1973 as the fund was winding down. Over US$50,000 still remained in the balance. Nacpil proposed two projects for funding: a region-wide interdisciplinary workshop on the Critical Asian Principle, and a series of colloquia on Asian perspectives in Christian theology.[50] One week after the final TEF meeting in July 1977, Chou gave this reply:

> With regard to your other request of US$23,500, from the same grant for a Workshop on "The Critical Asian Principle and Its Implications for Theological Education" to be held in April 1978, there was some serious discussion and questioning....First, is the Workshop the kind of doctoral-level study programme of GST [SEAGST], for which the grant was made? The second is a general query regarding the wisdom of another big and expensive conference so near to so many only recently held. In fact, there is uncertainty about the value of "big" conferences to justify the high cost.[51]

On May 12 of the same year, during the Consultation of Pacific Coast Seminaries on the Pacific Basin Theological Network, Shoki Coe (who at that time was TEF's director) had expressed his reservations about implementation of the Critical Asian Principle. The consultation report noted:

[49] Kim Hao Yap, *From Prapat to Colombo: History of the Christian Conference of Asia (1957-1995)* (Hong Kong: Christian Conference of Asia, 1995), 144.

[50] Nacpil to Chou, April 17, 1977, in Association of Theological Schools in South East Asia, *Minutes of 1977 Meetings, October 6-8, 1977, Pondok Sentosa, Jakarta, Indonesia* (1977), 93-97.

[51] Chou to Nacpil, n.d., ibid., 91.

> Dr. Shoko Coe...responded to Dr. Nacpil's report by tracing the stages of the changes in theological education in Asia from the end of the colonial era, with its demand for new forms of ministry. He expressed some other problematics about the Critical Asian Principle, especially the hope that it is not simply a slogan or a fad. Rather, it refers to the historical Asian realities within which Asian Christians must do mission, ministry and theology.[52]

Nacpil gave a spirited defense of the workshop method in the Critical Asian Principle's implementation at the ATSSEA meeting later that year:

> We must involve the constituency as widely and deeply as possible.... We are interested in a method which is both participative in its process and productive in its results. Our purpose is to produce models of contextual curricula which can be used by the schools in their own efforts at reform and renewal.[53]

Nacpil further underscored his defense with a strident attack on TEF (under the leadership of Shoki Coe, a former ATSSEA colleague and founder of contextualization). He asserted: "[TEF's hesitation in approving the workshop grant] is short-sighted, to say the least, and as far as TEF is concerned, a betrayal of its avowed aim of reforming and renewing theological education through contextualization!"[54]

Anyway, Nacpil pressed ahead with his colloquia on Asian perspectives in Christian thought. Workshops and conferences became the main preoccupation in the Nacpil and Yeow years. As we shall see, efforts to involve the wider constituencies did not end with closer links with the churches. Member schools began to pursue their own interests. The association's activities became more and more dependent on external support.

This was not unanticipated. In 1965, Henry van Dusen ended his accreditation report to ATSSEA with a frank observation:

> Before I visited the Schools, I would never have believed that the situation is, what prevailing, it is. That it is being perpetuated without serious efforts at correction can, I believe, be possible only because those responsible for the Schools in Asia and their

52 "Report of a Consultation of Pacific Coast Seminaries on the Pacific Basin Theological Network, San Anselmo, California," ibid. 86.

53 Ibid., 80.

54 Ibid., 79.

> friends in the West have never brought themselves to face its stark shame. Let me characterize it as "the scandal of dependency."... The nearly total dependency of Theological Education continues, widely, prevailing, unmodified....The dependence upon Overseas contributions might average over 90% of total costs....Here is the last vestige of Christian colonialism—at the very heart of the Church's life....Let us accept the harsh truth: not until the Churches of East Asia assume financial responsibility for the preparation of their own leadership can they claim to be fully Churches of Christ.[55]

Van Dusen deplored "the scandal of dependency" among churches and seminaries in South East Asia. His challenge, "not until the Churches of East Asia assume financial responsibility for the preparation of their own leadership can they claim to be fully Churches of Christ," underlined the association's ambivalent relationship with the churches. This link would become increasingly tenuous during the Nacpil and Yeow years.

Unquestionably, FTESEA from the start bankrolled the association. After all, ATSSEA was its child. In his May 20, 1959, report to the Board of Founders on his South East Asian tour, Raymond Morris went further than merely addressing library concerns. He warned against the dangers of Western dependency in theological education. At the same time, he recognized that realistically continued financial support "for some time" from the West was necessary: (1) to improve physical equipment of institutions; (2) to provide operating budgets; (3) to underwrite conferences and occasions when leadership can be drawn together; and (4) for grants in advanced training.[56] The Board of Founders met in November 1959. Fleming, who also served as the board's field representative, was able to announce to his South East Asian colleagues that the board undertook to continue support for the theological studies institutes and the journal; provide fellowships for advanced studies and short-term support for new Asian faculty appointments; continue scholarship aids for students; provide improvement of libraries; build up the writing and translation program of basic texts; and provide for faculty exchange professors within South

55 Van Dusen, "An Informal Report," 55-56.

56 Report of Raymond Morris to the Board of Founders, May 20, 1959, Records of the Nanking Theological Seminary, Board of Founders, 1940-1963, Special Collections HR1340, Folder 10, Yale University Divinity School Library, New Haven.

East Asia and occasional visits of professors from the West.[57] Clearly, the board adopted Morris's recommendations in their entirety.

The board was nervous about the prospect of long-term financial dependence. In 1962, Fleming announced the name change of the Nanking board to "The Foundation for Theological Education in South East Asia." He then reported:

> In connection with this change of name, the Executive Committee believed that the time was ripe to re-evaluate the present organizational and financial position of the Association. The work of the Association had largely come into being through the financial help of the Nanking Board. If and when it becomes possible to make use of these funds at Nanking, it would mean that the present Association could be without financial foundation. It was, therefore, requested by this body that the Nanking Board, or now the newly called "Foundation for Theological Education in South East Asia," explore means of laying a financial foundation which will not be so completely dependent on the Nanking funds, which might be diverted from this present project.[58]

Fleming's message was clear: FTESEA's support could only be temporary, depending on the political situation in China. So the FTESEA and ATSSEA had to lay an alternative "financial foundation" for theological education in the region.

Van Dusen's 1965 remarks made it clear that Fleming's plea was left unheeded. After all, South East Asian countries were in deep social and political unrest in the 1960s. Churches had little material foundation to attend to immediate needs, let alone funding for region-wide joint action for theological education. As we have seen, the financial needs were alleviated by TEF's support from 1958 to 1977. But once TEF reached the end of its Third Mandate in 1977, Van Dusen's question became more acute. This practical need illuminated the reasons behind the decision to establish the Joint Regional Planning Commission (JRPC) in 1974 and to change the association's name in 1980.

The Joint Regional Planning Commission was formed in 1974 by joint resolution of FTESEA and ATSSEA. Andrew Hsiao, chair of the

57 "Editorial," *South East Asian Journal of Theology* 1.3 (1960): 3-7. See also Cartwright, *River*, 41-43.

58 ATSSEA, "Association of Theological Schools in South East Asia: Report of the Executive Committee," *SEAJT* 4, no. 4 (1963): 51.

ATSSEA Executive Committee and of JRPC, gave this account of the commission's birth:

> FTE has a board in New York, and an office in London [under Ivy Chou]. It is understandable that for a number of years all important decisions such as determining priorities, allocating funds, etc. were made thousands of miles away from South East Asia. Realizing that this practice was no longer relevant to present trends of theological education, nor was it practical for the SEA situation, both ATSSEA and FTE began a few years ago to search for a new structural model.[59]

The joint commission was ATSSEA's first step in assuming financial responsibility in the post TEF era. In Hsiao's words, it "created in the theological schools a sense of responsibility never before found." The commission consisted of twelve members: six chosen by ATSSEA from among the membership, two by FTESEA, one Christian Conference in Asia representative, two representing the churches, and one Asian theological educator from outside Southeast Asia. The last three were to be chosen by the ATSSEA executive committee in consultation with the Christian Conference in Asia.[60]

Clearly the church-school and ATSSEA-FTESEA relationships were the joint commission's main concerns. In 1978 ATSSEA decided a new Resource Commission was to replace the joint commission.[61] ATSSEA underlined three important aspects of this move: (1) to expand funding requests to agencies beyond FTESEA; (2) to underscore the place "churchmen" assume in theological education; (3) to clarify the commission's sole accountability to the association. The purpose of the Resource Commission was "to be an instrument of ATSSEA in involving the churches to participate more deeply in the support of theological education and in coordinating the requests for and use of resources and funds." The twenty-member commission included six "churchmen"; six representatives from member schools; two members-

59 "Some Reflections on a More Desirable Structure for Theological Education in South East Asia," in Association of Theological Schools in South East Asia, *Minutes of the Triennial Meeting, March 23-26, 1977 Makati, Metro Manila, Philippines* (1977), 82-84.

60 Association of Theological Schools in South Asia, *Source Book on the State of Member-Schools 1975-1978* (1978).

61 Association of Theological Schools in South East Asia, *Minutes of the Special Meeting of the Executive Committee, February 18, 1978, Union Hotel, Kaoshiung, Taiwan* (1978).

at-large from outside the region; two consultants from Lutheran World Federation and WCC Programme on Theological Education; and four ex-officio members (ATSSEA executive director, ATSSEA chair, FTESEA and CCA representatives).[62]

To underline the churches' central position, the association changed its name to "The Association for Theological Education in South East Asia" at its 1981 General Assembly. Nacpil explained in his farewell report:

> [ATSSEA] had been an association of schools and of school heads. Churches and churchmen did not have much to do in the official bodies and decision-making process of ATSSEA. The restructuring of ATSSEA into ATESEA is precisely in acknowledgement of the fact that theological education is such a joint effort taking place at all levels and channels of the Association.[63]

But behind this official position lay a practical concern. Towards the second half of the 1970s, both TEF and FTESEA were anxious to have compliance measures in place. In the 1976 meeting,

> Drs. Ivy Chou [FTESEA executive director] and Paul Gregory [general secretary of the United Church Board of World Mission] reported on JRPC from the point of view of FTE. Dr. Chou outlined the possibilities, whether ATSSEA takes over JRPC functions or whether JRPC should be continued in its present form, or in an altered from (sic.)....Dr. Gregory pointed out that the Internal Revenue Service in the U.S. watches very closely the operations of foundations, to prevent their misuse and that putting the screening body and the beneficiary too close together, in terms of relationship, would engender the tax-free status of the foundation. Can more Church leaders participate, as in TEF? Guidelines need to be established for ATSSEA appropriations.[64]

The Policy Committee met in 1977 to consider the ATSSEA's relationships to WCC, CCA, and FTESEA and agreed that a

62 Association of Theological Schools in South East Asia, *Minutes of 1978 Meetings, October 11-18, 1978. Hotel Las Palmas, Malate, Metro Manila, Philippines* (1978), 190-91.

63 Association for Theological Education in South East Asia, *Minutes of 1981 General Assembly, June 26 to July 1, 1981, Philippine Baptist Theological Seminary, Baguio City, Philippines* (1981), 9.

64 Association of Theological Schools in South East Asia, *Minutes of the October 1976 Meetings, YMCA, International House, Hong Kong* (1976), 15.

"Resources Commission" be established "as a Fund recommending Body to FTE."[65] In other words, churches were drafted in to meet this regulatory requirement. Churches, however, were cool to this move. Later that year, the new executive director, Yeow Choo Lak, reported to the executive committee that national church councils had not nominated their Resource Commission representatives.[66] The Resource Commission's evaluation report in 1987 gave this assessment of the church representatives:

> Commissioners have conflicting interests, e.g. fund-raising. These church leaders have to raise funds for their own churches/seminaries, hence they are totally unable or unwilling to help ATESEA....Commissioners don't do anything for ATESEA in their denominations, e.g., they have said nothing about their ATESEA connections at Synod or Conference meetings.[67]

The Resource Commission then recommended that its size be reduced. The church-school relation receded to the background. Foremost was the concern for fund application to FTESEA. Whether the foundation saw the Resource Commission as legally necessary was the key to the commission's future. "If the Resource Commission is not legally essential in the eyes of FTE, then scrap the Resource Commission. The money saved can then be used for our member-institutions." Only six years after the Resource Commission's establishment, its expressed aims to engage churches and to assume responsibility fell by the wayside.

The FTESEA correspondences with ATESEA in the 1990s underlined this loss of vision. ATESEA saw the foundation as a grant agency, and the foundation became apprehensive and yet unclear what to do with its prodigal child, since Nanjing Union Theological Seminary had been reopened in 1981. In 1991 the China Christian Council joined the WCC, signaling China's firm commitment to international partnership. That very year the FTESEA's executive director Marvin Hoff wrote to reassure Yeow Choo Lak that support to South East Asia would not decrease because of new opportunities in China. Grant increases could be expected in 1992 and 1993.[68] At its

65 Association of Theological Schools in South East Asia, *Minutes of the Triennial Meeting, March 23-26, 1977 Makati, Metro Manila, Philippines*, 19.

66 Association for Theological Education in South East Asia, *Minutes of 1981 Meetings, September 4-6, 1981, Ambassador Hotel, Singapore* (1981), 86.

67 Association for Theological Education in South East Asia, *Minutes of 1987 Meetings, October 6-14, 1987, Hsun Chu, Taiwan* (1987), 189.

68 Hoff to Yeow, January 2, 1991, FTESEA Files.

annual meeting in December 1994, the FTESEA approved US$100,000 for ATESEA schools; members were, however, concerned that none had been requested for SEAGST, which they believed to be "one of the most creative and important programs of ATESEA."[69] The foundation began to question ATESEA on its audit procedures: Was it going to charge an administration fee for the various projects? How would it show grants from foundations in the annual audit? And did it want money for the endowment fund or annual grants for the various projects?[70] In mid 1995, with the prospect of funding from the Luce Foundation, ATESEA grant requests included: for SEAGST, US$800,000 for the endowment or US$50,000 annually for five years for scholarships for five doctoral students each year; US$600,000 in endowment or US$40,000 annually for five years for five scholarships for master's degree students; US$1,000,000 for an endowment for a regional professor of the SEAGST; US$200,000 to establish a revolving fund for the Chinese Theological Education Series; US$200,000 to establish a revolving fund for the Bahasa Indonesia Theological Education Series; an annual grant of US$15,000 for ATESEA for five years to fund the expenses of the accreditation commission; and US$800,000 for an endowment for the office of the executive director.[71]

Funding policies and mutual expectations became a central concern in the Hoff-Yeow correspondences. In December 1995 Hoff informed Yeow of the FTESEA's intention to reduce all of the Resource Commission's grant recommendations by 25 percent because of its own financial pressures.[72] In a follow-up letter two months later, Hoff underlined to Yeow that ATESEA already had a US$800,000 balance. Some of FTESEA's directors had not wanted to give funds to ATESEA in the past years, but "deferred to the decisions of the [Resource Commission]."[73] In March 1996 Hoff told Yeow pointedly that after nearly forty years FTESEA could no longer be the primary supporter of ATESEA. Hoff noted that 60 percent of ATESEA's budget went to "administration." He told Yeow frankly that he thought their predecessors at the American mission boards had "made a mistake of keeping ATESEA so dependent upon the FTE."[74]

69 Hoff to Yeow, December 20, 1994, FTESEA Files.
70 Hoff to Yeow, January 31, 1995, FTESEA Files.
71 Hoff to Charles Foreman and Ching-fen Hsiao, June 8, 1995, FTESEA Files.
72 Hoff to Yeow, December 21, 1995, FTESEA Files.
73 Hoff to Yeow, February 9, 1996, FTESEA Files.
74 Hoff to Yeow, March 5, 1996, FTESEA Files.

Yeow's frustrations became evident in his 1996 report to ATESEA. He began with a reference to "premier member-institutions," who by then had launched their own independent Master of Theology program; SEAGST's faculty and library development programs had made this possible. He then proceeded:

> We have been experiencing a deficit since 1994, primarily due to the fact that our major donor agency is experiencing some financial difficulty in making grants to several of its partners.... [After complaining about the tedious tasks in coordinating accreditation visit, he proposed:] All accreditation agencies charge a fee for each accreditation visit. In a way, we have been doing that, but because of financial difficulty faced by our member-institutions in countries with a less developed economy in the past we have not really asked for payment. Two developments seem to call for a review. More and more countries in our region are getting affluent....ATESEA itself is facing financial difficulty.[75]

Yeow's sentiments reflected the changed outlooks within the association's leadership by the mid 1990s. The FTESEA, the ATESEA office, member institutions, and churches had to deal with their own interests; increasingly, these priorities conflicted with one another. The 1965 Statement on Joint Action, which to a great extent served as the association's guiding policy, had in mind a region-wide partnership among ecumenically minded seminaries to equip churches for leadership amid the Asian revolution. By the mid 1990s, the member schools had developed tangentially; some became "premier schools," while others found it difficult even to meet their membership dues. There was little coherence in region-wide development in theological education. ATESEA had become more of an accreditation service and grant-processing agency that was beset by self-doubt when cash began to run dry.

Ironically, ATESEA's rapidly increased membership in the Nacpil and Yeow years exemplified this loss of vision. The association began with sixteen founding schools. Membership did not increase significantly in the Koyama years: twenty-two in 1969, increased to only twenty-nine by the time he resigned in 1974. As explained earlier, his energy was devoted mainly to SEAGST. SEAGST was the centerpiece

[75] Association for Theological Education in South East Asia, *Minutes of 1996 Meetings, October 25-29 1996, Dyana Pura Beach Hotel, Bali, Indonesia* (1996), 55, 58, 60.

in ATESEA programs, the embodiment of contextualization, and the tangible form of partnership among member schools.

Subtle shifts in priorities began to appear in the mid 1970s. Parallel to the ecumenical movement, evangelicals worldwide also began to network with one another, matching ecumenical conferences at every instance with their own gatherings. The Asia Theological Association (ATA) was established in 1970. Immediately upon taking office, Nacpil raised the question of whether ATSSEA was indeed "a representative body of theological education in the region":

> Should we deliberately promote the increase in the number of member-schools of ATSSEA so that it will become more and more a representative body of theological education and of theological schools in the region? The present Constitution offers regular membership "to institutions regularly engaged in training for the Christian ministry in Southeast Asia," and affiliate membership to "institutions involved in or concerned with theological education in Southeast Asia, such as study centres, lay training institutes or church bodies" (Art. III, Sec. 1 & 2). According to the TEF Directory (1974) of Theological Schools and related institutions in the Third World, there are some one-hundred theological schools and study-centres in Southeast Asia. Of these, twenty-nine are members of the Association....Not only is the present membership unrepresentative (in terms of sheer number), its growth has been rather slow. There were sixteen founding member-schools when the Association was established in 1957. Today there are altogether thirty-one member-schools, an increase of less than one member per year.[76]

Nacpil then recommended a proactive drive to increase membership. A remarkable increase in membership followed: forty-two in 1980 when Nacpil departed, forty-eight in 1983, fifty-four in 1986, sixty-one in 1990, sixty-nine in 1995, and eighty-one at the end of Yeow's term in 2001. Nacpil's membership drive, however, begged the question: was the association meant to be "the representative body" (in terms of numerical strength) or to serve as bearer of joint action for theological education in the region. It was meant to be the flagship of ecumenical partnership in South East Asia. This explained why Fleming excluded Bible schools from membership. Membership

76 Association of Theological Schools in South East Asia, *Minutes of 1975 Meetings, October 3-8, 1975, Taiwan, Republic of China* (1975), 39.

perceptions became increasingly unclear. By the end of 2001, cross accreditation appeared. ATESEA institutions that also received ATA accreditation included: in Hong Kong, China Graduate School of Theology and Lutheran Theological Seminary, a founding institution of ATESEA; in the Philippines Asia Pacific Nazarene Theological Seminary, Asia Pacific Theological Seminary, Asian Theological Seminary, International School of Theology Asia, and Asian Seminary of Christian Ministries; and Tung Ling Bible College in Singapore. A case can be made whether for some institutions ATESEA increasingly became merely an accreditation agency.

The ecumenical leaders involved in the joint action in the 1960s might have unintentionally paved the way for this loss of direction three decades later. The ecumenical movement was at its zenith. Fleming, C. H. Hwang, and others were confident that national churches would embrace the ecumenical understanding of mission and theological education. The newly established SEAGST would be a beacon of hope in equipping churches with the necessary intellectual and spiritual leadership in pioneering ministries. National church councils rather than denominational churches would be the primary ecclesial realities. The East Asia Christian Council and ATSSEA, in partnership with the FTESEA and TEF, would create a platform of creative theological thinking and regional coordination. But did the churches in South East Asia want to give up their denominational links and embark on this venture? Little attention was paid to the intransigent conservatism in churches. From the start, ATSSEA had excluded Bible schools from membership. By the end of the decade, Bible schools excluded from ATSSEA would form ATA, a rival association that was more able to appeal to the populace. One decade later, this sober reality would dawn on the ecumenical leaders as they appealed for greater church support. The churches' conservative outlook was a major concern in the Joint Regional Planning Commission's discussions:

> Theological education is a function of the church. The question "what is theological education" is related to the question, "what is the Church?" In the church we see an uncritical mixture of paganism and the Gospel. The Gospel as exercising a critical function on cultures, needs to be emphasised in theological education.[77]

[77] Association of Theological Schools in South East Asia, *Minutes of the October 1976 Meetings, YMCA, International House, Hong Kong*, 161.

In 1977, Nacpil lamented:

> The conviction has grown in me [Nacpil] that there is more to church-school relations than we have so far realized....If churches have thought at all about the thrust of their ministry or mission in their national setting, they have not gone so far as to find out what forms of ministry are required by such an understanding of their mission, let alone probe into the leadership and educational requirements of such a mission and ministry.[78]

The 1980 constitutional amendments restructured ATSSEA into ATESEA. It did not merely tidy up the 1974 constitution, but, importantly, it reversed the order of the first and second clauses in the association's aims. The first two clauses in the aims stated in the 1974 and the 1980 constitutions read:

1974:

1. To facilitate regional planning in theological education by schools in the service of the churches in South East Asia;
2. To promote creative relationships between member schools, other institutions and the churches in the region.

1980:

1. To promote creative relationships among institutions and agencies engaged in theological education and the churches in the region;
2. To facilitate regional efforts in theological education in the service of the churches in South East Asia.

The "school" focus in the original 1959 constitution faded. The roles member schools played in fostering "creative relationships" and in facilitating "regional" planning became increasingly tenuous. We already saw from the beginning that churches did not come into the picture; after all, ecumenical bodies in the main underwrote the association's program, as Van Dusen complained.

The 1980 amendments did not achieve their intended purposes in drawing churches to concrete forms of partnership; they in fact made ATESEA leadership increasingly detached from the schools that were the first reasons for its existence. Study centers, ecumenical bodies, and overseas partners became the main forums for pursuing "creative relationships." Yeow recalled:

78 Association of Theological Schools in South East Asia, *Minutes of the Triennial Meeting, March 23-26, 1977 Makati, Metro Manila, Philippines*, 42.

> It was rightfully felt that the seminary-church mix could be strengthened if social action activists in our churches could be included in working out a living theology in our region....The ten Theological Seminar-Workshops [from 1983 to 1992] galvanized the will of a younger generation of Asian church leaders, social action activists, and theologians to do theology contextually in Asia....[Together, they brought about] a procreative theological community in Asia....ATESEA went on a shopping spree, so to speak, to augment and popularize a body of contextual theological literature in Asia.[79]

But such forms of partnership were essentially short term and grant dependent. Collaboration among seminaries, churches, and social activists, generally speaking, was not a shared vision and reality at local levels, let alone throughout the whole region. So ATESEA's creative engagements ran the risk of not being able to be translated into the nuts and bolts of mainstream church life and seminaries, which of course were more concerned with longer-term and sustainable programs.

To some extent, Yeow Choo Lak and C. S. Song's plight poignantly depicted this sorry situation. We have already seen how Yeow, a Singaporean, worked without a church and seminary base in Singapore during his tenure. By 1993, Trinity Theological College Singapore began to offer its own postgraduate program and pursue its own regional network.[80] Ironically, ATESEA's chair in the early 1990s came from Southeast Asia Union College, a small college in Singapore with a much briefer history in theological education. C. S. Song provided the intellectual leadership during the Yeow years. By the time he took charge of the Theological Seminar-Workshops [TSWs] (1983-1992), he was already based in America, having left Taiwan in 1971. Song was based in Geneva from 1973; from 1985 he taught at the Graduate Theological Union in Berkeley. So the two key ATESEA leaders ran their programs without a concrete seminary base.

ATESEA's focus turned to producing "living theologies," but unfortunately with little impact on theological *curricula* in the "premier schools." Fleming's series of Theological Study Institutes from the late 1950s to the 1960s were more focused on developing the core theological curricula for the member schools. Trinity Theological

79 Yeow, *ATESEA Celebrates*, 93-95, 99.

80 Trinity Theological College (Singapore), *At the Crossroads: The History of Trinity Theological College, 1948-2005* (Singapore: Trinity Theological College, 2006), 141-46.

College Singapore was the center of these initiatives and was an obvious beneficiary. The same cannot be said for the Theological Seminar-Workshops. Tao Fong Shan Ecumenical Centre Hong Kong, the home of several TSWs, exemplified a twofold shift: from seminaries to study centers, and from developing core programs in theological education to probing theological frontiers. To be sure a burgeoning theological scholarship was evident across the region. It was unclear whether causative links could be established between ATESEA programs and such theological ferment. The ATESEA occasional papers published in the 1980s and 1990s did testify to the fruits of the TSWs. On the whole, however, these efforts did not result in any significant changes to the paradigm of theological *education* in the seminaries. And as we have seen ATESEA was also unable to solicit the churches' practical support for its programs.

The Theological Seminar-Workshops ended in mid 1990s, near the time when FTESEA financial support could no longer be taken for granted. ATESEA was at risk of turning into an unfocused accreditation agency, with huge membership expansion but little attention to the high ideals for which Shoki Coe and Koyama labored. Cross accreditation raised further doubts on the commitment of the whole ATESEA constituency in pursuing the original aims of the association. The continued availability of external funds from FTESEA and ecumenical bodies served to prop up these theological activities but perhaps was detrimental to the long-term objective of fostering local support and regional partnership.

The disconnect between ATESEA and the churches and between theological ferment and theological curricula that I have highlighted may in fact suggest a broader failure of the ecumenical movement in the post Pacific War era. As noted, the association's rise was connected with the birth of the East Asia Christian Council in the late 1950s. Church leaders played an active role in both enterprises. The official positions occupied by the participants in the 1957 Prapat Conference and in the 1959 Kuala Lumpur EACC Inaugural Assembly clearly testified to this. The EACC, however, adopted a twofold methodology to promote intraregional initiatives in its early developments that eventually alienated churches from the ecumenical movement. Harvey Perkins explained:

> Through consultations and conferences to create groups of people who share common ideas out of a common vision, and influenced by them, penetrate the normal work of the churches with them;

> To build up in the life of the churches and countries a group of people who are willing to probe the frontiers of the Christian enterprise, to encourage and nurture them and relate them in solidarity to each other.[81]

The history of the ecumenical movement in Asia indeed would be punctuated by many "conferences" organized and attended by those who were "willing to probe the frontiers." From the 1970s, the language of politicization, liberation, and transformation took hold of the ecumenical agenda. Those at the frontiers became increasingly impatient with church structures. Social activists began to dominate the agenda of intraregional meetings.[82] The "option for the people" became central to ecumenical programs. Conferences became occasions for making rhetoric-ridden statements on the world's ills. Looking back to the CCA's shift from a church-centered to a people-centered approach, Yap Kim Hao summed up its impact on churches:

> The ecumenical agenda was perceived [by the churches] as a foreign agenda, funded mainly from outside the region and, for the most part, unrelated to the agenda of the churches, with little consideration on how such can be adopted by the churches.[83]

He went on to underscore the importance of bringing churches back to center stage in the ecumenical movement in Asia:

> People's movements and action groups need to bring their experiences into the life of the churches. Their experiences with the people's struggles must be shared with the churches for the sake of renewal of the church and the building up of the body of Christ....Their participation in the CCA is of great importance, but it should not be at the expense of the virtual withdrawal of the churches themselves....In the years ahead the CCA should further develop its relationship with the churches and national councils, thus deepening their ecumenical commitment.[84]

Yap went further in his memoir. By the 1980s, Asia's ecumenism had lost Manikam's vision for coordinated efforts for the whole "East

[81] Harvey Perkins, "A Time of Vision and a Time for Vision," in *Minutes of the General Committee Meetings, April, 1982, Kuala Lumpur*, ed. Christian Conference of Asia (Singapore: CCA, 1982), 145.

[82] See Harvey L. Perkins, *Roots for Vision: Reflections on the Gospel and the Churches' Task in the Re-peopling the De-peopled* (Singapore: CCA, 1985), viii-xxxvi.

[83] Kim Hao Yap, *From Prapat to Colombo*, 170.

[84] Ibid., 173.

Asian" region, as we saw earlier. Caucus groups began to emerge, pursuing their own particular interests in the CCA.

> It must be admitted that concerned ecumenical leaders would form caucus groups to strategize and ensure good leadership in CCA....But there were some groups that worked in a mafia style. Cronyism was a problem and I call it ecumenical incest. The perception in the region was that CCA had a strong Korean mafia operating within.[85]

An Unfinished Journey: Come Wind, Come Weather

To conclude, what happened to the ministry to Chinese communities in South East Asia, which after all was the main reason for the Nanking board's involvement in South East Asia? In brief, from 1962 the Chinese Texts Translation Program came under a subcommittee that involved only the Chinese-speaking members of the association. In practice, Hong Kong and Taiwan took the lead. The program became the Chinese Theological Education Series, first under C. S. Song's direction in 1966, and then under James Pan in the 1970s. From the 1970s it became part of the publication program of the Chinese Christian Literature Council in Hong Kong.[86] The 1970s was a time of rapid growth in intraregional cooperation between theological institutions engaged in Chinese-speaking ministries. Seminaries in the region held their first region-wide Consultation of Chinese Theological Educators and Church leaders in 1972, during which the Association for Promotion of Chinese Theological Education was established.[87] The Chinese Congress on World Evangelization came into being in 1976, and it became the de facto platform for worldwide coordination

85 Kim Hao Yap, *A Bishop Remembers* (Singapore; Gospel Works, 2006), 112-13.

86 See ATSSEA, "Association of Theological Schools in South East Asia: Report of the Executive Committee," 53; *A Brief Look at the Association of Theological Schools in South East Asia*; James Pan, "The Chinese Theological Education Series (CTES), Director's Report, 1974-75," *SEAJT* 17, no. 1 (1976): 120-26. See also Nacpil's report in Association of Theological Schools in South East Asia, *Minutes of 1980 Meetings, October 20-25, 1980, Ambassador Hotel, Singapore* (1980), 64-65.

87 The Association for promotion of Chinese Theological Education, *A Report on the Consultation of Chinese Theological Educators and Church Leaders, 10th-13th Jan 1972* (Hong Kong: Christian Witness, 1973).

in ministry and mission among Chinese-speaking churches. Andrew Hsiao was able to report these growths in the association meetings.[88]

What then of the association? The immediate geopolitical, ecclesiastical, and mission contexts have changed since the 1950s. Yet the present need for regional cooperation amid common threats remains as urgent as the need was then. Can South East Asian churches cooperate in tangible ways across racial, political, and economic divides? The legacy that Shoki Coe, Kosuke Koyama, and their generation bequeathed may yet inspire radical discipleship among Asian Christians in the twenty-first century by offering a united witness and service among their fellows, who are suffering from unbridled greed in the globalizing age. Such initiatives may well come from the newer and powerful bases of Christianities that charismatic movements have created in South East Asia in the closing decades of the twentieth century. These charismatic forms of Christianity may well be the expressions of nuanced interplays between local values and Christian practice, meeting the needs of the populace in the time of nation-building and globalization. From Sarang Community Church in Seoul to City Harvest Church in Singapore, megachurches spread across Asia may well become the crucible for contextual theology and theological education in the twenty-first century. ATESEA's challenge and future may yet rest on whether it is able to speak to the real constituencies in Asia rather than to those in Geneva and New York.

88 Andrew Hsiao, "Chinese Theological Education in the 1970s," in Association for Theological Education in South East Asia, *Minutes of 1981 General Assembly, June 26 to July 1, 1981, Philippine Baptist Theological Seminary, Baguio City, Philippines*, 13-28. See also Andrew Hsiao, "The Past and Present of Chinese Theological Education," Association of Theological Schools in South East Asia, *Source Book on the State of Member-Schools 1975-1978* (1978), 127-43.

Conclusion

The twentieth century will certainly be remembered as one of extraordinary political, social, economic, and technological change, but in no region of the world was this transformation more apparent than in Asia. There the century was marked not only by changes common to all regions but also by the rise of nationalism, lengthy revolutionary ferment, the demise of imperialism, and creation of new political and economic institutions. These changes were felt particularly by Christian communities in Asia which, in most instances, had been created and sustained by Western missions. The rise of nationalism presented these communities with new challenges and new opportunities. Missions gradually but inexorably gave way to indigenous churches. Asian Christians became responsible for the development of their own theology and their own leadership. The history of the Foundation for Theological Education in South East Asia and of its predecessor, the Board of Founders of Nanking Theological Seminary, is the history of one American foundation's endeavor to understand and respond creatively and helpfully to these changes and to fulfill its mandate to support leadership development among the Christian communities of the region.

Ella Wendel, last surviving member of a very wealthy family, died in New York in 1931, leaving a significant portion of her estate to "the Board of Foreign Missions of the Methodist Episcopal Church...the income of which is to be used for the maintenance of the Nankin [sic] Theological Seminary in Nankin, China."[1] Wendel's sister, Rebecca Wendel Swope, had died the previous year, and her will contained identical provisions regarding the bequest for the benefit of Nanking Theological Seminary.[2] Though there is little indication of active church participation on their part, and though the sisters made generous grants to a variety of charities such as hospitals and schools, they were especially generous to the Methodist Episcopal Church and to Nanking Theological Seminary, an interdenominational seminary then operated by the Methodist, Presbyterian, and Disciples of Christ denominations.

At a time when other extremely wealthy Americans were endowing institutions which bear their names, the Wendel family chose for several generations to retain its wealth in family hands rather than to engage in large-scale philanthropies. Yet they lived frugally and had no interest in consumerism or conspicuous consumption. The sister who had dared to marry in defiance of their brother, Rebecca Wendel Swope, together with her husband managed the family's extensive real estate holdings after the brother's death. It is likely that she summoned a lawyer to write wills for Ella and herself, realizing that their vast fortune would go to the State of New York if they died intestate. Why they chose to endow the charitable organizations mentioned in their wills is anyone's guess. Only two of the charities enjoying the largess could confirm that the Wendels had made prior contributions: the Flower Hospital reported they had given $60,000 over the previous forty years, and Nanking Theological Seminary had received $5,000 after Harry F. Rowe, a Methodist missionary teaching there, had visited them and requested a donation. The bequests were primarily, but not exclusively, to Protestant institutions, and the sisters were known sometimes to attend a Presbyterian church near their summer home and an Episcopal church in Manhattan. Yet their lifestyle certainly reflected Methodist influence, and they chose to favor the Methodists in their wills. The gift for support of Nanking Seminary led to the creation of the Foundation for Theological Education in South East Asia and continues today to have an impact on Christian theological education in Asia and on the Christian churches in that region.

1 *NYT*, March 21, 24, 1931.
2 *NYT*, August 2, 1930.

Seventy-five years after Ella Wendel died, millions of Asian Christians can attribute some or all of the theological education of their clergy to the Swope-Wendel bequest. Their gift for the benefit of Nanking Theological Seminary had immediate consequences for theological students in China. Although the seminary's charter had been amended June 1, 1932, to provide for a board in the United States, none had been established. With the income from the Swope-Wendel fund to administer, one became essential. The Board of Founders of Nanking Theological Seminary was created June 5, 1937, quickly acquiring a charter from the State University of New York authorizing it to grant degrees to students who met that university's standards. Several American scholars who were planning trips to China were asked to assess the situation of Chinese theological education and report to the members of the seminary's supporting mission boards how the money might best be used, as it would certainly fund more than the fifty-nine students who were enrolled at the seminary when the gift was made known.[3]

Yet before any long-term plans could be made for allocation of income from the Swope-Wendel fund, World War II began in China. Except for one American missionary teacher, Hubert L. Sone, all of the seminary's faculty and students fled Nanjing before the approaching Japanese army in 1937. Sone remained behind to look after the property. He soon found himself absorbed in the task of feeding the thousands of refugees who sought protection at the seminary and, together with other foreigners who remained behind, laboring diligently to protect Chinese civilians from the onslaught of the Japanese army in a hastily created "international safety zone."[4]

Those faculty and students who had fled split up, some going to Shanghai and what they hoped would be the protection of the French Concession and the International Settlement and the others westward to Chengdu, where many of the universities had resettled behind Chinese Nationalist lines. The Shanghai group was cut off from foreign funds once America entered the war, but they survived by selling drafts on the Board of Founders in New York. In Chengdu things were better financially, since they were able to receive U.S. funds throughout the war. Although the faculty and students there endured severe deprivations due to wartime inflation and shortages, they could, and did, frequently ask the board for assistance, which was forthcoming thanks to the Swope-Wendel fund. Although the two groups were separated for seven

3 Cartwright, *River*, 9.
4 Ibid., 72-73.

years, once the war ended the faculty and staff reunited in Nanjing with few hard feelings resulting from the different decisions made and the different resulting wartime experiences.

The seminary resumed classes on its Nanjing campus after the war, but the growing strength of the Communist Party and the conflict between Communist and Nationalist armies interfered with its work. An interesting aspect of this unsettled period, however, was the spectacular growth in enrollment. Christians who earlier might not have considered a career in the church now looked to it for employment, as they assumed they would be ineligible on religious grounds to hold jobs under the new Communist government established in 1949. We can only guess at the suffering the seminary community endured with the many changes in religious policy adopted by the Chinese government during the 1950s, 1960s, and early 1970s. After the United States entered the Korean conflict in support of the south and China entered informally in support of the north, foreign missionaries were forced to leave China. Missionaries on the Nanking Seminary faculty thus left Chinese colleagues with whom they had labored long and with whom they had struggled together during the Second World War. The missionaries and the Board of Founders did not immediately consider new opportunities for their work nor seek to reestablish their Nanjing program in Taiwan since, like many Westerners, they did not expect the new government to last long, and they hoped to return to China in the foreseeable future.

As the expectation of return to China faded, the members of the Board of Founders turned their attention to the very large ethnic Chinese communities in South East Asia and considered options for extending their work to these communities. C. Stanley Smith, a missionary who had been the vice-president and for a time acting president at Nanking Seminary, was sent on a round-the-world tour, first to consult with mission boards and church leaders in Europe and later, joined by Sidney Anderson in India, to visit theological institutions throughout South East Asia. The Board of Founders had sent small grants to the schools in advance of the Anderson-Smith visit, and the seriousness of the board's interest in the region was understood by the schools, a fact which enabled Anderson and Smith to glean a great deal of useful information.[5]

Believing that the terms of the Swope-Wendel wills compelled them to spend money only on theological education for Chinese,

5 Smith, "A Report on Theological Education."

the Board of Founders initially limited its aid to schools with ethnic Chinese students. Yet it soon realized that such a restriction would hamper severely any contributions it might make to theological institutions in South East Asia. After an Indonesian protested that such restrictive gifts appeared un-Christian, the board reconsidered its options and gradually began to extend its support to Asian theological students and institutions without this restriction.

Since it had become impossible for the Board of Founders to direct funds to Nanking Seminary and thus to fulfill the specific instructions of the Wendel sisters' wills, the Division of Foreign Missions of the Board of Missions and Church Extension of the Methodist Church petitioned the Surrogate's Court in New York to decree that the monies bequeathed by Rebecca A. D. Wendel Swope and Ella V. Von Echtzel Wendel "for the maintenance of Nankin Theological Seminary in Nankin, China" should be paid to the Board of Founders of Nanking Theological Seminary. This petition was granted. Earlier the Board of Founders had received the approval of the University of the State of New York to amend and expand the statement of purpose

> to receive and disburse funds: (1) for any purpose contributing to Christian theological education (a) in China, or (b) in areas of Asia and the Western Pacific beyond the confines of China, and (2) for educational assistance to Chinese and other Far Eastern students preparing in these or other lands for the ministry or other services in the Christian church when said corporation shall deem the same advisable because of conditions existing in China.[6]

Although it appears that Smith and some of the members of the board initially wanted to support one theological seminary in South East Asia, which would absorb the former missionary faculty of Nanking Seminary and be modeled, as that school had been, on an American theological seminary, they soon realized that was impossible. Political, cultural, ethnic, nationalistic, linguistic, and even mission factors, all beyond the control of the Board of Founders, limited the board's freedom of action in the region. In the aftermath of the Communist victory in China and establishment of the new People's Republic there, many of the South East Asian countries forbade entry to Chinese nationals, even if a particular Chinese applicant wished to study at a theological seminary. The complicated ethnic mix in Burma,

6 Cartwright, *River*, 27.

the board realized, probably mandated that anyone planning to serve a church in that country should be educated there. Finding Chinese living in Thailand who both wanted to become clergy and had the educational qualifications to enter a theological seminary proved close to impossible, because the local Chinese educated their sons in Chinese vernacular elementary schools. This practice, *de facto*, eliminated them from places in secondary schools, which were instructed only in Thai. Students at the theological school in Singapore commonly appeared to be there because they had failed the entrance examinations to universities, a situation not unknown in other parts of South East Asia. Indonesia had the largest Christian population in the region, but its seminaries were staffed by Dutch scholars whose language few Indonesians wanted to study after independence. The Philippines had several theological seminaries, but none measured up to the standards of the former Nanking Seminary. When the board considered the institutions in Taiwan, it found that the Presbyterians had worked hard at establishing high academic standards, but, again, the students were largely those who could not win admission to government universities. The churches, which desperately needed clergy, generally could not afford to provide them adequate support. In Hong Kong the board found denominational seminaries that had fled the mainland, many of which were not interested in ecumenism.

An even more perplexing problem for the Board of Founders was what to do about the many Bible schools in the region, which admitted students with only elementary school education. Even though the board did not consider these schools academically adequate to merit board support, it had to recognize that the schools trained clergy who went out to serve rural churches and were welcomed by parishioners.

C. Stanley Smith became the Board of Founder's representative in South East Asia and worked diligently to organize the existing seminaries into a pan-national, ecumenical Christian community, while also increasing their admission standards. In the pre-Association of Southeast Asian Nations (ASEAN) days, when nationalism was rampant in the region, one Asian complained that only the church viewed South East Asia as a region. Because they had the Swope-Wendel funds to support their efforts, Smith and the Board of Founders were able to provide assistance for theological schools throughout the region and to encourage among regional Christians an ecumenical and international orientation. First through the 1956 conference in Bangkok and then through a series of study institutes, sponsored initially by the Board of Founders and later sponsored jointly with the Association of Theological Schools in South East Asia, Christians of the region gradually began to develop the knowledge, skills, and resources they required as they came to fill leadership roles earlier held by missionaries.

With the creation of ASEAN, the political realities of the region changed, allowing the citizens of each member country to visit other countries freely and member governments to cooperate on a regional basis. In this new situation, Christians observed that the exchange of people and ideas, which they had been encouraging from the mid-1950s, was becoming a reality in many other areas of life, to the great benefit of themselves and their fellow citizens. The church had helped lead the way toward this new regionalism.

Gradually, the board made one, two, and then many exceptions to its initial decision to fund only academic programs at the graduate level for otherwise outstanding programs, such as those at Jogjakarta, which educated Chinese and Indonesian students, and the one for aborigines in Hualien, Taiwan, which educated a clergy for a church with seventy thousand members. In this way, the Board of Founders began to accept theological education as it existed in South East Asia, instead of trying to mold it to meet Western standards or its own expectations. Instead of developing a union theological seminary similar to Nanjing Union, the board came to support a great diversity of seminaries, many of them denominational, in various countries. Smith and the members of the Board of Founders discovered that Asian Christians had different views of the Bible than did Westerners, and they began to encourage Asians to explore these views and the relevance of the Bible to life in Asia. Although still heavily influenced by Western ideas and standards, especially for libraries and accreditation, the Asian theological institutions also had their own ideas about what constituted appropriate curricula for seminary students. After the Bangkok conference, the Board of Founders relied increasingly on the recommendations of its Asian partners.

Through the study institutes and meetings of ATSSEA, which became the Association for Theological Education in South East Asia, leading theologians in South East Asia came to know one another and to exchange ideas regularly. Subsequent ATESEA theological seminar workshops and a variety of contextual theological literature generated from these workshops further undergirded Asian theological education and church development. Eventually, the generation educated after World War II moved into positions of leadership. Through various ATESEA committees, commissions, institutes, and teams, especially the

Resource Commission, Asians played an increasing role at the decision-making level regarding the use of the Swope-Wendel bequest. One observer noted that by the 1970s, the student helpers at the Bangkok conference were heading the theological institutions and holding leadership positions in the multinational Christian organizations of the region. Henry P. Van Dusen, president of Union Theological Seminary in New York, member of the Board of Founders from 1939, and chair of the FTESEA from 1963 until 1970, commented after one lengthy trip to the region that he had not seen one institution which did not have a distinctive, well thought out program that the other institutions needed to study. Although Smith once commented that C. H. Hwang of Tainan Theological College in Taiwan obviously believed in "ask and it shall be given you," Hwang was one of the many who implemented new programs to improve the understanding of Christianity in Asia. One of Hwang's ideas, startlingly simple, was to provide seminary graduates with a basic library of theological books to use in their parishes, something few graduates could afford on their own. Others implemented indigenous arts and music in their worship services and, eventually, this attracted the attention of many in the region.

The Board of Founders changed its name to the Foundation for Theological Education in South East Asia in 1963 to acknowledge the wider scope of its work in the region. It supported ATESEA's development of the South East Asia Graduate School of Theology when it discovered that the structure of theological education in the West was not well suited to conditions in Asia. Unique in its structure, the SEAGST placed individual students seeking master's degrees or doctorates with faculty members having expertise in the field of the student's interest, without regard to the nationality of either. From the 1970s on, visiting faculty from other ATESEA institutions, too, became a regular part of the seminaries of South East Asia, encouraged by ASEAN and interregional cooperation at a level unthinkable twenty years earlier.

Following normalization of diplomatic relations between China and the United States in the 1970s, it became possible for staff and directors of the FTESEA once more to visit Nanjing. The FTESEA was mindful both of its special obligations to that seminary deriving from the terms of the Swope-Wendel bequest and of the limitations imposed upon that support by virtue of the principles of the Three-Self Movement in the Protestant Church in China, as well as government policy there. In spite of these limitations, the FTESEA was motivated by its sense of obligation and found ways to resume its relationship with this school, now reorganized and named Nanjing Union Theological Seminary. Accepting the reality of the independence of the Chinese church and its schools and the unwillingness of the Chinese to re-establish dependence on mission ties with the West, the FTESEA assumed the role of partner with the church in China. Depending upon the advice and consent of the Chinese partners, the foundation began buying books ordered by the Nanjing Union librarian, providing grants for a library building and equipment, aiding in renovation of a music building, providing support for publication of journals, and providing grants for faculty and students to make trips to the West for attendance at professional meetings and for study and research.

The Protestant church in China began to grow rapidly during the final two decades of the twentieth century. As seminaries multiplied across that country, FTESEA searched for an appropriate way to relate to these many schools. When the China Christian Council established a Commission on Theological Education, that body became the link between the foundation and the regional and provincial seminaries. Nanjing Union remained the single national seminary, and FTESEA continued to work with it directly. The needs and requests of other seminaries were transmitted to the foundation through the commission, which became responsible for advising the foundation about the work of these schools and ways in which the foundation might help them.[7]

As the new century commenced, more and more decisions about how to use the Swope-Wendel funds were being made in Asia. Working primarily with three partners, the Resource Commission of ATESEA, Nanjing Union Theological Seminary, and the Commission on Theological Education of the CCC, FTESEA was committed to the use of its own resources and the development of additional resources in creative support of theological education in the region.

The Board of Founders was established in 1937 to implement the terms of a bequest by assisting Nanking Theological Seminary, an interdenominational Protestant seminary in China supported largely by American missionary boards. Through the following years, the turmoil of war, revolution, and the collapse of imperialism resulted in dramatic changes in the Christian communities in China and the rest of Asia. Missions gave way to national churches, and the Board of Founders found itself compelled to seek a change in its charter and to explore new ways of relating to churches and theological schools

[7] Minutes, Executive Committee, FTESEA, April 2, 1989, FTEA.

in China and South East Asia. What had begun in the 1930s as an effort to aid one missionary seminary in China had, by the beginning of the new century, come to assist many varied theological programs of the Christian churches in Asia and to influence Christian thinking worldwide. The generous bequest of Ella Wendel and Rebecca Wendel Swope was being used in ways that the members of the Wendel family never had dreamed of, but certainly they would have taken satisfaction in the significant role that it played in strengthening theological education throughout the region.

Bibliography

Archival Collections

Association for Theological Education in South East Asia, Papers, ATESEA Office, Manila, Philippines. ATESEAF.

Board of Founders, Nanking Theological Seminary/Foundation for Theological Education in South East Asia, Papers, Yale Divinity School Library, New Haven, CT, FTEA; and files of the executive secretary, privately held.

Board of Founders, Nanking Theological Seminary; Foundation for Theological Education in South East Asia; C. Stanley Smith Papers; Hubert L. Sone Papers; Nanking Theological Seminary Papers; Methodist Archives, Madison, N.J., and Record Office, United Methodist Church, Board of Global Ministries, New York. MA and MA/RO.

Fitch, George A. Papers, Harvard University, Cambridge, Mass.

Love, Harry Hauser. Papers, Coll. #21-28-890, Manuscripts Collections, Kroch Library, Cornell University, Ithaca, N.Y.. HHL.

Morris, Raymond P. Papers, YDS. MP.

Pope, Liston Papers. YDS. PopeP.

Price Family Papers, George C. Marshall Foundation, Lexington, Vir. PP.

Price, Frank W. Papers, Davidson College Archives, Davidson, N.C.

Warnshuis, Abbe Livingstone. Papers, Union Theological Seminary, New York. ALW.

World Student Christian Federation files, RG 46, folder 304-2828,2, Yale Divinity School Library, New Haven, Conn.

Published Works

Anderson, Sydney, and C. Stanley Smith. *The Anderson-Smith Report on Theological Education in Southeast Asia, Especially as it Relates to the Training of Chinese for the Ministry.* New York: Board of Founders, NTS, 1952.

Bays, Daniel H., ed. *Christianity in China: From the Eighteenth Century to the Present.* Stanford: Stanford University Press, 1996.

Biggerstaff, Knight. *Nanking Letters, 1949.* Ithaca: China-Japan Program, Cornell University, 1979.

Brook, Timothy. *Documents on the Rape of Nanking.* Ann Arbor: University of Michigan Press, 1999. Contains Hsu Shuhsi, ed., *Documents of the Nanking Safety Zone.* Chungking: Council of International Affairs by Kelly and Walsh, 1939, and *The Family Letters of Dr. Robert Wilson.*

Cartwright, Frank T. *A River of Living Water.* Singapore: Board of Founders, NTS, 1963.

Cheng Pei-kai and Michael Lestz with Jonathan Spence, eds. *The Search for Modern China: A Documentary Collection.* New York: Norton, 1999.

China Centenary Missionary Conference Records: Report of the Great Conference Held at Shanghai, April 5th to May 8th, 1907. New York: American Tract Society, n.d.

Crouch, Archie R., et al. *Christianity in China: A Scholar's Guide to Resources in the Libraries and Archives of the United States.* Armonk, N.Y.: M. E. Sharpe, 1989.

Education for Service in the Christian Church in China: The Report of a Survey Commission 1935, with supplementary chapter by C. Stanley Smith. Published by the Board of Founders, Nanking Theological Seminary, New York 1945. (Weigle Report).

Hunter, Alan and Kim-Kwong Chan. *Protestantism in Contemporary China.* Cambridge: Cambridge University Press, 1993.

Journal of the 117th Annual Meeting of the Board of Foreign Missions of the Methodist Episcopal Church, Newark, N.J., November 20-22, 1935. Newark: Methodist Church, 1935.

Lai, Pan-chiu, "Theological Translation and Transmission between China and the West," *Asia Journal of Theology*, 20, 2 (Oct 2006), 285-304.

Latourette, Kenneth Scott. *A History of Christian Missions in China*. New York: Russell & Russell, 1967 (reprint of 1929 publication).

Lodwick, Kathleen L., comp. *The Chinese Recorder Index: A Guide to Christian Missions in Asia, 1867-1941*. Wilmington: Scholarly Resources, 1986.

Lutz, Jessie Gregory. *China and the Christian Colleges 1850-1950*. Ithaca: Cornell University Press, 1971.

Moffett, Samuel Hugh. *A History of Christianity in Asia*, vol. 1: Beginnings to 1500, 2nd ed. Maryknoll: Orbis, 1998; vol 2: 1500-1900, 2nd ed. Maryknoll: Orbis, 2005.

Price, Frank Wilson. *History of Nanking Theological Seminary 1911 to 1961*. New York: Board of Founders of Nanking Theological Seminary, 1961 (circulated as a mimeographed document).

Record of Proceedings of the Conference on Theological Education in Southeast Asia, Bangkok, Wattana Wittaya Academy, February 21st-March 7th, 1956. Singapore: Malaya Publishing House, 1956?

Sandeen, Ernest R. *The Roots of Fundamentalism: British and American Millenarianism, 1800–1930*. Chicago: University of Chicago Press, 1970.

Sientje, Merentek-Abram, and A. Wati Longchar, eds. *Partnership in Training God's Servants for Asia: Essays in Honor of Marvin D. Hoff*. Jorhat, Assam, India: Association for Theological Education in South East Asia and Foundation for Theological Education in South East Asia, 2006.

Smith, C. Stanley. *The Development of Protestant Theological Education in China: In the Light of the History of the Education of the Clergy in Europe and America*, Part II: "The Development of Protestant Theological Education in China." Shanghai: Kelly and Walsh, 1941.

Stuart, John Leighton. *Fifty Years in China: The Memoirs of John Leighton Stuart, Missionary and Ambassador*. New York: Random House, 1954.

Su, Deci. "Theological Education in China," *Chinese Theological Review*, 11 (1996), 42-50.

Thomson, Alan. "A Note on the Development of the Association of Theological Schools in South East Asia," *SEAJT*, 16 (1975), 35-44.

Thurston, Mrs. Lawrence (Matilda S.) and Miss Ruch M. Chester. *Ginling College (Jinling nuzhi daxue)*. New York: United Board for Christian College in China, 1955.

Timperley, H. J. *Japanese Terror in China*. New York: Modern Age Books, 1938.

Ting, K. H. "Nanking Union Theological Seminary: Theological Education in New China: Part I: New Beginnings," in *Ministry by the People: Theological Education by Extension,* ed. F. Ross Kinsler. Geneva: WCC Publications, 1983, pp. 264-72.

Ting, K. H. "What Is a Theological Seminary," *Nanjing Theological Review,* 2003 (no. 56), 7-16.

Wickert, Erwin, ed. *The Good Man of Nanking: The Diaries of John Rabe,* trans. John E. Woods. New York: Alfred A. Knopf, 1998.

Yamamoto, Masahiro. *Anatomy of an Atrocity.* Westport, Conn.: Praeger, 2000.

Yao, Kevin Xiyi. *The Fundamentalist Movement among Protestant Missionaries in China, 1920-1937.* New York: University Press of America, 2003.

Yeow Choo Lak, *ATESEA Celebrates its Golden Jubilee: A Story of ATESEA in 50 Years (1957-2007).* Quezon City, Philippines: ATESEA, 2007.

Yu, Anthony C. *State and Religion in China: Historical and Textual Perspectives.* Chicago: Open Court, 2005.

Zhao, Fusan. "The Chinese Revolution and Foreign Missions in China Seen through the May 4 Movement," in Scherer, James A., ed., "Report of the Midwest China Consultation: Western Christianity and the People's Republic of China: Exploring New Possibilities." Chicago: Chicago Cluster of Theological Schools, 1979, 63-80 (mimeographed).

Periodicals

Asia Journal of Theology
Chinese Recorder
Chinese Theological Review
East Asia Journal of Theology
International Review of Missions
Nanjing Theological Review
New York Times
Sophia: The Magazine of Trinity College Singapore
South East Asia Journal of Theology
Tian Feng

Interviews

Chen Zemin. Interview with Samuel C. Pearson, Nanjing, China, July 1, 2005, and extensive conversations over the period 2002-04.

Hoff, Marvin. Interview with Samuel C. Pearson, July 2, 2005.

Ting, K. H. Interview with Samuel C. Pearson, Nanjing, China, July 1, 2005.

APPENDIX 1

Timeline of the Association

Year	Association	Christian world	Sociopolitical situation
1945			End of World War II; Japan surrendered Indonesia proclaimed independence
1946			The Philippines became independent
1948		World Council of Churches formed	Burma became independent
1949		Eastern Asia Christian Conference: The Christian Prospect in Eastern Asia, Bangkok C. H. Hwang became principal of Tainan Theological College	Founding of the People's Republic of China (PRC)

1950		The Declaration, "The Ways of the Chinese Christian Church to Exert Efforts in the Construction of New China," issued in the *People's Daily*, Beijing	Korean War began
1951		C. S. Smith's Report to the Board of Founders on the Program of the Nanking Theological Seminary with relation to work outside of China	
1952		Anderson-Smith Report on Theological Education in South East Asia East China Theological Education Forum convened; Nanjing Union Theological Seminary formed out of union of seminaries in East China. K H Ting became first principal	
1954		Consultation Regarding Theological Education in South East Asia, Williams Bay, Wisconsin National Committee of the Three-Self Patriotic Movement of the Protestant Churches in China established	Singapore Chinese middle schools clashed with police, opposing compulsory conscription against Malaysian Communist Party North Vietnam defeated the French colonial administration National Committee of the Three-Self Patriotic Movement of the Protestant Churches in China established

1955			First nation-wide election in Indonesia. President Sukarno defended a secular state based on *Pancasila* World nonalignment movement began under Sukarno's leadership
1956		EACC Conference on Theological Education in South East Asia, Bangkok	
1957	1st Theological Study Institute: Urbanization in Asia, Singapore; Provisional Constitution of the Association of Theological Schools in South East Asia (ATSSEA) drafted in Singapore	East Asia Christian Conference (EACC) formally established. Conference on "The Common Evangelistic Task of the Church in East Asia," Prapat, Indonesia	The Federation of Malaya (peninsular Malaysia) gained independence
1958		Theological Education Fund (TEF) established after the International Missionary Council Assembly at Ghana; Charles Ransom became the first TEF director The First Mandate of the TEF: 1958-1965	

1959	The South East Asia Theological Librarians' Workshop, Silliman University, Philippines Launch of the *South East Asia Journal of Theology (SEAJT)* First Meeting of ATSSEA, Singapore John Fleming became ATSSEA's first executive director 2nd Theological Study Institute: The People of God in the World, Singapore C. Stanley Smith died	Inaugural EACC Assembly "Witnessing Together," Kuala Lumpur	General election in Singapore; People's Action Party won Conversion of Chinese-medium school structure in Singapore into English-medium, multiethnic structure
1960	3rd Theological Study Institute: Christ and Culture–The Encounter in East Asia, Singapore		
1961	The Second Biennial Meeting of ATSSEA, Hong Kong	International Missionary Council united with WCC WCC Commission on World Mission and Evangelism formed	
1962	4th Theological Study Institute Christian Ethics and decision in a Rapidly Changing Social Situation of South East Asia, Singapore	Nanking Theological Seminary Board of Founders renamed The Foundation for Theological Education in South East Asia (FTESEA)	Burma under military government; beginning of isolation

1963	The Third Biennial Meeting of ATSSEA, Hong Kong 5th Theological Study Institute: Church History—Teaching and Writing, Singapore	EACC Situation Conferences held in Madras, Singapore, and Amagisanso	Operation Cold-store: left-wing leaders arrested in Singapore to advance a "non-communist, democratic and independent Malaysia" Sabah, Sarawak, and Singapore joined the Federation of Malaya to form Malaysia Indonesia-Malaysia Conflict (*Konfrontasi*) over the future of Borneo
1964		EACC Assembly, "The Christian Community within the Human Community," Bangkok	
1965	The Fourth Biennial Meeting of ATSSEA, Hong Kong Henry van Dusen's Accreditation Commission Report to ATSSEA 6th Theological Study Institute: Worship and Music in the Asian Churches Today, Hong Kong	EACC Consultation on Theological Education in South East Asia held in Hong Kong, resulting in A Statement on Joint Action for Theological Education The Second Mandate of the TEF: 1965-1970 C. H. Hwang left Taiwan and became TEF's associate director; Hwang adopted the name Shoki Coe. C. S. Song succeeded Shoki Coe as Principal of Tainan Theological College	Singapore became independent republic US sent combat forces to Vietnam Violence in Indonesia from 1965-1966: Communist Party (PKI) banned

1966	South East Asia Graduate School of Theology (SEAGST) founded 7th Theological Study Institute: Church and Society, Hong Kong	EACC Consultation on Theological Education in North East Asia held in Seoul Nanjing Union Theological Seminary closed from 1966-1980	The Great Proletariat Cultural Revolution began in China End of confrontation between Malaysia and Indonesia General Suharto assumed power in Indonesia
1967	The Fifth Biennial Meeting of ATSSEA, Singapore		The Association of Southeast Asian Nations (ASEAN) established
1968	Kosuke Koyama became executive director 8th Theological Study Institute: Missiology–Ecumenics–Church History, Hong Kong	EACC Assembly, "In Him all things hold together," Bangkok World Congress on Evangelism, Berlin Asia-South Pacific Congress on Evangelism, Singapore	
1969		John Stott founded Langham Trust Scholarship in the United Kingdom	Communal riots in Kuala Lumpur between ethnic Chinese and Malays. State of emergency imposed by the Malaysian Government (1969-1971)
1970	The Sixth Meeting of ATSSEA, Hong Kong	The Third Mandate of the TEF: 1970-1977 Shoki Coe became director of TEF Asia Theological Association established	

1971		C. S. Song left Taiwan John Stott founded the Evangelical Literature Trust	Admission of PRC to the United Nations President Ferdinand E. Marcos of Philippines (1965-86) declared martial law The New Economic Policy in Malaysia
1972	Critical Asian Principle adopted as guiding principle for doctoral program Offering of Th.D. program 9th and final Theological Study Institute: Christian Social Ethics, Singapore	The Association for Promotion of Chinese Theological Educators established First Consultation of Chinese Theological Educators and Church Leaders, Hong Kong	Anglo-Chinese School (Methodist) students in Singapore received "baptism of the Holy Spirit" Singapore Anglican Bishop Chiu Ban It received the "baptism of the Holy Spirit" while attending the World Council of Churches Conference (Salvation Today) in Bangkok (December 1972-January 1973) Beginning of the charismatic movement in Singapore
1973		EACC became the Christian Conference of Asia (CCA)	

1974	The Seventh Meeting of ATSSEA, Singapore ATSSEA headquarters moved from Singapore to Manila ATSSEA constitution amended. Regular meetings became triennial Emerito Nacpil became executive director Regulations and procedures for the FTESEA/ ATSSEA Joint Regional Planning Commission (JRPC) adopted by ATSSEA and FTESEA (1975-1977: three-year trial period) Commission on Non-traditional Study (1974-1977) established	Lausanne International Congress on World Evangelism John Stott's Ministries founded in the USA	
1975	Accreditation Commission Manual for 1975		Fall of Saigon to North Vietnam
1976		The First Chinese Congress on World Evangelization Hong Kong	Mao Zedong died; end of the Cultural Revolution in China

1977	ATSSEA Triennial Meeting, Manila: decision to reorganize ATSSEA Report of the Commission on Non-traditional Study	WCC's Programme on Theological Education replaced TEF	
1978	Resource Commission formed to replace JRPC		Social reform in China began under Deng Xiaoping
1979	Institute of Advanced Pastoral Studies established The Executive Committee proposed a revised constitution		U.S.'s diplomatic recognition of PRC The Formosa *Journal* initiated a Taiwanese reform movement
1980	ATESEA Constitution amended. General Assembly became quadrennial	China Christian Council established International Council for Evangelical Theological Education formed	
1981	ATSSEA formally became the Association for Theological Education in South East Asia (ATESEA) ATESEA General Assembly, Baguio Yeow Choo Lak became executive director ATESEA headquarters moved from Manila to Singapore	Nanjing Union Theological Seminary reopened	End of martial law in the Philippines

1983	*SEAJT* merged with the *North East Asia Journal of Theology* to form the *East Asia Journal of Theology (EAJT)* Programme for Theology and Cultures in Asia (PTCA) founded 1st Theological Seminar-Workshop: Doing Theology with Asian Resources, Hong Kong ATESEA Occasional Paper No. 1: Theological Education for Women.		
1984	2nd Theological Seminar-Workshop: Doing Theology with Asian Folk-Literature, Hong Kong		
1985	ATESEA General Assembly, Singapore 3rd Theological Seminar-Workshop: Doing Theology and People's Movements in Asia, Kyoto		The Communion of Churches in Indonesia withdrew from CCA membership, in protest of CCA's stance on East Timor

1986	*EAJT* became the *Asia Journal of Theology* 4th Theological Seminar-Workshop: Doing Theology with the Religions of Asia, Hong Kong		President Marcos fled the Philippines
1987	5th Theological Seminar-Workshop: Doing Theology with Cultures of Asia, Kyoto	Amity Press established in Nanjing	"Marxist Conspiracy" in Singapore Singapore government closed CCA headquarters in Singapore; staff deported
1988	6th Theological Seminar-Workshop: Doing Theology with People's Symbols and Images, Jogjakarta		
1989	ATESEA General Assembly, Manila 7th Theological Seminar-Workshop: Doing Theology with God's Purposes in Asia, Hong Kong		National Council of Churches, Singapore terminated membership of CCA Fall of the Berlin Wall
1990	8th Theological Seminar-Workshop: Doing Theology with the Spirit's Movement in Asia, Seoul		

1991	The Forum of Asian Theological Librarians (ForATL) founded 9th Theological-Seminar Workshop: Doing Christian Theology in Asian Ways, Chiang Mai	China Christian Council became a member of the World Council of Churches; CCA relocated to Hong Kong	
1992	10th and final Theological Seminar-Workshop: Doing Theology with the Festivals and Customs of Asia, Quezon City		Singapore's diplomatic recognition of PRC
1993	ATESEA General Assembly, Hong Kong		
1994	ATESEA Occasional Paper No. 13: Doing Theology with the Festivals and Customs of Asia (final occasional paper during Yeow Choo Lak's tenure)		
1996			The people of Taiwan elected Lee Teng-hui as president by popular vote
1997	ATESEA General Assembly, Hong Kong		Hong Kong returned to China
1998	ATESEA headquarters moved from Singapore to Manila		Anti-Chinese riots in Jakarta President Suharto resigned in Indonesia Asia's economic crisis

2000			Chen Shui-bian, leader in the movement for Taiwan's independence, elected president of the Republic of China
2001	ATESEA General Assembly, Seremban Resource Committee restructured		
2002	Sientje Merentek-Abram became executive director		

APPENDIX 2

Chief Officers of the Association

Association Chairs (1959-2001)

1959 Benjamin Guansing, Union Theological Seminary, Philippines
1961 C. H. Hwang, Tainan Theological College, Taiwan
1965 R. Soedarmo, STT Jakarta, Indonesia
1966 Ivy Chou, Methodist Theological School, Malaysia
1967 Jacob Quiambao, Union Theological Seminary, Philippines
1971 Peter Latuihamallo, STT Jakarta, Indonesia
1974 Hsiao Ching-fen, Tainan Theological College, Taiwan
1977 Andrew Hsiao, Lutheran Theological Seminary, Hong Kong
1981 Peter Latuhamallo, STT Jakarta, Indonesia
1985 Henry Kiley, Saint Andrew's Seminary, Philippines
1989 Koh Kang Song, Southeast Asia Union College/Southeast Asia Adventist Seminary, Singapore
1993 Zenaida Lumba, Harris Memorial College, Philippines
1997 Sientje Merentek-Abram, Fakultas Teologia UKIT, Sulawesi, Indonesia

Executive Directors (1959-2001) and SEAGST Deans (1966-2001)

1959 John Fleming
1968 Kosuke Koyama
1974 Emerito Nacpil
1981 Yeow Choo Lak

Index